THE GROWTH OF BRITISH
INDUSTRIAL RELATIONS

'ON STRIKE', BY SIR HUBERT VON HERKOMER R.A., 1891

THE GROWTH OF
BRITISH INDUSTRIAL
RELATIONS

A study from the standpoint of 1906–14

BY

E. H. PHELPS BROWN

PROFESSOR OF THE ECONOMICS OF LABOUR IN
THE UNIVERSITY OF LONDON

LONDON
MACMILLAN & CO LTD
NEW YORK · ST MARTIN'S PRESS
1959

MACMILLAN AND COMPANY LIMITED
London Bombay Calcutta Madras Melbourne

THE MACMILLAN COMPANY OF CANADA LIMITED
Toronto

ST MARTIN'S PRESS INC
New York

PRINTED IN GREAT BRITAIN

CONTENTS

CONTENTS

LIST OF ILLUSTRATIONS

ACKNOWLEDGMENT

THIS study has been made possible by the support of the Economic Research Division of the London School of Economics. Through this I received for several years the help of Miss Marjorie Alderson (Mrs L. Tivey), by whose sustained interest and scholarly care the materials were surveyed and abstracted. To the same support I owe the reading of proofs and the compilation of the Biographical Notes and the index by Mrs Meyrick Browne, a contribution by Miss Sheila Hopkins (Mrs L. S. Pressnell), and the skilful typing of difficult scripts by Miss Stella Adamson and Miss J. M. Robinson. I wish also to acknowledge gratefully Miss Helen Beven's willing help.

My thoughts have grown in discussion with many colleagues at the London School. Particularly would I record all I have learned from Mr B. C. Roberts and Professor Otto Kahn-Freund. Both have given precious time to the present script, they have saved me from errors and thrown fresh light on my arguments. But in contentious ground I have taken my own line, and they are not to be identified with any of my statements of fact or opinion.

There are others who have been generous of time and effort to help me with comment and information on particular points. Especially I would like to thank Mr R. O. Clarke, who read and annotated the whole script; and with him my uncle Mr Ernest Bibbing, Mr Alun Davies, Professor F. J. Fisher, Colonel Lyle C. Grimes, Mr Keith Hancock, Mr Harold Jolliffe, Mr J. Lawrence Milligan, Mr Leonard Murray, Mr Matthew Swainston, and Mr Herbert Tanner. To the kindness of the Lady Ellen Askwith I owe the sketch of Sir George Askwith.

The Appendix on Sources records the works on which I have drawn most directly. Sometimes I have quarried from them liberally, but I have not generally cited my authorities by footnote save where I have quoted their actual words. I wish to record here what I owe to their authors.

SYNOPSIS

Introduction. This study sets out to depict the state of affairs in 1906–14, but looks backward to ask how that state had come about, and forward, to ask how far it accounts for what goes on today.

Chapter I. THE CONDITION OF THE PEOPLE

1. *The growth of population.* The material well-being of the wage-earner in the past had depended most of all on the pressure of population, notably in the great Tudor impoverishment. In the mid-eighteenth century a vital revolution brought a renewed growth of population: this plunged Ireland into the cataclysm of 1846, but economic development in Great Britain kept its ever-growing numbers alive and after 1850 provided them with a rising standard of living.

2. *Changes in the size of the family.* A reduction became apparent at the top of the social scale in the 1870's, but it spread down slowly and unevenly. By the 1900's middle-class families generally contained fewer children than wage-earners', and among the wage-earners generally the rougher the father's work, the more children he had. This sharpened social contrasts.

3. *Internal migration.* The great shift of the balance of British population between south and north, and town and country, was coming to an end in the 1890's: in particular, the growth of the towns was checked until the coming of tram and motor bus. Yet people were still moving plentifully in all directions. Migration will have made for some loss of social inheritance, some insecurity and restlessness.

4. *Variations in the rate of rise of the standard of living.* There were three sorts of fluctuation: (i) long waves in the terms of trade — an adverse movement had set in during the 1890's, and this may have coincided with a pause in British technical advance; (ii) the pulse of the Atlantic community, bringing a cycle of twenty to twenty-five years in the rate of growth of the population and of

the stock of buildings and equipment within Britain — here too the movement was adverse in the 1900's; (iii) the trade cycle, with a period of about nine years, had its latest peak in 1907.

5. *Welfare in the home.* A substantial rise had been achieved since 1870 in product per head of the population. In the average household among the wage-earners dietary was adequate though stodgy, but the margin left for all other purposes was very narrow. Sometimes drink took an undue share — more so then than now. Clothing often had to be pinched: for many wage-earners it was a badge of inferiority. How much of his earnings a husband kept back and how much he handed over to his wife might be governed by local custom; perhaps on the average he kept a quarter. The well-being of the home depended essentially on good management by the wife, who was often overburdened. Any one household typically passed through various phases of stringency or sufficiency in the course of time. The last time of stringency, old age, was hard to provide against.

6. *The unskilled labourer* was relatively more numerous then than now. Social surveys revealed in the towns a mass of general workers living in primary poverty, that is, lacking the means to buy the minimum of food, clothing and shelter needful for the maintenance of merely physical efficiency.

7. *The farm labourer* had low money wages, but lower outgoings than the townsman, and various supplementary resources, and his physique and health were superior. But a class of casual labour in the villages was very poor.

8. *The wage-earner's house* in England was distinctive for being generally a separate two-storied, four-roomed building occupied by only one family. But nearly half the people of Scotland were in dwellings of one or two rooms only; and miners' housing often stood out by its squalor. The wage-earner could not be provided with the accommodation he was now demanding at a rent he could afford, because building had had no technical revolution. The contribution of local government so far was made mostly by slum clearance.

9. *Health.* The general death rate had been falling. But recent changes in dietary had not been helpful. There were big differences between the mortality rates of different occupations: generally the middle classes had lower rates than wage-earners,

but farm labourers, building craftsmen and coalminers had markedly low rates. Some medical attention was in principle available to all wage-earners, but many, and especially their wives, got less than they needed. There was a substantial difference in physique between the well-to-do and the industrial wage-earners, notably among the young. Medical inspection of elementary schoolchildren revealed many defects and diseases. Infantile mortality had remained very high until the turn of the century: here too there were big differences between classes. But improvements were now being made in the medical care and nutrition of children. Milk depots grew into infant welfare centres. The local education authorities developed a medical service in the elementary schools after 1902, and from 1906 began to feed hungry children at school.

10. *Education.* The strongest force making for social change was the extension of elementary education from 1870: where formerly only a quarter, now three-quarters of the adults of the country had passed through an efficient school. This reduced the differential between the earnings of the educated man and the labourer; raised the self-respect and subjective standards of the wage-earners; whetted their appetite for further education and wider reading; and made them resent their hardships more because they could now reason about them and see ways of removing them.

11. *The inequality of incomes* had become more conspicuous. Estimates became available which showed that the wage-earners, though they made up three-quarters of all occupied persons, got less than two-fifths of the national income. Inequality was greater then than now because the shares of rent and profits were bigger and taxation was not so progressive; and it was harsher when those who had least were not merely less well off than others, but were in actual poverty. It was felt to rest on the same privileges of ownership as gave the employer the whip hand over the workman.

Chapter II. THE CONDITIONS OF WORK

1. *The transition from school to a job.* Increased provision for technical training had been made from the 1880's, but only a minority could use it. The general school-leaving age was 14,

but under by-laws about a third of the children were withdrawn at 12 or 13. In the textile districts many children of 12 and 13 spent half their time in the mill and half at school. Children in full-time attendance did a good deal of work out of school hours. There was little guidance or training to help the boy or girl forward from school-leaving to the adult working life.

2. *The deployment of the working population.* Three out of four were wage-earners; the distinction between wage-earning jobs and others marked a difference of status and esteem. The 'middle class' occupations were increasing in relative number. Rather less than half the working population were in essentially industrial jobs, or in jobs where process and equipment had been radically changed by the industrial revolution; rather more than a quarter were in factories. The high proportion outside industry blanketed industrial discontent.

3. *Women workers* were divided about equally between the factories and workshops, domestic service, and occupations of higher social status. Various kinds of barrier closed some occupations to women and caused them to overcrowd those that were open. Among these there were sharp class distinctions. Domestic servants were 'respectable' and generally well paid and boarded, but their numbers were decreasing because the life lacked freedom. The shop assistant's life had many attractions, but the hours were very long. Working women usually had to discharge 'the double duty'. Those who took in work at home often toiled long hours for little money. Working women had accepted the special hardships of their lot apathetically, but now a new spirit was stirring.

4. *The workplace.* Many of its problems were simply the outcome of the increase of scale in the course of unplanned growth. The Factory Act of 1901 had set out the nation's standing orders for health and safety in workplaces, and there were separate codes for the mines, railways, and mercantile marine. The need for a code was marked by a fatal accident rate twice as high then as now; the wage-earner's risk of accident remained a source of resentment, despite the Employer's Liability Act of 1897. The factory code only followed the practice of good employers, but its enforcement showed the general run of employers in a poor light. Yet some employers of vision were making advances in the amenity of the factory, the housing around it, and in care for the

well-being and self-respect of their workpeople, that showed how the condition of the industrial wage-earner could be transformed.

5. *Unemployment* was felt to be a growing evil. Its causes have been classified as (i) the decline of particular industries or occupations, (ii) seasonal variations, (iii) the trade cycle, (iv) the building cycle, (v) intermittent and casual engagement of the unskilled. Behind the last lay the pressure of ever-growing population. A number of industries, and the greater part of the countryside, knew little of unemployment, but it fell on even the skilled man in the export and constructional trades that fluctuated in the trade cycle, and the unskilled suffered from it generally. The anxiety it brought the wage-earner depended not so much on the number out of work at any one time as on his own risk of finding himself one of them. The unemployed man might draw benefit from his union if he was skilled; the only general provision for his relief was that for the able-bodied pauper under the Poor Law, but from Chamberlain's circular of 1886 onwards endeavours had been made to organize relief works and employment agencies, and these led to the Unemployed Workmen Act of 1905.

6. *Changes in machinery.* The twenty-five years before 1914 brought few conspicuous or concentrated changes in British industry, and many of the innovations of the day made more difference to products than to processes. But the use of electricity was spreading in industry, and this was part of a continuous growth of equipment: the amount of equipment per worker seems to have doubled between 1870 and 1914. New types of machine were coming in, and extending the subdivision of processes, automatism, precision of working and standardization. These depreciated the craftsman's asset of versatility, and enabled many operations that he alone had performed to be done by 'machine men', women and boys. The higher speeds of the new equipment increased the fear of unemployment.

7. *Scientific management.* The movement, of American origin, began to affect British workshops in the 1890's. It applied scientific method to the study of management as a distinct function. In its bearing on the workman, it meant job analysis and design; time study; and incentive methods of wage payment, whether by progressive or regressive formulas — there

were several reasons for adopting the regressive. British work-men resented the new methods. To the craftsman they brought a loss of pride in work and of job control. The stop-watch threatened speeding up, and a breach of the tacit understanding on what was 'a fair day's work'. This threat was powerful because after incentive rates were introduced they were so often cut. Rate-fixing by-passed collective bargaining. The new earnings upset the wage-structure, and caused jealousies. Greater output by some men was seen to mean unemployment for others.

8. *Effects of the conditions of work on industrial relations.* In several ways the working life of the wage-earner was unsatis-fying or disturbing to him. The setting of the wage-bargain was formed by ever-rising population, and when there was any excess of applicants over vacancies the wage-earner was liable to get the worst of the wage-bargain because his need of the job was more immediate than the employer's need of him. He worked under the direction of the employer and to serve the employer's purpose. Their mutual dependence was masked by the assumption that the proceeds were limited so that the more the employer took the less there must be for the wage-earner, and by the outward form of profits, which appeared as an un-earned surplus. Accidents and business failure hit the workman harder than the employer, and he felt he was treated as expen-dable in the quest for profit.

These things bore less hard while firms were mostly small, but the growth of scale intensified them in several ways. Meanwhile there were changes in the type of employer. As he made money the employer, and still more his children, tended to move away from his workpeople into an existing contrasted social class and way of life. As the profession of management emerged a gap opened between the general level of education and training of employers and of the employed. As top management receded, more responsibilities fell on the lower grades, especially the foremen, of whom more was being asked at the same time by the increased subdivision of labour and use of automatics in the workshop.

In the quarter century before 1914 these last changes were bringing in some of the features of repetitive work in the factory that are most galling to human nature.

Chapter III. THE DEVELOPMENT OF INDUSTRIAL RELATIONS

1. *The first growth: craft unions.* The oldest unions extant in 1906 were typically founded in the last quarter of the eighteenth century. The impulse had been given by the widening of markets with consequently increased competition and instability. To keep going, unions had to function as friendly societies, but generally only the craftsman had the income and capacity to maintain these. Unions of craftsmen did in fact carry on through the times of legal repression, and might enforce a union rate and other conditions of work. Local clubs joined with others of the same craft, and the nation-wide craft union appeared.

This direction of development is not the only one unionism has followed. British unions followed it because the craftsman could run his union without administration by outsiders, did not want to merge it in any political movement, and found his effective allies not in his neighbours in other jobs but in his brothers of the craft elsewhere. The maintenance of apprenticeship gave him a special motive to link with them: he kept up the price of his labour by keeping it scarce, and this gave his unionism an exclusive and separatist occupational form.

2. *Operatives' unions and district bargaining.* Operatives who though not apprenticed had acquired a skill in mill and mine early formed unions, but these were more vulnerable to slumps and to blacklegs, and did not generally achieve permanence till about 1850. They followed the craftsmen in segregating by occupation. Their leaders were soon meeting a local committee of employers to negotiate a district rate. Employers who hotly resented any intervention by the union within their own works were willing to enter into a district agreement for wages and hours, and came to find it advantageous. This was the path of least resistance for the unions. The other line of action they found they could follow effectively was lobbying at Westminster.

3. *The joint board of conciliation and arbitration* took its rise in the 1850's and was signalized by the work of Mundella, Kettle and Dale in the 1860's. It provided for conciliation through an independent chairman: the conciliator has a distinct and useful function, but he can perform this best when called in *ad hoc*, and when he sat with the board regularly he tended to become an

B

arbitrator. The coalfields gave their independent chairman the arbitral function in the last resort by giving him a casting vote, and this might have proved a device for drawing the parties towards each other, but in practice the chairman simply gave his own award. Arbitration was often no substitute for the parties' own agreement with each other and might reduce the chances of their reaching it.

4. *The sliding scale* was used in coal, and iron and steel, to vary wages automatically according to the ascertained selling price of the product: it was found to bring adjustments about peaceably that were inevitable but had caused strife before. But the selling price was an inadequate measure of the industry's capacity to pay wages, and as unions grew stronger they thought the rises they could have got anyhow no compensation for the cuts they could resist. So the miners generally abandoned their scales between 1887 and 1902, though they continued to accept a national scale as a guide in the negotiations of their district conciliation boards. The iron and steel workers went on with the scale: they differed in that their earnings were tending upwards and their union allegiance was divided.

5. *The Birmingham Alliances.* Under the sliding scale it had been seen that wages might be kept up if the employers would form a cartel to keep up prices. In the 1890's the Alliances tried to arrange this institutionally in some Birmingham trades: at a costing conference the employers were to agree on setting prices to cover a 'fair profit' and good wages, and the union was to strike the works of any seller who undercut. But competition from within or without did soon break the Alliances, and employers generally were too competitive for the scheme to work elsewhere.

6. *Difficulties of the joint boards.* When the boards were new they had marked a changed attitude on the part of the employers and a higher status for the wage-earners. As time went on and the impact of this ceased to create goodwill, new claims of principle came up that were not so capable of compromise as a wage claim, and the men became impatient or distrustful, especially when a board agreed a wage cut. With the widening of the area of bargaining, boards ceased to be able to draw on the old fund of district loyalty and neighbourliness.

7. *The New Unionism.* The mid-Victorian unskilled labourers

had been incapable of maintaining unions without outside help, and the existing unionists saw their advantage more in keeping other men out than in bringing them in. But 1888–9 showed a new capability among the unskilled and a new spirit among the old unionists. There was recruitment in three fields — generalized unskilled labour; occupational groups in pockets here and there; whole industries like municipal employment and transport in which unionism had taken little hold so far. These joined in a third type of union, the general union, distinctive in that it halted at no occupational or industrial boundary: its dues were low, it set out to provide few if any friendly benefits, it felt itself part of a general labour and socialist movement. There was also at this time some development of industrial unionism by the new unions and the Railway Servants. The new unions were not aggressive for long: their membership fell off in the next slump, and they carried on as a kind of federation of occupational or industrial groups, and began to give friendly benefits.

But the New Unionism did bring a more assertive and aggressive spirit among the old unionists, and the belief that the whole structure of society had to be changed.

8. *Stoppages.* The rising phase of the trade cycle generally brought a good many short stoppages, the falling brought fewer but longer. The liability to stoppage was greater in the industries that felt the full force of the cycle, and in those where unionism was strong, except for printing, and iron and steel. There were also differences between regions apart from those consequent on their industrial composition. They may be ascribed to the factor of reverberation, areas of high industrial density having more stoppages than those of low; to differences in social structure and stability, especially the extent of recent immigration; and to the historical process by which an initial impulse in either direction tends to propagate itself. Though a few big stoppages accounted for most of the man-days lost, most stoppages were small and brief. The real causes of a dispute are often hard to seize on, but of the reported issues the chief were wages and hours, union security, and demarcation. Union headquarters rarely initiated a strike, but checked or released a movement of the rank and file. A prolonged stoppage brought great hardship; this had its mystique. The aggregate loss of man-days was small, but by 1900 stoppages were becoming more menacing, because of

greater militancy, and the extension of the area that would be stopped at one time: the stoppages in coal in 1893 and engineering in 1897–8 were landmarks. The thirty years from 1890 were to see the transition to general industry-wide bargaining. Where it was first achieved it brought in long periods of stability.

9. *Sources and centres of conflict.* More violent conflicts after 1889 were due to the extension of the area of disputes, which reduced strike pay; the increased participation of the unskilled, who more than others were drawn into conflict with blacklegs; the mingling of the mob with the unskilled in the towns; and especially to the clash between the new unionism and employers who resented having to deal with unions at all. Unions in this position had only the strike to resort to: the employers' riposte was to import blacklegs. Several agencies existed to supply them, especially the National Free Labour Association, maintained by the Employers' Parliamentary Council. The Shipping Federation, set up in opposition to Havelock Wilson's union, used a Federation ticket as a condition of employment, and brought in depot ships to break strikes against its use. The railway companies except the North Eastern long refused to recognize unions, though in 1896 the President of the Board of Trade mediated an agreement between the London and North Western and the Railway Servants. The men's unionism was divided by loyalties of grade and occupation. Many other employers, though not actively hostile towards the unions, did not want and had not been obliged to recognize them.

10. *Sectors with little unionism.* In middle-class employments there was little impulse towards unionism, because of the ethos of self-help, and relatively high social and economic status. Shop assistants enjoyed their work, had prospects of independence, worked mostly in small firms in personal contact with the employer, were divided by trade and scattered by location. Most of these factors also influenced domestic servants. Unionism had not got far in much manufacturing that was carried on in small workshops, even in centres of industry, and in some sizeable factories which were isolated. There had been notable upsurges of unionism among farm workers, but they had come to nothing. Since the villages had a rapidly growing supply of labour against a contracting demand, wage rises were hard to get except when labourers' wages in the towns were rising most;

some of the farmers, squires, and parsons were vindictive against unionists; work on the land and life in the village provided deep-going satisfactions.

Chapter IV. THE DEVELOPMENT OF PUBLIC POLICY

1. *Public provision for settling disputes.* Early provisions for arbitration really applied only to disputes about what was due for work already done, and though elaborated in an Act of 1867 remained a dead letter. British practice also failed to develop the arbitration of disputes about the application of an existing agreement, perhaps because it had not developed the detailed code of working practice that the plant contract provides in America. Also British employers and unions distrusted legal forms: this may be why none of them adopted a provision in an Act of 1872 for the legally binding arbitration of a third sort of dispute, that about future terms of employment.

2. *Findings of the Royal Commission on Labour, 1891-4.* The minority put in a socialist programme drafted by Sidney Webb, and said little about industrial relations. The majority found that these relations were at their best when strong organizations on both sides reached voluntary agreements by procedures they themselves had worked out: the one thing the government could usefully do was to provide conciliation where disputes proved obstinate. Accordingly Parliament passed the Conciliation Act, 1896. There was at the same time a movement for the setting up of local conciliation boards, but they were not used. Unions struggling for recognition advocated compulsory arbitration, but the majority disliked it. It had been adopted in New Zealand and Australia as a means of keeping the peace, and could conceivably have come in Britain had disputes been more extensive or unions weaker.

3. *The Courts and the strike.* In the 1870's Parliament had drawn up a code whose object was to maintain the effective right to strike while protecting those who would not take part; the Courts narrowed this settlement in several ways. They held that the lawful purposes of picketing did not include peaceful persuasion; that calling men out in breach of contract was a tort; that the predominant purpose of a secondary boycott by workmen was not to protect themselves but to hurt another, and

those who took part were actionable for civil conspiracy. Whereas actions on these or any other grounds could formerly be brought only against particular members or officers of a union, the Taff Vale judgment of 1901 held that they could be brought against the union itself. The effect was to make any strike liable in practice to involve the union in heavy damages. Unionists reacted politically.

4. *The enforcement of minimum wages.* The evil called sweating was investigated by a Committee of the Lords in 1889–90. Its cause was that particular groups of workers were helpless either to move to better jobs or hold out for a higher wage in their present ones. The apparent remedy was to apply a legally binding minimum wage, but there was a long-standing presumption that government should not interfere with prices in the labour market, and there were many practical difficulties, especially the possibility that at a higher wage these folk would get no work at all. One step that did seem practicable was to require Government contractors to observe recognized terms of employment: hence the Fair Wages Resolution of the Commons in 1891, and the adoption of the same principle by many local authorities. It implied that minimum wages could be safely enforced if they followed the rates arrived at in collective bargaining, and this in turn suggested that where agencies for bargaining had not grown up on their own the government might create them. This found an advocate in Sir Charles Dilke, whose ideas about it derived from John Stuart Mill, Alfred Deakin and David Syme in Victoria, and his own wife, a pupil of Ruskin. From 1900 he brought forward annually a bill to set up wages boards on the pattern of Victoria.

5. *Why had Parliament not provided a constitution for industrial relations within the firm?* In some ways this would have been a natural extension of what it had done elsewhere. Such a constitution would presumably have had to provide some element of employee representation. There had been many endeavours to set up self-governing workshops, but save for some small groups using simple equipment they had failed. The basic difficulty was that wage-earners had not shown the capacity to manage any business save co-operative retailing: some notable attempts by unions had failed disastrously. Also since risk capital was so scarce it could not be raised without giving the lenders control.

Though the unions increasingly tried to limit the authority of the employer they did not try to share it.

Chapter V. INSTITUTIONS AND PROCEDURES IN 1906

1. *The size of unions and union membership.* The craft unions were relatively big on the average because they contained some of the biggest unions in the country. Except for the miners', the operatives' unions remained small, being generally sectional and localized. Some of the general unions though young were already big. In 'white-collared' occupations only small beginnings yet appeared, save for two sizeable unions in retailing and one in the Post Office. Membership as a whole had grown in surges, with minor ups and downs in each trade cycle and major advances in 1871–3, 1888–91. The two million unionists of 1906 made up less than a sixth of all wage-earners, but were present in force in certain industries and districts where they were largely concentrated. Few were women, despite the Women's Trade Union League, for women wage-earners had less incentive than men to belong to unions and less capacity to maintain them, and would not join in large numbers until more men's unions were opened to them.

2. *Union funds and benefits.* With about £4 per member on the average, funds were low relatively to the claims on them for strike pay and, increasingly, friendly benefit. There was no actuarial accountancy, but when outgoings rose dues were raised. Dues averaged about 6d. in the £ of wages. All unions gave dispute pay. Though the new unions had eschewed other benefits at first, they came to adopt them. Most unions except the general ones provided 'out of work donation', a benefit they could administer as the friendly societies could not. The unions were almost alone too in providing superannuation, which they could offer because they did not have to fund it, but for the most part only craft unions provided it. There were also sickness and accident benefits. Members accumulated entitlement by their contributions, but could not withdraw accruals if they left the union, nor bring an action to enforce their rights. Administration was conducted with striking economy, was in fact starved. In all, the unions were already providing a comprehensive

system of social assurance, which the welfare state did but generalize.

3. *The government of the unions.* There were still many single-celled unions, but most unions were made up of branches under a central administration. Centralization of the executive function increased the union's power to act, but raised the problem of democratic control, and union constitutions had numerous provisions designed to limit executive discretion or retain the initiative for the branches. It became increasingly possible for branches to send representatives to periodic assemblies, to which the executive reported. But because many particular causes of discontent at the place of work could not be dealt with by and through headquarters, unofficial strikes would break out, and were thought to show that the leaders were out of touch with the rank and file, or could not control them. The branch did not provide the remedy; in most trades the shop steward had not yet taken on his modern role; district officers were too few and apt to be preoccupied or removed in sympathy. Union constitutions also lacked devices for reconciling the interests of different occupational and industrial groups within a common union.

4. *Conflict between unions; federations.* Conflicts arose over fields of recruitment; poaching of members; the claim that one union had the exclusive right to a certain job (demarcation disputes); and clashes between skilled men and their unskilled helpers. In particular, demarcation disputes were endemic in building, engineering and shipbuilding. They were too fierce and too technical to lend themselves to arbitration. But some potentially conflicting unions set up joint committees of adjustment. The settlement of demarcation disputes also became a main function of the federations of unions, which had been formed in large numbers at the time of the New Unionism, with the primary object of adopting and pursuing a common policy in collective bargaining.

5. *Trades Councils.* There was a wide scope for the trades council as the common purposes committee of the unionists in each town, and at one time it looked like becoming their general headquarters with some functions of initiative. But the loyalties of the individual member ran more readily to his brethren of the craft elsewhere than to men of other occupations alongside him, and on the issues most important to him he looked for help

not to them but to the union which linked him with those of his own occupation throughout a district or even the whole country. Also the trades council was liable to be split by rows between unions. So issues of trade protection generally ceased to be brought to it, and the local issues it was left with, often political, were of less moment.

6. *The Trades Union Congress.* By 1906 Congress had become an assembly of unions, forming its executive by electing representatives for twelve trade groups, and having its own administrative service. But this was starved: the one executive field in which Congress was effective was Parliamentary business, and the matters it debated were mostly demands for action by Ministers or Parliament. It avoided involvement in trade disputes, and diverted the demand for organized mutual support by hiving off the General Federation of Trade Unions in 1899. It also avoided commitment to support independent Labour candidates, and hived this off to the Labour Representation Committee in 1900. It then continued its own specific task of Parliamentary pressure, on a growing scale: the election of 1906 gave it a great opportunity to advance its programme and it did this well. But it remained a loose association for restricted common purposes: it could not become a federation with its own government, ultimately because the leaders of the unions could not delegate an authority over their members that they themselves did not possess.

7. *The General Federation of Trade Unions* had been given no power to control its members' actions but it did have power to withhold benefit from them, and this it used to husband its exiguous funds: the Executive constantly exerted itself for 'peace by all means', and in practice mostly supported only small local disputes. But thereby it did itself actually take part in negotiations with employers. There was real scope for development here, as also in union recruitment and re-grouping, and in linking with the trade union centres in other countries; but the funds of the Federation were too small, some of the big unions never entered it, and it did not attract any leader of the first rank.

8. *Employers' Associations.* There are instances from early days, but for the most part these associations did not exist until trade union action induced employers to combine, and even so they

met their competitors reluctantly, and often broke away again. Existing associations varied widely in formality of constitution. Most were local, but there were some national federations of local associations. The main object was to keep a common line and help one another in resisting the unions, particularly to help one of their number who was singled out for union attack. The shipowners had been particularly active against the closed shop. But generally British employers combined only under pressure, and developed no strategy of their own: they worked uneasily with their competitors, they were not much interested in industrial relations, many of them were by no means hostile to the unions. The main function of many associations was to provide the employers' side of a joint board. Employers set up no counterpart to the T.U.C.: one or more national councils to combat the unions were launched but got little support.

9. *The fixing of wages within and without collective bargaining.* Four out of five employees made their own bargain. When applicants were more numerous than jobs, the wage could conceivably drop to 'the fodder basis', but this pressure bore hard in practice only on unqualified labour, and custom and relativity held wages up. The trade cycle brought phases of full employment for semi-skilled and skilled workmen. Demand and supply exerted a persistent and pervasive if slow-working pressure to change the relative pay of different occupations and to raise real wages as productivity rose. Combination brings in the possibility of backing a claim by a stoppage, but this does not inherently work more in favour of one party to the bargain than another, and generally the effect of collective bargaining has been only to move the wage rather sooner or farther in the direction in which market forces would have taken it in any case. The unwillingness of employers to combine and the strength of actual and potential competition inhibited the collusive potentialities of collective bargaining.

10. *The arrangements of collective bargaining.* Provision for regular meetings was found to promote agreement. For wages and hours the bargaining unit was generally delimited by district and occupation, but on grievance procedure and working practices there were some near industry-wide agreements. The subjects included in one agreement or another were: detailed provision for wages and hours; grievance procedure; procedure to vary

the agreement; workshop rules. When an agreement was made
to run for a fixed term of years the object was to avoid change
for as long as possible. Agreements had to be drafted in terms of
general application which often gave little guidance in particular
cases. The issues discussed by contemporaries were whether
voluntary agreements should be made legally binding on all
employers, and what could be done to check the disregard of
agreements by the rank and file of the unions.

11. *Relations at the place of work* remained remarkably unregulated. The one usual provision for them was by way of
grievance procedure, and this took the issue out of the hands of
the parties to it. Nor, save among the miners and printers, was
there a unit or organization that could represent the unionists in
any one firm; there were some shop stewards, but they did not
generally treat with management. But the workpeople upheld
practices whose functions were: to maintain the union and the
right to belong to it; to make employment more secure by
limiting access to jobs, restricting output, and resisting labour-
saving innovations; and to regulate the amount of effort that
they should provide in return for a given wage. Recent changes
in the workshop had upset customary arrangements, and the
growing size of the factory put more distance between manager
and men, and laid more responsibility on the foreman, who was
often ill prepared to bear it. Workshop committees grew up to
protect union members against pressures so arising, but they
were regarded by the union leaders with a distrust they
reciprocated.

Chapter VI. STRIFE 1906–14

1. *The Trade Disputes Act, 1906.* The Royal Commission which
reported in 1906 was agreed that the unions could not be
exempted again from all liability to be sued, but the majority
recommended that an action should not lie against a union
unless the act complained of was committed with the authority
of its executive. The government brought in a bill on these lines;
it dealt also with civil conspiracy, picketing, and interference
with a man's business as a ground of action. On the main issue
the House with the concurrence of the government preferred to
say outright that actions in tort should not lie against trade

unions. This anomalous immunity was conferred because it was thought to be the only sure way in practice to uphold the right to strike; and because it did but restore what had been the *de facto* position for thirty years before the Taff Vale judgment. It might have been better to have safeguarded the right to strike while outlawing unfair practices.

2. *The railwaymen, 1907.* The relative position of railwaymen had worsened since the 1880's and their prospects of promotion had declined. An Act of 1894 had virtually frozen railway rates, but since then costs of fuel and materials had risen, and the consequent downward pressure on wages was a reason for the unwillingness of management to recognize the unions. In November 1906 the Railway Servants drew up a national, all-grades programme. Three approaches to the companies were rejected: in October the members voted for a national strike. Lloyd George intervened and got the companies to accept a scheme of conciliation boards, though they still avoided recognizing the unions. The settlement showed how the stoppage of a basic industry would bring the government in: it had acted now to coerce the employers and impose an industry-wide settlement.

3. *The foundations of the welfare state, 1908–11.* When Lloyd George went to the Exchequer and Churchill to the Board of Trade in 1908 the government began an attack on destitution along the lines advocated by the T.U.C. and commended by the practical experience of the unions. Asquith's budget of 1908 had made financial provision for the Old Age Pensions Bill that Lloyd George brought in. Both reports of the Poor Law Commission recommended a national system of Labour Exchanges, and this was set up by an Act of 1909: in applying the Act Churchill worked closely with the T.U.C. A scheme of unemployment insurance which though limited in scope was 'a daring adventure' was embodied in Part II of the National Insurance Act, 1911. Part I applied health insurance on the German model to virtually all wage-earners. A number of measures helped children, notably the free place system in secondary schools. Trade Boards on the plan of Victoria were now seen as an extension of the Factory Acts, and a limited experiment in their use was made by Churchill's Act of 1909. The inequality of wealth was attacked by differentiation of tax between earned and unearned income in 1907, and by land

value duties and super tax in Lloyd George's budget of 1909.

4. *Wage cuts and the miners' Eight Hours, 1908–9.* In a sharp recession employers in shipbuilding and engineering on the North East Coast gave notice of cuts of about five per cent to take effect early in 1908. In the shipyards the woodworking unions held out for four months, in engineering three unions held out from February to August. In each case the federated employers eventually resorted to a general lockout of the unions concerned, and with Churchill's help agreement was then reached, virtually on the employers' terms. A dispute in cotton followed a very similar course. The strength of the men's resistance may be ascribed to their sense that a living wage should be a first charge on industry and to their unwillingness to give way to a demand in the absence of an accepted criterion of wage adjustment. It was a virtue of the 'machinery' the Board of Trade always tried to get adopted that its ritual did reduce this sense of arbitrariness. The disputes of 1908 show the area of bargaining being extended by the employers' action.

The Miners' Federation had made the statutory eight hours day its aim since 1888, but bills were opposed not only by the coalowners but by the Durham and Northumberland miners. The Act at last passed in December 1908 provided only for eight hours exclusive of winding times, and it led to many strikes when the men were confronted with consequential changes in working practices promulgated by management.

5. *The Cambrian stoppage, 1910–11; the seamen and dockers, the railwaymen, 1911.* The Cambrian stoppage marked the increasing economic tension in the coal industry caused mainly by falling productivity and the Eight Hours Act. It arose on the issue of the 'con' in the hard place: greater stringency in granting allowances encountered a greater militancy, especially among the younger men, who demanded a guaranteed minimum wage, and were moved by the syndicalist doctrine applied in *The Miners' Next Step.*

In June 1911 there was a spontaneous outburst of strikes of seamen, dockers and others in the ports, generally settled by raising wages. In August a strike of railwaymen in Liverpool quickly led to the threat of a national strike: the railwaymen were incensed by lagging wages, the ineffectiveness of the scheme of 1907, the non-recognition of their unions, the Osborne judgment. People felt that a revolutionary outburst impended. But Lloyd George got the railway companies to depute two spokesmen actually to meet the union leaders, and the men went back to work pending the report of the Royal Commission on the working of the scheme of 1907. When this report came out in November a resolution of the Commons led to the companies meeting the union leaders, and they adopted a modified conciliation scheme. As part of the settlement the Railway Traffic Act, 1913, permitted rises in rates needed to cover the cost of improved labour conditions. The Osborne judgment was reversed by the Trade Union Act, 1913.

6. *The coalmines and the Port of London, 1912; the Triple Alliance; the Midlands, 1913; the growth of unionism.* The whole Miners' Federation struck on 25 February 1912 to enforce a claim for a national minimum. Their rapid use of the industry-wide strike followed on the success of the railwaymen in 1907 and 1911, and their own success in getting the Eight Hours Act. But the government could not meet their present demand for a schedule of district rates and a national minimum of 'five and two'. It decided to go ahead with its own bill which provided only for district boards to fix minima. When the bill became law the miners' leaders availed themselves of the smallness of the majority for continuing the strike to call it off.

Some drew the lesson that industry-wide action was powerful but the front should be broader still. The Transport Workers' Federation had been formed in 1911, the N.U.R. was formed in 1913. But the Transport Workers were beaten in a big strike in the Port of London in May-August 1912, mainly on the non-unionist issue: they lacked support from outside. A general lock-out of the Irish Transport Workers by the Dublin employers in the autumn of 1913 also seemed to point the need for greater unity. On the initiative of the miners the Triple Alliance of the miners, railwaymen and transport workers was formed in January 1914.

In 1913 came 'the prairie fire in the Midlands', a spontaneous widespread outbreak of strikes centring on the claim for a minimum of 23s. a week. The unsuspected strength of unionism it revealed was part of the movement which raised total membership by two-thirds in 1910-13.

7. *The causes of the strife of 1910-14.* It seemed the more

ominous at the time because it reverberated with other conflicts — over the House of Lords, Home Rule and Ulster, votes for women — and with rising international tension. It also seemed part of an international movement of industrial revolt. But in fact the strife in Britain was mostly confined to two sectors — unskilled labour generally; and all grades in two industries, mining and the railways. For the unskilled 1911 was the second wave of the surge that had risen first in 1888: very likely the wave came now because of the rise in the cost of living from 1908. In the mines and railways management was caught between rising costs and insufficiently rising prices, and reacted sharply to any suggestion of higher wages. The concentration of disputes in these sectors largely explains why there was fighting: this broke out mainly over blacklegs. It is remarkable that other sectors were so little disturbed in a period when the advance of real wages was checked for near twenty years: perhaps the change was not clearly realized at the time. But an actual fall in real wages would surely cause unrest, and at this time the money wages particularly of the general worker did not rise readily to keep pace with the cost of living, because of the pressure of growing numbers, and because there was little organization that would enable competing employers to make a common advance of wages.

8. *Public policy towards disputes.* The tried and tested policy was to work for an immediate settlement through conciliation and then set up new or improved 'machinery' — a joint board of conciliation. This worked well when there was willingness to make some advance in wages and what had been lacking was co-ordination; but not in other tempers or on other issues. It was used to settle the two great industries that were in upheaval at this time because it was a device by which an extension of collective bargaining could be enforced on the employers from without. There was also a general faith in the curative power of the joint board, which shewed itself in the setting up of the Industrial Council after the troubles of 1911.

A different method was used to deal with disputes that involved the national stoppage of a basic industry. Here the government itself intervened, and what it did was to coerce the employers by the legislative power: mainly because employers are capable of coercion as the men are not. These improvised steps opened a new chapter in industrial relations: especially they seemed to show that the national strike of a basic industry would put irresistible pressure on the government, and they strengthened the tendency to widen the trade union front.

Chapter VII. SEQUEL AND SURVEY

1. *Why no revolt followed.* One reason was that after the war a rise in real wages came about through a rise in productivity in home industry, a favourable turn of the terms of trade, (probably) a generally lower rate of profit, and a reduced share of rent in the national income. This rise was not shared by the miners, the men in cotton, and the skilled men in engineering: big stoppages in all three industries were lost by the men. But the lower-paid wage-earners made a relative as well as an absolute advance, and poverty was greatly diminished. Other factors contributed, such as smaller families, social insurance, better housing. Class differences were reduced by the effects of tax on inequalities of property and income, and by a change of attitude and manners, which found practical expression at the place of work.

2. *The weapon of the stoppage of essential industries.* Lloyd George's policy in the disputes on the railways in 1907 and 1911 and in the mines in 1912 and 1915 indicated that the stoppage of an essential industry would oblige the government to impose a settlement acceptable to the men. The threat of such stoppages was used for political as well as industrial purposes in 1919–20. The government prepared to make a stand, by the Emergency Powers Act, 1920. On 'Black Friday' in 1921 the railwaymen and transport workers withdrew their undertaking to strike in support of the miners. Once the government had taken its stand the danger of a strategy that must end either in the defeat of the unions or the overthrow of constitutional government was apparent, but it was invoked to help the miners resist a wage cut in 1926: when the General Strike was called off a chapter was closed.

3. *How far have the basic problems of industrial relations been solved?* These problems take their rise when population grows so that many men cannot get access to land and have to seek jobs which can be offered only by those who have capital and technical

knowledge. This brings difficulties, through subordination of those who take orders to those who give them, inability of workers to identify themselves with their work, clash of economic interests, and fear of getting the worst of the wage bargain. But the expectation that the advance of industrialism would confound all other social differences in one great cleavage between capital and labour has been falsified: partly because industry has provided higher standards of living and with these has come a reduction of social inequalities generally, partly because within the field of industrial relations proper there has been a growth of effective institutions and procedures. The improvement in British industrial relations since 1914 must be attributed to the circumambient changes rather than the internal.

4. *The negativism of British public policy towards industrial relations.* In the Factory Acts and the like, Parliament regulated the conditions of employment in detail, but in disputes it confined itself to conciliation, and it did not try to impose settlements, only help the parties to set up their own 'appropriate machinery'. This contrasts with compulsory arbitration in Australia and New Zealand, and co-ordinated action towards a national wages policy in Holland and Scandinavia; but these do not make so much difference in practice as to call British policy into question in these respects. It is otherwise in the regulation of the institutions and procedures of industrial relations, where Britain is conspicuous for the absence of a positive code of law. The case against providing this is that it is contentious, and cannot ensure good relations in the absence of goodwill, whereas if that is present it is unnecessary. But many issues calling for the definition of rights and redress of wrongs mark out industrial relations as proper to the rule of law.

5. *The predominance of industry-wide bargaining in Britain.* In 1914 some industries had what were at once district and nearly industry-wide agreements, and there were industry-wide agreements on procedure, but most bargaining about wages was by districts. But both employers and unionists had some instigation to widen the area of the bargain; and when disputes broke out in 1906–14 it was usually found easier to reach and maintain a settlement if 'machinery' was set up that would assure all employers that their competitors would be paying the same rate. The war removed competitive restraints on the widening of the

c

area, and hastened it by the need to raise money wages generally. The Whitley Committee assumed that organization should be industry-wide, and the Trade Boards Act of 1918 provided for 'regulation of wages throughout the trade'. Industry-wide bargaining has also been promoted by the occupational divisions of unionism, and by the employers' recognition that it made rises easier to grant and did not encroach on the 'prerogatives of management'. But it left a gap in the firm, which the shop steward and joint consultation mark the effort to fill. It has also concentrated wage negotiation on a point where little can be done to raise real wages, which experience shows depend chiefly on productivity. Meanwhile managers and unions alike have not sufficiently developed the possibilities of joint action to raise the status and real earnings of the workpeople firm by firm.

INTRODUCTION

'Humanity is like the sea,' Lloyd George said in 1910 [1] 'It is never quite free from movement, but there are periods of comparative calm and others of turbulence and violent disturbance. Everything points to the fact that the storm cone has been hoisted and that we are in for a period of tempests.' It was of social strife that he was thinking, and he proved right. Even when he spoke a dispute had begun in the Rhondda whose obstinacy and bitterness marked a new temper. The four years that followed showed it to be widespread. Strike followed strike. Though disputes were mostly small and local, their mounting frequency revealed an increasing impatience; and some great strikes stood out, threatening for the first time in our history to bring all the wheels of the country to a standstill for lack of fuel or transport, and so effectively challenging the authority of government itself. There was an impact in the mood as well as the extent of the conflict that made some observers believe they were being borne onwards to an hour of destiny. In the quieter light of retrospect those years still stand out as one of the critical phases of tension and transition in our social history.

As such they challenge diagnosis. Why did such a head of resentment and intransigence build up at all, and why just then? What shift had come about in the balance of social forces, and how did it impinge on attitudes and institutions? The first object of this book is to answer these questions. It endeavours to portray the condition of the people and the state of industrial relations in 1906–14, so as to account for the pressures generated in that setting, and their outcome.

But there is another question, particularly concerning industrial relations in Britain, which this study may help to answer — how they came by some of those peculiarities which mark them off to-day from those even of kindred countries. Unlike the trade unionists of Sweden and Western Germany, those of Britain are not marshalled industry by industry, but segregated

[1] Address to the Liberal-Christian League at the City Temple, 17 October 1910.

according to affinities of locality and especially of occupation, so that those in any one industry commonly belong to a number of different unions. Yet, unlike the unionists of the United States, they do predominantly join one another in negotiations that cover a whole industry; and unlike the unionists of Holland, France, or India, they are not divided into constellations of conflicting political or religious adherence. This unity, however, does not extend to wage policy: British unions will not accept, as the Scandinavian and Dutch unions do, the guidance and participation of their national congress in their negotiations with employers. There are contrasts too in what is negotiated: collective bargaining in Britain commonly arrives at agreements about the particular issues in dispute from time to time, but seldom at comprehensive and detailed regulations of the conditions of employment and the working relations of management and labour, such as the American plant contracts provide; nor do British agreements usually have a fixed date of expiry as the American do. There is a deep-going difference, again, between the British attitude to the proper role of government in industrial relations, and that held by the community, and in great measure by the unions too, in some countries whose political traditions and social structure do not prepare us for so much divergence. Unlike the American Congress, the British Parliament has not enacted any code to regulate the dealings of employers and unions with one another, or of the unions with their members. New Zealand and Australia have long banned strike and lockout, and provided for the compulsory arbitration of industrial disputes: in Britain it is the right to strike that Parliament has been concerned to preserve, and save in time of war arbitration has been looked upon mainly as an expedient to be adopted, if at all, only with the consent of both parties and at the final stage of negotiation. When with such differences as these in mind we look at a cross-section cut fifty years back, we shall naturally ask how far they had already appeared, and what forces had already shaped them or were shaping them then. Since societies having many similarities with ours have developed such contrasted systems of industrial relations, we must suppose that our own could conceivably have come out differently, and in tracing its growth we must pause to think of what might have happened as well as of what actually did.

The present study is therefore something more in purpose than an account of one period alone, and its title expresses a prevailing interest in origins and development. It does not only depict the state of affairs in 1906–14, but looks backward from it to see how it had been reached through the years before, and forward, to ask how far it accounts for what goes on to-day.

When our aim is to single out what is crucial in a long story of growth and change, there are advantages in fixing our viewpoint in this period which is removed by half a century from the present yet has so much in common with it. It lies in its own continuous relation with the Victorian expansion, but was also the time when powerful forces broke surface that have shaped the British community of to-day, and in that sense it is contemporary. The general election of January 1906 is a landmark in our social history. The Liberal majority and the return of twenty-nine independent Labour candidates were not simply the swing of a familiar pendulum, but marked the opening of a new era. It had been brought in by general elementary education, votes for wage-earners, and a heightened resentment against the industrial system. Ways of dealing between master and workman and differences in wealth and opportunity between classes that had been taken for granted when most workmen were uneducated now appeared as oppressive and unjust. Hardships no greater than before were felt more keenly. They were the more resented because they were believed to be gratuitous. Illiterate men find it hard to see how things, however harsh for them, can be different from what they are, but now education had diffused among wage-earners the capacity to conceive of a new social order.

Their resentment and faith bore mainly on the contrast of poverty and riches, and the relations between employer and employed. We shall begin by asking how these two matters stood when the new House of Commons met in 1906 to consider the stormy prospect they afforded.

CHAPTER I

THE CONDITION OF THE PEOPLE

I

The greatest influence on the material welfare of the British people in 1906 was the vast increase in their numbers. In the middle of the eighteenth century England and Wales had had not much more than six million inhabitants; the census of 1901 enumerated more than thirty-two million. That was multiplication by about five in a century and a half: a rate of growth whose extraordinary magnitude is suggested by the reflection that if no more than two hundred thousand people — only as many as live in Plymouth to-day — had started to increase like this at the time of the Conquest, and the rate had been sustained, their successors in the early twentieth century would have been as numerous as the whole actual population of the world at that time. A vital revolution had come about in the eighteenth century. About 1740, the death-rate in England and Wales seems to have begun a fall which, persisting with only minor intermissions, halved it by 1900; but the birth-rate probably did not go well below its level of 1740 till after 1880. That level had once been no higher than would make good the ravages of disease: in the course of the eighteenth century those ravages fell off — we do not know why — but the old habits of procreation persisted. So it came about that decade by decade through the next century the population of England and Wales rose never by less than eleven per cent, sometimes by as much as fourteen. The Victorians faced a problem as big for them as that of finding houses, jobs, and food for another six million people within the next ten years would be for us. It was remarkable that they solved it at all. It was a miracle that the bulk of the people in 1906 were better off than their forbears had been when the vast expansion began.

In the usual course of history, such an unbalancing of birth-rate and death-rate as had happened here would have led to an outpouring of hordes over other lands, or a great famine and killing off, or, less drastically, a progressive reduction of the original impetus by the increasing misery it brought. This last consequence had probably been experienced once already in these islands. The fifteenth century, for all the Wars of the Roses, had been a high plateau of economic prosperity: we know that the wage of a mason or carpenter then would buy him as much of the basic materials of consumption as his successors in the same crafts were getting around 1880, and it is very probable that this material well-being was general. But at Henry VIII's accession, a decline set in, and it went on relentlessly through Elizabeth's reign, until at the worst, under James I, the building craftsman's wage would only buy two-fifths or less of what his predecessor's had commanded a century before. We cannot be sure, but the evidence agrees with the assumption that the cause was a great growth of population, pressing ever harder on in-expansive food supplies: and if that was so we might attribute the checking of the fall in the wage-earner's dietary to the progressive tendency of that fall itself to reduce births, or in-crease deaths, or both, and so restore the balance that had been upset in Henry VII's time. At any rate, we know that though men died of hunger in a year of bad harvest, the fall was halted without any cataclysm of famine.

But more recently, in Ireland, there had been a cataclysm. In the eighteenth century the Irish people had begun to increase at much the same time as the English: possibly for different reasons, probably no less rapidly. A population of about four millions in 1781 added as many again to its own numbers in the next sixty years while sending out another million and three quarters to Britain and America. The doubling of the number of mouths to feed within Ireland itself was made possible largely by growing more potatoes. But in 1817 there began a series of partial failures of the crop, followed by epidemics of fever. In 1846 disease destroyed the harvest: there was absolute famine. 'Generally speaking the actually starving people lived upon the carcases of diseased cattle, upon dogs, and dead horses, but principally on the herbs of the field, nettle tops, wild mustard, and watercresses, and even in some places dead bodies were found with grass in their mouths.'[1] In the five years beginning

[1] *Census of Ireland*, 1851, V, p. 243.

with 1846 perhaps a million people died in Ireland in excess of the normal mortality, and another million and a half fled the country. The prodigious increase of numbers in the island was not merely checked, it was sharply reversed: the eight millions of 1841 receded decade by decade through the rest of the century, to only four millions and a half in 1901.

Britain, less dependent on the potato, was less exposed to sudden and utter destitution; but those who saw how population was growing there had reason to expect that checks just as powerful if not so abrupt would be imposed there too. For the growth had begun independently of food supplies, and was going on without regard to them. The empty stomachs came first, the food for them had to be found afterwards, if it could be found at all.

But we know that the worst never came to the worst; the rate of growth that in Ireland reached and passed breaking point, in England went on and on. The reason we know too: the biological revolution was followed by agrarian and industrial revolutions, that greatly increased the yield of British fields, but above all increased the ability of the British people to bring food in from overseas. They saved themselves from the fate of the Irish, by manufacturing with ever improved machinery products they could barter for the harvests of other lands ; and carried both by ever improved means of transport over land and water. There was a race between population and productivity; for a time population led; then productivity caught up and drew ahead.

So industrialism and international trade not only saved an ever-growing population from starvation, but after a time brought it a rising standard of living. Our most continuous record of wages is for the building craftsman and labourer; the two kept a fairly steady proportion, with the craftsman getting half as much again as the labourer, and it is unlikely that this labourer's wage will have differed much from the wage of unskilled labour generally. When the rise in population set in, about the middle of the eighteenth century, builders' wages in the Thames valley were buying about two-thirds as much of the materials of consumption as their predecessors' wages had commanded in the fifteenth century. Then came a fall, steepened in the Napoleonic Wars, from two-thirds to less than a half of the old basketful — little more than in the worst days under

James I. With peace came a recovery that proved progressive. To the builders the Hungry Forties brought at least as much purchasing power in return for a day's work as had the best part of the century before; about 1880 they even recovered, and passed, the fifteenth century level; by 1906 they were a third above it. There were many changes meanwhile in the relative standing of wage-earners in different callings, and different parts of the country, but we can take the builders as sufficiently representative of the general run to give us at least the order of magnitude of its movement: then we can say that since the growth of population began, the amount of materials that prevailing wages would buy had about doubled at the same time as the numbers to be fed within a small island had increased fivefold. We know of nothing like this in the history of the world before. It was achieved through technical innovation and improvement in agriculture, industry, and transport, and the opening up of new lands overseas.

2

More babies were being born in Britain in the first decade of the twentieth century than ever before. We can now add, than ever since. In fact, there had long been signs that a change was coming, and the births of those years were more numerous because there were more married couples and not because these had more children apiece. On the contrary, they had fewer: the Victorian family in its heyday had typically had five or six children, but the couples who married in 1900–7 were only going to have little more than three children each on the average, and those who married in 1910–14 less than three.

The change had become apparent in the 1870's, but only at the top of the social scale. It took time to spread. Meanwhile, it increased the difference between the way of life and material well-being of different social types and groups. The divergence was already apparent among the families whose children had all been born by the 1880's: the miners, farm workers, and unskilled labourers had more than the average number of children, the professional and administrative classes far less. After that the number decreased in all walks of life, but most rapidly where it was already smallest, so that the divergence widened: there was much more difference between the average doctor's family and the average miner's in 1906 than thirty years before. Among the brides of the 1850's, for instance, the miners' were to have about eight children each, to the six of the doctors' and lawyers'; among those of the early 1880's the miners' were still to have about seven, but the doctors' and lawyers' now not even so many as four.

This marked a social cleavage. It was a movement towards greater inequality. In 1850 the families to be supported by the incomes of the professional man and the labourer were of much the same size: the professional man would have had six children on the average, the labourer seven, but a higher rate of mortality among the labourer's children would have reduced this difference. By 1900, however, the children of the professional man would now typically number no more than four, whereas the labourer would still have six, and their dependence on his earnings had been extended by their mostly being forbidden to go to work before they were fourteen. If a child made only half the claim of an adult on the family purse, then this divergence would have been equivalent to a rise of a quarter in the incomes of professional men without any change in those of labourers — a shift we should reckon dramatic if it actually had come about in that way. Yet, in its own way, it did actually come about, and it was apparent to contemporaries, who noticed it in an increased ease of living among the middle classes, a greater ability to spend on personal services, on dress, travel, and pleasure generally. There were the golf-course and the weekend; the mock-Tudor house with its tennis court; the prep school and the public school; and, most conspicuous of all, the motor-car, which made so great an impression of affluence, and even of arrogance, with its noise and choking dust and lethal speed. Middle-class families found the money and time for these things more easily because they had fewer children. For the labourer and his wife there was no corresponding relief and indulgence.

But why did the gap open? Why were the families of most of the wage-earners not reduced as much as those of the clerk, the shopkeeper and the professional man? The Census of 1911 showed that some wage-earners were in fact having no more children than the middle classes. These were the men with indoor jobs other than factory work — the domestic servants, caretakers, and waiters; men in the textile trades, where it was so usual for the wife to be going out to work too; and, perhaps, the alert men who were taking up the new trades of electrical work and motor manufacture, though not a little allowance is due here for there being more young men among them, and so a higher proportion of families which were uncompleted at the time of the census. Most of these occupations did not require a high standard of education, or pay high wages, and the small families in them are evidence that there was nothing in the position of the wage-earner as such to prevent him from limiting the number of his children. Perhaps the factors which none the less did keep up the size of most wage-earning families will be brought out if we look to the other extreme. The biggest families were those of men doing rough muscular work in the open air — dock labourers, dustmen, coal heavers, building labourers, navvies, fishermen, and farm labourers — or in arduous conditions — the men in the coal mines, in the iron and steel furnaces and mills, in glass works and gas works and potteries. Many of these were among the lowest paid, but by no means all of them: not the miners, nor the iron and steel workers. One thing they had in common was that they did not call for booklearning; but here again, though some of the occupations with small families needed a good education and kept the mind exercised — that of compositor, for instance — most of them did not. Only the roughness of the work — the bodily exertion, the exposure to heat and dust and weather — seems to provide a factor that is consistently different between the two groups. Perhaps it can also be traced in a gradation through the families of intermediate size, with coopers, oil millers, soap and manure and tannery workers, blacksmiths and painters among the larger; and then, with smaller families, the railwaymen, the tram and bus men, the factory trades and the building craftsmen.

What explanation does this suggest? It may be that rough and hard work increases desire, as danger does, or makes men want children more. But a stronger reason is probably that it makes men conservative in the social sense — less ready to change their ways and take up new ideas. In 1873 the Cambridge economist Alfred Marshall[1] had stressed how bodily fatigue inhibits thought among 'those vast masses of men who, after

---

[1] 'The Future of the Working Classes,' reprinted in *Memorials of Alfred Marshall*, ed. A. C. Pigou (1925).

long hours of hard and unintellectual toil, are wont to return to their narrow homes with bodies exhausted and with minds dull and sluggish'. 'We have all heard', he went on, 'what rude manners have been formed by the rough work of the miners; but even among them the rougher the work of the body, the lower the condition of the mind. Iron miners, for instance, are a superior race to colliers.' It happens that the Census of 1911 found that the number of children born to a hundred couples was 360 for the coal miners, 343 for the iron miners.

But whatever the effect of exhausting work, it is apparent that of the reasons generally accepted for family limitation in more recent years, a number will have acted only so far as people were aware of new ideas and responsive to them, or were quick to follow those changes in fashion that usually begin at the top of the social scale and travel down it. Such are the growth of a personal responsibility for the well-being of the children one has brought into the world; the spread of the scientific outlook, breaking down inhibitions, and increasing men's belief in their power to control their lives; the extension of the small family simply as a fashion with which men conform to avoid appearing unusual; and especially the rising status of women, which made wives less willing to be exhausted by pregnancies and worn out by family cares, and (though this more slowly) raised the cost of children by giving a daughter nearly as great a claim on her parents' purse as a son.

There were two vicious circles that help to account for the family limitation coming more slowly where families were bigger to start with. One centred upon the age of marriage. Generally, the more numerous the children, the younger the mother had been when she wed. At the extremes, in 1911, less than a third of the wives of professional men, but three-quarters of the wives of miners, had married before they were twenty-five; and a fairly steady relation runs through the intermediate occupations — where the families are bigger, a higher proportion of the wives married early. Early marriage made a bigger family more likely: a young bride would be a wife during more of her child-bearing years, and during more of those earlier years, moreover, in which fertility is greater. But bigger families might themselves be a cause of earlier marriages among the children who grew up in them. Parents would not be loath to see the elder children leave overcrowded homes. Children whose upbringing had given them little ability or incentive to look ahead, and save or work for a distant object, would not find waiting easy for anything. Those whose standard of living was already so low that an early marriage could hardly lower it further, who could hope to put by very little even by severe self-denial, and who could not expect to be earning more later on, had little rational inducement to wait.

The other vicious circle centred on infantile mortality. The more babies were born, the higher the proportion of them who died. With few exceptions, this connexion was close and regular throughout the range from small families to big, so that if we know the size of family prevailing in a given occupation we can predict accurately the rate of child mortality there; and conversely. In part, the connexion must have been direct, and reciprocal: where many babies were born, there could have been less care for each; and where many babies died, there was more room for more. But the size of family and the rate of infantile mortality will also have undergone a common influence in the habit of life, the way of thought of the parents. The grouping was by occupation rather than by income: and in the occupations where infantile mortality remained high, people were backward — not so much aware as others of ideas in the air, not so used to taking an initiative in their own interests, not so capable of changing their habits, or working for distant aims. It is at least probable that these were also the substantial reasons for their not limiting their families.

But from the turn of the century the gap between the classes no longer widened, for the decrease in the number of births became no less rapid now among the manual workers than in middle class families — among the miners, indeed, it was more rapid. So by 1939 the difference in size of family between different social groups was to become rather smaller than it had been in 1914, and since the number of children had decreased again meanwhile all round, the remaining difference would not have been felt so much. If the backwardness of some occupations was the cause of the divergence opening, we can attribute the change that set in about 1900 to the progressive effect on mental alertness of the elementary education which had advanced so far since 1870 in extent and quality. Stephen Reynolds, living among Devon fishermen at this time, wrote that 'the older-fashioned working man will not consider voluntary limitation of the family. To his mind it is unnatural and wicked. But the younger generation is keenly interested in its possibilities and personal advantages, and its advantages to the children who are born.'[1]

3

The growth of population that was still going on fast in the first decade of the twentieth century had made a great internal migration necessary. Though there had been little movement over long distances, there had been much over short. The over-spill of the ever-growing population in the countryside moved, where it could, into adjacent centres of industry, in search of better jobs, or any job at all. This exodus seldom brought an absolute fall in numbers in the regions which it left, but it did reduce the pressure there, so that these regions in their turn received an inflow from rural districts further out. Thus a succession of short moves shifted the balance of the whole population: the towns everywhere grew faster than the country, the north of England grew faster than the south.

Towards the end of the nineteenth century, the shifting of the balance came, for the most part, to an end; in some respects it was even reversed. The one exception was the continued growth of some of the coalfields, and especially of South Wales: the population of Glamorgan more than doubled between 1881 and 1911. But otherwise the movement of more than a hundred years came to an end.

The towns as a whole ceased to grow at the expense of the countryside, largely because the villages, having lost so many potential parents in the migrations of earlier years, had fewer children now. 'In a single decade,' Cairncross says,[2] 'as many as forty per cent of the young men aged 20–30 might migrate from some rural districts, and the final loss from one generation might come to nearly two out of three.' None the less, there was gener-ally no absolute decline: only in the 1880's had there been an absolute fall in the population of the English countryside as a

---

[1] *Seems so! A Working Class View of Politics*, by Stephen Reynolds and Bob and Tom Woolley (1912), p. 266.
[2] A. K. Cairncross, *Home and Foreign Investment, 1870-1913* (1953), p. 75.

whole, and there were more people living in it on the eve of the First World War than there had been before the repeal of the Corn Laws. By the turn of the century the rural population had reached a level not greater than could be supported by a more prosperous agriculture, and by contacts with the nearby town facilitated by bicycle and bus.

The growth of the towns was also checked because they were becoming congested, and this was raising the costs of industry, and inducing firms to set up their new plants in smaller places, or even to move out from the city in which they had long been established. The cost of living was generally higher for the workman in the town for two reasons: higher rent, and the daily journey to work. Trade unions being stronger in the towns obtained a differential to compensate these costs; sometimes perhaps rather more than this. So though the towns continued to attract manufacturers by the size of the labour market they afforded, their higher labour costs were beginning to repel them. 'The employers of trade union labour', said a surveyor who gave evidence before the Royal Commission on London Traffic in 1904,[1] 'have already in many instances withdrawn from London, where the highest rates of wages obtain,' and he gave a list of ten printing firms who had moved to the country; some engineering firms, too, he said, had gone.

About 1890 it must have seemed likely that our cities were nearing saturation point: they could hardly find room for more people in their central districts, and the cost of local transport was so high for the workman of those days that they could hardly grow by extension either. There was a consequent agitation for more and cheaper local transport. In 1883 a Cheap Trains Act had obliged the railway companies to run more workmen's trains as the Board of Trade might direct; the new London County Council began to press for more services: there was a National Association for the Extension of Workmen's Fares. Workmen's trains did in fact greatly increase in number, but even when the journey by steam train was cheap it was still likely to be tiring, with a long walk at either end, and an infrequent service. Looking forward, an observer of the time might well have held that the cities had reached their limit, that

---

[1] Memorandum of Evidence by Mr H. T. Scoble, Appendix No. 66 to *Report of Royal Commission on London Traffic*, (Vol. III, Cd. 2752 of 1905).

industry must begin to spread more evenly over the country, that any further urbanization could come only through the expansion of the country towns. But then came two new techniques which revolutionised local transport: the electric railway, and the motor bus. With these, local transport could be more frequent, more flexible, and, especially, far more pervasive than ever before. By 1895 workmen's trams were running throughout South London; the London County Council developed a housing estate at Tooting, and the number of workmen's tickets sold on the trams that served it rose in the ten years before the War from half a million a year to near nine millions. The constraints on the great towns were off; they set out on their most rapid and extensive consumption of the green fields.

Meanwhile, however, the congestion of the towns was still bad enough to check the inflow to them, and perhaps accounted also for an outflow which now arose, so that after 1900 some towns had a net loss of population by migration. London was one of these, but most of the other southern towns continued to grow, and the contraction was mainly in the towns of the north. No longer was the north growing faster than the south. The reversal of the balance of industry and population that was to become prominent in the years between the two great wars was already apparent in the 1890's.

But the British remained a migratory people. More than a third of the men born in England and Wales who remained there to be enumerated in the Census of 1911 had by then left their native county. The proportion of the natives who went away was highest in the rural counties — Rutland, Huntingdon and Radnor sent out more than half, quite apart from those who left the country altogether; Berkshire and Oxfordshire, Hereford and Brecon very nearly half. At the other end of the scale were the industrial, and especially the mining counties; but of all the counties south of the Border, only three — Lancashire, Durham, and Glamorgan — sent out less than a quarter of their sons. It was the other side of the same penny that more than a third of the people of England and Wales in 1911 had moved into the county in which they were found then from another county in which they had been born. The proportion of immigrants in the local population naturally varied even more than that of the natives who had moved away. It was generally higher in the

D

towns than in the country; in those towns whose recent growth had been rapid it was more than a half: they were congeries of strangers. But this apart, there was no bias of movement. It was not the case, for instance, that the most rural counties which had sent out a high proportion of their own sons generally received few of other counties': on the contrary, there was much movement into them. Nor was it the case that the more industrial counties generally held a higher proportion of immigrants than did the rural counties: at one time that must have been so, but in 1911 the proportion of immigrants was high in Rutland and Berkshire, for instance, and relatively low in Yorkshire and Durham.

So there was much movement into and out of most parts of the country; and though, as before, most of these moves were over short distances, it is hard to find any two districts between which some movement cannot be traced. Take, for example, three county boroughs, Canterbury, Exeter, Wolverhampton: the Census of 1911 found at least one man native to each of these in every county and county borough of England and Wales, with negligible exceptions — of some four hundred and fifty possible moves, only nine had not been made. It may seem unlikely that any natives of Canterbury would be found in South Shields or Wigan, Anglesey or Montgomery; but they were. Or again, from each of three counties, Berkshire, Huntingdon, and Westmoreland, some natives were found in 1911 in every county and county borough of England and Wales, with only this one exception, that there was no one from Huntingdon in Tynemouth.

This general post, moreover, had recently quickened. In 1901 the men who were found in some part of England and Wales other than their native county made up some twenty-eight per cent of the whole; ten years later the percentage was thirty-six.

The effect of this movement on the life of the British people must have been profound. It would be too much to say that it made them an uprooted people, for not many more than a third of them were leaving the region of their birth, and of those who did many moved too short a distance to cut off their old ties and make them altogether strangers in their new location. But it seems likely that so much internal migration must have had some at least of the disturbing effects which are known to

attend international migration: have brought with it some lone-
liness, and strangeness, some loss of the arts of living and the
supports of kith and kin. For a young man setting out to seek his
fortune, migration can be an opportunity and a liberation; but
most of the British migrants, if moved by an impulse of adventure, and attracted by the higher wages to be earned in the
towns, were impelled also by the sheer necessity to find any sort
of job at all. ' "There was more mouths to be fed at home than
could be fed" ' old Alice said, in Mrs Gaskell's *Mary Barton*.
' "Tom . . . had come to Manchester, and sent word what
terrible lots of work was to be had, both for lads and lasses. So
father sent George first . . . and then work was scarce out
towards Burton, where we lived, and Father said I maun try
and get a place. And George wrote as how wages were far
higher in Manchester than Milnthorpe or Lancaster; and, lasses,
I was young and thoughtless, and thought it was a fine thing to
go so far from home." ' That sums up the motives; and then —
' "Eh, lasses! ye don't know what rocks are in Manchester! . . .
I often wonder if the hawthorn is standing yet, and if the lasses
still go to gather heather, as we did many and many a year past
and gone." '

4

The race between productivity and population had been won
by productivity, and the standard of living of the British people
had risen despite the continued increase in their numbers; but
the rate of improvement had been variable. Over a century the
advance was great, but there were times when many people
found their progress halted or reversed. Since the repeal of the
Corn Laws the wage-earner had suffered little from the great
affliction of his forbears, the dire dearth, the starvation even,
that followed a failure of the harvest. But he was still sorely
beset by the ups and downs of trade. Economic forces bore upon
him just as the currents of tide and river water, the rolling in of
the waves and the gusts of the wind, bear on the surface of an
estuary. In these movements we can trace three sorts of fluctuation.

The first was in the terms of foreign trade. The produce
annually available to the British people depended not only on
the skill and vigour with which they worked at home, but also

on how much foodstuffs and raw materials they were able to get from time to time in exchange for the part of their output that they sent overseas. This part was substantial: in the 1900's it was a sixth of the national product, and it was rising. But the wage-earners had more at stake than these proportions of a national aggregate would by themselves suggest, for they spent some seven-tenths of their income on food, drink, and clothing, and the terms on which they could obtain wheat and meat, wool and cotton in exchange for their own labour mattered to them accordingly. These terms were made up of two elements. The first was the productivity of British labour in manufacturing the goods Britain exported: how much could the wage-earner turn out in a day's work? The various forces of economic progress at home had greatly increased this amount in the course of the nineteenth century, and at its close the day's work was yielding the wage-earner a far bigger product of manufactures. He then, in effect, took the greater part of this product to barter it for foodstuffs and raw materials, and here the second element came in: how much of these things would be available in the markets of the world in exchange for each bar of steel or bale of cloth Britain sent out? There had in fact been a periodic swing in the answer to that question, and it had been big enough to make marked changes in the rate of growth of the amount of imports the wage-earner could win by a day's work. From one end of the nineteenth century to the other, that amount had increased almost fourfold; but a period of rapid rise after the Napoleonic Wars had ended in a setback in the 1850's and 1860's, and the renewed rise that followed had in its turn been broken off in the 1890's. The wage-earners became very conscious of that turn of the tide. The twenty years before had accustomed them to a persistently falling cost of living, while their own money wages altered little on the whole; now the changed balance of the markets of the world came home to them through rising prices in the shops, and their wages did not rise in proportion. They had been used to getting a little better off year by year, and now it seemed they had only impoverishment to look forward to. They resented this the more keenly because meanwhile their subjective standard of living, the livelihood to which they felt themselves entitled, had been raised by the continued extension of education among them. The recent worsening of their condition seemed to bear out the prophecies of Marx, whose work was becoming increasingly known. But in fact it arose from forces beyond the power of anyone in Britain to control, from the long pulsation of the balance of supply and demand in the markets where the manufacturing peoples of the world exchanged their wares for the foodstuffs and raw materials of the farmers, planters, and miners. By multiplying their numbers in a small island, the British people had given hostages to fortune.

It seems likely that the adverse movement of the world market that set in against Britain in the 1890's was aggravated because there was some check at this time to the rate at which the British wage-earner was getting the benefit of technical advance. The secular rise in the amount of manufactures that he could make in a day had been made possible first and foremost by the ingenuity of the inventor and the skill of the engineer, but the benefits of innovation were enjoyed widely only in proportion as the new methods were given widespread and massive application, and this was often not till many years after the pioneers had made their break through. The heroic age of the steam engine was in the eighteenth century, and Bessemer's way of making steel had been announced in 1856, but it was in the great rise in the standard of living after 1870 that the great harvest of Steam and Steel was reaped. 'It has been said, and it may be with truth,' said the report of the Royal Commission on Gold and Silver in 1888,[1] 'that the development of machinery was as great in the fifteen or twenty years which preceded 1874, as in the subsequent years, and that steam transport has been also largely developed in the earlier period. But not only has the actual extension of railways and the cheapening of land and sea freight been greater in the subsequent years, but the effect of railways which had been previously made has been more felt.... Large new districts of great natural fertility, and rich in minerals, have been opened up, and consequently civilized countries have been furnished with an unprecedented quantity of raw vegetable and mineral products.' So great a stride forward in technique as the substitution, for example, of a steel steamship for a sailing ship, makes a great and immediate difference to output per man; but then the rate of progress must fall off, unless new technical advances are reaching the stage of widespread application in

[1] Cd. 5512 of 1888, Pt. II, para. 26.

time to take up the running. In the 1890's the great harvest of steam and steel came to an end, and we entered upon a pause in economic growth: not that new ideas — the internal combustion engine, the new chemical processes, the manifold uses of electricity, the synthetic fibres — were not being developed, but that not till during and after the First World War did they reach the stage of widespread application.

The second sort of fluctuation in the rise of the British wage-earner's income seems to have arisen ultimately from variations in the rate of growth of America. It has been explored by Brinley Thomas.[1] There was a constant interplay, in what he calls the Atlantic economy, between a Europe that provided migrants, equipment, and capital, and a North American continent that attracted them. But the rate at which they were drawn in fluctuated, and this imposed a reciprocal fluctuation on the rates at which equipment and population accumulated within Britain. At one time, between 1870 and 1914, the westward flow would be strong, and in America the rate of growth of population, and income, and the stock of buildings and other fixed capital, would all be high, while in Britain they would be checked just because so much was going out of the country. Then the flow would fall, and with it the rate of expansion in America, while the check to the export of men and capital would raise the rate of growth of output and equipment within Britain. These forces bore especially on the British building industry, and may account for the cycle of twenty to twenty-five years that has been traced in its activity: a trough in the 1880's, a rise persisting to a peak near the end of the century, and then a recession down to 1914 — the industry was sadly short of work in some of those years. This pattern for building indicates the course of variation in the other sectors that felt the forces of the Atlantic economy.

It will be seen that these forces brought a check to the rate of economic growth in Britain just at the time, at the end of the nineteenth century, when the world market was turning against Britain too. A recent study[2] has found that between 1900 and 1913 there was little change in the quantity of goods and services consumed by the average Briton. The national total of consump-

---

[1] Brinley Thomas, *Migration and Economic Growth* (1954).
[2] A. R. Prest, *Consumers' Expenditure in the U.K. 1900-1919* (1954).

tion appears to have risen by about fifteen per cent, which is not much more than the eleven per cent by which an ever-rising population increased meanwhile; and the food and clothing that mattered so much to the wage-earner did not show even that small improvement. This is very different from the record of the thirty years before, in which the basketful of goods that the average British wage would buy had increased by two-thirds. There is no doubt that wage-earners felt the contrast, resented it, and increasingly blamed capitalism for it.

The third sort of fluctuation in the British economy had a shorter period than the first two. The trade cycle, as it was called, had an average length of about nine years. Within that span would fall some years of rising activity, in which employment and output increased; then came a turning point, not necessarily sharp enough to be called a crisis, followed by some years of decline, to a trough where unemployment was severe and enterprise subdued; and then a recovery came about, and brought in the rising phase of the next cycle. This kind of rhythm can be traced in the eighteenth century; after the middle of the nineteenth it was clear cut. Like the other two fluctuations, it seems to have been transmitted through foreign trade, for since 1850 the first sign of the onset of a depression had usually been a drop in exports. It was understandable that the loss of income in so big a sector of the British economy should have depressed the home market in which the other sectors were selling. But the internal changes that followed had their own pattern and self-perpetuating propensities. When activity fell, it was investment — making of buildings and equipment — that fell most. The demand for products declined in proportion as they were durable: unemployment rose higher in shipbuilding than in clothing, and higher in furniture than in foodstuffs. Two sources of fluctuation were cumulated, when durable goods came to constitute an increasing proportion of British exports. As in the fall, so in the rise, it was the export trades and the constructional trades that moved most. In these trades, employment fluctuated by about an eighth below and above its average level: or, what is the same thing, unemployment at its worst amounted to about a fifth of the labour force in work at the preceding peak. Other trades were less disturbed, and in the worst year of a cycle the unemployed did not usually number more than eight or nine per cent of all wage-earners. In the better half of the cycle there was full employment, if this is reckoned as attained when the rate of unemployment is below three per cent. The national product rose and fell within the cycle to about three per cent above or below the line of advance it was following at the time. It was therefore also about three per cent lower, taking all years together, than it would have been if — though the case is artificial — the same rate of advance had been maintained without any lapse from full employment. This shortfall is of the order of magnitude of only one year's economic progress, and may not appear formidable: but it covered much anxiety, hardship, even destitution, where the blow of unemployment fell.

The movement of this cycle had acted at first to offset the adverse turn of the other tides in the 1890's, for employment rose from a low point in 1893 to a peak in 1899. Then it fell, and though unemployment was not severe, the public were now made increasingly aware of it: the unemployed marched, they demanded work from town councils, they trooped into church on a Sunday morning and stood silent in the aisles. A not very powerful revival began in 1905, but was cut off in 1907, when a crisis in the United States led to a fall in British exports. The severe cyclical unemployment of the next two years fell upon wage-earners to whom other kinds of fluctuation had already brought a setback to their standard of living and a shortage of work in the building trades. We can understand it that these were years of perplexity, resentment, and conflict.

5

The standard of living that the British wage-earner had reached by the turn of the century, but was hardly holding on to through the years that followed, can be envisaged if we compare it with the more familiar standards of recent years. In such comparisons it does not come out well: the basketful the average wage would buy in 1906 was not much more than half — at the most three-fifths — that of fifty years later. Yet it was still bigger than any, so far as we know, that the wage-earner had ever had before. After 1870 there was no doubt that the national product was rising faster even than population. The comparative plenty of the fifteenth century was recovered, and surpassed.

Especially the steam engine, running on steel rails or driving the steel ship, was now bringing to the British housewife ever more cheaply a share of the ever growing output of foodstuffs in the Americas and Australasia. Old folk remembered the Hungry Forties; the U-boats lay unseen ahead; in the meantime the threat of famine was banished. The English wage-earning household of average size and income had a dietary now that might be stodgy and monotonous, but was certainly substantial.

This average household was by no means that of husband, wife, and three children, which is sometimes taken as typical. In fact, that particular family made up not more than one household in twenty, mercifully, for unless its head had at least a skilled man's wage it was bound to lead a life of penury. The actual bill of fare in most wage-earning households was made possible by their containing more than one wage-earner. The average household in fact contained two, whose joint earnings amounted to about one and a half men's wage packets, and this income had to support those who earned it together with two or three others — the housewife, the old, the young. Outside agriculture, it would have averaged about 45s. for a full working week in 1906 — the equivalent of about £10 10s. in 1958. It served to provide the household with some such weekly rations as the following:

32 lb.	bread and flour;
3 lb.	rice, tapioca, oatmeal;
17 lb.	potatoes;
9 lb.	meat, of which about 1½ lbs. was bacon;
¾ lb.	cheese;
12 eggs;	
2 lb.	butter;
10 pints	fresh milk;
5 lb.	sugar, with a small amount of jam, marmalade, treacle, or syrup;
small	amounts of fish, currants and raisins, vegetables and fruit, pickles and condiments;
½ lb.	tea, and small amounts of coffee and cocoa.

We notice the relatively large weight of meat, and the small amount of fruit and vegetables — people feared these as the source of summer diarrhoea in children, and vitamins began to be traced only after 1906. On the average of the whole population such supplies provided a rather higher total of calories than the British people obtained in the time of stringent rationing after the Second World War.

The narrowness of the wage-earner's livelihood in those days was to be seen not so much in dietary as in what was left for spending after the food had been paid for. At the prices of 1914 the weekly rations listed above would have cost 20s. at least. Rent with fuel and light would have taken another 7s. 6d. That left only 17s. 6d. in all, or an amount per head equivalent to from 16s. to £1 in the money of 1958, to cover all clothing, furnishings and hardware, soap, matches, drink and tobacco, medical charges and insurance, papers, stamps, the journey to work, outings and entertainments.

Sometimes — more often then than now — drink took an undue share. At the end of the nineteenth century the consumption of beer amounted to nearly two pints a man for every day of the year. If we could go back to the streets of 1906, the drunkenness would startle us. It was alarming to contemporaries, who noticed that in half a century in which most crime had diminished substantially charges of drunkenness had gone up by a half. On the average of the country they amounted to about thirteen a week for every hundred thousand people (the corresponding number for 1950 was two), but in the seaports and manufacturing cities they were more numerous. In the towns a third of the drunks were women. A change was becoming apparent: at the outset of the new century the use of beer and spirits both began to decline, and looking back now we can see in this the beginnings of a revolution, in which education, and the bicycle, the bus, the Saturday afternoon football game, the cinema, transformed the leisure of the British wage-earners in the towns. But in 1906 life remained dull and constricted for too many of them. There was a saying that getting drunk was the shortest way out of Manchester. The average spending of wage-earners' households on drink before 1914 was put at not less than six shillings a week.

When margins were narrow it was often outlay on clothing that was pinched. Even for the higher-paid wage-earner, buying one garment or a pair of boots meant paying away a large part of one week's earnings. Sometimes these payments could be made out of occasional overtime, or extra earnings at Christmas, or the annual shareout of a sick club; but what the housewife needed was a way of making sure that something was put aside for clothing each week regularly. One such way, but an expensive one, was to buy 'on the never-never', and make the weekly payments afterwards to the tallyman who came to the door. Another was to pay into a clothing club or boot club organized by a local shopkeeper. But often the provision was not properly made. The streets saw greater contrasts of dress before 1914 than those who have grown up since can readily conceive. The well to do were glossier then; poverty shambled in misfits and came out at the elbows: even for Sunday best there were accepted patterns of what was fitting to the wearer's station in life. For many wage-earners their clothes were a badge of inferiority.

What chance the housewife had to look after her family depended in part on how much of her husband's wage he handed over to her. There were two customs. He might hand all his earnings over to her and get back a fixed sum for his own pocket money — that was the 'tip up' of the mining villages, sometimes performed before the front door so that the neighbours could see fair play. Alternatively, he might hand over a fixed allowance, and keep whatever the difference was from time to time. An intermediate plan was for him to hand over his basic or normal pay but keep any bonus or overtime money for himself. On any plan, what proportion did he get? It must have varied widely. Farm labourers on twelve to fourteen shillings a week kept as little as sixpence. Inquiries during the Second World War suggested that in the wage-earning homes with one, two, or three children in Glasgow and Leeds the husband commonly kept a quarter of his net earnings. Our calculations of the household budget before 1914 make this appear a possible proportion then too.

Even when the wage-earner's wife got most of a good wage, the home could not be well found nor the children well fed and clothed unless she was a good manager. Minor lapses from frugality and foresight that would have mattered little in a house with servants came home sharply to her. Many a comfortable and cheerful home was maintained by her hard work, self-denial and skill. Where those were lacking she and her home were easily dragged down. 'Everything depends on her,' Lady

Bell wrote in a book about the ironworkers of Middlesborough;[1] 'the husband's steadiness and capacity to earn are not more important than the wife's administration of the earnings. . . . The man's wages, which before marriage generally left him a margin after paying his lodging or contributing to his parents' expenses, need careful handling in his own home to make them go far enough for two. The young wife often does not understand how to do it. She does not know much about cooking, she is not skilful at sewing, she does not know how to organize. At first, however, she may be able to encounter life with tolerable success. Then she has a child, and let alone the fact that during the time preceding the birth of the child everything is more difficult to her probably than before, she afterwards, usually long before she ought to do any work, begins struggling with her daily duties again, plus the baby this time, whom she generally nurses, and whom she has to look after entirely. And then, possibly, before this first baby is able to walk, or when it is just able to do so, while she is still having to carry it about and look after it incessantly, another one is coming or come, the mother herself, perhaps, being still in her teens. As the time goes on her energy slowly ebbs, and with it her courage and her hope. One's heart aches at seeing a girl of twenty-four or twenty-five, when she ought to be at her best, most joyous, most hopeful . . . already appearing dulled, discouraged, her form almost shapeless, her looks gone, almost inevitably becoming more of a slattern day by day from sheer incapacity to keep up with her work.'

The strain that a brood of young children put on the mother and the household income was one of several phases through which any one wage-earner's household would commonly pass in the course of its life history. So far we have been looking at an average household, as a central point on which to fix our attention when we are comparing the prevailing standards of living of different times; but one and the same household might stand in very different relations to this point at successive stages. When it was first set up the husband would probably be at the height of his earning capacity, and his wage had only two to support. Within five years there might be five mouths to fill, and clothes for three growing children to find, but no greater in-

[1] Lady Florence Bell, *At the Works: a study of a manufacturing town* (1907), Ch. VIII.

come: a household that had had a small margin for comforts before could be plunged in poverty now, could be actually short of food. As the children grew up, the older ones began to earn, and that brought some relief. As they left home, a room might be let to a lodger, and the household would now have climbed out of poverty again. But the earning power of a manual worker often began to decline before he was fifty; illness would increase with age; there was no age of retirement, but the time was coming when the husband would not be able to work any more.

This is the contingency that was at once most probable and most difficult to provide against. It could be seen ahead, but while it was still remote much present self-denial — and denial of the children — would have been needed in most wage-earning homes to make adequate provision for it. Probably this was the reason why few friendly societies provided old age pay: though there was also the administrative complexity of the annuity, but for which more societies might have pressed its advantages on the attention of their members. The trade unions, it is true, were not hampered by actuarial tests of solvency, and could simply pay each year's pensions of retired members out of each year's dues of active ones: if actually only a few craft unions provided pensions, that must have been because the others' members could not face the cost. The main support of old age had to be the children, and they did generally accept an obligation to take the old folk in. The house might be crowded with grandchildren already, the old folk might feel that their room would be valued more than their company. But generally the only alternative for them, and the sole resort of the childless, was the dreaded workhouse.

6

There was another and even more evident way in which looking at the average household alone fails to bring significant facts to notice: its income was higher than that of a good many more than half of all wage-earning households. This was so, because wages were not evenly distributed. Above the mean was a long range of higher rates, containing a minority of wage-earners, yet these between them received half the whole wages bill of the country, because some of the rates were relatively very high. On the lower side was a larger number of wage-earners.

Their rates did not diverge so far from the mean as many of the higher rates did, but divergence on the lower side did not have to go far before it brought families into poverty. In particular, there was a mass of unskilled labour subject to irregular employment and receiving when in work only about a pound a week — say £4 13s. od. in the money of 1958.

This unskilled labourer is a man on whom our eye must rest for a moment, because he made up so great a part of the wage-earners before 1914, and in our own day has become comparatively rare. The extension of education, and the increased amenities of the homes in which young wage-earners grow up, have greatly decreased the proportion of the entrants to the labour market who have only their muscular strength to offer, and has correspondingly increased the supply of those who have some technical training before they come in, or have had an education which will help them to acquire skill on the job. Their doing that has been made the easier because mechanization has provided a greater number of semi-skilled jobs. The result has been to establish a gradation where there used to be a gulf. Before 1914 the skilled man got half as much again as the labourer in building, two-thirds as much again in engineering; by the 1950's he got only about a sixth more; and not only has the span become narrower from end to end, but there are more intermediate rates spread along it. The general rise meanwhile in the standard of living of all wage-earners, and the benefits of the welfare state, have made most difference to those who were worst off.

A contrast has disappeared. But we must carry our minds back to a time when it was conspicuous, when skilled and unskilled wage-earners were almost two different races, set apart from one another by wide disparities in income, dress, and personal bearing. The skilled wage-earners maintained many a comfortable home, where the family enjoyed an ampler diet, could get away for a week's holiday by the sea, owned a bike or a pram, paid a child's fees at the secondary school, and put something by pretty steadily against misfortune or old age: they might have a house with a bow window, five rooms, a garden, a piano in the parlour. But the unskilled were far from all this; in their homes there was hardship in the best of years. Together with those households already considered whose proportion of resources to needs, though not always low, was low in certain phases, they made up the poor.

In fact, if the York that Seebohm Rowntree studied in 1899 was a fair sample, more than forty per cent of all the urban wage-earners with their wives and children were living in poverty. We can define poverty as he did, as lack of the means to buy 'the minimum of food, clothing, and shelter needful for the maintenance of merely physical health'.[1] In this minimum nothing is included 'for the development of the mental, moral, and social sides of human nature', nor for sick clubs and insurance: only the cheapest dietary that will keep up the strength of men in moderate work, with their wives and children, together with the rent of a working man's house, and the barest essentials of boots, clothing, fuel, and light. Those who had less than this not only suffered sometimes from hunger and cold, but were at all times kept below a normal level of energy, because they did not have all that was needed simply to maintain the physical efficiency of a man at work. 'And let us clearly understand', Seebohm Rowntree wrote,[2] 'what "merely physical efficiency" means. A family living upon the scale allowed for in this estimate must never spend a penny on railway fare or omnibus. They must never go into the country unless they walk. They must never purchase a halfpenny newspaper or spend a penny to buy a ticket for a popular concert. They must write no letters to absent children, for they cannot afford to pay the postage. They must never contribute anything to their church or chapel, or give any help to a neighbour which costs them money. They cannot save, nor can they join sick club or Trade Union, because they cannot pay the necessary subscriptions. The children must have no pocket money for dolls, marbles, or sweets. The father must smoke no tobacco, and must drink no beer. The mother must never buy any pretty clothes for herself or for her children. . . . Should a child fall ill, it must be attended by the parish doctor; should it die, it must be buried by the parish. Finally, the wage-earner must never be absent from his work for a single day.'

On that definition Rowntree found that about fifteen per cent of all the wage-earning folk in York in 1899 were bound to live

[1] B. S. Rowntree, *Poverty, a study of town life* (4th edn., 1902), Ch. IV.
[2] op. cit., Ch. V.

in poverty, even if their every penny was spent with strict economy on the essentials alone. Another twenty-eight per cent appeared, from the want and squalor evident in their homes, to be failing to provide themselves with those essentials, although their income would have sufficed for them if nothing had gone on drink, tobacco, and gambling, or the indulgence of impulse and fancy in spending.

There is no reason to suppose that other towns were, for the most part, very different from York, or that conditions changed for the better before long. Rowntree's findings for York in 1899 agree closely with those of Charles Booth in London in 1887–92, and those of Bowley and Burnett-Hurst in Northampton, Warrington, Stanley, and Reading, in 1912 and 1913. In fact these were years when the earnings of the unskilled labourer were at all times insufficient to keep a family of three children above the poverty line. Of the households whose income was too low to maintain them however wisely they spent it, about half had been brought down because many children had been born into a home whose income could have provided for a smaller number, or because of the sickness, or unemployment, or death of a breadwinner, and the advance of old age; the other half were in poverty because the earnings of the breadwinner were so small, even when he was in regular work. In 1914, when the poverty line for a man, wife, and three children lay at about twenty-four shillings a week, nearly a quarter of all the adult male wage-earners in the country were earning less than twenty-five shillings.

There was little furniture in homes of the unskilled labourers: if it could have been afforded, there still would not have been room for it. 'It is difficult', wrote Mrs Pember Reeves,[1] 'to say whether more furniture or less furniture would be the better plan in a home consisting of three rooms. Supposing the family to consist of eight persons, most people would be inclined to prescribe four beds. As a matter of fact, there will probably be two. In a double bed in one room will sleep father, mother, baby, and ex-baby, while in another bed in another room will sleep the four elder children. Sometimes the lodger granny will take a child into her bed, or the lodger uncle will take a boy into his; but the four-in-a-bed arrangement is common enough to

[1] Mrs Pember Reeves, *Round about a Pound a Week* (1913), Ch. IV.

need attention. It must be remembered again that these people are respectable, hard-working, sober and serious. They keep their jobs, and they stay on in the same rooms. They are not slum people. They pay their rent with wonderful regularity, and are trusted by the landlord when for any reason they are obliged to hold it back.' There was nowhere else to lie when someone was ill: a child might have measles or whooping cough, the mother might have been delivered that day of a baby, but when night fell the others must go in alongside. The baby might have a banana crate cot, but in London in 1912 that would have cost 3s. 6d.: crate with sacking bottom, 1s.; bag of chaff for mattress, 2d.; blankets, 2s. 4d. 'As a rule it would be safe to say that the new baby does take its share of the risks of the family bed, legislation to the contrary notwithstanding.'[1] There was usually at least one room with no one sleeping in it — because there was no bed, or no bedclothes. Blankets were few and thin on what beds there were, and that meant keeping the windows shut to keep warm. On the night of Wednesday, 12 September 1900, the air temperature in York was 50° F. In the best houses inhabited by wage-earners, 10 per cent of the front windows were open; in the middle class of houses, 5 per cent; in the poorest, only 3 per cent.

Some people achieved miracles of good management in the poorer households; many women kept the house neat and clean. But it is always difficult to use a small income economically. Food had to be bought at the costly rates charged on small quantities, for there was no money in hand for more, and little space for storage. Broken grates were heavy on coal. The cooking which makes the best of simple ingredients was not possible when all there was to cook in was two or three burnt saucepans.

Life was hard for these poor — not for those only whom dire misfortune had brought down, but for those who day after day, year after year, had to make do on the earnings of the unskilled. A nurse who worked among them remarked that they rarely feared death. 'It is rather the certain hope of death that makes life tolerable to them both in its bitterest moments and in its long-drawn-out struggles against weakness, poverty, ill-health, and sin. Often what is called their callousness to the sight of death should rather be traced to envy of those who are dead and

[1] ibid.

E

at peace. Have they shed few tears? For themselves they wish none to fall.'[1]

7

It might be thought that the farm labourers shared the poverty of the unskilled men in the towns. Their weekly wages were actually lower: though men who had the care of animals got somewhat more, the ordinary labourer's wage varied from twelve shillings a week in Oxfordshire to a pound in County Durham; the average for all Britain in 1906 was probably something more than eighteen shillings. Those eighteen shillings then went as far as rather more than £4 in the money of 1958, but what is that to bring up a family on? Yet families were brought up, and healthy ones too. Evidence we shall set out later shows that farm labourers as a body had a lower death-rate than any other manual occupation except the gardeners and the railway engine drivers — a rate lower even than the schoolmasters' and the civil servants', only a half that of the coal heavers and glassworkers, little more than a quarter that of the general labourers. The lad beginning work on the farm had an expectation of life little shorter than the ordinand's, and longer than the office boy's. When he had a family, the mortality of his babies would be as low as in clerks' families, and lower than in those of skilled workmen who were getting two and three times his money.

The explanation is partly that the country was a healthier place to live in, partly that the farm labourer had much less to pay out on rent than the urban workman and usually nothing on fares, but probably most of all that the weekly money wage made up a smaller part of his effective income than of the townsman's. The children would earn something, a not inconsiderable proportion of the father's wage, by odd jobs while they were still at school, and going out to work as soon as they reached the early leaving age. A garden or allotment and a pig in the sty would provide substantial supplies of food. Various perquisites and boons would come from the farm. Clothing would be handed on from the rectory or the house where a daughter was in service. Making do still meant constant hard work and vigilant management; but granted these, and the fresh air and

[1] M. Loane, *The Queen's Poor* (4th impression, 1910), p. 33.

the fields to run in, the various supplements explain why the country children stood out by their chubby cheeks, and the doctors in the recruiting stations of the First World War remarked on the physical superiority of the countryman over the townsman.

But there was one type of labourer in the villages who did drag out his life in griping poverty — the day labourer, who had not got on to the establishment of a farm but picked up what casual work he could, now on the land, now on the roads. His existence marked the pressure of population in villages which year after year had to send their natural growth away. It would have been better for him if he had gone too; but he had not, and he had become imprisoned in his own penury.

8

To a contemporary observer who had studied housing in the industrial cities of Germany and America, that of the English wage-earner seemed relatively good. 'In England and Wales,' wrote Dr Shadwell,[1] 'eighty-four per cent of the population live in dwellings of four rooms and upwards, which means broadly separate houses. Now the prevalence of small houses involves spreading out and the covering of much ground with many little streets, which produces a monotonous effect; a smoky atmosphere makes them grimy, and dull skies contribute to the general dinginess. . . . The whole presents to the eye a vast area of dreary meanness and monotony. Thus the best feature of English national housing turns to its apparent disadvantage and the impression is gained by superficial observers that the bulk of our working-class population lives in "slums". The word "slum" has no precise meaning, but if it implies serious sanitary defects it is not applicable to most of our town housing. There are real slums still, but the bulk of the working class population do not live in them; they live in small houses, often of a mean and dingy exterior but in essential respects more sanitary than the large and often handsome blocks to be seen in foreign towns, which are not put down as slums because they do not look dirty.'

On an international comparison, the English wage-earner's house had in fact two distinctive features — it was a two-storied, four-roomed building, standing in a paved street of such

[1] Article on Housing, *Encyclopaedia Britannica*, 11th edn. (1911).

buildings; and the whole of it was occupied by one family alone, save often for a lodger. Sometimes the front door gave on to a passage, from which a parlour opened in front, and the kitchen at the back; this kitchen, which was also the living room, was hardly more than twelve foot square. Sometimes the front door opened directly into a kitchen and living room at the front, and then the back room was a scullery, with a sink, copper, and tap. Beyond the back room was the yard, where in houses recently built there was a water closet, but in others an earth privy. Upstairs there were two bedrooms. The cooking was by a coal grate, and if the parlour or a bedroom were warmed it was by an open coal fire; the lighting was by candles, paraffin lamps, or gas. The floors were laid with linoleum, the walls were papered.

This general type was varied by local and industrial tradition. It was remarked how the craftsmen of Bristol, where wages were relatively low, reckoned to have a house with six rooms, or five and a scullery, whereas the better-paid craftsmen of the industrial north accepted four small rooms, or even three and a scullery, but expected more outings. Scotland was very different from England and Wales. In 1911 only 7½ per cent of the population of England and Wales were living in dwellings of not more than two rooms, but in Scotland the proportion was nearly a half. In England and Wales, less than one tenth of the population were packed in more than two in a room, in Scotland more than four-tenths. Two-roomed dwellings predominated in Edinburgh and Glasgow, three-roomed in London and Birmingham, four-roomed in Manchester, and five-roomed in Liverpool. There may have been some compensation in that the Scots rooms were generally bigger: it was reckoned that a two-roomed house in Edinburgh or Glasgow would generally have as much floor space as a three-roomed house in Birmingham. Yet it remained remarkable that a country which had taken no less active a part in industrial development than the rest of the United Kingdom should have retained so much lower a standard of housing. Sir John Clapham thought the explanation lay in tradition ' — a tradition in stone, traditional domestic habits — of astonishing persistence.'[1]

Perhaps that was also the explanation of the over-crowding in

[1] J. H. Clapham, *Economic History of Modern Britain*, Vol. III (1938), Ch. VIII, p. 463.

the adjacent counties of Northumberland and Durham, where it was worse than almost anywhere else in England and Wales. But this also marked the general tendency of miners' housing to be bad wherever it was. Some colliery companies had built good housing estates, but these were exceptional: over the coalfields as a whole the large families of the miners were packed into small and dingy cottages. Rows of these cottages had sometimes had to be run up quickly when a new pit was sunk. Even the more solid buildings often suffered later from the subsidence of the ground. In some coalfields the pits were scattered through a farming countryside, and the miners' houses formed part of the villages there, and had the benefit of their pleasant surroundings. But two districts stood out for their grimness. In the steep-sided valleys of South Wales, there was little space for terraces of houses beside river and road and rail, pithead and tip, along the narrow floor; there was a shortage of houses. The hillsides, cut back to make room for the houses, rose sheer on east and west, and shut the sunlight out; in several valleys it happened that the ground most practicable for building was on the darker side. Because the buildings had to be strung along many miles of the valley floor, there was no natural civic centre, no group of church and hall hallowed by old associations; there was little ground for park and playing field, nor when one of these was made could there be many houses within walking distance of it; there was little ground either for garden or allotment. The other grim places were round the Scots pits. The houses here, built of the cheapest materials, were commonly arranged in the cheapest form, the dismal lines of 'Miners' Rows'. On the mud between them stood the dilapidated washhouses, and the privies, or the privy-midden, which was a walled dump into which the ashes and night-soil of the cottages were thrown together, with a row of latrines down one side; 'and the children just run about there.'

Part of the miner's trouble was that his family remained generally so large. He shared the vicious circle that afflicted large families generally: the more there were to find room for, the more there were to feed, and the less there was to spare for rent. This would have caused trouble even if the fathers of the bigger families had not often been among the lower paid. It was this, together with the existence of slums limited in extent but appalling in squalor, that made up the core of the housing problem.

This problem could not be attributed simply to the growth of population. That growth, it is true, demanded an increase in the number of houses by not less than a tenth in each decade, if only existing standards were to be maintained; but this was in fact achieved. Wage-earners generally depended on houses being built to let as private investments, for few of them owned their own houses — in York the proportion was less than six per cent; but local savings went into bricks and mortar, the speculative builder found buyers, the houses did go up. What was lacking was an advance in the technique of building that would have made house-room available to the wage-earner in the same increasing plenty as other products. Revolutions in manufacture and transport had substantially raised the supply of food and clothing to each family, and the amenity of accommodation expected must have been raised in sympathy; but there had been no revolution in building — 'the industry capitalism forgot'. Only two processes, sawing and brickmaking, had been mechanised. That was why it was impossible to provide the lower-paid wage-earners with a house which was adequate by the standards they were now acquiring but whose cost was covered by a rent they could afford. A separate house, not a flat or tenement; five rooms for an average family; a piped water supply, a water closet, perhaps even a bathroom; not too many houses to the acre, so that there could be air and light around each, and park or playground at hand; and yet a site not too far from the place of work — this specification was costly. The skilled wage-earner and the clerk could pay a rent which covered it, and the rows of bow-windowed houses built in the boom of the 1890's show how private enterprise provided it. But the middle and lower grades of the wage-earners could not afford it.

The question arose whether public enterprise must not supplement private here. Experiments by municipalities and philanthropic associations were showing that under careful administration sanitary if graceless quarters could be provided at a rent within the reach of the unskilled wage-earner, by buying up old houses and setting them in good order, or by putting up 'buildings', as they were called, that is, big blocks of tenements; and such schemes could return perhaps as much as four per cent on their capital. In 1904 Liverpool was trying to build three-roomed tenements at a cost of about £100 apiece, by prefabricating the walls and floors out of cement and crushed clinker from the refuse destructors. But decent new houses for the middle and lower ranks of the wage-earners were generally possible only by subsidy.

After the First World War this was accepted, and the subsidy was provided by ratepayer or taxpayer. Before 1914, though the principle aroused more opposition then, it had in fact been introduced, for the Housing of the Working Classes Act of 1890 empowered local authorities, if they chose, to build houses and bear the net annual cost out of the rates. But outside London few did choose; in all Great Britain, down to the end of 1906, only some 20,000 dwellings were provided under the Act, and of these more than four-fifths were tenements or flats. The main difference local governments did make to housing, and it was a great one, they made by forcing the owners of dilapidated properties to repair them, by acquiring and reconstructing or clearing some of the worst houses, and by bringing all new building up to the requirements of improved by-laws. In this way some of the worst slums had been completely cleared, and a great many particular buildings here and there had been reclaimed from slumdom; in the ten years before 1906 Manchester had closed nearly ten thousand 'back-to-back' houses, and made five thousand better houses out of them. This sort of clearance was especially effective in reducing the urban diseases.

9

The health of the British people was indeed rapidly improving, and not only by the clearing out of the plague-spots. Between 1870 and 1914 the death-rate fell by a third, and this must be ascribed not only to the continued advance of medical knowledge but to the whole vast improvement since 1870 in the condition of the people. Public health had won its first great battle, against the diseases of dirt. A better educated people looked after itself better. The food of the wage-earners had been increased by rising imports.

But with these improvements there still went much that was distressing. We know now, for one thing, that recent improvements in the quantity of the wage-earner's dietary had been accompanied by some adverse changes in its quality. An increasingly urban community found it difficult, and therefore costly, to get fresh milk. From about 1870 the tin of condensed milk provided a cheap substitute; but it contained little fat, and little therefore of vitamins A and D. The doctors did not yet know of these vitamins, but they noticed that the children fed on this milk though they grew plump lacked vitality, and often had rickets. Each tin had to bear a label stating that it was not suitable for infants; but it was much cheaper than fresh milk, and the wage-earners continued to rely on it. One 4d. tin would last a family of five or six for a week. At the same time the protective value of their bread had been decreased through the supersession of stone-grinding by roller-grinding in the flour mills. Sir Jack Drummond calculated that within ten or fifteen years this reduced the average intake of vitamin B by two-thirds; what was left was sufficient, but by no ample margin, to save the population from beri-beri. With this went a fall in the intake of bone-forming salts, and of iron. The loss of iron made for anaemia. The loss of calcium in both bread and milk made for bad teeth.

There were also marked differences in health between different sections of the community. Some indication of these is provided by the figures of mortality in different occupations. We cannot simply compare the death-rate among lawyers, for instance, with that among seamen, for it may well be that there is at any time a higher proportion of elderly men among the lawyers, and in all walks of life the elderly have a higher death-rate than the young. But we can clear the influence of age away from that of occupation by forming on paper a group made up, in fixed proportions, of men at the different ages of life, and then calculating how many deaths would occur within it in a year if it were made up wholly of representatives of this or that occupation. It is convenient to choose as these fixed proportions those of the whole male population, and to adjust the total number in the group so that if it were composed not of representatives of one occupation only but of all occupations, it would suffer the loss of just one thousand men by death during a year. Calculations of this kind have been made for England and Wales according to the death-rates for each age of life in each occupation in 1900–2.[1] They show wide differences, and a ranking which is sometimes unexpected. Some wage-earners, notably the farm labourers, the builders and the coalminers, were healthier not only than the average of the whole population, but than the physicians and surgeons. The good standing of the coalminers is specially remarkable: their lot had been improving rapidly in recent years, in respect both of disease and of accidents. The tin miners were at the other end of the scale, with the potters, the seamen, and the unskilled labourers: these lost about twice as many of their number in a year as the healthier callings did.

England and Wales, 1900–2: relative number of deaths occurring within a year from all causes, including accident, in a group of fixed size and age-composition, when it is made up wholly of men at work in or retired from the occupation shown.

Clergy	524	Printers	994
Gardeners	563	Tailors	1027
Farmers	596	Plumbers, painters, glaziers	1114
Railway engine drivers		Cotton manufacture	1114
and stokers	610	Butchers	1148
Farm labourers	621	Coach, cab, omnibus	
Schoolmasters	665	service	1157
Civil servants	723	Hairdressers	1196
Grocers	729	Lead miners	1206
Lawyers	750	Coalheavers	1221
Tanners	774	Glass manufacture	1260
Carpenters and joiners	820	Chimney sweeps	1343
Gas works service	878	Brewers	1393
Coal miners	885	Dock labourers	1481
Bricklayers and masons	906	Potters and earthenware	
Domestic indoor servants	927	manufacture	1493
Blacksmiths and strikers	937	Seamen and merchant service	1646
Physicians and surgeons	952	Innkeepers and publicans	1781
Wool and worsted manuf.	984	Tin miners	2131
Commercial travellers	988	General labourers	2235
		All occupations together	1000

These differences are the joint outcome of several factors. There is the physique of the entrants into each occupation and the standards required of men if they are to continue in it — the low mortality of railway engine drivers, for instance, may be due in great part to the high standards required at recruitment and in periodical re-examination. There is the influence as life goes on of the habitat and personal morale of those in particular callings, and this may account for part of the healthiness of the

[1] *Supplement to the 65th Annual Report of the Registrar-General, Part II,* (Cd. 2619 of 1908). Letter by Dr John Tatham. Table IV.

clergy and the morbidity of innkeepers: we do not know how far these differences in behaviour are stamped by the job itself upon men otherwise less differentiated, or merely display those existing differences of constitution which originally drew them into the jobs. Beyond these factors again are the work itself, and the place of work: in the healthiness of gardeners and farm labourers we may see the effects of varied bodily exercise in the open air, in the high mortality of potters those of dust, and heat, and lead. Other differences will have stemmed from differences in income, and consequently in dietary, housing, recreation, and medical care.

In this last respect the wage-earner was generally at some disadvantage. When illness came, a friendly society or trade union would sometimes pay for the doctor, or a hospital bed, as well as issue sick pay. But usually it did so only for the member himself, not his wife and children, and if they were to be insured it had to be by paying weekly dues to a medical club, or 'contract practice', run by one or more of the local doctors. Those who could not or did not insure would have to pay the doctor's bill out of savings, or some extra earnings when they came — harvest money in the country, overtime or Christmas bonus in the town. Some could get free consultations as outpatients of a voluntary hospital, or be admitted to a bed there. Those with no other resource, and willing or obliged to accept the stigma, fell back on the relieving officer's order for the services of the District Medical Officer appointed by the Guardians, or attended a Poor Law dispensary; and when they had to go into hospital went to the sick wards of the workhouse, or a Poor Law infirmary. There were few nurses as yet to come to the home, but some help was being given to the women and children there by the health visitors the town councils and the like as public health authorities were now appointing. The medical care these various agencies enabled the wage-earner and his family to get in practice varied widely from place to place. No one in principle was left without any, but many — especially the women — will have gone without what they sorely needed. Much of the attention that was given could not go beyond the single consultation and prescription of that consolation and fetish, the bottle of medicine — 'my mixture'.

The differences in health between different sections of the

community went with big differences in physique — much bigger than today. The Oxford and Cambridge undergraduates of 1908–10, at the age of about twenty, were more than thirty pounds heavier, and about three-and-a-half inches taller, than the lads of eighteen in the West Midlands and the North-West who were medically examined on conscription in 1918, and only a minor part of the difference can be attributed simply to the difference in age. The 'Belisha boys' called up at the age of twenty in 1939 weighed about fifteen pounds more and stood about two inches taller than the conscripts of 1918: they still were smaller than the Oxford and Cambridge undergraduates of their age before the First World War, but the difference had been halved.

There were similar differences among school children. The elementary school children in the industrial cities of Edwardian England were apparently only about an inch taller at thirteen years of age, and not more than six pounds heavier, than the children of the factory districts of Lancashire, Cheshire, and the West Riding had been in the 1830's. They were considerably smaller than children of the same age in the public schools: a committee of the British Association found that about 1880 public school boys at eleven years of age were two inches taller than their contemporaries among the children of agricultural labourers, and nearly three-and-a-half inches taller than those among the children of factory workers in the towns. In Dundee, in 1904, the thirteen-year old girls in the elementary schools were fourteen pounds lighter and three inches shorter than the girls of the same age in Harris Academy. These differences too seem to have been reduced by the present day. We know that in Glossop the thirteen-year old boys and girls in the elementary schools in 1944 were around three inches taller, and fourteen pounds heavier, than their predecessors of 1911 — just the difference between the girls of the elementary and secondary schools in Dundee in 1904.

The rapid advance which the elementary school child has made in the last fifty years is some indication of what his health was like when the advance began. When in 1908 the medical inspection of elementary school children became obligatory for all local education authorities, the prospect so revealed was thus described by the Chief Medical Officer of the Board of

Education:[1] 'Speaking generally, it may be said that out of the six million children registered on the books of the Public Elementary Schools of England and Wales, about 10 per cent suffer from a serious defect in vision, from 3 to 5 per cent suffer from defective hearing, 1 to 3 per cent have suppurating ears, 6 to 8 per cent have adenoids or enlarged tonsils of sufficient degree to obstruct the nose or throat, and thus to require surgical treatment, about 40 per cent suffer from extensive and injurious decay of the teeth, about 30 to 40 per cent have unclean heads or bodies' (in 1908 about 30 per cent of the children in the London elementary schools were recorded as 'badly fleabitten'), 'about 1 per cent suffer from ringworm, 1 per cent from tuberculosis in readily recognisable form, from 1 to 2 per cent are afflicted with heart disease, and a considerable percentage of children are suffering from a greater or less degree of malnutrition.' 'Defective nutrition stands in the forefront as the most important of all physical defects from which school children suffer.' The proportion found to be suffering from it varied much from one district to another — from under one per cent, to over twenty; and no doubt some of this variation was due to differences in examiners' standards. The proportion recorded for London was eleven per cent. Perhaps ten per cent can be accepted as representative for the country as a whole.

The special difficulties of the children showed themselves most of all in a rate of infantile mortality which was high not only by the standards of a later generation but in comparison with the contemporary mortality among adults. The infantile rate had begun to fall with the adult rate in the 1870's, but in the 1880's, for reasons which remain obscure, its movement was reversed, and by the end of the century it was back at the level of thirty years before — a level we might find today in a village of the Indian plains. At its worst, indeed, it was higher even than that. An inquiry was made into the families of 331 out of the 364 children who died in Dundee under one year of age in the second half of 1904. '240 mothers, who had been working both before and after marriage, had borne in all 885 children and no fewer than 520 . . . were dead. The remaining 91 mothers had either worked before marriage only or not at all, and out of a

---

[1] *Annual Report for 1910 of the Chief Medical Officer of the Board of Education*, (Cd. 5925 of 1911), p. 256.

total of 460 children 195 . . . had died. There were 630 living children and 715 dead for the 331 families, and all of the dead children, with seven exceptions, lived less than five years, and no fewer than 630 less than one year.'[1]

There was a great difference in infantile mortality between different social classes: in the homes of the miners and the unskilled wage-earners in 1911 it was twice as great as among 'the upper and middle classes':

England and Wales, 1911. Mortality of legitimate children under one year of age, according to the occupation of the father.

	Deaths per 1,000 babies born
1. Upper and middle classes	76
2. Intermediate between middle class and wage-earners	106
3-8. All wage-earners	133
3. Skilled workmen	113
4. Intermediate, mixed skilled and unskilled	122
5. Unskilled workmen	153
6. Textile workers	148
7. Miners	160
8. Agricultural labourers	97

Source: 74th Annual Report of the Registrar-General (1911). Cd. 6578 of 1913, Table 28B, p. 88.

These differences were apparent in the deaths at all stages of the first twelve months, but with few exceptions they were much wider in the later months — in the first month, for instance, the mortality rate among the babies of unskilled workmen was less than half as great again as that among those of the 'upper and middle classes', but in the last quarter of the baby's first year it was between two-and-a-half and three times as great. This points to the difficulty of weaning and artificial feeding in poor homes, with their lack of clean whole milk, and the ignorance of the mothers. Sometimes the trouble was that weaning was put off even when the mother's milk was failing, because breast feeding was easier, and cost nothing, and was thought to be a safeguard against conception. Beyond that, 'once weaned, the child of a labouring man' (here that means, of an unskilled wage-earner on a pound a week) 'gets its share of the family diet. It

[1] Dundee Social Union: *Report on Housing and Industrial Conditions*, 1905.

gets its share of the 4d. tin of separated milk, its share of gravy and potatoes, a sip of the cocoa on which 3d. or 4d. a week may be spent for the use of everyone, and, if its father be particularly partial to it, a mouthful of fat bacon once or twice a week, spared from the not too generous "relish to his tea". Besides these extras it gets bread.'[1]

The relatively low mortality among the agricultural labourers' babies was specially marked in the latter part of their first twelve months, and this suggests the value of their supply of whole milk; while the very low incidence of diarrhoea and enteritis among them shows by contrast how much harm the privies and the flies did to the town babies in a hot summer. In that of 1911, the deaths of babies from diarrhoea and enteritis were nearly trebled.

It was usually a bad thing for the mother to be going out to work: it meant strain during pregnancy — the deaths of babies from congenital malformation were especially numerous among textile workers — and it meant the baby being left during the mother's working hours without the breast and in the charge of someone who might be more or less incompetent or unconcerned to feed it. But these things do not explain the exceptionally great loss of babies in the miners' homes, for the miner's pay was relatively high, and his wife seldom went out to work: an especially high rate of death from 'convulsions' there suggests a tradition of poor handling and unsuitable feeding; and then there were the miners' bad housing, and their exceptionally big families. Moreover, a detailed study of infantile mortality rates, occupation by occupation, shows so continuous a gradation, and so close a connection with the size of family — the more the births, the more the deaths — that the governing factors must be sought in the whole attitude and way of life prevailing in each occupation.

But about the turn of the century there had begun an advance on more than one front towards better care for the health and nutrition of the children. An Act of 1902 provided for the training of midwives, and the exclusion of unqualified women from practice. The corporation of St Helen's in Lancashire gave a lead to the country by setting up an infants' milk depot in 1899. One milk depot set up by a voluntary committee in

[1] Mrs Pember Reeves, *Round about a Pound a Week* (1913), pp. 102-3.

Finsbury in 1904 developed into a school for mothers, and the mothers' schools in turn developed into infant welfare centres, especially under the stimulus of the first national conference on infant mortality, over which John Burns, as President of the Local Government Board, presided in 1906. By 1917 there were nearly a hundred infant welfare centres in London alone; most of them had been set up by voluntary workers, but in 1914 the Local Government Board began to make grants in aid of them to local authorities.

While in these ways better food and, especially, better guidance were being provided for the babies and the toddlers, much was also being done for the children as they came on into school. The School Boards could appoint a medical officer as a 'necessary officer' under the Act of 1870, though very few of them did so; sometimes the local Medical Officer of Health took an interest in the schools, or the teachers tested the children's sight; but the development of a medical service in the elementary schools was almost wholly the work of the local education authorities newly constituted by the Act of 1902. By 1905 a system of medical inspection had been set up by the London County Council and nearly fifty other authorities; the inspectors caused many fears and misgivings among parents at first, and had to walk delicately, but an Act of 1907 made it obligatory for the local education authorities to provide for the medical inspection of all elementary school children, though not for parents to let their children be examined. It also empowered the local authority to provide medical treatment for school children, and pay for it out of the rates, and a school medical service now began to grow up around the school doctor and the school nurse. One of its first tasks and achievements was to cleanse the children and get rid of ringworm, fleas and lice. In 1908 the parents of children who after having been cleansed got lice again were made liable to prosecution; but the main thing was that the co-operation of suspicious parents was gained by the patience and tact of teachers and nurses. So the proportion of London elementary school children who were fleabitten or lousy was greatly reduced, until by 1913 of the older girls only a third had verminous heads. Moreover, it was reported, 'the children come better clad and where, at the first glance almost, the nurses used to find all the garments infested with vermin, they need now carefully to examine undergarments to discover the conditions.'

In the schools in the poorer districts, many children could not learn just because they were hungry. Some warm-hearted people were trying to help them. In Birmingham Mr George Hookham spent £1,380 out of his own pocket in 1904 to provide breakfasts in fourteen schools, on five days a week through the school year, for 1,600 or 1,700 children a day in the winter, and 800 or 900 in the summer: a cup of hot cocoa made with half a pint of sterilized skim milk and sugar; and five ounces of the bread 'known in the trade as "seconds" ', in two slices, one spread with butter, the other with jam: for a total cost of elevenpence for every ten breakfasts. 'There is not a superfluity of breakfasts given — never quite as many as there are applicants, and if a child gets a breakfast whose father is in work some other child who does not get a breakfast and whose father is out of work is always ready to inform the teacher.' In Deptford the Rev. J. Gregory Mantle, hearing that a boy who fainted in school had had no food for two days, raised over £400 by subscription, and provided seventeen weeks of free breakfasts. In London in 1904–5 nearly 27,000 children were being fed in the schools, most of the money coming from a fund raised by *The Referee* newspaper. The need was not disputed, but what was to be done if the child was hungry only because his parents drank? Or if the trouble was just that the father's earnings were low, would not feeding the child be the Speenhamland system again, a supplementation of low wages from the rates, and an invitation to employers to reduce wages? Again, 'it is a matter for grave consideration whether the valuable asset to the nation in the improved moral and physical state of a large number of future citizens counterbalances the evils of impaired parental responsibility.'[1] A circular of the Board of Education in 1905 said that when children were hungry because of temporary difficulties of their parents, such as illness or unemployment, they had best be fed by 'the various voluntary and charitable agencies which exist for the provision of meals for children who are sent to school hungry'; but if the parents were permanently impoverished, or though capable of feeding the child were

[1] *Report of the Royal Commission on Physical Training (Scotland)*, (Cd. 1507 of 1903) paras. 161-8.

BOYS OF THE SAME AGE IN A SCHOOL IN BERMONDSEY, LONDON,
IN 1894 (*Above*) AND 1924 (*Below*)

neglecting it, the teacher or school managers could make a special application to the Guardians or Relieving Officer, who were empowered by the Relief (School Children) Order, 1905, to recover the cost of the child's meals from the parent when it seemed to them he could pay.

But the next year the issue of parental responsibility was decided by Parliament in favour of the immediate feeding of the children, at whatever cost to morale: an Act of 1906 empowered local authorities to provide meals at school for children who needed them, and to provide them free if the parents could not pay, the cost to be borne by the ratepayers up to the limit of a halfpenny rate. By 1911 about £150,000 a year was being spent in England and Wales to provide meals completely or to serve food which was supplied by charity; the cost of a meal averaged about 4½d. Here, as elsewhere, the young welfare state had its teething troubles. An inspector found in one school that 'the children are not restrained from hasty eating, and immediate application for second helps'; in another many children sang grace 'in a repulsively loud shout'.

Meanwhile physical training was going ahead, in those schools at least which having playgrounds could drill in the open air. From 1895 the higher grant for discipline could be earned only by schools that used the Swedish system of exercises.

10

The spread of education was of all recent changes the most revolutionary, the most destructive and the most creative. The effects of economic changes on men's ways and aspirations were small in comparison.

It is true that the British society which had carried through the industrial revolution stands out in contrast with the 'under-developed' countries of today by reason of the schooling it provided. Even at the time of Waterloo perhaps as many as a quarter of all the children in the country went to some sort of school, and by the days of the Great Exhibition the proportion was probably a half. Some of these schools, moreover, if only some of them, gave a good grounding. So it came about, from the end of the eighteenth century onwards, that British wage-earners were able to find among themselves the leaders, organisers and administrators of their own movements: though

F

the orators of Chartism were middle class, the draftsman of the Charter was the carpenter William Lovett, and he, born in 1800, had been schooled in Penzance — he went 'to all the dame schools of the town', was taught to read by his great-grandmother, and went to two boys' schools, where he 'learned to write tolerably well, and to know a little of arithmetic and the catechism'. Had it not been for such schooling as that, the British wage-earner would have depended for his organization, as the Indian does today, on outsiders — zealots from the middle class, firebrands or party agents or saints; lawyers in search of business, and political aspirants in search of publicity; and jobless men in search of a living, and sometimes just gangsters. Yet, by the standards soon to be attained, the extent of illiteracy in Britain was still appalling. When the wage-earners in the towns got the vote in 1867, probably about a half of them had not had any schooling at all, though many would have picked up some smattering of reading and writing. At this time more than a fifth of the men who signed the marriage register in England and Wales could only make their mark. In Scotland the proportion was only half as great — a sign of the superiority in education with which Scotland was habitually credited in the nineteenth century. In both countries, the proportion of the brides who could not write their names was higher than of the grooms.

Within forty years this illiteracy was to be abolished. The Act of 1870 which set up the School Boards to fill the gaps between the voluntary schools began a rapid development, first in the amount, and then, increasingly, in the quality, of elementary education. There was an inrush of pupils: a million and a half new school places of some sort were provided in the first six years; many of the children were simply crammed by rote for the grant-earning examination in the three R's, which even in 1880 only a quarter of the candidates passed. But the number and quality of teachers improved. In 1893 there were still only sixteen teachers for each thousand children in the London elementary schools, but within ten years there were twenty, and the proportion went on rising. These more numerous teachers were better trained, not only in particular subjects, but in the art of teaching, and from 1890 they were working under a Code whose aim was 'the development of interest and intelligence and the acquirement of real substantial knowledge'. The infant schools led the rest in the improvement of their class-rooms and their methods of teaching, and this mattered all the more at a time when far more toddlers than in later years were sent to publicly-maintained schools. As school became more interesting and humane, children actually began to like it — that was noted as something new — and truancy decreased. Part of this decrease was due to a change in the attitude of the parents too: many of them at first had resented compulsory attendance as an imposition, but as time went on an increasing number came to see the good of schooling for their children, and demand more of it.

In part, their demand was met by the development of secondary education: Balfour's Act of 1902, which laid the responsibility for that on the county councils, began a course of development hardly less remarkable than that begun in 1870 for the elementary school. In 1907 the grant-aided secondary schools were required to give not less than a quarter of their places to 'free place' scholars from the elementary schools.

By 1914 this extension had made no difference to those who were already employed as manual workers, and not much even to the clerks. Yet meanwhile the growth of the elementary schools alone had made a profound, pervasive difference to the wage-earners, to the kind of people they were and to what they expected of life. Of all the statistics of the day, none were more eloquent than these:

Estimated proportion of the population of London within the ages 25–55 who at the date shown had passed through an efficient school.

			%
1891	-	-	23
1901	-	-	52
1911	-	-	78
1921	-	-	90

Source : *New Survey of London Life and Labour*, Vol. I, (1930), Ch. VIII, Table II.

These figures are probably representative of the country at large. Within the short span of twenty years, the grown men and women of Britain changed from a predominantly illiterate to a predominantly literate people.

The effects of this were revolutionary. In a developed indus-

trial society, illiteracy is not a deprivation merely, but a defor-
mity. The harm it does is not measured by what a literate man
would suffer if some accident deprived him of the ability to read
and write, for his mind would have already been developed by
the use of those skills. The illiterate man may rather be compared with a primitive tribesman in a land ruled by men with
telephones, radio sets, and no less mysterious laws and regulations. He sees these other people communicating with each
other in a way he cannot share, and acting on principles which
remain a closed book to him. Their powers seem superhuman.
He must treat them with deference, for they are so much
stronger and cleverer than he is; but he readily supposes also
that they are using and abusing him for their own ends, and his
subservience is interrupted by outbursts of violence. Riots apart,
however, he is conservative; he has never had the experience
which reading brings of seeing things which are not in front of
his nose, he has had no practice in abstracting and combining
ideas; so he finds it hard to conceive the world as ever being
different from what it is, even when it is a harsh world for him.
He is not easy to reason with, for he is not used to handling
argument, which perforce must use some abstractions, and in
any case he suspects the literate man of trickery. Since also he is
not used to handling information, he is at the mercy of rumour.
These traits, which are most marked when the whole mass of a
labouring population is illiterate, were moderated when the
literate and illiterate worked alongside each other as they did in
Britain, and, in a community of neighbourly and paternal
traditions, were separated from each other by no bar of race or
colour or religion. But they were not overlaid altogether. The
virtual extinction of illiteracy by 1914 revolutionized the
character and outlook of the British wage-earner.

One thing which education did was to make him a better
workman. There were some who thought that schooling would
make boys set too much store by soft hands, that they had better
be broken in to industry before they got into easy-going ways.
But the increase which took place after 1870 in the relative
number of the more skilled workmen would not have been
possible without the elementary school. It had been a difficulty
in an engineering works in the 1870's that some even of the
apprentices had to go to night-school simply to learn reading

and writing, but by the turn of the century that was a thing of the past. 'A good education', said Alfred Marshall,[1] 'confers great indirect benefits even on the ordinary workman. It stimulates his mental activity; it fosters in him a habit of wise inquisitiveness; it makes him more intelligent, more ready, more trustworthy in his ordinary work; it raises the tone of his life in working hours and out of working hours.' The ability to work to simple written instructions, or read about the tricks of one's trade or one's hobby in a technical journal, which nowadays are taken for granted in any alert workman, had to be developed in a community where it was rare. Education was worth while simply as a business investment, and the wonder is that a business-like community did not see its value before: but there was a reason. 'The difference between the value of the labour of the educated man and that of the uneducated,' Marshall[2] had pointed out in 1873, 'is, as a rule, many times greater than the difference between the costs of their education. If the difference between the value of the work done by a good breed of horses and a bad one be much greater than the difference between the costs of maintaining them, can there be any doubt that the good breed will drive out the bad one? But no individual reaps the full gains derived from educating a child.' It was a gap among the incentives in a system of private enterprise and free labour, that no one could make a profitable business of the proper schooling and training of the nation's young entry, of its annual intake of manpower. Nor was there any war sufficient to make the country fully conscious of its neglect, until the Boer War brought it up sharply. Yet there must have been many who thought, what Marshall went on to say, that 'if the State work for this end, the State will gain'. From 1870 the State did increasingly work for this end, and the industrial quality, not of its best workmen but of the average, was raised.

The elementary school affected the labour market in a number of ways. We have seen already how it reduced the numbers of those who had to enter on their working lives without qualifications, or much hope of acquiring any. This was one of the ways in which poverty was to be overcome, and a sure

[1] *Principles of Economics* (8th edn., 1920) IV, vi, 5.
[2] 'The Future of the Working Classes,' reprinted in *Memorials of Alfred Marshall*, ed. A. C. Pigou.

way in the long run, though it worked slowly. At the other
end of the scale, it increased the numbers of the best qualified
wage-earners, and provided an increasing supply of entrants to
the lower grades of the clerical and administrative occupations.
Here, where scarce abilities used to command so much more
than the unskilled labourer, greater plenty lowered the relative
pay. Literacy and skill became relatively cheaper, unskilled
labour relatively dearer. Women's wages rose more than men's,
young people's more than adults'. Marshall estimated in 1885
that 'for each pound invested in education, there is perhaps not
more than half as much returned in extra earning in after life as
there used to be. . . . If we take as our standard the wages of
unskilled labour, there is a steady fall in the earnings that an
expensive start in life will secure to people of average ability,
whether they be musicians, or painters, or medical men, or
lawyers, or, lastly, business men.' Thus education made for
greater economic equality. At the same time it opened more of a
career to the talents of wage-earners' children.

More conspicuous at the time than these economic consequences was the effect on manners. The wage-earners became
cleaner in their persons and their homes, better spoken, more
carefully dressed. The school-mistress helped to refine the manners of not only her pupils but their parents; and her effect on
them grew as more and more of them came to be her former
pupils. They had more self respect, higher standards for their
homes and a deeper sense of responsibility for their children.

With these went wider interests. There were many signs of
increased mental activity. One of them was the demand for
adult education. The university extension movement had done
something to meet this, since Cambridge, London, and Oxford
went into it in the 1870's: in many of the larger towns university
teachers were now giving courses of lectures each winter, with
perhaps a class after the lecture, and written work, and an
examination at the end of the course. The sense that education
could be a form of enjoyment and social intercourse appeared in
the summer meetings which the extension movement began
in 1888. But for the most part this suited the taste of those who
had had a fair education already, or the middle class women
who wanted to improve on their schooling and occupy their
leisure. The needs of the wage-earners were mostly met else-

where. For a very few of them, who were able to follow a full-time course, there was Ruskin College in Oxford from 1899 onwards. For the many more who wanted to study in the evenings, and work out their problems together in groups of their own forming, there were the branches of the Workers' Educational Association, founded in 1903. When six years later this Association began to organize tutorial classes, it provided the most intensive and scholarly of all forms of adult education. Here when controversial questions arose they were discussed without prior commitment to any doctrine; but meanwhile the Plebs League had arisen from a split at Ruskin, to provide courses designed to fit the workers for class warfare.

These agencies exercised the minds of not a few men who were to make their mark in the world, and sway the destinies of their country, after the First World War; but the number thus kindled was, considered merely as a number, a minute part of all the millions of wage-earners, and it was the increase in reading, reading of all sorts, many of them trivial, but reading where there had been none before, that leavened the mass. There had been a growth of public libraries. Local authorities had had some limited powers to maintain libraries ever since 1850, but did little until — a mark of the times — many of them chose a library as their way of commemorating the Jubilee of 1887. Then about 1900 the benefactions of Andrew Carnegie began throughout the country, and the hundred and fifty municipal libraries open before the Jubilee were augmented by another four hundred by 1910. Not all the wage-earners felt able to use them: some were frightened of filling up the form of application, or ashamed to enter in their shabby clothes. For these, as for all other wage-earners, there was some alternative in the increasing supplies of cheap editions, some of them, like Stead's Penny Poets, very cheap. But books were not the staple reading of the wage-earner. Lady Bell reported of Middles-brough in 1907 that more than a quarter of the workmen read books as well as newspapers, nearly a half read the papers only, and a quarter did not read at all. This was the time of the great expansion of the popular press; part of its secret was that for the first time it made newspapers interesting to women. Yet even a halfpenny for a paper was more than many a home could afford every day, and the great standby was the Sunday paper. This, said Lady Bell, helped 'to make the Sunday pass quite harm-lessly, at any rate, for many among the workmen, who spend the day in bed, reading and smoking. . . . Even in households where each penny is an important item of expenditure, 1d., 2d., 3d., and sometimes as much as 6d., is set apart for this delectable Sunday reading.' It must be remembered that the Sunday papers of those days gave a summary of the whole week's news.

The reading of different papers sharpened wits, and induced, along with not a little scepticism, a new habit of acquiring information. Stephen Reynolds, writing in 1911 of the fishermen of Sidmouth in Devon, said that 'among some of the younger men here it was one of the jokes of the recent elections to get hold of rival halfpenny journals and to compare their headlines; and the verdict usually was: "They're all of 'em liars together. They only does it to deceive the likes of us. They ought to be muzzled or put a stop to, I reckon." ' But he added: 'The importance of working-class fairness in weighing up facts lies in this: that the body of facts, genuine or spurious, accessible to them had so enormously increased of late; and they undoubtedly tend to examine the sources of their information more critically. Who, before the last two elections, ever heard of Board of Trade returns bandied about among working men? Was there ever, in Southern England, at any rate, such an amount of keen and comparatively dispassionate argument?'[1]

Education also increased the capacity for discontent. It made men see old conditions with new eyes. That was remarked especially of the miners. One of their leaders, John Cairnes of Northumberland, when asked to give a reason for the unrest of 1911, replied, 'Our men have been under the thumbs of the schoolmasters from at least 1870 until now and our men are more refined than they were forty years ago; they desire better homes, better food, better clothing. . . .' The great conciliator G. R. Askwith spoke in 1913 of 'a spirit abroad of unrest, of movement, a spirit and a desire of improvement, of alteration', and he gave as his first reason for it that 'the schoolmaster has been abroad in the land'. He was speaking in Bristol, and perhaps his words were read by a Bristol van driver named Ernest Bevin, who had recently become a union organiser, for when

---

[1] Stephen Reynolds, *Seems So! A Working Class View of Politics* (1912), pp. 146, 150.

Bevin gave his purpose in standing for Parliament in 1918, he said, 'You cannot have the schoolmaster abroad for fifty years and still keep the working classes at only a living wage.' So to the peroration of his address to the court of inquiry into the dockers' claims in 1920, the inquiry in which he won the title of the dockers' K.C.: 'If you refuse our claims then I suggest you must adopt an alternative. You must go to the Prime Minister. You must go to the Minister of Education and tell him to close down our schools and teach us nothing. We must get back then to the purely fodder basis. For it is no use to give us knowledge if we are not to be given the possibility of using it, to give a sense of the beautiful without allowing us ever to have a chance to obtain the enjoyment of it. Education creates aspirations and a love of the beautiful. Are we to be denied the wherewithal to secure these things? It is a false policy. Better to let us live in the dark if our claims are not to be met.'

II

Education was making for a reduction of the differences between social classes in attainments, manners, and earnings. As time went on this effect would become powerful. But in the meantime the outcome was a heightened resentment of existing differences.

We have noticed some ways in which these differences had become more obtrusive. The size of the middle class family had been limited while most wage-earners had as many children as before, and this had widened the disparity in the margin of expenditure available for the amenities of living. One of these amenities was the motor-car. This enabled employers to move out of town: instead of being neighbours of their workpeople and familiarly known to them, they now increasingly removed their households, not into another place merely, but another society. The car itself was a loud, aggressive thing, roaring and tooting where there had been quiet, scattering the hens from the lane and the children from their playground in the street, pushing humbler folk aside and on a dry day covering them and their gardens with dust. The passengers who swept past, sitting high in their wraps and goggles and veils, seemed to be showing off their brass, in more ways than one. There were other ways in which manners had taken a turn to the ostentatious and unneighbourly. Women's fashions were ornate, conspicuous in their costliness, with a huge impracticality that vaunted the wearer's idleness. King Edward was not much seen in mine or mill, but a set around the court took the popular eye with a lavish display, that was pictured in the new popular press.

These things seemed to mark the mounting wealth of the nation, and political orators confirmed the impression as they pointed to the ever-rising total value of this or that. Wage-earners drew the inference. A third of them in the towns were living in outright poverty. 'Why are the many poor?' asked Fabian Tract No. 1. 'We live under a competitive system with Capital in the hands of individuals. What are the results? A few are very rich, some well off, the MAJORITY IN POVERTY, and a large number in misery. Is it a just and wise system, worthy of humanity? Can we or can we not alter it? Hitherto the system has escaped condemnation only because we are so ready to accept established custom — and because such general ignorance prevails both as to the evils to which this state of things inevitably gives rise — and as to our power of altering it.'

One way in which that ignorance was being reduced was by the spreading of information about the division of the national income. A census of wages in 1886 had for the first time supplemented the returns of incomes assessed to tax so as to make possible a tolerable estimate of the aggregate of all incomes and the division of this aggregate between different classes of recipient. The Fabians seized on the implications of these studies, and *Facts for Socialists from the Political Economists and Statisticians* made them known. It showed, in effect, a cake whose size represented the whole national income; out of this were cut successively a slice for the share of rent, another slice for interest, a third for profits and salaries; there remained less than two-fifths of the cake for all the wage-earners. A work which was first published in 1905 and ran through edition after edition, *Riches and Poverty*, by L. G. Chiozza Money, displayed 'the equator of British incomes': this was the income tax exemption limit of £160 a year (say £750 in the money of 1958), which was shown to divide the national income into two equal parts; one half was shared among thirty-eight million people with incomes below the exemption limit, the whole of the other among a mere five million with incomes above it.

More thorough studies made later have shown these estimates to have been fair enough: Chiozza Money indeed may well have understated the extent of inequality in one way, for the number of the well-to-do who received half the national income between them was probably less than the five million he gave.

If the facts of the distribution of income are not such dynamite today, it is because so much about them has changed. It is no longer plausible to separate all salary-earners from the wage-earners in the Fabian way, as members of the endowed class who, when they elect to work, enjoy a monopoly of ability. If we joined salaries with wages to make up the earned income of those days, we should find that this amounted to sixty per cent of all income produced at home. Since then the proportion has risen to seventy, for the shares of rent and profits have fallen. Meanwhile, taxation with far higher rates and steeper gradu-ation than was conceivable then, and discrimination against income from property, has reduced still further the inequalities in what is left after tax is paid. These taxes have helped to provide benefits for those who were worst off. A great rise in productivity has made more available for all. Together, these changes have virtually abolished poverty among wage-earners. The luxury of the few used to be made possible by the hardships of the many, but now inequality means only that some are better off where all are provided for; and the measures taken to reduce inequality have gone far enough to make us aware of their limitations.

But in 1906 all this was unforeseen. What stood out then was the contrast of poverty and riches; and the connexion between inequality of wealth and the inequality of status between employer and employed. 'The manual working wage-earner', the Webbs wrote in 1912,[1] 'has lost faith in the necessity, let alone the righteousness, of the social arrangements to which he finds himself subjected. He sees himself and all his fellow-workers toiling day by day in the production of services and commodities. This toil is continued without cessation year in and year out, under the orders of persons of another social class who do not share his physical exertion. He sees the services and the commodities that he feels that *he* is producing, sold at prices

---

[1] S. and B. Webb, *What Syndicalism Means*. Published as a supplement to *The Crusade* by the National Committee for the Prevention of Destitution, August 1912.

far exceeding the amount which he receives in wages. He has, of course, been told that this price has to pay large salaries to managers and other officials, and has to cover payments of rent and interest to the owners of the land and the capital. But today, in his disillusionment, this statement seems to him merely another way of describing the fact: it does not satisfy him of the reasonableness of the enormous and constant inequality between the wage that he receives and the incomes enjoyed either by the owners of the instruments of production, or by their managers and agents who rule his life. And this inequality of income is not personal to himself and his employer: it is true of all wage-earners and all employers. It results in a society in which one-tenth of the population own nine-tenths of the accumulated wealth; in which one-fifth of the adults take to themselves two-thirds of the annual product, and allow only one third to be shared among the four-fifths who are manual working wage-earners,[1] in which, as a consequence of this inequality, and in spite of a wealth production greater than the world has ever known, one-third of all these manual working wage-earners have scarcely a bare subsistence, whilst most of the other two-thirds are so little removed from this low level that the slightest interruption or dislocation of industry reduces many of them to destitution. In dramatic contrast with this penury and desti-tution he sees hundreds of thousands of wealthy families wasting in idleness and senseless extravagance, literally hundreds of millions of pounds annually out of the wealth that is produced. Something is radically wrong with a society that produces this inequality, universally and eternally, without relaxation or redress. To all the wage-earners who think about this matter, to all who are, in fact, "class conscious", the explanation seems simple. Whilst they and their fellows are contributing the whole of the physical toil involved in the production, distribution, and exchange of commodities, they are excluded from the ownership both of the instruments of production and of the products of their labour. But this is not all. The ownership of the land and the other instruments of production carries with it the power of giving orders as to how they shall be used. The manual working

---

[1] This was somewhat overstated: about 1910 the wage-earners made up three-quarters of the occupied population, and their wages were about thirty-five per cent of national income.

wage-earner finds himself spending his whole life in subjection to the arbitrary orders, even to the irresponsible caprices, of the employers and their agents. If they chose to close the mines and quarries, the fields and factories, of which the law gives them the ownership, the wage-earner and his family may starve. And in law and government the position seems much the same. The mere manual working wage-earner feels himself out of it all.'

CHAPTER II

THE CONDITIONS OF WORK

I

A people that could escape starvation only so long as it could sell its industrial exports in competitive markets had done little for the industrial training of its young people.

The old way of training by apprenticeship went on, but was felt to be in decay, because there were now so many jobs it did not fit. It was a good way of learning the skill of a craftsman, where the essential was not dexterity but know-how — the ability to solve problems out of a fund of experience not reduced to the principles of science. It was the function of apprenticeship, with the lad working alongside the craftsman, to impart this experience. But technical progress called for instruction in technology, that is, the application of the principles of science to industrial processes, and this the old style of apprenticeship did not impart.

The gap was seen, the technical and trade schools of France and Germany showed it up, and the foundation of the City and Guilds Institute as a central examining body in 1880 had been followed by a Royal Commission on technical instruction. This resulted in an Act of 1889 that empowered the new county councils to promote technical instruction, within the limit of a penny rate; though in deference to the trade unions' fears of a flooding of their market, it also said that such instruction should 'not include teaching the practice of any trade or industry or employment'. Further encouraged by a grant from the central exchequer, the county councils now began to provide various technical institutes and evening classes, and so learned their own trade as local education authorities for thirteen years before they were made such for all purposes in 1902. But the provision was patchy, and only a very small proportion of each year's entrants to industry could have benefited by it, for only those who were going to become technicians or set foot on the managerial ladder would be able to use the technology taught, and those who had only an elementary education were in any case not able to learn it. The lad who was going to acquire only the machine-minder's knack picked that up by going through the mill, unless he was lucky enough to join one of the firms that had their own training programmes for their recruits. Notable among these was Cadbury's, who from 1902 onwards developed a comprehensive scheme of education for their boys and girls, with first a compulsory continuation course to carry their general elementary education forward, and then a choice of voluntary courses in commerce and technology; though they came up against 'the extraordinary apathy of both boys and their parents towards the learning of a trade'.

So most boys and girls got no teaching after they left the elementary school. An Act of 1876 had provided in effect that no child could be removed from school before he was ten, but the school boards could make by-laws providing conditions on which he might be removed before he was fourteen, which otherwise was the effective school-leaving age. Though many boards made no provision, nearly three-fifths of the families of England and Wales were brought under by-laws allowing the early removal of children who had got on far enough with the three R's. So it was possible for an eleven-year-old named Ernie Bevin to leave the village school in 1892, he being then able to read and write, to work on a farm for his board and sixpence a week, paid quarterly. But in the 1890's the lowest age at which removal could be permitted was raised to twelve. In the 1900's the position was that where there were by-laws they generally required early leavers to have attained at least the sixth standard, and more often the seventh, and many children did not do this till they reached fourteen in any case; but still about one child in three did leave when twelve or thirteen.

But beside full-time exemption there was part-time. When that began it had been a victory for the educators, for what it brought in was not part-time absence but part-time attendance. The Factory Acts had said that factory children must attend school, in 1833 for two hours a day on six days a week, in 1844 for half of each of five. That was the first compulsory education in Britain, and schools were built because of it where there had been none before. But as general requirements of school attendance were imposed and raised, the half-time system stood out and made a break in them. Some parts of the country did not have it at all — London and Birmingham, for instance; but it had taken deep root in the textile districts. It was now working in this way, that the school boards could make by-laws allowing the part-time exemption of children aged twelve or thirteen, provided they had attained a standard that was set lower than for full-time exemption — usually the fourth or fifth standard only. In 1906 there were getting on for 50,000 half-timers. Sometimes they spent alternate days in the mill and at school, sometimes they went to the mill in the morning and school in the afternoon for one week, with the next week the other way round. There was a variant in Scotland, where a child who was let off all school during the day could still be required to attend continuation classes: in Dundee children of thirteen were working in the jute mills from 6 a.m. to 6 p.m., with two hours off for meals, but their attendance at school from 7.15 to 9.15 p.m. on four evenings of the week was 'rigidly enforced'.

One of the Lancashire half-timers was later to be Minister of Education. In 1902, at the age of twelve, George Tomlinson began to work thirty hours a week as a weaver, while still attending school, one week from 9 a.m. till noon, the next from 1.30 p.m. to 4 p.m. The next year, being thirteen years old, he began to work a week of $56\frac{1}{2}$ hours. In 1939, speaking in the House of Commons in a debate on nutrition, he referred to the Spens report, which told how the formation of bone takes place mainly between the ages of eleven and sixteen, and said: 'I asked myself, after reading that in the report, whether it was an explanation of the difference between my stature and the stature of some hon. Members who adorn the benches opposite. It tells us of the things that will make bone, and of what should and should not be done by children between the ages of eleven and sixteen. I was working in a cotton mill then, carrying heavier weights than I ought to have been carrying.'

The system was called the Shame of the North, but it went on because the parents wanted it. David Shackleton, the president of the Weavers' Amalgamation, and later first permanent Secretary of the Ministry of Labour, had been a half-timer himself from the age of nine, and used to defend the system by pointing to his own burly frame. In 1908 a meeting of representatives of the cotton trade unions voted in favour of ending, not the whole system, but the inclusion of twelve-year-olds: when the members of those unions balloted, they rejected even that by much more than four to one. Not till Fisher's Act of 1918 was the system to be touched, and then it went root and branch.

But without getting any exemption many children started paid work before they left school, by working out of school hours. It was found in 1902 'that in England and Wales a substantial number of children, amounting probably to 50,000, are being worked more than 20 hours a week in addition to $27\frac{1}{2}$ hours at school, (and) that a considerable proportion of their number are being worked to 30, or 40 and some even to 50 hours a week'. An Act of 1903 on the employment of children — defined as those under fourteen — prohibited the employment of any child at night, the use of any child under eleven in street trading, and more generally the employment of any child 'in any occupation likely to be injurious to his life, limb, health or education, regard being had to his physical condition'. The local authorities were empowered to limit children's work more closely. But few of them did so, nor were the rules of the Act itself enforced effectively. There was in any case little possibility of controlling the industrial work children were made to do in their own homes, and when a sweated industry was being carried on some of them were shockingly overdriven there.

The child who left school for full time work did not get much help or guidance. The Factory Act of 1901, and the Mines Acts, had put up some fences to keep children and young persons out of dangerous places and employment at night and for excessive hours — generally, no one under nineteen might work in a factory for more than $10\frac{1}{2}$ hours, exclusive of meal times, on five days of the week, with a half day on Saturday. But for vocational guidance, and training in the ways of man's estate and working life, there was little provision. A minority still got such induction through apprenticeship; others entered the training schemes provided by some big firms; many will have been helped on by the kindly interest and example of the small employers and older workpeople they went to work with. But it is a distinctive feature of industrial and urban, in contrast with traditional and rural societies, that children do not generally make their way

G

forward to adult skill and stature by helping their parents in
their work, learning by their example, and eventually taking
their places. On the contrary, a boy may never see his father at
work in the factory, and when he gets his own first job, very
often it will be somewhere else. So most young people had to go
out into working life on their own, to sink or swim. Some of
them were rebuffed, disheartened and demoralized. A boys'
club leader who saw much of that has remarked, 'The discipline
and order secured by the elementary schools was almost mira-
culous; but within two or three years the well-trained schoolboy
degenerated into the larrikin of the streets, ignorant, foul-
mouthed and predatory.' Hence 'the Ragamuffins and Hooligans, who made copy for the new journalism when it was new;
the Scuttlers and Ikes of Manchester; the Peaky-Blinders of
Birmingham; the Forty Gang, the Bengal Tigers, the Dockhead
Slashers and the Bermondsey Street Yoboes.'[1]

That was the great towns at their worst. Most young people
found more to belong to, more to do. In the family, and neighbourhood, in church and chapel and club, they found com-
panionship, interest, outlets, and a natural support and guide
in the task of growing up. By trial and error they found their
way into a job they could settle down to.

2

Most of the young people who were entering on their working
life around 1906 were going to become and remain wage-
earners. There was a line that was clearly marked then, though
it has become blurred since, between wage-earners and others.
In a factory, it separated the operatives, the men and women
'on the clock', from the staff — the administrators, technicians,
and clerks — who commonly kept different hours and used a
different entrance. Beyond the factory it could be extended to
divide manual workers generally from clerical, and employees
from employers. But here it entered some debatable ground —
on which side, for instance, should shop assistants lie, or nurses,
or the police? The very attempt to put every occupied person
into one or other of two camps seems not merely perplexed but
pointless nowadays, and it has in fact been given up, but it used
to mark a real contrast of status and outlook. Those on the one

[1] W. McG. Eager, *Making Men* (1953), pp. 365, 339-40.

side were felt to be superior to those on the other, in education and gentility as well as income; and just as the members of a multiracial society, for all the mixtures there may be around, know whether each man is 'white' or 'coloured', so English people of those days generally knew whether a man was a wage-earner — 'working class' — or not.

About three out of four of all the gainfully occupied were wage-earners in 1906. The proportion was falling, as it had been for a generation, because the ranks of the clerical, administrative and technical workers had been growing the faster. In the 1870's they had made up less than a sixth of the whole working population, and we wonder today that the world ever went on with so few to administer its services and apply and advance its technique. The growth of such services was now giving an opening to a rapidly increasing number of children. But of all the young people who entered the labour market each year, two out of three were still becoming wage-earners.

The working population that they joined was probably the most industrial in the world: there can hardly have been any other country, then or at any other time, in which so small a part of the whole working population was on the land—no more than eight per cent. That could be so only because most of our food was imported as the return on our past investments overseas and in exchange for our current exports. These exports were mainly of coal, textiles, machinery and ships. The central bastion of the economy that made these contained a quarter of the whole working population. Other forms of manufacture, with the public utilities of gas, water and electricity, occupied another fifth.

But industrial relations would probably have taken a different course if everyone had been industrialized. As it was, even in Britain, less than half the working population was engaged in industry, if by that we mean the wresting of fuel and raw materials from nature and the working with them in forge and factory, workshop and mill. The others were variously occupied, not in agriculture only but in building, in transport, in trade retail and wholesale, and in providing all manner of services, governmental, professional, clerical and personal — there were more people in domestic service alone than in all the branches of engineering. Alternatively we might ask what part of the working population was in jobs where process and equipment had been created or radically changed by the industrial revolution. We should then include transport and the public utilities with manufacture, and on balance take the mines too, but not building: again less than half the working population would be covered. The rest, outside agriculture, were in jobs where the firms were often bigger than of old, and the skill and knowledge required of the worker himself had changed in the last hundred and fifty years, yet the processes he performed were of the same kind, and there had been no great change in the quantity or type of his equipment — desk, counter, ledger, trowel, or saucepan. The impact of industrialism on the working life is seen at its most distinctive in the factory, and a third question we might ask is what proportion of the working population was employed there: the answer, if we take all the factories, workshops and laundries within the purview of the Factory Acts, is somewhat more than a quarter. So there was little resonance to industrial discontents. A small grievance felt by many people can work more powerfully than a big one felt by a few: when we see our own resentment mirrored in the faces of others, we feel it more strongly and with a deeper conviction of its justice. But those whose working lives were dominated by the relatively new techniques of industry were living among others who though of the same income and status as themselves were going on in the old ways. These others, moreover, were no less numerous. They would not spontaneously understand what it was that irked the factory hand; the flames that sometimes swept through him met a firebreak in them; his outcry was deadened in their apathy. That is why the great preponderance of the wage-earners as a whole in the working population did not bring an overwhelming force to bear upon industrial relations: they differed too much among themselves in the mode and mood of their working lives. Those who were discontented were only a discontented element. Over against any such, and tuned to other wave-lengths, there stood another, larger, inert body, 'the community'.

We have seen how the salaried or middle-class workers were increasing relatively to the wage-earners: there were also some sustained changes in the deployment of the wage-earners themselves. Agriculture had long been contracting; better prices since the 1890's checked and even reversed the fall in absolute numbers there, but the relative decline went on. There was a relative decline, too, in the textile mills and the clothing trade, and most markedly of all in domestic service — all of these predominantly women's work. The building trade, fluctuating in its own long rhythm, entered early in the new century on a prolonged decline, and was shrinking not relatively only but absolutely. On the other side the growing industries form a list familiar in more recent years: defence; power; transport and communications; engineering and chemicals; food, drink, and tobacco. But in none was the rise greater than in coal — a rise of nearly a quarter of a million, or about thirty per cent, in a decade. Looking at such changes, some contemporaries saw a worsening of the working life, a growth of the gimcrack brummagem trades calling for little more than unskilled labour, and a recession of craftsmanship. But their alarm seems to have been unfounded. The market for some skills contracted, and some semi-skilled employments widened; the growth of mining meant an increase in an exacting but very unadaptable proficiency; yet there is no doubt that the course of change, at this as at other stages of economic growth, was widening the market for trained ability.

3

About three workers in every ten were women. The proportion was rather lower then than now, partly because women were only beginning to make their way into the more qualified callings. In all England and Wales in 1911 there were less than five hundred women doctors; in the offices of central and local government the women were a sixth of the whole staff against more than a quarter now, in banking and insurance less than four per cent against more than a third. Of all the occupations requiring education and training, only teaching and nursing gave openings to women in large numbers. After them, in point both of training and gentility, came the occupations of shop assistant and domestic servant. Factories and workshops were separated from such callings as those by a wide gap in the scale of refinement and respectability, but it was to them that the many girls went who were not sufficiently educated or refined in speech and manners to go into the other occupations, or whose parents could not afford to wait for their earnings while they trained. The industries that took them in the largest

numbers were textiles and clothing, but they did unskilled work
in factories of most kinds, and they were more numerous relatively to the men within the factories generally than they were
outside. In all, about a third of all working women were there;
another third were in domestic service; and the remainder were
in occupations of higher social status, the shop assistants the
most numerous, and then the teachers.

In their search for jobs girls came up against more barriers
than their brothers. Their lack of muscular power was a drawback in some work. The Factory Acts fixed not only the number
of hours but also the times of day within which they might work
— in particular, they were forbidden to work at night — when
there were no such restrictions on the employment of men in the
same jobs. Because most girls expected to get married and give
their work up then, the employers had little inducement to train
them, nor did they themselves see much point in training. But
very generally also they came up against barriers set by prejudice, custom, and the active opposition of the men. Sometimes
the customer would not want to be served by them, sometimes
the employer would just not think of trying them on work they
had never done. Propriety was often felt to require that their
departments should be kept separate from men's. Even where
the sexes worked alongside one another, a line was drawn
between men's work and women's. The women seem to have
accepted this as simply being in the nature of things, or they felt
it would be wrong in any case to take work away from those on
whom whole families depended. 'I have met with cutting re-
proofs from forewomen and others in the bookbinding houses
when I tried, in my innocence, to find out why they did not turn
their hands to simple and easy processes which were being done
by men. "Why, that is man's work, and we shouldn't think of
doing it!" is the usual answer given with a toss of the head and
a tone insinuating that there is a certain indelicacy in the
question.'[1] If the women had had no such compunction the
men would still have held the line. Jobs were at stake where jobs
were often scarce. Even men who did not fear to lose their own
jobs would see a threat to their wages wherever women competed with men for employment, for the women were like black-

[1] *Women in the Printing Trades: a sociological study*, edited by J. Ramsay MacDonald
(1904), pp. 65-6.

legs, willing to cut the rate. Hence a vicious circle: because so many women had to seek employment in a limited field, their wages were low; because their wages were low, the men enforced the limits. They took an instinctive stand on the existing lines of demarcation, and a manager could move a woman across them only under peril of an immediate strike.

None the less, new machinery was enabling work to be given to women that used to be done by men: not only was machine-tending substituted for handicraft, but the processes of the craft itself were broken up. The authors of a survey of women's work in Birmingham in 1906 gave a long list of trades in which women had replaced men in this way — chain making, cheap jewellery, tailoring, press stamping, and so forth. But where women were working already on traditional processes, their low wages delayed the introduction of machinery: in Warrington newspaper offices women compositors were paid one-third of the men's rate, and the cheapness of their labour was stated to make it unnecessary to introduce linotypes.

The field of women's employment was subdivided by class distinctions, many of them not the less strongly felt for resting on no grounds apparent to outsiders. Most sorts of factory work still imposed a stigma as such: in the textile districts women's work in the mills had long been part of the social order, but elsewhere people often felt that no decent self-respecting girl could ever work in a factory. One difficulty about factory work for women was that they were liable to molestation by the men, or would hear their bad language, and it was the mark of an enlightened employer that he kept the sexes apart: at Port Sunlight the girls came later and left earlier than the men so that they should not be subject to annoyance in the street, and at Cadbury's only 'red badge men' of proven character were allowed in the women's departments. The factory girls were liable to have to walk home with dirty faces — sometimes employers fined them if they were caught washing in the factory: if that was so, they might as well go to work with their hair in curlers too. Generally there was an impression that they were a rough lot, or liable to be led into bad ways. The warehouse was a different place, and the girls who were sorting and packing there, it was said, rarely mixed with the factory girls. But there were also distinctions within the factory itself.

'Most kinds of work are performed by distinct classes of girls,' it was said of Birmingham; in one factory a proposed dining-room had to be given up because the lacquerers would not eat in the same room as the dippers. 'In Manchester, up to 1870, to be a folder was looked upon as being next door to being on the streets', but now 'folding and sewing girls look down on the machine girls tremendously, and would not sit at the same table with them for anything'.[1]

Domestic servants escaped the stigma of coarseness. 'When a girl goes into service at a gentleman's house,' one of them wrote in Birmingham, 'she is more liable to get into better company than factory girls. To be a servant is much more healthier and comfortable. Girls who are in service are generally much more quieter and more ladylike than those which work in a factory. In gentlemen's houses there are proper lavatories and ventilators. There is another reason why servants are much more healthier, they have the more time for their meals than factory girls have.'[2] The good quarters and the unstinted and wholesome food that most girls in service enjoyed were a great amenity, so much so that they were thought to unfit girls for coping with what they would have to put up with when they were married. Servants' wages had been rising for the last thirty years, both absolutely, and relatively to women's wages in industry, and when women in industry were commonly getting about £30 a year with everything to find from it, the servant with £20 to £25 over and above her board and lodging was regarded as well off. This rise in relative pay had come about without the least formal trade unionism on the servants' side, simply by the working of demand and supply. On the side of demand, the number of middle-class households was rising faster than the population. On the side of supply, education was giving an increasing number of girls the chance to go into other respectable occupations, and it was a chance they took — the number of girls under twenty-five in domestic service actually fell between 1901 and 1911. The reason lay in a great drawback, a stigma almost of the job, that had to be set against its comparative comfort and its stability — it lacked freedom. The

---

[1] *Women in the Printing Trades: a sociological study*, edited by J. Ramsay MacDonald (1904), p. 67.
[2] E. Cadbury, M. C. Matheson, and G. Shann, *Women's Work and Wages* (1906), p. 115.

A Strikers' Meeting in Millwall, London, 18 March 1914

servant had to live in another woman's house and be at her beck and call all day and every day; and not all mistresses were considerate. People spoke of skivvies, and slaveys. As another essayist in Birmingham wrote: 'Why I prefer to work in a factory. — Because there is a fixed time for meals and you do know when you are done, you are not all hours of the day, and you have only got one to serve and you can go to as many classes as you like in a week, you have got Saturday and Sunday to yourself and you can see a bit of life and we are not shut up all day.'

Meanwhile, another 'respectable' occupation for women — that of shop assistant — was expanding. The pay was generally good, as one would expect in a job that required some education and refinement from its recruits and was seeking more of them — women were generally earning between 15s. and 21s. a week. The work was attractive to most women, moreover, because the setting was clean and sometimes elegant, there was variety in the working day, and above all it gave personal contact with the customers, and the satisfaction of helping them. But the hours were long. A shop assistant who was later to be the first woman to enter the British cabinet, Margaret Bondfield, set out some of the hours that assistants were working in London in 1899:[1] in a general wholesale and retail store that employed nearly a thousand assistants in the West End they were working from 63 to 69 hours a week, less an hour a day for meals, in a middle-class outfitting shop in north-west London $67\frac{1}{2}$ hours, and so on. These hours were not exceptional. It was common for shops to be open from eight in the morning until half past six or seven in the evening on five days in the week, and until two o'clock on the sixth, and the assistants might have clearing up or stock marking to do after the doors were shut. Sometimes on Saturdays the shop stayed open till ten or even eleven at night. A law of 1892 had laid it down that young people under eighteen must not be employed in a shop for more than seventy-four hours a week, including meal-times. Another law in 1904 empowered local authorities to make an order fixing the hours at which shops must stop serving customers; but this must not be earlier than seven, or one o'clock on one early closing day, and a two-thirds majority of the shopkeepers — not their assistants — was

[1] Margaret Bondfield, 'Conditions under which shop assistants work,' *Economic Journal*, June 1899.

required. This was hard to get, and few orders were made. Without an order, any one employer who shortened hours on his own would lose trade to his competitors; and meanwhile he could fill his vacancies. This was so even when it was a condition of employment not only to work the long hours but to live in — to live as a boarder over the shop, under house rules laid down by the employer, and to accept the board and lodging he provided as part of the wage.

For many women, the claims of paid employment competed with or were mounted on the claims of housework. Some of the married women who went out to work were wives of unskilled labourers, and desperately needed more money even when their husbands were in work; if the children suffered from the mother's being away, they did not starve outright as they would without her earnings. Others who went out to work were wives of unemployed men, or of men who squandered their earnings on drink and betting. Some just wanted to get out of the house, like the one who said to Mrs Ramsay MacDonald: 'D'yer think I could stop at 'ome all dye and mind the blessed byby — it 'ud give me the bloomin' 'ump!' She earned 10s. a week in her jam factory, and paid her mother 5s. to mind and feed the baby. 'In districts where married women's work is very common,' Mrs MacDonald observed, 'the idea that a young woman should look after her own home and children seems sometimes quite strange. That kind of work devolves upon the older generation, and in family after family one finds the grandmother making clothes, cooking the meals, minding the babies, whilst the mother's energies are used in some factory.'[1] The proportion of working women who were married was much higher in the textile mills than in the country as a whole, and the mortality of textile workers' babies was higher too — especially from congenital malformation, and also from diarrhoea, which was thought to be due to the artificial feeding of babies while their mothers were in the mill.

The same motives that made some women go out to work led many others to do outwork in their own time at home — sewing and machining of all sorts, carding and packaging, making paper boxes and brushes, burnishing metal with soap suds and

---

[1] *Wage Earning Mothers*, by Mrs J. R. MacDonald and others (The Women's Labour League, undated).

beer. Here was an underworld where appalling hours were sometimes worked for very little money, and the children were pressed into service too, getting up early to stitch on hooks and eyes before they went to school, getting a few more cards done in the dinner hour, sitting up late to do more at night — a whole family might earn five or six shillings a week.

Whether working women were married or not they had their share of the housework to do as well as their work in the factory. This was 'the double duty' that their brothers escaped. Annie Kenney the suffragette had begun as a half-timer in Lancashire at ten years old, and had a finger torn off in the mill. 'I saw men, women, boys and girls, all working hard during the day in the same hot, stifling factories,' she said later.[1] 'Then when work was over I noticed that it was the mothers who hurried home, who fetched the children that had been put out to nurse, prepared the tea for the husband, did the cleaning, baking, washing, sewing, and nursing. I noticed that when the husband came home, his day's work was over; he took his tea and then went to join his friends in the club or in the public house, or on the cricket or football field, and I used to ask myself why this was so.'

But most women did not ask that. What struck one of the early women factory inspectors[2] first and foremost about the women workers was their 'mute sense of industrial inferiority, outside the great textile industries'. Their apathy was borne partly of the hopelessness of attempting improvement, partly of the inability to conceive that improvement was possible. In this passivity they bore not only those ills of factory life that they shared with the men, but some others peculiar to themselves: 'in spite of protective laws, a working day and week in which the standard hours worked by women frequently exceeded those for which men, in certain great trades, had by means of trade unions secured recognition from employers; a frequent lack of suitable or even decent and sufficient sanitary accommodation, of cleanliness of a domestic nature, and of other hygienic requirements, sometimes injuriously affecting conduct and morals; not only low average and individual wages, but on the part of pieceworkers an intolerable uncertainty as to what their

[1] Quoted at p. 22 of E. Sylvia Pankhurst, *The Suffragette* (1911).
[2] Dame Adelaide Anderson, *Women in the Factory* (1922), pp. 24-5.

rates really were; and, for all, a liability to arbitrary deductions for fines and alleged damages to work, which often brought earnings below subsistence level.'

But now there were stirrings of a new spirit. The original stronghold of the suffragettes was among the women textile workers of Lancashire and Yorkshire. The question to Sir Edward Grey that led up to their first prison sentences ran: 'Will the Liberal Government give votes to working women? Signed on behalf of the Women's Social and Political Union, Annie Kenney, member of the Oldham Committee of the Card and Blowing Room Operatives.'[1]

4

The factory like the industrial town had 'just growed' — in 1801 in all Britain there had been only twenty towns with more than twenty thousand inhabitants apiece — and many of the troubles of both arose from the failure to realize at some stage of growth that explicit provision had now to be made for much that had looked after itself so long as things were on a smaller scale. As the town spread, the workman and his family could no longer walk out into the fields on Sundays or on a summer evening. As the shed or attic grew into the factory, all manner of needs made themselves felt to the worker, though to the employer it seldom seemed part of his job to attend to them. There were housekeeping needs, for washrooms, latrines, lockers, canteens; and hygienic needs, for ventilation, dust extraction, lighting, and heating — matters which the two or three workers in a small shop could arrange tolerably for themselves, but which called for special design and equipment in a big one. There was the effect of lay-out on human relations — what freedom of movement it left the men, what possibility of talking with one another. There was cleanliness. There was working dress. There was the dignity or squalor of the building, and the effect of that on the self-respect of those who worked in it. Many of these things have their counterpart in the village blacksmith's shop, or the back-yard shed, but there they do not matter so much. Bring large numbers of workers together, fit them in more tightly, make their workplace not a room they adapt to their needs but an iron frame they themselves must be

---

[1] E. Sylvia Pankhurst, *The Suffragette* (1911), p. 27.

fitted to, and these things cause trouble unless thought and money are spent on them. A factory is the house of a working community: as such it has human needs to satisfy, and a functional beauty to achieve. What grows piecemeal by accretion and contortion is unlikely to do that, nor what is planned for the machinery and not for the men. But it was young firms that needed new factories, and young firms were short of capital.

By degrees Parliament had confronted these problems, and put together an industrial code. The latest of the Factory Acts, in 1901, had set out the nation's standing orders for health and safety in workplaces. It laid down standards of air space and air movement, and required lavatories to be provided, floors to be drained, walls to be limewashed. It ordered the fencing of dangerous machinery, forbade the cleaning of machines while they were running, and laid down special precautions for boilers. It continued the power which the Home Secretary had had since 1891, and which Asquith had used vigorously, of making special regulations for dangerous and unhealthy industries, twenty-two of which were dealt with by 1910. There were two other major issues. One was the hours of work of children, young people, and women: for these the Act laid down the maximum number of hours they might work, and the times of day that the work must be done in — women, for example, must not work at night. There was no limit as yet on the hours of adult men, save possibly on a railway or in a dangerous trade. The other major issue was that of cheating in the payment of wages: the Act required that wages must be paid in coin of the realm and not in truck, they must not be handed over in a public house, and pieceworkers must be given a written statement of the rates at which they would be paid.

The Factory Acts now covered not factories only, but many workshops, and docks, and laundries. Alongside them were other laws for the mines, the railways, and the mercantile marine. The impact on public opinion of the degradation of women and children in the pits, and the recurrent death roll of disasters there, had early brought the mines under detailed statutory control in matters technical as well as human, and the code now in force had been largely enacted as far back as 1872. The railways, too, had early been brought under technical regulation, but that more to protect the passengers than the staff. But at last in 1893 the Board of Trade was empowered to act on complaint of excessive hours and require the company to submit a reasonable working schedule, and that was the first legal limit ever set in Britain on the working hours of grown men; and then a Royal Commission on accidents to railwaymen was followed in 1902 by a statutory code of rules especially concerning shunting, brakes, and the safety of the permanent way gang. The seaman's life was far more dangerous than the miner's, but its disasters were generally less concentrated and not so near home, and Plimsoll had had a struggle to get his loading line through in 1876; but the Merchant Shipping Acts of 1894 and 1906 were comprehensive — the former was the longest in the statute book. Notably they contained provisions against taking coffin ships to sea and against overloading and undermanning, and they laid down scales of life-saving equipment.

Parliament's regulation of the mines and the mercantile marine was conspicuous in its requiring that no one might take charge there unless he had obtained by examination a certificate of technical proficiency. The reason was simple — incompetence would lead to great losses of life and equipment. But incompetence in other industries also led to losses: we might think now that the principle, once admitted, would have proved pregnant, and been extended, both in the range of subjects the young manager had to study — human nature for one of them — and in the industries comprised. But elsewhere, the effects of bad management were not so dramatic. Mining engineering and navigation, moreover, were definite bodies of knowledge that could be taught and examined; there was not yet a subject, in that sense, of administration, or management, or leadership.

One indication of the need for an industrial code is given by the accident rate. We have no trustworthy measure of the course of non-fatal accidents, because the standards of reporting will have changed, but that does not apply to the fatal ones, and these gave a death-rate from accidents at work that in the early 1900's was double and more than double what it has become fifty years later. Out of each ten thousand men at work in 1952-6, the factory operatives lost about one killed a year, the railwaymen less than four, the coal miners less than six, the seamen less than eleven. In 1902-6 the corresponding losses were rather more than two factory operatives, nearly eight railwaymen, more than twelve miners, and fifty seamen. Those higher rates must be put down in part to the lower personal quality of some of the workpeople then, in particular to their drinking more. Probably also they mark equipment designed with less regard to safety, and the use of the human hand for movements that the machine has taken over since. But they must also mark a difference in the activity of management, in the attention it gave to safety and the training of workpeople who were often careless or wilfully disregarded existing precautions. It was more natural to take less trouble to prevent accidents, when most people regarded them as inevitable. In Birmingham it was common to see women with hands mutilated from a mishap in the press shops. One of the first women welfare workers related how her girls often lacerated their hands or had fingers severed, and when one had an accident she would walk to the hospital holding her bleeding hand for all to see: it was a revelation for both managers and girls to find that a small adjustment of the job reduced the number of these accidents. The Welsh miner who was injured was carried home and laid on his kitchen table top for the doctor to operate on him there. The valley knew when a man was killed, for the whole shift came up, and walked behind his body till it was laid in his front room.

Accidents might be accepted as part of life, but only because it was a hard life anyhow and there was no justice in it. They typified how the scales were weighted against the wage-earner. No need to make a fuss, he was told, accidents were bound to happen from time to time, and he took the risk when he took the job. But he felt he was doing that job for another man's profit, so why should it be he and his family that had to bear the cost? If injuries were an inevitable cost of production, then the relief of the injured should be paid for out of the product. But there was no social insurance: any cover a man got he must pay for wholly himself. Nor, down to 1897, was he able to recover from the employer unless he could show both that the employer had been negligent and that neither he nor any fellow workman had been. But in 1897, thanks to Joseph Chamberlain, the law was changed, and Parliament accepted the principle that the compensation of the victim or his dependents must be a charge on industry, almost regardless of what caused the accident. Even then, the principle was not at first applied to seamen, or farm workers, or domestic servants. In any case, it was still the workers whose bones were broken; the employers and shareholders had only to pay a premium. Industrial injuries remained a mark of the difference in privilege and status between employer and employed.

There is another, less overt way in which they may have worsened industrial relations. Danger generally makes men more combative, more attached to their mates and more hostile to outsiders. If industry is liable to hit out and maim or kill me, I want to hit back at industry, or those who own it. Working in the presence of lurking danger, moreover, imposes a constant need to be careful, a constraint often the more pressing because it is a responsibility for other men's lives; and this may have its repercussion in impatience and readiness to have a row elsewhere.

It was in any case significant for industrial relations that there was difficulty in enforcing the code of health and safety. True, this code often did no more than follow the existing practice of good employers, and resistance to it came from workpeople as well as employers; yet still it must be said that its day-to-day administration did show much contemporary management in a poor light. There had long been an inspectorate, and since 1893 it had contained some very hard worked women. What is striking now in the inspectors' experience is not so much the cases of crass incompetence or inhumanity, as the more prevalent attitude that the law was too grandmotherly and they were too fussy. G. R. Askwith, who had seen more than most men of British employers between 1900 and 1914, said that most of them did no more than comply with the bare requirements of the Factory Acts, and did not interest themselves in the amenities of their workpeople. Anyone who wanted to draw up an indictment of employers would find shocking cases enough in the inspectors' reports, which were an arsenal for socialists. Most employers deserved no such condemnation, and yet were little aware of one of their functions and opportunities as managers. In this indifference to the amenities of the working life, moreover, they were overlooking a source of efficiency as well as of satisfaction. When some of the railway companies had shorter hours for their staff forced on them by the Board of Trade, they found that discipline was improved and services became more punctual: did it then take the Board of Trade to teach them their own business? In engineering, British employers were contrasted with the German. G. N. Barnes[1] as secretary of the Amalgamated Engineers was in Germany in 1898. 'In the application of science to industry,' he wrote later, 'they were ahead of Great Britain, and had in fact, as I thought, in some places, overdone it, as for instance, in supplying the tiniest machines with separate electric power and in guarding runing machinery to the extent of unnecessarily hampering the operative. I was astounded to see how the comfort of the worker was provided for in the way of supply of food and drink, baths, and in some cases, houses. . . .' Sir Andrew Noble,[2] who managed the biggest works in Britain, Armstrong Whitworth's at Elswick, noticed the same two features — 'the way in which their shops were warmed, their having the tools supplied to the machines, so that the men need never leave their machines, and certain comforts for the men . . .'; he sent a dozen of his foremen over to see for themselves. By contrast, the enforcement of the Factory Acts in Britain showed the state as having to intervene not only to make employers less rapacious but to make them more competent. It strengthened the faith of those who held that public ownership would substitute not justice only, but efficiency, for the squalid muddle of private enterprise.

But there were exceptions, and they were pregnant. G. R. Askwith also found 'many employers with vision, who consistently examined their stocks of machinery and were continuously out for improvements and who thought of the welfare of their men in and out of the shops, and strove for good ventilation, cleanliness, amenities, and recreation'.[3] In the early days of the Industrial Revolution there had been some notable employers of that kind, and some instances crop up here and there later. Wedgwoods maintained a tradition of attention to welfare, Courtaulds had a day nursery in 1852, Colmans in 1868 started a works kitchen to provide a pint of coffee for a penny when the men were assembling for work at 5.45 a.m., and a hot meat

---

[1] G. N. Barnes, *From Workshop to War Cabinet* (1924), p. 54.
[2] *Minutes of Evidence of the Royal Commission on Trade Disputes and Trade Combinations*, (Cd. 2826 of 1906), Q. 2530.
[3] Lord Askwith, *Industrial Problems and Disputes* (1920), p. 353.

H

dinner for threepence or fourpence. Sir Titus Salt had built what was for the times a model village imaginatively planned around his new mill at Saltaire, in the 1850's. But the line had run thin. Now new employers had arisen who were to transform the nation's conception of what a factory and the community around it could be like. There is little in the modern design and housekeeping of the factory that had not already appeared in one place or another by 1906.

The landmarks here are, first and foremost, Lever's start at Port Sunlight in 1888, and then Bournville village in the 1890's, and the estate by Loch Ness that the British Aluminium Company were to lay out with guidance from the Garden City Association. In 1890 Joseph Rowntree had moved to a new factory at Haxby Road, and New Earswick village followed in 1904. Hull Garden Suburb was begun in 1908, partly for Reckitts' workpeople. Great changes were signalized here in the conception of what was not merely desirable but practicable. The factory itself was designed for light, air, and cleanliness. It was set in pleasant surroundings. The needs of its workpeople were provided for as well as those of its machines: there were lockers, wash rooms, dining halls. For those workpeople too a township was planned, with good houses and good gardens, parks and playing fields and swimming baths, schools, libraries, churches and halls. But all this was done by competitive firms who continued to make profits and expand. It was not philanthropy only, it was good management. It would survive, and extend. Here, moreover, the prevailing relation between business and the state was reversed: in standards of housing and in imaginative town planning, it was business that gave the lead to local government.

The three examples we have named were outstanding, in their scale and impact, but there were others. A contemporary survey of 'model factories and villages' noted at Dartford 'the creeper-clad works of Messrs Burroughs and Wellcome, surrounded by gardens with seats on the lawns', and at Glasgow the carpet factory of James Templeton and Co. — 'this they have rendered a thing of beauty and an added attraction to the neighbourhood, by facing it with coloured brickwork after the design of the Doge's Palace at Venice'.[1] In Hans Renold's new

[1] Budgett Meakin, *Model Factories and Villages* (1905), pp. 76, 80-1.

chain factory begun at Burnage in 1906 'well lit and ventilated single-storey buildings were sited among trees thoughtfully left to provide pleasant shade and scenery'.[1] It was something new that visitors were conducted around some factories, though generally only those where proprietary brands were made. The amenity that was most usually added to the factory was the playing field, for this could be provided, albeit at a distance, even where the factory was old and the site was cramped: it was recorded that Brunner, Mond had built an athletic pavilion, Huntley and Palmers had provided fourteen acres, and most of the big wholesalers and retailers of London had their fields in the suburbs.

With this went greater care for the welfare of the worker within the factory. Some firms had long been giving sick-pay, or helping their workpeople run a sick club, but now Cadburys had a surgery with a doctor in daily attendance whose services were free, and Rowntrees provided the free services of a whole-time dentist. Pretty & Son of Ipswich had a day nursery at their corset factory. Thos. Adams & Co., lacemakers of Nottingham, introduced rest pauses, with 'a break after 10 a.m. when a hawker visits the warehouse with refreshments approved of by the management, and again after 4 p.m., when batches of girls go down to the tea room in turn to partake of their own supplies'[2]. Sometimes an organ played at mealtimes in the canteen. Many firms helped their young workers to attend technical courses, or provided classes and lectures for the older ones. One of the first house journals was *The Thames Ironworks Quarterly Gazette*, which started in 1895; Lever's *Progress* began in 1899.

Various activities of this kind began to be brought together under the care of a new kind of manager, called first, after American practice, the Social Secretary, and then the Welfare Manager. Rowntrees appointed a woman as Social Secretary in 1891, and later took a male graduate to look after their men. By 1906 the duties of the welfare manager were generally considered to be: engaging new workers, suggesting improvements in factory conditions, organizing clubs, and editing the magazine.

At the same time something was being done here and there to provide holidays with pay. In 1886 the Gas Light and Coke Co.

[1] B. H. Tripp, *Renold Chains* (1956), p. 85.
[2] Budgett Meakin, op. cit., p. 140.

of London began a week's holiday with pay and a gratuity of
4s. 6d. for all men who had been continuously employed in the
carbonizing department for the previous twelve months and had
not been absent for more than seven days except for illness: 'the
holiday is to be spent', the Company's announcement said, 'in
the country or at the seaside'. About the same time the South
Metropolitan Gas Company announced double pay for a week's
holiday for men with three years' service. E. S. and A. Robinson,
the Bristol colour printers, and Manders the ink manufacturers
of Wolverhampton followed with a week's holiday with pay in
1889. The South Metropolitan Gas Co. in London had gone
further, with two weeks for employees of three years' standing.
Brunner Mond's gave a week's holiday on double pay to all who
had not been absent without leave for more than two days
during the year. Lever also issued double pay in one sense, but
half of it had been collected from the worker himself at the rate
of one hour's pay deducted from each week's packet through
the year.

There was also a growth of pensions. Some employers had long
been making *ex gratia* payments to old hands, or their widows.
Constituted schemes came in first for clerks, with the Gas Light
and Coke Company apparently leading the way with a contributory scheme in 1842; Prudential Insurance had established
widows' pensions by 1866 and retirement pensions by 1872.
Perhaps the first scheme for manual workers was again that of
the Gas Light and Coke Company, about 1870. Siemens
Brothers, the cable manufacturers of Woolwich, adopted a
pension scheme from their German parent in 1872, with an
endowment fund for widows and orphans. Now in 1904 Lever
began a fund to provide pensions for widows and those who had
to give up through illness or injury, and also retirement pensions
at sixty-five for men who had twenty years' service; all the
money was found by the firm. Rowntrees followed in 1906 with
a contributory scheme.

Nothing bore the stamp of intelligent management more
clearly than a reduction in working hours. The factory had
brought about appalling hours, out of the wish to spread the
fixed cost of expensive equipment over as many units of output
as possible; and in the early days when mills depended on intermittent water power there was the added motive of crowding as

much work as possible into those days when the power was there. But this took no account of the human factor, of the possibility that lengthening the worker's day would not increase his output in anything like the same proportion, or even raise it at all. A drastic reduction in the hours of work of textile mills, brought about by the Ten Hours Act of 1847, had shown that this possibility was actual: there were mills that cut their working week from seventy-two to sixty hours, and found after a while that their output was as big as before. One might have thought that the example would have been found instructive, and that the movement would have spread. But employers hesitated: they might agree there was a good chance of their faring as well as before, and yet feel they could not risk it unless their competitors did the same. It was hard for them to make a compact to this end, as it was for shopkeepers in the twentieth century — there would always be someone who stood out; so in practice the reduction of hours depended on trade union pressure. From time to time the unions did press for shorter hours, notably in the boom after the Franco-Prussian war, when the week of fifty-four hours was generally won in the sectors of industry that the unions had organized. By the end of the century, indeed, the organized trades were more consistently marked off from the rest by their shorter hours than by any other difference. Some unions had now adopted the eight hours day as an aim. But few workmen could yet afford to buy daylight by giving up earnings: if hours were reduced, the pieceworkers might perhaps be able to keep their earnings up by turning out as much as before in the shorter time, but the hourly paid could not do it unless they negotiated a compensatory rise in the hourly rate, and that was putting a double burden on the employer — raising his direct costs at the same time as his indirect. When the Amalgamated Engineers actually had offered to take some cut in pay in return for the eight hour day, the employers had told them they could hardly think it was meant seriously. None the less, there were some employers who, like Robert Owen in earlier days, took the initiative in reducing the hours of their own workpeople, in the belief that with less fatigued workers and with their own better management they would not lose ground to their competitors. Mundella and Joseph Chamberlain had done this in their day, bringing the weekly hours down to fifty-five or fifty-four; but in the 1890's a number of engineering firms went on to the forty-eight hour week, and the government followed them, in Woolwich Arsenal — 'a careful comparison had been made', Campbell Bannerman said, 'of the results obtained elsewhere, and the conclusion (confirmed by the Department's own experience) had been formed that any increase in wages would be compensated for by a saving in fuel, etc., by the increased energy of the workmen, and lastly, by the prevention of lost time owing to the suppression of the breakfast hour.' That might have been expected to give an impetus. But it did not. Most industrial wage-earners remained on a normal working week of over fifty hours until after the First World War; they began each day with a spell before breakfast, on an empty stomach or on drink they bought on their way to work. The firms which were regularly working a forty-eight hour week for men before 1914, though well-known, remained exceptional.

What such firms were doing, in that way and many others, made up a movement that came to be called 'industrial betterment'. It is easy now to undervalue it. Certainly it had its limitations. Where it was in many ways at its most imaginative — in Port Sunlight — it went with an unrelenting autocracy. There might be smugness and an air of patronage about the conferment of benefits, some of which seem small to us now compared with the pride that was taken in them. But there are other and weightier considerations. If much was made of improvements that do not seem remarkable now, it was because they were remarkable at the time. They stood out from the grey and grimy ruck of industrialism, they showed that the working life to which the growth of population had irrevocably committed most of our people need not be sordid or unhealthy. They showed that a factory town could be a good place to live in and work in. That was revolutionary: but it was a practical revolution, for the firms whose workpeople were best treated were vigorously managed, technically progressive, profitable, thoroughly viable. Many of them, moreover, not least the Quakers, thought of the amenities of welfare not as an opiate for discontent but as an outcome of their respect for their workpeople as human beings, and this found its deepest expression in good manners and fair dealing. The future lay with that kind of management. In the years to come its combination of imaginative vigour in technology and administration with understanding of the workman's feelings and concern for his self-respect has done more than any other force or faith to advance his welfare.

5

There was a risk that cast a darker shadow even than injuries over the life of the wage-earner — the risk of being out of work. It had come to loom larger of late, whether because there was rather more chance of it than before, or men being better educated resented it more; or just because in an ever-growing population even a constant rate of unemployment meant a greater absolute number of men unemployed in each town at any one time, and so echoed and amplified the hardship, and gave everyone more sense of the magnitude of the problem. That magnitude appeared in the streets. Orderly, gaunt, silent, the unemployed filed into churches during Sunday service and stood in the aisles; they passed in long procession around the floor of the Glasgow stock exchange; with their blankets they marched up to Westminster. In the winter of 1903–4, the President of the Local Government Board told the Poor Law commissioners, 'there were crowds besieging the offices of the Relieving Officers and Boards of Guardians in London, in Leeds, in Liverpool, in Manchester, in Birmingham, and all our great cities where the unemployed difficulty arose in an acute form; the Boards of Guardians could hardly sit in some places without safeguarding their doors, which were besieged by a crowd of people demanding assistance.'

It was at that point, where it arose most urgently, that public opinion had taken the problem up. It was seen as one of relief and rehabilitation. Here was a man who was destitute because he could not find a job: what could be done to make work for him, or retrain him, or help him to migrate? But when William Beveridge published his *Unemployment: a Problem of Industry*, in 1909, the very title marked a new approach. Men were out of work because in various ways the demand for labour and the supply did not match place by place. The task was to chart those ways and improve the design of the system. Besides the unemployed man there was unemployment to deal with. Besides the problem of relief there was one of industrial organization.

Beveridge's work and the studies he and others have made since have made clear various mechanisms by which the number of jobs can fall short of the number of applicants. One that had always been evident — the decline of an established industry, or the by-passing of established skills by new processes — was found to have attracted more attention than its actual extent deserved. Occasionally some districts suffered much in that way, and in any part of the country some men with a life-time of experience in one occupation might lose their stock in trade to a new machine. But changes in the relative sizes of industries went on gradually, and the machines were creating new openings as well as closing old ones. There was no great source of unemployment here before 1914: these once for all changes in the demand for labour were less troublesome than its fluctuations, even though these rose and fell about an ever-rising trend. The shortest in period came from the changes of the seasons, conventional and climatic. The printers got short of work when Parliament rose. The dressmakers who were working all hours in May and June had little to do in August. Young people set up house in the spring, and little furniture was sold in the winter. In the winter months, too, builders were more held up by bad weather, and the householder's mind did not turn to getting his painting done, even indoors. Some trades were busier then — the gasworks, for instance, and some parts of the docks — but on balance jobs were fewer, and it was a hard time in more ways than one. There was next a fluctuation of longer span, not widely reckoned with as yet in an age when statistical records were fewer and less familiar than now; but when Beveridge charted 'the pulse of the nation', he showed how a rhythm of about nine years' period had long run through it. This was the trade cycle, conspicuous at its high and low points as boom and slump, but at most times keeping demand and output above or below their trends of growth. It bore especially on two sectors — on the export industries, where its movements generally began; and on the industries making durable products of all kinds, especially those providing the materials for the construction of new plant and equipment — iron and steel, engineering and building. This trade cycle had risen to a peak of activity during the Boer War, in 1899; then employment declined until 1904, when it was bad; by 1906 an improvement was apparent, and continuing. But one big industry did not share in this revival. We have seen how building, though affected by the trade cycle, had long also followed a rhythm of its own, with a longer period, as much as a quarter century long, that was bound up with the swing of the resources of growth between the eastern and western shores of the Atlantic. British builders had met a brisk demand for houses in the 1890's; but about the turn of the century they entered upon a decline that persisted till the war; while the working population as a whole was growing fast, their own numbers actually diminished.

But beyond these fluctuations lay a kind of unemployment that persisted even in the boom, and accounted for most of the distress in a slump. The unskilled man was under-employed at the best of times. He worked on short engagements, and there were gaps between them. The sort of work he did fluctuated from day to day and the fluctuations were thrown on him. 'Has there ever,' Beveridge asked, 'in the big towns at least, been a time when employers could not get practically at a moment's notice all the labourers they required?'[1] In that way the supply created the demand; there was no need for managers to arrange a steady flow of work, or for buyers to look ahead — when they could do with another man he was waiting at the gate. ' "In the case of a warehouse it is utterly impossible as a rule for the warehouseman to tell from day to day how many men he may require the following morning. He may have a heavy stock of any particular class of goods in his warehouse, the owner of which may sell it, say late in the afternoon, the order is passed through and the carrier applies for delivery first thing in the morning. The warehouseman thus requires a considerable number of men; but for days on end, even although he has a heavy stock in his warehouse, he may not require more than one or two hands beside himself to attend to sampling orders." Every railway company has, for the goods traffic of its principal stations, its set of extra men, who get taken on for a few hours, or for a day or two, whenever there is pressure of business. . . . In London "a large body of men is always required for the Friday night baking". . . . In busy marketing neighbourhoods, a whole class of butchers' assistants are engaged only for Fridays

[1] W. H. Beveridge, *Unemployment: a Problem of Industry* (1909); new edn. 1930, p. 69.

and Saturdays.'[1] Conspicuous among these workers on short
engagements were the building labourers, following some cart-
load of materials to find a site where work was starting, being
taken on without selection or reference, to be turned off in a
couple of days if they did not prove up to the job. Best known of
all were the dockers; but their lot only dramatized that of many
others. ' "To go in" for one half-a-day, one day, two, three,
four, or five days out of the five and a half is common to boot-
making, coopering, galvanizing, tank-making, oil pressing,
sugar-boiling, piano-making, as it is to dock labouring, steve-
doring, crane lifting, building.'[2] These men were partly needed
to take the place of absentees among others of their kind. It was
on them that most of the unemployment fell when trade was
bad: obviously so when they were only wanted for the peak load
in any case, but also even when they were in regular employment in good times — the employer would choose the least
qualified men to lay off first; and he would want to keep his
skilled and experienced men together even when there was not
enough for them to do, but he could turn the unskilled away
without any fear of not being able to replace them the moment
he wanted to.

There was a mechanism, it was said, whereby a fluctuating
demand caused a bigger reserve of labour to be retained than
was needed to meet that demand at its peak, and the actual
average earnings of the men to be lower than the prospective
earnings that attracted them. This mechanism depended on
employers taking men on independently, so that the momentary
high demand of the one could not be set off against a low
demand from another as it would be under central engagement;
and on such men as actually were taken on at any one time
being taken at random, so that however little work a man had
been having, the next time he applied he had as much chance
of getting into the money as anyone else. It was specially for the
docks that this mechanism had been described, but its linkages
were found widely elsewhere. What seems remarkable now,
however, is not so much that the demand worked in a particular
way, as that the supply was there. Of much unskilled labour in

---

[1] S. and B. Webb, *The Public Organization of the Labour Market: being Part II of the
Minority Report of the Poor Law Commission* (1909), pp. 186-8.
[2] ibid.

the towns everywhere it could be said, here is a body of men underemployed at the best of times, earning year in and year out less than a subsistence wage, recurrently dependent on relief: why do they stay there? why do they not move to better prospects elsewhere? The answer is, they could not. The casual engagement of dockers was not just a gambling saloon device that held men in dockland against their own interests: if what they actually earned had been paid them as regular weekly wage, small though it was, they would have had to put up with it, for most of them had no alternative. We come here again upon the existence in those days of a mass of unqualified labour, such as recent years give us no conception of. Its numbers were still being recruited from the many boys who were pushed into the first job they could get the day they left school. It was the homes that gave the worst start in life that were now having the most children. Here was the overspill of the remorseless flood of population, rising by more than ever before — the natural increase was now more than four hundred thousand bodies a year. Many occupations went on behind dykes natural or contrived that kept the increase of new entrants down; those who could not get in there overcrowded what jobs there were elsewhere.

The unemployment which arose in these various ways was of very different consequence to different wage-earners. There were many occupations where the risk was slight — the railways, for instance, agriculture, retailing, the offices of central and local government, domestic service; also the coal mines, which traditionally met a fall in demand by short time rather than by laying off, and which in any case were expanding now so strongly that a check only meant halting recruitment for a while. In other occupations, though men were laid off when trade was bad, the steady-going experienced man had little ground in practice to expect discharge himself. That left two sectors in which unemployment was concentrated. One we might call the trade cycle sector — the export industries like textiles and ship-building, the constructional industries like iron and steel and engineering, and building, though we have seen that this had another rhythm of its own. The distinctive mark of this sector was that here the experienced and qualified man was liable to be out of work from time to time — though printing was a trade

outside it where that was true too. The second sector was
marked off by a horizontal line between social classes rather
than vertical boundaries between industries. In it fell the unskilled everywhere. It was they who made up most of the
numbers.

Of wage-earners as a whole, the proportion unemployed
probably varied from less than three per cent in a good year like
1899 to ten per cent and more in a bad year like 1904 or 1908.
The rate recorded by the trade unions that paid benefit to their
unemployed members was actually below three per cent on the
average of the better halves of the trade cycle, making up
twenty-five years out of the forty-seven from 1866 through 1912:
that could not have come about without spells of really full
employment and local shortages of labour. But average rates,
low or high, tell only what proportion of the workers are unemployed at any one time, and this is the product of two factors
— the proportion who lose their jobs within the year, and how
long these have to wait before they get another. At the one
extreme, an annual average rate of five per cent would appear
if only five per cent of the workers lost their jobs but these
remained unemployed throughout the year; at the other, it
could equally appear if every man lost his job once during the
year but had to wait only a twentieth of a year before he got
another. Actual experience fell between those extremes. Among
the London Compositors, on the average of ten years, the rate
of unemployment was under five per cent, but more than
twenty per cent of the members were out of work at least once
in any one year. In a bad year like 1894, the Scots Blacksmiths
had had less than thirteen per cent of their members out of work
at any one time, but more than forty-five per cent had had a
taste of unemployment at some time during the year. The
reader may ask himself, if he had been one of the Scots Blacksmiths then, would it have been the thirteen per cent or the
forty-five that was the measure of his anxiety? Moreover,
though the other side of the forty-five per cent was that even in a
bad year more than half were never out of work, very few could
have been sure that they would be among the lucky ones. If a
battalion going up the line could be assured that not more than
one man in ten was going to be hit, the men's faces would still
look strained. Most wage-earners seldom lost their job in

practice, and could get another if they did; but the prospect of being out of work will have cast its chill on them for all that. Unemployment was a major hazard, and humiliation, of the wage-earner's lot.

When he did fall out of work, there was no general public means of support for him except what the Poor Law provided for the able-bodied pauper. The skilled man would have none of that except in utter extremity, when he had lost all hope of keeping his status anyhow. It was seldom, moreover, that he came to that pass: he was not out of work so much as the unskilled man, and when he was he often had savings to draw on, he might have relatives still earning a skilled man's wage, and above all, his trade union generally paid 'out-of-work donation'. The unskilled man had none of these supports. The problem was how to relieve him without opening a wide breach in the defences painfully erected in 1834 against indiscriminate doles and the subsidising of wages. Some mitigation there was in practice of the strict workhouse test: men were given out-relief for their families if they themselves went into the house, or were even allowed to sleep out themselves provided they attended each day to do some prescribed task, often stonebreaking. There was, moreover, a clause that allowed the relieving officer to give an able-bodied man out-relief in 'sudden or urgent necessity', and that was stretched a long way. But the main channel — apart from private charity, of which there was a great deal — was by way of relief works. These had been instituted to help the qualified workman tide over a spell of bad trade. There was a tradition that they had done this well in Lancashire during the cotton famine, and when Joseph Chamberlain saw the distress among the jewellers and silversmiths of Birmingham in 1885, his mind turned to them, but the local Board of Guardians would have none of them. The next year, as President of the Local Government Board, he sent out a circular urging the Guardians to 'confer with the local authorities, and endeavour to arrange with the latter for the execution of works on which unskilled labour may be immediately employed'. These works were meant to save the self-respect 'of those who do not ordinarily seek parish relief', but these would have nothing to do with them, and it was the unskilled who swamped them. They were exposed to every familiar objection against hastily improvised make-work schemes: they were costly, they lowered men's standards of a fair day's work, to the extent that they got anything useful done they only deprived other men of their jobs. None the less, they went on, and as unemployment mounted in 1903 they were resorted to ever more widely, for there was no other ritual by which out-relief could be given legally to large numbers — they were a kind of extension of the stoneyard. In the winter of 1904 Walter Long as President of the Local Government Board tried to make something more of them than that in London, when he brought representatives of the boroughs and Boards of Guardians together, and set up a scheme by which respectable men temporarily distressed should be singled out from the general run of applicants for relief, in order that a real endeavour might be made to get them jobs. Information about vacancies they might fill was to be collected through local labour exchanges. Special works might be put in hand of kinds they could do. Colonies might be set up in the country, to give them useful work and train them for settlement on the land at home or overseas, or they might simply be helped with the expenses of removal or emigration. These ideas were embodied the next year in an Unemployed Workmen Act. A Distress Committee to carry them out was to be set up in every town of fifty thousand or more inhabitants. The principle that the unemployed might be a charge on public funds outside the Poor Law was admitted for the first time, by the authorization of a halfpenny rate to meet certain expenses. In this respect the Act made history. But its purpose failed as Joseph Chamberlain's had done: there was little effective selection of the men assisted, most of whom continued to be unskilled men in casual employment at the best of times.

It was they who dominated the problem of unemployment, and this it is that explains why obvious methods were not used. These men could not be granted benefit subject simply to the requirement that they must be genuinely seeking work, for how could that test be applied to those who were almost always more numerous than the jobs they could take? Could such men be paid a dole without their simply being made available at still lower wages for such jobs as were open to them? Even less, it seemed, could they be brought under a scheme of insurance. The Webbs were to find that in 'trades where discontinuous employment is the rule, and where the employment is sporadic and ever shifting in locality, no system of insurance is either financially or administratively possible'; and 'if the provision of out of work pay by trade union insurance is impossible for the men of discontinuous employment, it is obviously still more out of reach of the under-employed'.[1] The problem of unemployment was submerged in the sea of poverty.

6

The industrial development of the twenty-five years before the First World War brought no conspicuous or concentrated change in the working life of the British people. The great centres of industry were not now spreading out so fast as before. Only in South Wales was one industrial region growing much more quickly than the rest of the country, and drawing in a great net immigration. Only one industry, that of boots and shoes, underwent a thoroughgoing technical transformation. There were striking innovations, but most of them made more difference to products than to processes: the bicycle, the rubber tyre, the motor car, the aeroplane, artificial silk, radio telegraphy — these were bringing the consumer new amenities, but were mostly produced simply by adaptation of existing types of labour and equipment in existing industrial communities. It had been different when steam and steel were transforming the pattern of the working day in a hundred trades, creating new concentrations of industry, and scoring lines across the face of every county.

The new industries, moreover, were small as yet. Even electricity grew slowly. This was surprising, when the electric motor provided a new and adaptable application of power, the electric cable had revolutionized its transmission, and the dynamo driven by the steam turbine had equally revolutionized its generation. Sir Charles Parsons had patented his high speed dynamo on the same day as his turbine, in 1884. But for long electricity continued to be thought of mainly as the source of a luxury light. Potential users in the home, the factory, and the town council were unwilling to scrap their present plant for producing light by gas, or power by the reciprocating steam engine. None the less, the electric motor was making its way

[1] S. and B. Webb, op. cit., pp. 180, 202.

into the factory, here and there in the big mills, and very generally in the light manufacturing trades and new trades, that could use power increasingly but did not need it on the great scale, and had been getting on hitherto in their small workshops with the treadle, or a gas engine, or the rented use of shafting that someone else's engine drove. In this way workers previously scattered in small workrooms were brought together in what now became a factory in the eyes of the law. This was one of the reasons for the increase of a half in the number of factories in the country in the course of less than eighteen years from 1895.

This increase, however, was also part of a general process of accumulation and change, that was progressively raising the amount of equipment per man throughout most of industry. The available evidence suggests that this amount doubled between 1870 and 1914. Moreover, there were not only more machines year by year, but new types of machine. These are not remembered now, most of them, by the name of an inventor, and they were not path-breaking; they made no bound forward but advanced somewhat beyond what had been achieved already; they would run rather more quickly, or grind rather more finely, or carry out some operation themselves that had depended on the workman's mind and hand before. Many of them were American. Year by year they kept up a flow of innovation. In a quarter century it brought in a new order. There had been no turning point; but, looking back, men felt the change had been profound.

The craftsman also felt it had been much for the worse. The essence of craftsmanship is not sleight of hand but versatility. Great skill in carrying out some one manual operation can be acquired in time even by mental deficients: what distinguished the craftsman was his ability to turn his hand to anything. He could size up a problem, decide how to set about it, adapt his methods to peculiarities of material or design, and carry out in succession each operation in the chain that linked the raw material with the finished assembly. Requiring no direction but holding all needed knowledge in his own head, he looked out on the chances and changes of the market-place from a stronghold of indispensability. But recent tendencies were undermining it. They were most apparent in engineering. Versatility ceased to be needed when the chain of operations was subdivided and each link was made the sole job of one man: it might take ability and long training to be able to do all of ten jobs, but no one of them was beyond the reach of an unskilled man given time to learn it, if he had not to learn anything else. This kind of subdivision, as Adam Smith noted long ago in the pin factory, is possible in proportion as the total output is large, and it may have been on the increase simply because the size of the factory had grown. But it had been specially advanced by the new machines. Sometimes, as in boot-making or gear-cutting, these appeared where there had been no specialized machine before. Sometimes they were of familiar function but were now made to perform automatically a process to which they became specialized. Both types made less demand than before on the understanding and dexterity of the operative. The turner used to do not only turning, but boring, reamering, milling, screw-cutting and drilling: these other operations came to be given over each to a special machine tool, and at the same time, in turning itself, the marking out of the work, the setting of speed and feed, and the grinding of tools, were transferred to specialists. The new automatics, once a job had been set up in them, could be run by a newcomer, and jigs were increasingly used to enable him to work accurately despite his lack of training. He was called a machine man, or handyman. Sometimes a woman did the work, or a boy. 'In all highly-organized engineering shops most of the boys are taught to do one part of an engine and nothing else,' a witness told the Royal Commission on the Poor Laws, sweepingly, but making clear the contrast with the past. With subdivision and automatism there went a third development inimical to the craftsman — increased precision, and the standardization that went with it. When no two units were quite the same, the fitter was an artist, who had to size up each part, and see where and how much to work on it himself to make it fit. As automatic machines turned out a less variable product, his skill became less needed, and the work of assembly could be passed to an assembler — a man who could not take a file to the parts he handled, but could put them together if they fitted to start with. This change was taken farther by those trades, especially the new manufactures of the sewing machine, the bicycle, the motor car, and electrical equipment, which

I

worked to tolerances rather than to the more exact adjustments of the old workmanship. A mere machine tender could use a limit gauge; if the part passed the gauge it could be assembled.

Such changes as these gave new openings to women in many trades. They gave the man who had missed being apprenticed a chance to earn more than a labourer, and acquire the status of the semi-skilled. But craftsmen who had grown up in the older world of freedom and artistry felt them to be a degradation, and they frustrated and embittered the lad who went into engineering because he had 'a mechanical bent', which means an unmechanical one, a desire to devise and construct. It may be more than a coincidence that the Tom Mann and John Burns of 1889, the G. N. Barnes of 1897, and many of the militant shop stewards of the First World War, all came out of the engineering shop.

One other feature of the new machines disturbed labour of all grades — the very speed they ran at. The new high speed steels in cutting tools, the windy hammer or the electric drill in the shipyard, the sheer r.p.m. of new and rackety machines built to be run to death, threatened 'technological unemployment'. With the pneumatic chisel, it was reported from the Clyde in 1902, a boy could do in a few hours the day's work of a man; and boys had never been so plentiful. The fears that this aroused, and the consequently increased attachment of the worker to restrictive practices, were enhanced by a new drive by management for faster work by the men too.

7

This new drive was part of Scientific Management. That name did not gain currency until the end of 1910, but the change in attitudes and methods it connotes began to be felt as a wind blowing through British workshops, especially the engineering shops, in the 1890's. It was a wind from the west. No doubt the time was ripe in any case for a closer attention to the functions of management in Britain, but the immediate stimulus and continuing example came from America. Here a number of efficiency engineers, or industrial consultants as we should call them now, had emerged and begun to proclaim and demonstrate that management was a distinct function with its own applied science. It may seem strange to us now that this had ever had to be discovered, for in every workshop the function must always have been discharged somehow. But the discovery of 'communication' in recent years is an example of something that people have always been doing being newly apprehended as an object of study with its own problems, jargon and potentialities. While business was on a smaller scale the man at the head did many jobs which had to be divided between specialists only as scale grew, and not until the function of organizing was separated from the technical, commercial, and financial functions were its tasks grasped and the possibilities of improving it displayed. In particular, an epoch of rapid technical advance tended to bring to the top men who were technicians to their finger-tips, and they by temperament and training were fascinated by the problems of equipment but often impatient of 'the commercial side' as they called it — costing, job-routing, human relations, planning and organizing generally. But in the 1890's American precept and example began to show how much could be done to raise efficiency by applying scientific method to management as a distinct function.

The new attack bore on a number of points. The lay-out of the plant was scrutinized to eliminate unnecessary movement. Jigs, fixtures, and tools were looked at with a severe regard to the economy of skill and effort. Operations which had been left to custom or improvization were planned, and planners were appointed, and given desks — here began a notion that was to be extended to whole economies in the inter-war years, first and foremost in Russia. The progress of planned production was recorded and controlled. Organization charts were drawn, and the great debate was opened on the merits of functional executives as against line and staff. But for the wage-earner what mattered most was that each job was studied.

The first step was to record the job as it stood, and divide it into its components. One purpose was to eliminate unnecessary movements; another, to break the job up, so that each part could be done as economically as possible. Many parts of a skilled man's job did not themselves demand skill: let them be separated and given to the unskilled. In operating a machine, especially the growing class of automatics, the workman might need skill only in setting up, or maintenance: let these things be entrusted to specialists, and then the manual routine of feeding, starting and stopping can be performed by a labourer. All this was called 'taking the brains out of the job'. It carried the division of labour in the workshop farther than ever before, and must sooner or later have come about as a response to the workshop's growing size.

When jobs had been re-designed and re-allocated in this way, two further steps remained. The best known leader of the new school, F. W. Taylor, had noticed when he was a gang boss in a steel mill that the men under him were not exerting themselves nearly as much as they could without cumulative fatigue. His reaction was interesting: he did not upbraid them as slackers nor threaten them with penalties, but as a scientist he asked two questions — how can we measure the amount a man can do in a day without over-exertion? what gimmick can we build in to induce him to perform that amount? The answers he found in time study and incentive methods of wage payments.

Time study brought the stop-watch into the workshop. The object was to find how long a man needed to perform a given operation, if he was of average proficiency and worked at a rate he could maintain day in day out — a rate often exemplified by a man walking at three miles an hour, not strolling but not exhausting himself. Any one operative when studied was likely to diverge somewhat from the desired standard, and then it was for the judgment of the man with the stop-watch to make the due allowance for the divergence, and produce a corrected time. Such times were taken for parts of an operation separately, and the time for the whole would be arrived at by adding the times selected as applicable to the parts when each was performed without a hitch. The object was to find how many operations could be completed in the working day, and dividing the time now obtained for the single operation into the number of hours in the day would give that, but only if the operator never needed to straighten his back, stop the machine to clear swarf, or go to the lavatory: so again the judgment of the man with the stop-watch had to be invoked, to add to the time for the operation an allowance for these needs and contingencies. None the less it was held with conviction that the outcome was a scientific measurement of the time needed to do the job, and so of the number of jobs that the workman could do in the day.

The way was now clear for an incentive method of wage payment. Piece-rates were as old as wages themselves, and in Britain they were the predominant method of wage payment in many of the industries that by the end of the nineteenth century were strongly unionized — in cotton, for instance, in ship-building, the boot and shoe industry, and much of coal-mining. But now payment by results was to be extended, and take more complicated forms. The books of rates in which the traditional piece-rates were codified might be complicated, but one simple principle connected the rate for the unit of product with the workman's pay — he got the same rate per unit of product whether he turned out much or little, so that his earnings were proportional to his output. Now a host of variations from proportionality were devised, and sometimes like sauces were known by the names of the chefs who concocted them.

They had two alternative objects. One was to provide a special stimulus to attain and hold a certain level of output: the workman who reached it by a final five per cent rise in his output obtained a rise of much more than five per cent in his pay, the workman who let his output fall below it suffered a sharp reduction, virtually a fine. Here, over a certain range at least, a rise in output raised earnings more than propor-tionally. But the other object of variation was to effect the oppo-site, and prevent earnings from rising in the same proportion as output, especially when this rose greatly. Evidently any formula that did this would cost the employer less than the ordinary piece-rate, and by the same token would give the workman who raised his output less for each additional unit than he had been paid per unit previously. That could be and was represented as barefaced robbery, but two considerations gave it substantial justification. One was that as time went on the output a man could achieve with a given effort was commonly raised by improvements introduced by management — better tools, minor but cumulative improvements in jigs and fixtures, more accurate components, more reliable materials. These would all reduce somewhat the time that would be allotted to the job if it were re-timed, but in practice jobs could not be continually re-timed, and it was simpler to provide that part at least of the gain from improvements should automatically accrue to management. The other consideration was the weightier. Time study was liable (though this was not proclaimed) to go wrong.

If the time allowed was too short, the workman soon brought the mistake to notice; but if it was too long, he found himself holding a 'gravy job', and kept the news to himself. The time study men had in any case a bias to set rates on the loose side, in order to ease the introduction of an often unwelcome innovation and avoid the rows that tight rates caused. Especially in engineering, moreover, many rates had to be set simply by guesswork because there was not a long enough run of the job to warrant a time-study, and these too would err on the loose side. This bias was offset by the use of a regressive formula which reduced the average payment per unit of output as output rose. The jealousies which 'gravy jobs' set up among the workmen were mitigated if the loose rate was not allowed to raise earnings in proportion to its looseness.

In so far as Scientific Management meant job study, British workmen loathed and dreaded it.

To the craftsman it brought loss of self-respect and loss of job control. Where he had been master, setting about the problem in his own way and time, he became a subordinate who had to do as he was told. The pressure for output, output, meant scamped work instead of true craftsmanship. Parts of the job that it had been his pride to do were handed over to unskilled men and boys. He had been vigilant to mend the fence that kept 'unlawful men' out of the jobs his craft alone might do: now parts of those jobs were thrown open to outsiders.

Few men, craftsmen or not, but disliked the stop-watch. If the aim had really been only to get the time of an average man working at an accepted pace there could have been little objection, though to be observed closely as an exhibit, and measured as a kind of machine, might still not be pleasant. But the real aim was felt to be to work the pace up, and raise the required minimum. 'One young "understrapper" I knew,' Alfred Williams wrote of the railway shops at Swindon,[1] 'is in the habit of standing over the boys at the lathe, watch in hand, for four hours without once moving, and, by his manner and language, compelling them to run at an excessive rate so as to cut their prices.' That may have been exceptional, but it typified a general anxiety. Time study in fact threatened a breach of the contract between employer and workman. In its essence that

[1] Alfred Williams, *Life In a Railway Factory* (1915), p. 61.

contract always has to provide that so much pay shall be given in return for so much effort, but since effort cannot be measured the amount to be put forth cannot be specified in the contract, and has to be left to a tacit understanding or convention that defines 'a fair day's work'. The phrase seems empty if we ask, what do you mean by fair? but at any one time and place there was a consensus that defined an acceptable level of exertion, and stigmatized those who gave more and also those who gave less. Since the wage-earner, unlike the sub-contractor, put himself under the employer's direction, he was sensitive to the threat of being hard driven, and the standard of the fair day's work was a vital safeguard to him. The stop-watch threatened to undercut it.

What made this threat so powerful was that after the time study men had set rates and the workman had responded to them, again and again the rates were cut. Given the opportunity to increase his earnings by working harder a man did, and began to take home a quarter or a third more than before. Management generally did not like this. Since the rise in earnings was obtained only by a rise in output at least as great or, if a regressive formula was used, even greater, the labour cost per unit of output was no higher than before or even less, but a confused notion persisted that the men could not be earning more without labour costs having gone up. This apart, there was always the thought that the extra earnings were unnecessary — if the man had long been getting 30s. a week, why should he need 40s. now? Moreover, this 40s. upset the wage-structure: not everyone in the shop, still less in the factory, could be put on incentive, and the earnings of those that were rose sharply relatively to the others. These others included the foreman. When in a particular case the higher earnings arose from a loose rate there was a further reason for feeling that a mistake had been made. So rates were cut. Then the wage-earner had to work harder than before to earn as much as before. He felt cheated, and he had been.

The experience made clear to him a danger always implicit in the new method of wage payment — it by-passed collective bargaining. In industries long accustomed to piece-rates, those rates themselves were the subject of the bargain; but where the new method was brought into an industry where the union rate was a time rate, it substituted a rate fixed arbitrarily by the time study man or the foreman. True, the workman would get not less than his entitlement under the union rate for the number of hours he had worked, but the old implicit bargain that governed the effort he must give for his pay was evaded, and a new amount of effort was fixed without negotiation.

In other ways the new method upset settled habits of the workman's mind. Men who had hitherto been earning the same now earned different amounts. That awoke jealousies, and the fear of not holding the line — those who earned the most were setting a pace that would soon be demanded of everyone; someone would turn informer, or curry favour with the foreman, to get one of the gravy jobs. To raise output, moreover, even if everyone did it, was to threaten other men's jobs, and very likely one's own. The 'lump of labour fallacy' was no fallacy in the experience of the workman. He found himself often enough in a position where there was only so much work going, and the more any one man did of it, the sooner the others would be sacked.

It will be seen that Scientific Management in its first impact on the wage-earner conflicted with some basic precepts of trade unionism. It threatened to break into the craftsman's exclusive control of certain jobs. By paying different amounts to men who had the same time-rates it departed from the principle of 'the rate for the job', the same for all who did it. By getting men to work harder for what was in practice an uncertain rise in pay, it broke up the existing bargain on 'the fair day's work'. It by-passed collective bargaining, and returned wage-fixing to the fiat of management. It asked men to forget that it was shameful to get more for oneself by working someone else out of a job.

8

The conditions of work are central to the problem of industrial relations. That problem arises from the wage-earner's discontent, and this is not created by particular grievances nor assuageable by particular benefits, but pervasive and persistent, drawn in by him with the very air he breathes. In several ways intelligible to us all his working life is inherently unsatisfying or irritating to him.

For one thing, 'master and servant' was long the plain English for 'employer and employed', and the usage shows how the relation between the two parties to a contract of employment was felt to be inherently different from that in a contract of sale, even in the days when employment was on the small and simple scale, when the wheelwright or blacksmith just took on a man to help him in his shop, or the master mason who had undertaken to build a house got his team together. The distinctive marks of the contract of employment were that it was usually made between men of unequal resources, and that the workman put himself under the direction of the employer.

The inequality of resources makes the workman liable to get the worst of the bargain. The trouble is not, as is sometimes said, that his labour is perishable, so that every sale of labour is a forced sale: for the use of the employer's equipment is equally perishable, and the day it stands idle for lack of labour is lost as much as the day the workman is unemployed. What puts him at a disadvantage is rather that, in practice if not in principle, the employer has more in hand to live on while he bargains, so that he is not under such pressure to come to terms. As Adam Smith said, 'A landlord, a farmer, a master manufacturer, or merchant, though they did not employ a single workman, could generally live a year or two upon the stocks which they have already acquired. Many workmen could not subsist a week, few could subsist a month, and scarce any a year without employment. In the long run the workman may be as necessary to his master as his master is to him; but the necessity is not so immediate.'

But this brings no disadvantage to the workman if he is selling his labour in a wide market, or if, whatever the extent of the market, business is profitable and the demand for labour brisk. A unit of War Loan sold on the Stock Exchange will command the price of the day like any other, even though its own seller is distressed: it is only in the narrow market that the forced sale is liable to have to take the lower price. Even the workman who would be starving within the week if unemployed could get not a job only but a rise, if his labour at the going rate would be highly profitable to employers, and several were competing for it. But the workman has not been able to rely on either of these saving conditions. Because at any one time he wanted to find work within reach of his home, and work moreover in his own trade, he might well have only one or two employers to deal with; he could offer himself to more if he could go farther afield or take up another sort of work, and many a man did this, but it had its costs and limitations. Trade was sometimes brisk, but not always, and when it was not, instead of two employers after one man, there were two men, and more than two, after one employer. The risks to which a way of life is subject colour even its sheltered reaches, and the workman who is for the time being in a wide and rising labour market still sees himself as inherently a suppliant not able to argue about the terms of an engagement if he is offered one at all.

From the middle of the eighteenth century onwards he was the more likely to form that image of his position, because the competition for jobs was continually sustained by the increase of population. Decade after decade the working population rose by not less than ten per cent, sometimes as much as fourteen, even after the emigrants had gone. Let the labour market reach equilibrium, with supply equal to demand at the going rate of wages: within the year there would be jobless men trying to get places. At times of boom, it is true, the demand for labour rose faster even than that ever-rising supply; but the other side of that medal was the depression, when the demand fell absolutely, and there would have been unemployment even if the number seeking work had not risen meanwhile: but it had. Often there were men literally waiting at the gate for the employer to take on at the going rate of wages the moment he wanted them. That was the labour market as the wage-earner saw it. It was once pointed out that a difference of sixpence either way in the balance of income and outlay makes all the difference between serenity and misery. The labour market is like that. Whether there is one more vacancy than there are applicants or one more applicant than there are vacancies decides which of two worlds the wage-earner shall live in, and makes all the difference between two industrial systems. It was in the system of excess applicants that the British wage-earner saw his own life set.

He therefore thought of the employer as inherently having the whip hand over him, so long as he stood alone. Not always by any means, yet more often than not, that was so in fact. Only in a broad market could he reckon on a wage that would be independent of his own power to hold out in the bargaining.

Only in the rising phase of the trade cycle was the demand for labour brisk enough to remove the continual overspill of rising population. Where the market was not broad and the demand was not brisk, he needed his job more urgently than the employer needed him.

Though it was in the wage bargain that he dreaded the employer's whip hand most, he might also feel it as work went on day by day. The second distinctive feature of the contract of employment is that the workman puts himself under the employer's direction. It is this that distinguishes the employee from the sub-contractor. The difficulty is only partly that the employee has to do without the independence, spontaneity, and agreeable irregularity, that a man can enjoy who is working on his own. True, herein lay one of the reasons why, when factories were first set up, country people were loath to go into them. They were accustomed to great exertions, but only at times and seasons, or as they chose themselves; to rising at four in the morning often enough, but not early every morning when the hooter blew. Yet this sort of regularity and discipline becomes accustomed in time. Though a few people never can accept it, most men can, and without resentment, because they see it as a requirement that arises out of the situation and not out of any one man's love of power: tasks have to be carried out systematically and orders have to be given wherever men work together. What wage-earners generally resent is not having to work under another man's direction but working for his purpose and his profit. The end for which they have to work is his and he has chosen it without consulting them. They are taken on solely to serve it, and will be laid off as soon as they cease to. It is a short step from this to the conviction that the relationship is inherently one-sided, that the employer is getting something out of them that has no counterpart in what they get from him, in a word that they are being exploited.

But is not this only a peevish illusion? is not the relation essentially reciprocal, a partnership between two men neither of whom can get on without the other? What jobs would the wage-earners have now if the business had not been built up? and so long as they want to stay in those jobs, what prospects of betterment have they save as the business thrives? Each party can prosper only as the other does. That is profoundly true, and yet the conditions of the wage-earner's working life can easily persuade him of the opposite. He can seriously believe that he can prosper only in so far as he can keep the bosses on the run.

One simple reason for this is that at any one time, the product of an industry being what it is, the employees' receipts can be increased only if the proprietors' is diminished: indeed, if we think of proportionate shares, it is always and for ever true that the only way to raise the one is to reduce the other. The now familiar instance of the cake reminds us of the pitfall there, but in all the vast threshing out of social problems before 1914 there was an extraordinary absence of the notion that the cake could be made bigger. In any case, at any one time of bargaining its size is limited and future increases are uncertain: what one party gains here and now seems simply to be taken from the other. It is an easy inference that the employer would like to reduce wages in order to increase his profit. We are all of us apt to project into others impulses that we dare not acknowledge in ourselves, and see those impulses as attacking us from without through those others' agency. For any wage-earner who has acquisitive and aggressive impulses to project, the employer at the bargaining table provides a natural lodgement and bearer.

This sense of a head-on collision of interests is heightened by the very nature of profit. Wages connote deserts, but all down the ages profits have attracted the critical attention of the moralist, because somehow they obstinately appear to be un-earned and undeserved. This is so at the most superficial level, simply because they arise as a surplus and there is no contract stating the service for which they are rendered: but a surplus is inherently suspect of being unnecessary. It is fair to reply that profits are the return to factors of capital and enterprise that are no less necessary to the creation of the product than is labour itself. But when one penetrates that much deeper, the difficulty still remains. For the services of putting up money and getting the business going were provided in the past, and yet are found to be levying a perpetual rent-charge on the annual product. It is clear that the buildings and machinery contribute to that product, but were not they in their day the product of labour, and do they not have to be continually renewed by labour? That management plays a necessary present part is no less clear, but managers receive salaries. What is not clear is why those who provided the original funds should go on receiving a return, they and their heirs and assigns in perpetuity.

Once again, it is fair to point out that since savings cost an effort, they have to be paid for, as certainly wage-earners themselves allow when they are asked to contribute to War Savings; and that since it is savings alone that make the construction of equipment possible, their use is productive and commands a return in that right. Such a return takes the form, let us say, of an agreement to repay £110 in one year's time for £100 lent now; and if at the end of the year the capital sum is still required in the business, it may be convenient to both parties for the lender to receive £10 and allow the £100 to remain for a further year in return for a further £10; and so on. And this does make sense: there can be no objection to the annually renewed dividends to shareholders, unless one objects to the giving and taking of any interest at all. But still the argument seems contrived; what is written on the face of things is all against it. The profit-taker (not to write profiteer) is like the actually innocent man who happens to be found with a gory knife in his hand not far from a bleeding corpse: given a calm attention and a measure of credence he will be able to establish his innocence, but appearances are against him.

If readiness to believe the worst of profits needed any fostering, moreover, it would get it from the inequality of hazard between employer and employed. The employer has his capital at risk, or some of it; the wage-earner commonly has his whole livelihood. We have already seen one instance and advertisement of that, conspicuous and frequently renewed: the workman was exposed to injury, and sometimes death, as the employer was not, yet until 1897 he or his dependents were commonly unable to enforce the payment of any compensation by the employer. But the same inequality shows itself in the human cost of the rise and fall of industrial fortunes. Shipyards are built where there was once only a fishing harbour; workers come in, street after street extends, the migrant makes a home there and puts down roots. Now the trade is depressed; very likely this is not the employers' fault, but it is they who decide to close the yards down; and the men whom they drew in and who made their homes there say, 'for all they care we can rot'. What would the morale of a battalion be, if the men knew that in any tight corner the officers would take the unit transport and clear out, leaving them on their flat feet? It was the quest for profit that built the town, it is the drying up of profit that has ruined it. So it has come to seem to the wage-earner that the very destinies of his life may be decided for him by the profit-taker. What is more, he has no power to reciprocate. From time to time management calls on him to accept some change, to make some effort, and why? always in order that higher profits may be earned; but he can put no pressure on management in order that higher wages may be earned. So long as his work adds something to profit, he is used; let it cease to, and he will be thrown out. Profit-seeking and the right to hire and fire seem to be bound up together: the boss can sack you and you cannot sack the boss.

There is an answer to this, and a substantial one: the contract of employment can be terminated by either side; in practice, if a workman sees a chance of bettering himself, he will leave, sometimes without even the formality of notice; a business can be carried on only if it pays its employees sufficient to retain them in the presence of alternative opportunities. But that is not how things commonly appear to the wage-earner. Between his employer and himself he sees an inherent difference in power and status. The employer can discard him as he cannot discard the employer. He has that in mind when he considers how the employer makes his profit. Profit looks like the return to the whip hand.

The workman resents his subordination at the place of work more keenly when he is no longer one of a politically subordinate class, but has become a voter in a democracy. One of the unions' positivist sympathizers, Henry Crompton, put the point well in the 1870's. 'When the Radical manufacturers preached political change to the working classes,' he wrote, 'and set up before them political independence as a goal to strive for, they ought not to have been surprised to find that the ideas they had taught with reference to the outer civic actions were at once applied to the inner industrial life. . . . If the right aspiration for every citizen is to be independent and free, that is, not subject to arbitrary power but dependent only upon just laws, the same aspiration must inevitably appear right to him in his capacity as a workman.'[1]

[1] Henry Crompton, *Industrial Conciliation* (1876), pp. 2-3.

The anxieties and resentments we have been considering are inherent in the very position of the wage-earner, but they are felt with very different intensity at different times and places, and they were less active so long as the average firm was still small. We can understand why. In the small firm, the master commonly worked, if not alongside the men as their leader in a common task, at least near by them, in daily contact with them, well known to them as a human being. He was not set apart from them by differences in manners and class, nor was his capital invested widely so as to insulate him from the misfortunes of the establishment where they worked for him: the slump that cost them their jobs laid him low too. The difference between them was in function more than in class. But the mere quantitative growth of scale brought a qualitative change in human relations. True, that growth was a necessary condition of higher productivity and so of higher real wages, and it brought with it other potentialities of benefit to the wage-earner; but in several ways its immediate effects on him were adverse.

One adverse effect arose simply from the numerical change in the ratio of employers to employed. The proportion of applicants to vacancies as a whole might not be changed, and the growth of industrial centres meanwhile would have brought more firms within the reach of any one workman there; but so far as a given number of jobs came to be administered by a smaller number of employers, each workman would know fewer employers personally. That would decrease a factor of security in his working life. The workman who knows a number of alternative employers personally will always have in mind whom he would turn to if he were in need of a job or found himself unfairly treated where he is now. By the same token, he will be personally known to a number of employers, and the man who has a local reputation as a good workman has little reason to fear unemployment or oppression. Relations of this kind add much to the security of workpeople in trades where the unit of employment is small, and may help to explain the little headway that trade unionism has ever made among shop assistants, domestic servants, and farm labourers. But as the representative unit grew in size, these links of personal knowledge were broken, and the wage-earner became more insecure.

At the same time he came to have less chance of becoming a

master himself. Marshall remarked in the 1870's that in some districts more than half the employers had begun as workmen; but the economic forces that were raising the average size of the firm were also making it harder for the small man to get a start. That took away a source of hope, and hope is a vitamin without which most of us cannot live in health of mind. It is true that the workman had a new sort of advance open to him, namely working his way up inside the firm, but he had much less chance of achieving independence. It was natural that he should turn upon the employer he could not escape, and demand more from him. Gambling was said to be a growing evil: it meets a need of those who see no chance of bettering themselves by their own efforts.

As firms got bigger there was also bound to be less personal contact between master and man. Certainly where that contact existed in the small firm it was not always peaceful. There were masters who were renowned for their hot tempers and rough tongues; the angry workman could and did let the boss have it now and then. But all these rows were rows between one man and another, face to face, and the possibility of having them, far from causing anxiety, must have relieved and prevented it. We can see how this will have worked if we contrast what happens when the employer is remote, little seen around, hardly known as a man. At once the workman feels a sense of powerlessness and insecurity. He may have some minor difficulty that he could clear up readily enough if he could speak to the boss in person, but he finds himself confronted instead with a procedure, a channel. What he claims may be refused him by someone who expresses no personal opinion and can enter into no argument, because it conflicts with a ruling that has been laid down by a head office he has never seen; or he may just be told that his claim will be duly reported and the answer will be communicated to him in due course. In a South Wales valley the difference was noticed when the miner who had had a dispute with the deputy or under-manager could no longer walk across the fields and see the owner at the door of his house, but must deal with a manager who was tied down by instructions from the head office of the combine in Cardiff. This having to deal with a poker-faced man whose relation with you was dehumanized and straitjacketed was as infuriating as not being able to deal with the ultimate boss himself. But the fact that this boss was himself remote made for a special anxiety. Here was a source of power that could reach out and change all the workman's life, but that the workman himself could not get to know, understand and depend on, argue with. The position of the wage-earner in the big business might have been specially designed for the projection of paranoid anxieties. That the remote power is malevolent seems infinitely more probable than that it is kind. Let its intentions be of the best, it will be a miracle if they are understood.

Perhaps this is why the term 'absentee landlord' is practically a term of abuse. One could argue that if a man who lives in the village can fairly charge a rent for the use of his land, his removing to a distance cannot make the payment iniquitous; but the tenant is apt to distinguish. It is related that there was a landlord in Ireland who was not an absentee, but in the troubles two men were told off none the less to shoot him; they waited behind a wall to catch him on his way back from market, and when he did not come by at his usual time one said to the other 'Sure an' I hope nothin's happened to the dear old gentleman'. We find it much easier to expect the worst from people we do not meet than from those we do, especially when they have some power over us; and hate them accordingly. The value of the meeting does not lie in any cordiality it may generate but in its discharging the static anxiety that will otherwise be building up. In business the amount of personal contact varies inversely with the size of the firm; and the amount of anxiety directly. The source of the trouble does not lie in ill will, but simply in scale. As firms grow bigger, human relations in them become more difficult, simply because of size.

This growth as it went on in Britain before the First World War was accompanied by some changes in the type of the employer. One such became apparent, and opened a divide between him and his men, as soon as he ceased to take his own jacket off and labour alongside them. The work that was specially his to do as the firm grew was done in a different place, in different dress, and at different hours. The silk hat that he wears in the cartoons of the time he wore in common with some of his clerks, but still it marked him off from the men, and he commonly came to work later in the morning than they, and

K

went in by a different and cleaner entrance. As he grew richer, moreover, there was a traditional upper class for him to enter, that was not so much in conflict with the industrial workmen, as cut off from them by differences in residence, speech, and sport. The sons and grandsons of the self-made man were even more likely than he to 'go county'. It was noticed how the motor-car increased the social distance between the employer and his workman by enabling him to move out into the country; the factory became the place where he made the money to support the life of a country gentleman. He and his family no longer worshipped on Sunday in the same church or chapel as his workmen. To them it was clearer than ever that he was not 'one of us' but 'one of them'.

This increase in social distance was accompanied by an increased disparity in training and ability. The masters in the small firms, taking them as a whole, will have had some superior qualities of character and mind to account for their having set themselves up and taken the lead as their men had not, but they had much the same start in life, and as long as they worked on the small scale their superior capacity could not be made manifest by any great difference of function or scope. As firms grew, however, the function of the employer became more distinctive, and the impact of his abilities wider. A profession of management arose. Its own requirements were ill-defined, but men entered it who had qualified in an established profession, law, engineering, accountancy. Technical training apart, the employer was increasingly likely to have had more general education than the wage-earner. There would still be incapable men among the employers, and men of high innate ability among the employed; but the growth in the size of the firm made it more likely everywhere that the posts of direction and management would be filled by men with more education and brains than their workpeople. Thereby it created a basic and obstinate problem of industrial relations. It is hard not to be jealous, and suspicious, of those who are visibly abler than oneself. In one way, equality was the conscience of the age in Church and state — the equality of all men before God, before the law, and in 'the verdict of democracy'; but how could there be equality in the dealings between bright men and dull men? The clear mind confronted with the stupidity that cannot even recognize its own interests can hardly express goodwill except by a self-imposed fairness and artificial patience that are felt, and resented, as condescension. The slow mind confronted with the quick one expects to be outsmarted, searches simple statements for hidden meanings, fears that to agree will reveal its own helplessness, and keeps its end up by being difficult. If you co-operate you may be taken for a ride. The way to hide your perplexity, uphold your interests, and protect your self-respect, is to be awkward.

But as the scale of business grew the personal employer sometimes disappeared altogether, and his place was taken by a board of directors. This brought its own difficulties. Often where the structure was formally that of a public company there was some one man, the chairman or managing director or general manager it might be, who figured for good reason in the workman's eye as the boss. But this was not necessarily so, and the decisions on which so much might depend for the workmen were taken in practice as well as principle by a board many of whose members were not working directors known in the shops, but representatives of this or that financial interest. It might even be hard for anyone in the business to know where the ultimate control really lay, for the immediately visible board might be only part of some system of interlocking or superimposed interests. Interests they were called, and as they became more remote from the workman he saw ever more clearly what they were an interest in: the sense of community of purpose was gone, and it seemed plain now that those who controlled the business were concerned only with what money they could make out of it. As management became separated from ownership, profits seemed more like rent, 'God's gift to sleeping man'. Put together the two notions there — that the workman is being used as a means to another man's end, and that this end is to take as much as possible out of the product — and what appears is the definition of exploitation and the bedrock of Marxism.

As the employer receded from the workshop, his place there was taken by managers of various levels, from the general manager or works manager down to the foreman. These were themselves employees, under instructions, under pressure. There was always the need for results to make them spur the workman on. They had their own jobs to keep, and had been told what showing was expected; they looked for promotion, and would be judged by their success in keeping output up and costs down. It is usually easier to be hard with other men when one does not deal with them directly but issues orders for others to enforce on them, and the remote employer was to that extent more likely to be hard. The manager or foreman who was himself disposed to press, or who feared he would miss promotion or even lose his job if he did not, could always put the blame on those above him. Remote and indirect control is biased towards inhumanity.

But it was not only the general increase in the size of the firm that was putting more strain on the manager: the changes in equipment and methods that had been coming with it were also asking more of him. Especially was this true of the foreman. So long as he was in charge of craftsmen he had had relatively little to do. The craftsman carried his methods in his own head, and had to be left to solve his problems in his own way and time; the foreman did not have to set work up for him nor provide him with aids, and he could no more usefully stand over him to urge him on than he could over a doctor making his diagnosis at the bedside. But as the craftsman's work was broken down into components that were entrusted to handymen or machinists, their work needed to be co-ordinated and assisted. The new machines they ran could perform automatically what had once depended on the trained hand, but only after they had been set up properly, a new and sometimes exacting task. As operations became repetitive the rate of output came to depend as never before on the sheer pace of the operator's application, and the foreman was expected to see that this was fast. He would hardly have been made a foreman unless he was able to learn his way quickly about the new machines, but what he needed to know about his new tasks of administration and man-management he could not pick up like that, and he was given no training to help him with it. His was a hard job: put in charge of men much like himself, given no training in administration, at once technician, rate-setter, and ganger, a shock absorber between the drive of management and the obstinacy of the men — no wonder if he was sometimes fearful of his authority, artful, harsh or unfair. For many men he was effectively the boss. 'In most works, in the engineering trade at least,' one employer wrote in 1917,[1] 'the whole industrial life of a workman is in the hands of his foreman. The foreman chooses him from among the applicants at the works gate; often he settles what wages he shall get; no advance of wage or promotion is possible except on his initiative; he often sets the piece-price and has power to cut it when he wishes; and, lastly, he almost always has unrestricted power of discharge. These great powers are exercised by men chosen generally for their energy and driving power. They are usually promoted workmen, with no very marked superiority in education, outlook, or sympathy over those whom they command. It is not surprising, therefore, that these powers are often abused; and a tyranny, both in matters of detail and principle, established, which the higher management, even if it has the desire, has very little power to soften or control.'

The other side of this medal was a harder life for the men. Some of them had lost the independence that craftsmanship gives, and with it the status that set them apart from mere hands. The more intelligent when reduced to repetitive operations lost the satisfaction that problem-solving, planning and building had given. All had more sense of being driven. The changes of the day had not yet brought in the moving belt or assembly line, but it was in these years that the spirit and method of workshop organization came in that were to be satirized in the nightmare factories of *À nous la liberté* and *Modern Times*. Alfred Williams, a poet and rural philosopher by bent, condemned himself to work for twenty years and more in the Great Western Railway engineering shops at Swindon. Writing of them in 1915, an embittered but observant witness, he said:[2] 'A decade and a half ago one could come to the shed fearlessly, and with perfect complacence; work was a pleasure in comparison with what it is now. It was not that the toil was easy, though, as a matter of fact, it was not so exhausting as it is at present, but there was an entirely different feeling prevalent. The workman was not watched and timed at every little operation, and he knew that as the job had been one day so it would be the next. Now, however, every day brings fresh

---

[1] 'Industrial Reconstruction: an Employer's View,' *The Athenaeum*, March 1917; quoted here from Sidney Webb, *The Works Manager Today* (1917), pp. 27-8.
[2] Alfred Williams, *Life in a Railway Factory* (1915), Ch. XVIII, p. 304.

troubles from some quarter or other. The supervisory staff has been doubled or trebled, and they must do something to justify their existence. Before the workman can recover from one shock he is visited with another; he is kept in a state of continual agitation and suspense which, in time, operate on his mind and temper and transform his whole character.

'At one time old and experienced hands were trusted and respected, both by reason of their great knowledge of the work, acquired through many years, and as a kind of tacit recognition of their long connection with the firm, but now, when a man has been in the shed for twenty years, however young he may be, he is no longer wanted. There is now a very real desire to be rid of him. For one thing, his wages are high. In addition to this, he knows too much; he is not pliable. It is time he was shifted to make room for someone lower paid, more plastic and more ignorant of the inner working of things.'

The belief that there were good old days that came to an end shortly before one reached man's estate oneself is recurrent in many ages, and is less likely to arise from any actual changes of the times than from those within the observer, and particularly from his own disappointment as the hopes of youth give way to the drag and plod of middle age. But what we know independently of the changes that were going on in size and management, machinery and methods in the quarter century before 1914 suggests that there was more than this common projection of inward disenchantment in the statement several men have made who worked in mine or factory then that the work which once had given pride and satisfaction had become a burden. In the interwar years Peter Donelly was in the steelworks at Barrow-in-Furness. 'From what I was told by the old hands,' he has written,[1] 'I reached the conclusion that workmen in the early days of the steelworks had a better understanding of the nature of work and the nature and use of machines than is common now. . . . Work was not then considered as a necessary evil to be escaped from or whittled away and finally abolished. Men came to the steelworks to make something and making was a pleasure. Although the processes of industry had been broken down even then, the specialisation of work was no more than an elementary study. No one had yet attempted to change the human notion

[1] Peter Donelly, *The Yellow Rock* (1950).

that a man can do more work with the help of a machine, for the inhuman notion that a machine can produce more if the man can be integrated with it. . . . It was only by the men of my own age and younger ones, that work in the steelworks was strongly denounced as a vocation, or denied to be an integral part of life which could enrich life in any way, except by providing the money to pay for living.'

The stress that has been laid here on the effects of changes in the size of firms and in their management, equipment, and workshop practice, is a stress, and not an evenly weighted balance. Such a balance would find a place for all the work-shops that remained small and all the trades that followed their traditional ways, as well as for all that was being done by good will and common sense in every walk of life to make new ways more tolerable and leaven industrial relations with mutual respect. But strong effects suggest strong causes. We have to explain why those who can prosper only as partners have so often been at daggers drawn, and why the wage-earner has so often chosen as his leaders men who were combative or obstinate by temperament. The stress laid here on what was galling to him in his working life is no more than commensurate with the resentment he has shown.

CHAPTER III

THE DEVELOPMENT OF
INDUSTRIAL RELATIONS

I

The story of modern British industrial relations begins with the beginnings of the unions.

If we consider only unions that proved viable, able to maintain a continuous organization through the ups and downs of many succeeding years, those beginnings may be placed in the last quarter of the eighteenth century. Of the unions in existence in 1906, the oldest traced their origins to those years: the Gold Beaters were established in 1777, the Brushmakers in 1778, the London Bookbinders in 1784, and seven others before 1800.

It may be that some enlargement of means, and ideas, promoted unionism at this time. We know that the basketful of goods that the builder's wage-rate would buy had increased gently but persistently for a hundred years since the Civil War, so that by 1750 it was more than half as big again; and probably this was a general movement. At the same time there seems to have been an extension of schooling — at least men behaved as if there had been: they showed more interest in political ideas and made more use of the printed word; the times of Tom Paine, the Corresponding Society, and Twopenny Trash were coming in.

In this setting various changes had occurred since 1750 to make the wage-earner's position less stable and secure. A great and sustained growth of population set in, and soon showed itself in the poverty of surplus labour in the villages and an increased competition for jobs in the towns. The migrant overcame the barrier of distance that had once insulated many local markets, at the same time as those distances were being reduced by revolutionary improvements in transport by land and water. The sheltered local market had been subject to the variations of the harvest, but those apart it had maintained steady sales and customary relations. But life in the cloth-making districts that made for distant markets was very different: they had long experienced the changes in fortune that arose from fluctuations in aggregate demand, the varying success of different competitors, and the merchants' speculative changes in the size of their stocks. With the extension of other markets these fluctuations now became felt more widely, and many trades began to experience in common the ups and downs of boom and slump. The wage-earners of one town had less of a local monopoly, being more exposed to competition from other labour moving in, and from the imported products of manufacturers elsewhere; it is to this that scholars have attributed the beginnings of unionism at this same time in the eastern cities of the United States. The wider market also disturbed the working life of the wage-earner by fostering an increased division of labour and a bigger size of firm.

Amid these disturbances wage-earners had an evident motive to unite for self-protection. Trade clubs had been formed throughout the century, and from time to time there were strikes. Yet those who could keep a union going year in year out were few as yet, and all craftsmen. There were several reasons why they alone could do it. Any union was liable to draw the fire of the authorities, and be repressed under one of the many statutes against combinations, or simply as a criminal conspiracy at common law: but the craftsman was respectable, not suspect of sedition, and able to carry on his unionism under cover of the mutual benefit societies and clubs for jollification that had long had their meetings at the Bricklayer's Arms and the like. In 1906 the names of some unions still suggested how they had begun in that way — the Hand in Hand Coopers, the Amicable Woolstaplers, the Edge Tool Trade Protection and Death Society. These functions of the friendly society — funeral benefit, sick pay, even 'out of work donation' — proved essential to keep members together and paying their dues in hard times when the union had to lie doggo and money was scarce. But at first it was only the craftsman who could keep a friendly society going. He could afford his dues more easily, out of earnings at least half as big again as the labourer's. He was more likely to have the developed faculties, the book-learning, and the experience of affairs, without which the union could not find efficient officers from its own ranks, conduct its meetings, write its minutes and letters, and keep its accounts. Whether for mutual benefit or trade unionism, he was bound to his brothers of the craft by the strong sense of kinship that arises not from any calculation of advantage but from the spontaneous identification of oneself with those who have been through the same school and are practising the same art.

So unions of craftsmen were formed and carried on year after year, not as friendly societies only but effectively as trade unions, even while it was still a crime to attend a union meeting. Their members did not have to come forward as unionists, or try to treat with the employers through their officers: enough that each in making his own bargain should refuse to work for less than the union rate, and that all should help maintain him if he found himself out of work in consequence. This was a method still being used in the twentieth century, when the Journeymen Silk Hatters had their own 'glazed price list hanging on the wall of every hatter's shop',[1] and the Journeyman Curriers were still working to a bill of prices dated 1812. But more than a rate of pay could be made effective in this way: the prohibition of piece-work, the limitation of the number of apprentices, the stint, and the closed shop, are all said to have been enforced by the Liverpool Shipwrights before 1824. The knowledge that there was a union behind this may have been a relief rather than an anxiety to the employer, who was assured that whatever was being imposed on him was being imposed on his competitors too. It was not unknown for a committee of masters to meet spokesmen of the men, and negotiate a collective agreement. But such committees were more often formed to fight a union.

Before long local trade clubs were being linked to form unions covering a town, a region, or even all England. A club in one town would begin to correspond with the clubs of the same craft in others, make mutual arrangements to help tramping members, and send contributions when a struggle broke out. It was a natural next step to form an association of which the clubs became branches. Early in the nineteenth century such associations were found with their carefully drawn constitutions, printed rule books, and annual congresses. The 'Rules and

---

[1] Frederick Willis: *101 Jubilee Road: a book of London yesterdays*, (1948), c. XII.

Articles to be observed by the Journeyman Paper Makers throughout England' divided all England and Wales into five divisions, each with its centre; one of these, Maidstone, was also the national headquarters, and the other centres were to remit funds to it. The rules provided for the payment of clerks, required the divisions to hold quarterly meetings, and laid down a scale of weekly dues varying according to the rates of pay in different parts of the country.

The direction of this development is so familiar that it may seem inevitable, but it is not the only one that unionism has followed, and even in Britain the unions might have taken another path if they had come later — have grouped by industry, for example, rather than by occupation, or have been organized from the centre instead of having the springs of their energies in their branches. One reason why they took their actual road lies in the personal quality and social status of the craftsman. In a country like India unions have not been viable unless maintained by outsiders — careerists, or social workers, or agents of a political party — who provide an indispensable element of administrative ability and continuity, but impose their own conceptions and purposes. Something like that seems inevitable if unions are to exist at all in countries where most wage-earners are low paid and illiterate. But the craftsmen of eighteenth-century Britain had enough administrative ability in their own ranks. There were many among them who could write letters, conduct the business of a meeting, administer an association constitutionally, keep accounts, and hold funds without embezzling them. The capacity for communication and the instinct for the forms and proprieties of procedure that the early unionists showed startled contemporaries and remain remarkable. They explain why British unions stood on their own feet, seldom beholden to outsiders, concerned only with the interests of their own members.

There is another way in which this source of strength explains why these unions kept clear of politics. Where early unionism has not been controlled by political parties it has sometimes, as in Sweden and Belgium, felt itself none the less part of a political movement, and early strikes have had political objects such as the extension of the franchise. But the craftsman in Britain had his status in the community, wore his top hat, stood apart from the mob, and had no thought of using his union for political ends: he often identified himself with the actually governing classes sufficiently to join one or other of their camps, and he did not want the division between them to split his union. If he did support the middle-class radicals his union would still not merge itself in Owenism or Chartism. Political unionism is the unionism of the dispossessed, but the craftsman had a stake in the country.

It is his personal quality also that explains why his club joined with those of the same craft in other towns rather than with those of other crafts in its own. In wide sectors of France, in the years before the First World War, the only effective organ of unionism was the bourse du travail, the centre in which the trade unions of a town, whether or not they were branches of a wider union, came together not only for common services such as education but for common action in the local bread and butter issues of unionism, the negotiations and disputes with employers and local authorities. It was the same in Greece in the interwar years. In Britain, it is true, trades councils grew up, to bring the local leaders of unionism together for common counsel and mutual support, and sometimes they were active. But the lines of communication of the branch of the masons, the carpenters, the engineers, never ran through them. Partly this was because the branch was strong in itself, and did not need nursing by what other leadership there was in the town. But mainly it was because the loyalties of the craftsman went up, like his dues, to his own headquarters: when he needed help he looked for it to a man of the same trade two hundred miles away and not to someone in another trade next door. One reason was that he identified himself more closely with the brother of the craft, who through the servitude and ritual of apprenticeship had been inducted into the same mystery. But there were also economic reasons. He would expect to change his employer from time to time, and not infrequently he moved from place to place, but always in the same craft: so the conditions in which men of his craft were working elsewhere were of more interest to him than those in which men were doing other jobs beside him. Again, the price he could get for his labour depended on his keeping it scarce, and to prevent his trade being flooded with 'illegal men' he had to hold the line of apprenticeship everywhere. We might think this would have been reinforced by a wish to protect his own wage-rate from being undercut by men doing the same work for lower pay elsewhere; but regional differences in wage-rates were wide, and accepted by the unions, which continued to fix rates locally even when organized nationally; and the employers in different regions were not always selling in competition with one another — the builders, for instance. The main consideration was the control of entry to the trade. Granted the ability to communicate and administer over distance, this motive decided that the early unionist in Britain would organize by occupation rather than locality.

Because this was an exclusive and separatist principle, it made independence an object of policy. The craftsman felt he strengthened his union not by bringing men in but by keeping them out. It was a natural corollary that what wages and conditions of work the union sought were matters for itself alone, and outsiders must not interfere. Other objects — Parliamentary measures, for instance — might be common purposes which unions should associate to pursue, but the main object was essentially a private one, for which it had to contend not with employers only but with other labour. Because its function was to maintain privilege, any influence of outsiders on its claims would be not to help on but to hold back. Men who felt this would not easily agree that their own wage claims should be concerted with those of others, still less, as was to come about in Scandinavia, that an association of unions should arrange a programme of wage changes for all its members.

Nor would the craftsmen readily join with other men working for the same employer. So far as those others were labourers, they were separated by a social gulf, and there was little prospect of their making good union members. So far as they were craftsmen, they too were more concerned with the terms on which they might have to work elsewhere than with those on which other men were working alongside them at the moment. There was, moreover, a ground of conflict: it was useless for a craft union to exclude 'illegal men' unless it could also maintain its exclusive right to do certain work, but some of the jobs it claimed as its own might be taken by men of other crafts. Hence disputes about demarcation. The upshot was that each union saw more hindrance than help in tying itself up for a three-legged race, and preferred to run alone.

Thus two circumstances of its beginnings gave British union-ism a characteristic direction. It began when only the craftsmen were strong enough to maintain a union. Good communications in a small country were available to enable these craftsmen to follow their bent and interest, and link up with each other rather than with different kinds of men. The outcome was a movement that turned away at the outset from the paths that would have led to industrial unionism or a centrally co-ordinated unionism, and took instead the independent, clannish way of occupational unionism.

2

So far we have been speaking of the craftsman, but there was a growing number of men who were like him in possessing a particular ability, and came early to unionism. They acquired their ability not by apprenticeship but just by 'going through the mill': this meant that they did not have the control over entry to the trade that the craftsman had when he could enforce his regulation of apprenticeship, but they did have a skill. We may call them operatives. It is not surprising that their unions began to appear already in the eighteenth century. Conspicuous among them were the miners and the jenny spinners. In 1812 the cotton weavers were able to stop every loom 'from Carlisle to Aberdeen'. There is said to have been a durable union of framework knitters from 1760. The woollen workers of the West Riding formed a union in 1794 that still existed in 1806.

But of the operatives' unions which survived in 1906, very few had been founded before 1850. The advantages which the operative shared with the craftsman he shared only partially. Like the craftsman, he earned more than the labourer: but the industries he worked in were subject to fluctuations, and as trade fell off dues became harder to find just when the union was least likely to get a rise. Operatives' unions were laun-ched in years of brisk demand for labour; they grew and were soon a power in the land: a depression followed, and they were no more. They were vulnerable, also, when they came into conflict with the employer. To be a craftsman was to belong to the craftsman's club, but the operative might or might not be a unionist, and employers reacted hotly against attempts 'to dictate whom they should employ', that is, to refuse to work with non-unionists. Contemporaries laid much stress on skill as an essential condition of unionism, because in a world where many unskilled men were available to take over any job within their scope, there was little hope of the present holders of those jobs winning a strike; and if the unskilled man could not do the operative's job at once, he could at any rate be put on to learn it, and employers made vigorous use of blacklegs.

The passage of the first half of the nineteenth century did not diminish these obstacles, but it increased the ability of the operative to overcome them. By 1850 his real income was about half as big again as in 1800. Meanwhile he grew in experience, learning the hard way not to expect too much or strike against the set of the tide, finding by trial and error the structure that would give his union direction and control, accepting the need for self-discipline and a steady loyalty. Durable unionism, made possible only by certain personal qualities, fostered them in its turn. When Marshall came to draw up a balance sheet of trade unionism he laid much emphasis on this. 'Unionism', he wrote in 1892, 'must be judged mainly by its influence on the character of the workers. . . . The power of unions to sustain high wages depends chiefly on the influence they exert on the character of the workers themselves.'[1] So from 1850 onwards the formation of viable unions of operatives went on rapidly, and half of such unions existing in 1906 had been formed before a new impetus and type appeared in 1889.

The operatives followed the craftsmen in grouping by occupation: spinners joined with spinners, and weavers with weavers. The force of example was sufficient to account for much, for the one type of union that had proved able to survive hitherto was occupational. The operatives had in any case some of the same inducements as the craftsmen to reach out and link up: if they had no apprenticeship to control, they had no less strong a motive in the need to stop men of their occupation in other districts being brought in, as they so often were, to break a strike. Meanwhile, too, the communications on which occupational grouping depended had been transformed. What was in any case a small country, in which big industrial cities were separated by short distances, was now equipped with means of rapid communication throughout its length and breadth by

[1] Alfred Marshall, *Elements of Economics of Industry*, (1892), VI, xiii, 16.

railway, telegraph, and penny post. The farthest branch could keep in easy touch with headquarters, a national officer could get down to it within the day. Ties of mere propinquity were at a discount.

But in another respect the operative's union differed from the craftsman's. The craftsman's did not necessarily have to negotiate with employers, because it could rely on its members to hold out for the union rate in their own individual bargains; but the operative's could not do that. Instead, it had to win its way through to collective bargaining. In *Mary Barton*, Mrs Gaskell has given a picture of how this began. In a time of depression, some Manchester manufacturers have the prospect of a large export order, but think they can be sure of it only if they turn the work out at a very low price, and they offer a low wage accordingly: the weavers refuse to work. 'The day arrived on which the masters were to have an interview with a deputation of the work-people. The meeting was to take place in a public room, at an hotel; and there, about eleven o'clock, the mill-owners, who had received the foreign orders, began to collect. Of course the first subject, however full their minds might be of another, was the weather. Having done their duty by all the showers and sunshine which had occurred during the past week, they fell to talking about the business which brought them together. There might be about twenty gentlemen in the room, including some by courtesy, who were not immediately concerned in the settlement of the present question; but who, nevertheless, were sufficiently interested to attend. They were divided into little groups, who did not seem unanimous by any means. Some were for a slight concession, just a sugar-plum to quieten the naughty child, a sacrifice to peace and quietness. Some were steadily and vehemently opposed to the dangerous precedent of yielding one jot or tittle to the outward force of a turn-out. . . . The door was now opened, and the waiter announced that the men were below, and asked if it were the pleasure of the gentlemen that they should be shown up. They assented, and rapidly took their places round the official table. . . . Tramp, tramp came the heavy clogged feet up the stairs; and in a minute five wild, earnest-looking men stood in the room. . . . Had they been larger-boned men, you would have called them gaunt; as it was, they were little of stature, and their fustian clothes hung loosely upon their shrunk limbs. . . . At the request of a gentleman hastily chosen to officiate as chairman, the leader of the delegates read, in a high-pitched, psalm-singing voice, a paper, containing the operatives' statement of the case at issue, their complaints, and their demands, which last were not remarkable for moderation. He was then desired to withdraw for a few minutes, with his fellow-delegates, to another room, while the masters considered what should be their definite answer. When the men had left the room, a whispered earnest consultation took place, every one re-urging his former arguments. The conceders carried the day, but only by a majority of one. The minority haughtily and audibly expressed their dissent from the measures to be adopted, even after the delegates re-entered the room; their words and looks did not pass unheeded by the quick-eyed operatives; their names were registered in bitter hearts. The masters could not consent to the advance demanded by the workmen. They would agree to give one shilling per week more than they had previously offered. Were the delegates empowered to accept such offer? They were empowered to accept or decline any offer made that day by the masters. Then it might be as well for them to consult among themselves as to what should be their decision. They again withdrew. It was not for long. They came back, and positively declined any compromise on their demands. . . .'

That was in the 1830's. Galsworthy in his play *Strife* represented the same sort of thing as still going on in the twentieth century. But by then it was exceptional: the spokesmen of the union were no longer kept waiting below stairs; the reception of a delegation had given way to negotiation between parties who met on an equal footing. Several circumstances promoted this. The unionists were at least strong enough to bring a number of mills out together, and would go back only when a common settlement had been made for them all. If the employers had begun by feeling that the wider the combination was, the greater the threat to them, they soon found it was really the other way round: except where they were pinned down by foreign competition they might have little to fear from a wage settlement if only it was enforced on all of them alike, and a strong union was their guarantee that it would be. Not a few reached the con-

L

clusion that it was a positive advantage to them to have a floor put under price competition in this way. Those who had little love for the union were still willing to meet it to negotiate a rate, because of all union activities this interfered with them least. They would resent hotly any encroachment on their prerogatives as managers of their own businesses, but collective bargaining only meant that they were paying the same price as their competitors for one factor of production, just as they did when they bought a raw material in the same market. By the same token, in one way or another they would victimize one of their own men who came forward as a union spokesman with some demand in their own works, but neither pride nor policy gave them any objection to meeting the officers of the union as equals in a district wage negotiation.

By 1860 this kind of negotiation had become the main channel of British industrial relations. What had not come about also deserves notice. In the United States today the main stream of industrial relations runs through the negotiation and application of a plant contract between the management of one plant and the workpeople in it. Since the district bargaining of Victorian Britain was later to widen into industry-wide or national bargaining, we might be tempted to carry the movement backwards and suppose that the first stage had been bargaining plant by plant. That would be quite wrong. There were strikes, of course, of one employer's men at a time, and settlements confined to one firm, but these forms of action were transient or peripheral. It was never a main function of the unions to conduct negotiations between the workpeople of one plant and their employer. Such negotiations raise more issues and touch more sensitive nerves than district bargaining. Because this has to cover many firms at once, it can deal only with a short list of common factors, and cannot enter into the detail of the conditions of work firm by firm. The building itself, its lighting, heating, and ventilation; the processes and machines used, which men, and how many of them, are put on each; promotion, suspension, dismissal; the very way a foreman speaks to his men — questions like these are important to the wage-earner, but district bargaining cannot go into them. That made it all the more acceptable to employers. When unions of operatives were struggling for recognition in Britain, the employers were under no legal obligation to recognize them, as they were in America under the New Deal. The unions had to take the path of least resistance. It led them to district bargaining about wages and hours. Issues that often mattered more to men at work they had to leave untouched.

In any case the unions seldom brought the wage-earners of any firm together: rather they pulled them apart by stressing the occupational ties of different groups. In engineering, and especially in shipbuilding, any one employer would have to deal with many different unions, and these sometimes were at daggers drawn with one another. Alongside the unionists worked the many less skilled men, and women, who were not unionized at all. There was no common organization, and matters of common interest in the firm went by default.

But there was one other line the unions had struck out on, and with outstanding success. Already in 1824 Francis Place, by organizing what may be called a trade union lobby, had brought off a *coup* at Westminster, and secured the outright cancellation of all the statute and common law by which unionism as such was criminal. The Short Time Committees of the textile operatives led by John Doherty, secretary of the Cotton Spinners' Federation, found support and leadership from sympathizers in many walks of life: a Royal Commission set out the facts, and in 1833 Parliament passed a Factory Act that was a landmark not because it placed new limits on the hours a child might work but because for the first time it appointed inspectors to enforce them. In 1847 the same movement achieved a triumph when Parliament accepted a Ten Hours Bill that by limiting the hours of women in the mills would in practice limit those of men too, and did so when evasion was prevented by another Act in 1850. Nothing like it was within the unions' reach through their own bargaining power. It was plain for them all to see that in some important respects they could get more done through Parliament than by direct action. They could count on effective support and guidance from middle-class sympathizers of several schools of thought. If the facts were investigated they could give telling testimony. If a case was made out at the bar of common humanity, the opposition of the employers would not stop Parliament from legislating.

So by 1850 the two procedures the unions had found they

could really make work were collective bargaining for a district rate, and campaigning for Parliamentary action.

3

The collective bargaining gave rise to a new institution. This was one of the few inventions that have been made in industrial relations, a device, it seemed, which would make them run more smoothly than, with the same men and problems, they ever could without it. It was to be the characteristic form of organized British industrial relations for the thirty years from 1860 to 1890, then to be taken over by governments in Australasia, and to return thence to the British statute book. It was generally known as the Board of Conciliation and Arbitration.

It arose when employers who were in practice meeting spokesmen of the unions from time to time as issues arose began to think their discussions would go better if both sides took part with the common status of members of a formally constituted and permanent board. This belief went back at least to the 1850's, when boards had been set up in shipbuilding on the Wear and the silk trade at Macclesfield; but the board that caught the eye of the country, and was to be the model for many others, was that set up in 1860 in the hosiery trade of Nottingham. William Felkin, the historian of that trade, had long been advocating boards; A. J. Mundella, son of an Italian refugee and a Welsh mother, a humane and imaginative employer, took the initiative in convening a meeting of employers and employed, which after five hours of debate brought an obstinate dispute to an end by setting a board up. It proved to put an end to the whole successions of strikes and lock-outs which had troubled the trade hitherto. Four years later, Rupert Kettle, a judge of the Worcestershire county court, who was often called in to arbitrate in trade disputes, persuaded the Wolverhampton builders to follow suit. Again the board worked well and ended a long recurrent strife, and it was copied by the building trade in other districts. Then in 1869 David Dale, a Quaker ironmaster of Darlington, joined with the union leader John Kane to set up a board for the iron and steel trade of the north of England: through the next two decades it was to bring about nearly sixty wage settlements. Thus three men, two of them humane employers and one a lawyer known as the Prince of Arbitrators, put the idea of the joint board into practice in the 1860's, and showed the benefits it could bring. Their example was followed widely. The next thirty years were the heyday of the joint board.

Its essential form was a council composed of an equal number of representatives of employers and workmen. In Mundella's board the workmen's representatives had at first been elected by all employees, whether unionists or not, but in practice they had all been the union's men, and the constitution was changed before long to provide explicitly for the union finding the workers' side. This was the general practice. Sometimes there was an independent chairman, more often the board found chairman and vice-chairman from its own members, or each side provided the chairman at alternate meetings. The chairman might have a casting vote, or unresolved issues might be submitted to arbitration — to decision by two arbiters, for instance, one from each side, and, failing their agreement, by a single umpire whom they chose. There was also often a sub-committee to deal with particular claims and disputes as they arose in one workplace or another, mostly about the interpretation of an existing agreement. Where there was an independent chairman, or an umpire, he might be from the law — the chairman of the Durham coal board was the judge of the county court — or a respected employer in another industry, like Joseph Chamberlain or Lord Brassey.

We know that negotiations did often, though not always, go much better when a board was set up. Its distinctive device seemed to be the independent chairman, or provision for calling an outsider in if the members could not reach agreement among themselves. The third party might be in the chair at all meetings, or be called in to preside only if the two sides failed to reach agreement by themselves; or he might appear as an umpire, chosen by representatives of the two sides to pronounce upon some particular issue, or nominated by a public figure such as the Speaker of the House of Commons. If as was often the case the chairman was given a casting vote, or the umpire was empowered to give a binding award, then conciliation went over into arbitration, and the last possibility of deadlock was provided against. It is natural to ask whether these arrangements did not make a contribution to the art of industrial relations.

That conciliation itself was useful there can be no doubt. The conciliator has several functions, of which the common element is that he helps the parties to communicate with each other more effectively. He can keep the temperature of the discussion down by confining it to the points at issue, and stating them in unemotive terms. When the parties lose their tempers with one another too easily to be able to talk face to face, he can go backwards and forwards between them. He may be able to devise proposals new in form or substance, which go some way to reconcile conflicting claims, or provide a rough compromise, or make it easier to give ground without losing face. He can save one side from trying to call the other's bluff when in fact it is not bluffing. Especially, when both sides have stuck fast, thinking it a sign of weakness to be the first to climb down, he can get them to make concessions, because he can tell each what the other will do in return, and can make what is given up appear as a favour to him rather than a concession to the other side.

An independent member could certainly help a board in these ways to reach its own agreements. But the process probably goes on more easily when the conciliator is not always in attendance, but is brought in only when he is needed, and is then not always the same man. One who is always sitting with the board has the great advantage of getting to know the technicalities of the trade, and the personalities in it. But by the mere fact of continuity he will find himself pushed over from the role of conciliator to that of umpire. Though he acts solely as a conciliator and is careful not to obtrude his own opinions, these are bound to influence his actions — what points he selects for compromise, what extent of wage adjustment he regards as reasonable in a given state of the market — and the parties will soon form a shrewd impression of what they are. Part of his success as a conciliator, indeed, is due to the respect which his own judgment commands, for it is this that warrants as reasonable a concession which otherwise would be avoided as a sign of weakness. But as the picture of his working stock of principles fills out, the parties will come to look on him more as an umpire than a go between, and their approach to him will change accordingly.

Thus the permanent independent member was likely to take on willy nilly something of the arbitrator's role; and often when a board was set up this role had been provided for from the first — the outsider was empowered not merely to help the parties reach their own decision, but if need be make one for them, and serve not as their conciliator only but their umpire.

In the coalfields, it is true, an arrangement was used which came betwixt and between, and might conceivably have made the best of both worlds: the independent chairman with a casting vote. For here the district boards of conciliation usually had an outsider as chairman, who was to try to bring the two sides into agreement first, but if that failed must vote with one or the other. If this procedure could have been followed strictly, it would have been a most ingenious device. The independent member would himself promulgate no terms, nor modification of terms, so the parties could not shuffle out of their own responsibility to negotiate by leaving the outcome to him; and in adjusting their final proposals, they would each be drawn towards the other, lest through lack of moderation they deflect his vote to the other side. But the inducement to converge would not have worked in all cases: if one side thought the other's terms were stiff, it would not expect to lose the casting vote, and if it thought them easy, would not much mind if it did: only when they were of middling severity would it be much concerned to underbid them. In any case, convergence was not possible where not shillings and pence but issues of principle were in dispute. The spokesmen of the unions, moreover, would have to justify any concession they made before rank and file who knew less of the theory of games than of the smart of their own grievances. Either side, moreover, by standing pat, might induce the other to be the first to move and show its hand. Either side, too, would not only be trying as usual to find out the real sticking point of the other, but would want even more to sound the opinions of the independent member: if it were going to make some concession, it would not want to go farther than it must to win him over; until it knew his mind, it would be left in the position which employers and employed alike always detested unless they felt too weak to fend for themselves — committed to accept terms before they knew what they were. So under the system of the casting vote the two sides would in practice treat the independent member much as they did when he was solely a conciliator; and he for his part would have to negotiate with them step by step.

That still might seem an ingenious and fruitful blend of two principles. Arbitration would be tempered by an element of conciliation, in that the independent member could not simply announce the terms that seemed fitting to him, but must if necessary modify them so as to gain at least one party's agreement. Conciliation would be strengthened and expedited by an element of arbitration, because the agreement had to be obtained from one party only, but would then be binding on the other. In practice neither of these possibilities seems to have been realized. The independent member could hardly conduct a dutch auction in two directions, moving away from his starting-point (supposing this in the middle) ever a little farther, now this way, now that, until he got a bid on one side or the other: instead, he had to state his views as they were. In fact, it appears that the chairman's casting vote in the coalfield boards did not mean voting at all, but the making of an award by an umpire; indeed the Miners' Federation used to refer to the chairman as the Umpire. So the element of conciliation counted for little in practice. On the other hand, that of arbitration was limited because either side could withdraw from the board. This they sometimes did: employers withdrew when a claim of principle was staked that they would not concede; the men, when they would not take a wage cut. Thus the independent member could make a settlement only if he could devise terms not too different from those which either side expected to get by fighting it out. His ability to do that depended not only on his own skill, but on how far apart the expectations of the two sides lay to start with. There will also have been some issues on which one side would sooner fight and lose than settle even for better terms without a struggle.

These were in fact also the limits within which arbitration proper operated in those boards which provided for it in the last resort. One might think that the limits were in practice fairly wide, because both parties had an interest in peace, and had undertaken to seek and ensue it through the board, for whose sake they would therefore accept some sacrifice of possible advantage in this or that particular settlement. There is force in this, and yet the arbitral award had its own drawbacks, and accepting it might be more distasteful than volunteering a concession in negotiation. 'The umpire', said the secretary of

By courtesy of Messrs. Stewarts & Lloyds Ltd

THE BOARD OF CONCILIATION AND ARBITRATION FOR THE MANUFACTURED STEEL TRADE OF THE WEST OF SCOTLAND.
OCTOBER, 1904

the Northumberland and Durham coalowners,[1] 'must of necessity be a man who has no direct interest at stake: but this does not necessarily prevent his having a personal bias, while it precludes him from having the least technical knowledge of the interests he is called upon to decide. The umpire may have a pet idea like restriction to advertise; he may have a peculiar training, which may cause him to exclude a certain class of evidence; he may have all, or a certain number of defects; but he can never have a perfect knowledge of the absolute wants of both sides, and this often causes mischievous awards.' If an umpire could not have principles of his own, neither could he take to splitting the difference, for then either side could go on raising claims in the expectation of at least getting something. The very fact, moreover, that arbitration would come in the last resort could prevent the parties from arriving at an agreement that they would have reached otherwise: for a concession made in negotiations might go further than the umpire himself would prove to do, and it would count against one in the subsequent arbitration. This was especially an embarrassment for the spokesmen of the unions: when they reached an agreement, they often had to take it back to their members for confirmation, and if it was rejected they would return with a strengthened hand if it was to renewed negotiation, but with a much weakened one if it was to arbitration. Again, their members could call them to account for anything they conceded voluntarily, but not for what the umpire might impose, however great. They would therefore be extremely reluctant to make any concession in negotiation, that is really to negotiate at all. The reluctance would be all the greater if proceedings were in public, and they sometimes were. Until 1894, the Webbs have related, the affairs of the boot and shoe industry had been dealt with by a board in which 'nine chosen leaders of the Federated Associations of Boot and Shoe Manufacturers of Great Britain met, in the council chamber of the Leicester Town Hall, an equal number of elected representatives of the National Union of Boot and Shoe Operatives. These elaborate debates, conducted with all the ceremony of a State Trial, were presided over by an eminent and universally respected solicitor, sometime mayor of the town. If no agreement

[1] Mr T. W. Bunning, at a meeting of the Royal Statistical Society in March 1880, *JRSS*, XLIII, p. 57.

could be arrived at, the conference enjoyed the services, as umpire, of no less an authority than Sir Henry James, formerly Attorney-General, before whom, sitting as a judge, the issue was elaborately reargued by the spokesmen of each side. Finally as a means of influencing the public opinion of the trade, there were published, not only the precise and authoritative decisions of the conference or the umpire, but also a verbatim report of all the proceedings.'[1] Evidently neither side would find it easy to make a concession when every word was going out to constituents.

For these reasons the bringing of independent persons into the joint boards as conciliators or umpires proved of limited use at the time, and achieved no real advance in the methods of industrial relations. Conciliation proper was and remains of great usefulness, but it is effective only in so far as it leaves open the possibility of failure. When the boards went beyond it, in order to make sure of a decision even when the parties themselves could not agree, they spoiled negotiation without ensuring a settlement.

4

In two industries the boards installed another piece of machinery: wages in many parts of the coal and the iron and steel industries were made to vary with the price obtained for the product. This was the sliding scale. It was hailed as a sovereign specific for the endless wrangle over the division of the proceeds.

How it worked we can see by taking an example from South Wales, where the miners were working under a sliding scale of some kind from 1875 onwards. This scale could not fix a general rate of wages, because the hewers were paid according to the tonnage they got, and the rate per ton varied from place to place according to the difficulty of working, but what it did was to provide that each man should get the rate ruling for his present working place or its like at some basic date, raised or lowered by a percentage dependent on the present price of coal. Thus the scale obtaining at the turn of the century provided that for each change of $1\frac{1}{2}$d. from the basic seaport price of 7s. 8d. a ton there should be a change of $1\frac{1}{4}$ per cent in the rate of wages being paid in each place in December 1879. Since $1\frac{1}{2}$d. on 7s. 8d. represents

---

[1] S. and B. Webb, *Industrial Democracy* (1920 edn.), p. 186.

1·63 per cent, there was a reduction gear — the variations of the wage were smaller than those of the price. Even so, they were big: in 1892 wage-rates had been more than 46 per cent above standard, by the end of 1896 they were only 10 per cent above, by the end of 1899 they were up again to 30 per cent above; thus they were brought down by nearly a quarter within four years, and then rather more than half the loss was restored in the next three.

Such changes were acceptable only in trades where experience had shown that there would always be wide fluctuations in wages in any case. These were the trades in which, for one thing, the price of the product rose and fell greatly in the trade cycle, and was largely fixed by international competition, so that there was little possibility of reducing the falls, albeit at the cost of unemployment, by restricting output. It was also requisite that much of the fluctuations of selling price should have to be transmitted to wages because these formed a large part of the cost of production. Where these conditions held, it was claimed, the sliding scale transformed industrial relations. The inevitable adjustments had once been brought about only by costly strife; now they were made reasonably and peaceably. In the first twenty-five years' working of the board for the northern iron trade that had been set up in 1869 in Darlington — once 'the cockpit of the north' — there were 60 wage settlements, 7 by agreement, 20 by arbitration, and 33 by sliding scales, without a single stoppage affecting the whole region. It was reckoned an advantage for both employers and workpeople that the scale brought about small changes frequently instead of big changes at long and indefinite intervals. It was also an educative device: 'before the adoption of the sliding scale,' said the secretary of the Northumberland and Durham coal owners,[1] 'could any miner be got to *believe*, that while coal was selling for 25s. a ton in London, and 15s. in some of the local depots, the coal owner was only getting 4s. 5d. a ton over the output of 26 million tons in the counties of Northumberland and Durham? but this has now become an acknowledged fact; the working of the sliding scale has thus done more to gain the men an insight into the necessities of the owners, than worlds of political economy.' The

[1] T. W. Bunning, at a meeting of the Royal Statistical Society in March 1880, *JRSS*, XLIII, p. 57.

insight was helped by the average price being ascertained by an independent accountant: the mere fact of the employers' opening their books to an investigator whom the men had had a voice in choosing was an earnest of their good faith and raised the status of the men.

So it came about that the sliding scale, whose origins in single instances go far back, came into much more general use in the coalfields and iron and steel trade at the time when so many joint boards were being set up, in the 1860's and 1870's. But it was practicable only where the product was sufficiently homogeneous and constant for a single typical or average price to represent fairly the receipts of most of the producers at any one time and from one time to another. When the cotton industry did consider adopting a modified form of scale in 1899 it failed, not surprisingly, to agree on it. The scale was also less attractive, even where manageable, if the fluctuations of selling price were not so great, or so closely linked with wages — less attractive therefore in the coalfields that found the house coal for the home market than in those which raised the coking and steam coals and supplied export markets. In these exporting coalfields, however, and in the iron and steel trade as a whole, its use had become general by 1880.

But even where it was feasible it had its limitations and drawbacks. The selling price gave a tolerable measure of changes in the capacity of the industry to pay wages only when costs other than wages were small, or in practice varied in close proportion to the selling price, and in many industries these things were not so. A way round was to base the scale not on the selling price but on the amount by which that exceeded the cost of raw materials per unit of output, but this was complicated. Another difficulty was the effect on the capacity to pay of changes introduced in methods and equipment. The remedy was to take the accumulation of all such changes into account from time to time by negotiating a new scale, but then all was in the melting-pot again, and there might be trouble. Meanwhile, even while a given scale was still serving its purpose, the men came to dislike it. If they had only weak unions when it was instituted, or, as in South Wales, none at all, then they would reckon the advances it brought them promptly in the rising market a more than adequate offset to the cuts which they would anyhow be unable to stave off in the slump. But as their power to resist picked up, when they saw in a rising market that the spot prices in the local paper stood well above the average ascertained prices which their wage followed, they reckoned they could drive a better bargain without the scale, and when it brought cuts they resented them as altogether too big. In particular, they began to assert the principle that their own minimum standard of life must be a first charge on the industry, and if it was more than the industry could pay in a year of slump, the fault lay with weak selling: wages ought to determine prices, and not prices wages.

For this reason the great growth of the miners' unions that began in the 1880's brought an opposition to the scales that resulted in a general abandonment of them, from Northumberland in 1887 to South Wales in 1902. When the Midland Federation of miners' unions had been formed in 1885, one of its two great objects was their abolition — the other being the eight-hour day. Three years later it expanded into the Miners' Federation of Great Britain, which within a decade came to speak for, or have a working agreement with, all the organized miners in the country outside Durham and Northumberland, and this great new power in the land maintained the same two objects: its first great struggle, a milestone in our social history, was fought to resist a reduction of wages claimed in consequence of the fall of the price of coal in 1893. After 1902 only the Forest of Dean was persisting with a scale of the old kind. But the objection was not so much to wages varying in some measure with prices — that was accepted as inevitable — as to the limit-less reduction in the slump that the old kind of scale implied — 'the bloody thing has no bottom.'

When the old scale went, therefore, the essential change was the fixing, save only in Durham and Northumberland, of a lower limit below which the wage should never fall. To get it, the miners had been willing to concede an upper limit too, even though this did lose them money in a good year; in any case, the range of variation allowed under the new arrangement was less than had occurred under the old — the new agreement in South Wales in 1903, for instance, allowed a range of only about ten per cent on either side of its midpoint. Given the minimum, the miners were willing to let wages continue to be adjusted by reference mainly to the selling price, but left the conciliation boards discretion to take into account other factors affecting the current capacity of the pits to pay. The Scots board, reconstituted in 1902, for example, was empowered to adjust wages within a range of a little over twopence in the shilling on either side of the midpoint, on the following principle: 'The net average realized value of coal at the pit-bank for the time being, taken in conjunction with the state of trade and the prospects thereof, is to be considered . . .; . . . in current ordinary circumstances a rise or fall of $6\frac{1}{4}$ per cent in wages on 1888 basis for each $4\frac{1}{2}$d. per ton of rise or fall in the value of coal is reasonable.' In this modified form, the organized adjustment of wages according to the state of the market actually spread, and was adopted in the strongholds of the Miners' Federation which had been obdurate against the old scale. By 1906, district conciliation boards working along these lines were providing the means of wage adjustment in almost all the coalfields of the country.

But in the iron and steel industry the old sliding scale went on, to the apparent satisfaction of all concerned. One reason for this contrast was probably that the ironworkers' real earnings were rising at this time and those of the miners were not. The output of coal per miner reached its highest point in the 1880's, and then declined; in the early 1900's it had fallen off by an eighth, a serious fall; what improvements there were in methods or equipment at this time were far from offsetting the exhaustion of the easiest seams. Nor was this offset by a rise in exchange value: the price of coal was rising, but not more than wholesale prices generally. In furnace, rolling mill, and foundry, however, the output per man continued to rise: in an active year like 1906 it was already about a sixth as great again as it had been in a similar phase of the cycle, less than twenty years before; and this great advantage was not reduced by any loss of value in exchange. The ironworker's scale could be adjusted from time to time to yield him an ever higher real income. He did not feel, as the miner did with reason, that market forces were pushing him back, and he must dig in for a defensive battle against them, and establish a claim of right that would transcend them. The fluctuations which the scale brought meanwhile were tolerable, because the cuts did not go to the bone.

There was another reason. The miners who were opposed to the sliding scale had effectively a single union, and this could negotiate wage changes when the scale had gone, but the allegiance of the ironmen was divided, there were conflicts and jealousies between grades and occupations: an industry in which the unions would not or could not associate effectively for general wage negotiations accepted the sliding scale as a way of making general wage changes.

5

There was another expedient that went with the joint board, and received some acclaim in the 1890's as the way to reconcile employer and employed within a new industrial order. This was the Birmingham Alliance — the bedstead alliance, as it was sometimes called.

It may have been suggested by the sliding scale. In South Wales this had shown that wage-rates could often be kept up if only supplies to the market could be kept down. When this was not done, and the market fell, we have seen how there had also been critics who said clearly that wages should determine prices, not prices wages. In the early nineties Havelock Wilson, the spokesman of the seamen, had proposed a combination of union and owners to keep up freights and so make good conditions possible for the crews the union would provide. About the same time the miners within the Federation had given themselves a week's holiday, to let stocks run off and so keep sagging prices up, and when prices continued to fall they proposed a joint cartel of owners and men to restrict output; a little later the example of the Westphalia Coal Cartel was explicitly urged on the Scots coalowners by the men's spokesman. In 1896 D. A. Thomas proposed a cartel in South Wales in which the miners should take part, but the other owners would not have it. The previous history of 'the limitation of the vend' among the northern collieries suggests that such schemes were unlikely to succeed, even if they could ever be started, in an industry that was now widely dispersed, competing internally, and selling much of its output against foreign competition.

But there were more compact trades, with more sheltered markets, and the idea of the double-barrelled cartel had its attractions wherever the wages of the workers seemed to be threatened by competition between their employers. The Royal

Commission on Labour had seen in it the threat of a monopolistic and abusive development, perhaps near at hand. Others were drawn to it because it promised to establish identity instead of conflict of interests between employer and employed. In Birmingham it took practical shape for a time in the 1890's. Alliances, as they were called, were formed between combinations of employers and workpeople, in which the employers undertook to sell only at prices which would yield them a profit and enable them to pay a bonus over present wages, and the workpeople undertook to strike the works of any employer who failed to do this. The leading case was the metallic bedstead trade, but Alliances were also formed for china electrical fittings, china door furniture, fenders, metal rolling, and metal and cased tubes; at one time there were said to be five hundred employers and twenty thousand workmen in them.

These trades were marked by some peculiarities which explain the attraction of an Alliance to them. They were not highly mechanized and they did not have big factories, but were the trades of small men, sub-contractors and garret-masters. So they were easy to enter: only a small capital was needed, and the factors who did the marketing would advance much of that. There was a constant supply of new garret-masters, moreover, because the sub-contractors, being paid piece-rates themselves but paying day rates to their own labour, sought this in its cheapest form, and took on school leavers whom they would turn loose at the age of sixteen, with the trade at their finger tips but small prospect of employment as wage-earners. By the 1890's these conditions of the supply of enterprise had been subjected to some twenty years of that general downward pressure on prices which contemporaries called the Great Depression. The small masters proved weak sellers. The professional buyer could easily beat them down, one at a time, by assuring them that if they did not make his price, someone else would — nay, was making it already. They were the less able to hold out for a price which would cover their costs, because they did not know what these were: when they costed an article at all, their methods were slipshod, incredibly so as it seems now, and since they were producing a small number of each of many different designs and types of article, the question of how much of their general expenses should be allocated to any one of them was in any case difficult. The low prices imposed and accepted in this way seem to have brought neither of the two usual correctives. On the one hand, they did not choke off the supply of effort and enterprise. On the other, despite an expanding national market, they did not stimulate sales so as to raise the factors' offers again — the products were not articles of continuous consumption, but were bought by any one consumer only occasionally, and often — like the doorhandle — formed only a small part of a composite unit, so the demand was inelastic. Thus these small Midland trades found themselves essentially in the same fix as the sweated sempstresses of East London, unable to hold out for a reserve price, and without the correctives that the market forces both of supply and demand usually apply to a price driven too low.

But they were more capable of seeking the remedy in combination. One of their number, E. J. Smith, came forward to advocate it in an ingenious and imaginative form. Its two essentials were both intended to stop weak selling. First, the manufacturers must get together, and agree on a set of standard costings for their main products: Smith appears as the pioneer of uniform cost accounting in Great Britain. These costings must include 'a fair profit', and all members of the Alliance must agree to sell only in accordance with them: it is not clear whether each having reckoned his own costs in the standard form was obliged only to add a minimum percentage for profit to them, so that if he could manufacture more cheaply he could sell more cheaply, or whether, as seems more likely, a single price in shillings and pence was to be agreed in the costing conference and thereafter observed by one and all. But experience showed that professional buyers would be ingenious and unscrupulous in getting particular manufacturers to evade their undertaking covertly, and the second essential was to provide a sanction against the weak seller by bringing in the men's union to strike his works. If a union did not exist already it must be created. It would be assured that wages and conditions should never be worse than those ruling at that time: and as soon as the Alliance brought its price list into action, every man should get a certain bonus, which would be automatically raised by any later increases of the profit margin. There was to be a joint board of conciliation to adjust complaints, with an ultimate

M

appeal to arbitration. The union was also promised that none but its own members would be employed. In return, it undertook to strike the works of any employer who ratted.

The great danger of price-raising, everyone said, was the competition it would stir up, and E. J. Smith was at pains to show in all innocence how an Alliance could deal with competition: at home, by using the yellow dog, the exclusive contract and the deferred rebate; abroad, by systematic dumping. But in one way or another it was competition that broke the Alliances. The showpiece, the Alliance in Smith's own metallic bedstead trade, was broken when the furniture stores went over to wooden bedsteads. When some of Arthur Chamberlain's workmen joined an Alliance he said he did not believe in it and refused to follow them; the employers in it called the men out on strike and maintained them, but he would not give in; the employers got tired of finding the money and called the strike off. Most likely other Alliances succumbed to the same disintegration as Smith himself describes[1] overtaking a gentleman's agreement of the old and simple sort, 'to cease from underselling': 'It was very seldom that all the members of a trade could be got together for such a purpose. Still, many of them would come, and would readily enough consent to an arrangement which the honest man would intend to carry out to the letter, but which the dishonest man would resolve to ignore as soon as possible. It afforded a splendid opportunity for taking part of the trade of a competitor. . . . Buyers immediately laid themselves out to invent the most elaborate account of the manner in which members of a new association had broken their pledges. Some of the stories told were correct, but most of them were pure fabrications. Unfortunately the travellers and agents believed everything, and were careful that the stories should lose nothing in their transmission to their several houses. When these reached their principals the same credulity was exercised, until the whole trade was up in arms, and the majority resolved not to be sold by their competitors.' None of the Alliances survived the century.

These small midland trades were said to be specially propitious to Alliance because there was so little social difference between employer and employed there: Smith himself had been

---

[1] E. J. Smith, *The New Trades Combination Movement* (1899), pp. 10-11.

a workman before he set up on his own account. But there were many other trades and places in which employer and employed were sufficiently close together socially, and on good enough terms with one another, to have been able to form an Alliance if other circumstances had permitted it. The fatal obstacle was the unwillingness of the employers to accept permanently the restrictions on their own freedom of action which that sort of combination required, particularly when its very formation had greatly raised the profits of piracy. When Havelock Wilson made his proposal for keeping up freights, a trade journal remarked: 'Mr Wilson knows uncommonly little of shipowners. . . . I should like to see an undertaking by a hundred representative shipowners not to accept less than a minimum freight, which would survive longer than the period necessary for at least one of their number to get to the nearest telegraph station from which he could instruct his agent abroad to ease off to the extent perhaps of threepence a ton, more if necessary.'[1] This, moreover, was in an industry renowned for its propensity to form cartels. Will Thorne, secretary of the Gas Workers and General Labourers, told a public enquiry in 1912 about the same difficulty with employers. 'You cannot get them to agree to what we call a minimum selling price,' he said. 'They get round the board, and as soon as they get outside they go and cut one another's throats in the commercial market. . . . They say they have tried many times, but they cannot agree, and, if they do agree, as soon as they get outside, when they have had their lunch, they get on the telephone and carve one another up.'[2]

This seems to have been the basic reason why so little came of a scheme which, whatever its threat to the rest of the country, seemed to promise so much for the ease and harmony of employer and employed in any trade which would adopt it.

6

The discontent with the sliding scale that ran high in the nineties was part of a deepening disenchantment with the board of conciliation itself. There was no other plan before the public

[1] *Fairplay*, 20 June 1890.
[2] Industrial Council Enquiry into Industrial Agreements, Minutes of Evidence (Cd. 6953 of 1913), Q.9763.

for improving industrial relations by voluntary action, and the formation of new boards went on; but existing boards were running into too many difficulties for men to believe there was sovereign efficacy in them.

Yet did they not in fact have some special virtue? Did they not supply industrial relations with a constructive element that was lacking in mere *ad hoc* bargaining? The evidence is conflicting. On the one hand, there is no mistaking the force and sincerity with which contemporaries testified to the difference this or that board had made. On the other, as time passed the charm seemed to fail. Some disputes were not brought to the board at all; others were brought only to be remitted to the disputants through failure of the board to agree; decisions reached by the board were repudiated or evaded by the parties. Some boards broke up, or were silently abandoned. Mundella's own board, the archetype, came to an end after twenty years. How can we account for this?

The explanation may be that what made the boards work so well at first was not their constitution and procedure, but two changes that came in with them.

The first was that a substantial part of the employers agreed to observe a common minimum wage. The great obstacle to getting an advance from one employer or section had been the threat of underselling by the rest: the setting up of a board must often have brought firms into line for the first time. As the leader of the Birmingham brassworkers put it, 'The respectable manufacturers said to them, as trade unionists, "We don't mind how much in reason we pay you if the same price is paid all round." They replied, "Then have a Board of Conciliation." '[1] But employers could observe a common minimum without the formalities of a board, and if some were minded to break away, the existence of a board would not restrain them.

The other change was in the employers' attitude. A board could not come into being without a shift from the old relation of master and man. To see this signalized must have brought the men a fine sense of achievement: that they should sit by right and not by grace with the employers, as equal members of a council, at which one of their own number might sometimes be in the chair, had been unthinkable not long before. In this immediate

[1] W. A. Dalley, *The Life Story of W. J. Davis, J.P.* (1914), p. 213.

satisfaction they may well have rested for a time, at least not ready for the moment with any new claim of principle. It was a common experience, moreover, that the new arrangements were not only made possible in the first place by a change of attitude, but deepened and reinforced that change as time went on. The men's representatives gained understanding of the market forces which limited the actions of the employers; the employers gained insight into the hardships and anxieties of life for the men; and both found a greater respect and liking for one another as human beings.

But when events moved on, new and contentious issues inevitably arose; when the ground once newly gained came to be taken for granted, men began to look out beyond it towards fresh claims to stake. The setting up of a board had marked a stage in social development, a new status for the unions, and a less unequal relation between those who directed work and those who carried it out: 'master and workman' began to give way to 'employers and employed'. But this change could be brought about without the creation of boards; and when its effect had been absorbed, and new issues arose, the existence of a board had of itself no great power to resolve those issues peacefully. Tempers had been rising since the turn of the century in the South Wales coalfield, and the men had begun to press an issue of principle, the minimum wage, which the employers refused to accept: there were thirty strikes about wages there in 1903, and every one of those cases is said to have been before the Board of Conciliation. Wage claims, claims for advances at least, suited the boards well for two reasons — they were 'district matters', not felt to affect the prerogatives of management within its own works; and being issues of quantity rather than principle, they were amenable to compromise. But by the turn of the century it was clear that the men were also advancing claims of another kind, that these were claims of principle, and that they did affect the prerogatives of management. The increasing difficulties encountered by the well-established conciliation system of the Durham and Northumberland coalfields showed how this would make a board ineffective — there were many 'local strikes affecting single collieries. In most of these cases the workmen at the colliery concerned act in opposition to the rules either written or unwritten, which regulate the action of the Owners' and Workmen's Associations, and in such cases they act without, or in opposition to, the advice of the agents of their own association'.[1] Typical issues were, refusal to work with non-unionists; a demand for the reinstatement of two men dismissed for sending up dirty coal; and a demand that a hewer be dismissed who had agreed to undertake extra work, of a kind that hewers did not usually do, in return for extra pay. The boards belonged to the era when it was an achievement for the unions to gain recognition and take an equal part in reasoned negotiation. As industrial relations moved on to a new stage, they had less meaning to the men and less work that they could do.

In the story of particular boards there were various other causes that made for disenchantment and decay. The board had often been set up after years of recurrent strikes, culminating perhaps in some especially protracted stoppage which had purged the combative propensities of both sides for a while and left a vivid appreciation of the cost of conflict; but as time passed the memory of that grew dim, and a new head of aggression built up. The very fact of a board working well was sometimes its downfall: so long as the men were satisfied, they ceased to feel that they needed the union to fight for them, and they fell away from it, so that when the board made a decision which they did not like their leaders found they could no longer control them; or, if the board got on too well, the men might come to feel that their leaders were in the masters' pockets. A board might have its honeymoon in the rising phase of the trade cycle when wage advances were the order of the day in any case; then came the slump, and wage cuts, and the men had no more use for it — that was how the board in the Potteries was broken up, twice. The working of a board always depended on the cohesion of both sides, and whatever fractured that — whether it was strife within a union and the outbreak of unofficial strikes, or rivalry between unions, or the defection open or covert of a section of the employers — made the board useless, because its decisions would not be observed in practice. The Leicester Hosiery board, it was said, after many successful years, broke up because 'the employers had lost confidence in themselves, and

[1] Royal Commision on Trade Disputes and Trade Combinations, Minutes of Evidence (Cd. 2826 of 1906), Q. 1412 seq.

the workpeople had lost confidence in the employers, and in themselves.'[1]

There was also a way in which these boards, even those that went on tolerably well, were now falling behind the times. From the 1890's onwards the area of negotiation was constantly extending: districts were linking up, and some trades were making agreements which covered most of the country. But the board lost much of its virtue as its coverage widened. The growth of confidence and the blend of bargaining with mutual trust which had come about in the successful boards had owed much to their being local: their members spoke the same dialect, had the same local interests, sometimes went to the same chapels. The district board whose formal constitution proclaimed a faith in equal status and friendly dealing was a means of drawing on and developing these ties of neighbourhood. A board that covered a wide area did not have the same resources to draw upon. 'At the national level' the difference between the formally constituted board and other ways of meeting for bargaining became inconsiderable. In fact, only two or three boards covered a whole trade. The increasing number of industry-wide agreements were mostly to be arrived at by direct negotiation.

7

The militancy of the men that was making trouble for some of the boards was felt to be a sign of the times, a manifestation of the New Unionism. The name connoted a flood of energies and ideas that poured through two channels: it changed the spirit of established unionism, and it swept into unionism many who had not come near it before. The second process brought into being a type of union which, at least as a viable and continuing organization, was virtually a new one, the general union.

The members of this type of union were typically unskilled. They had not been able to maintain unions before because, in a word, they lacked the resources themselves and no one else would supply them. Underemployed and low paid at the best of times, they could not keep up a subscription. Illiterate, they could not find secretaries and treasurers from their own ranks. They were a helpless class, a class apart: though craftsmen and

[1] Royal Commission on Labour, Summary of Evidence, Gp. C., Pt. I (Cd. 7421-I of 1894).

operatives shaded into one another then as they do now, a gulf that exists no longer divided the operatives from the labourers. These were set apart by their lack of schooling and their rough manners, drunkenness, and inability to look after themselves. They received the continual overspill of population, the lads for whom there were no vacant niches in the existing structure and no resources to train them in a skill. They were the sink, too, into which the failures in other walks of life seeped down, the neurotics and the handicapped. Their own families, among the largest in the community, continually added to their number more ill-nourished and untrained youngsters. Not the administration of a union merely, but being a member of its rank and file, requires resources of money and character that appear formidably great when one looks at the mid-Victorian labourers: everyone took it for granted that unionism was beyond them.

Yet they would often have kept their own union going if only they had some help with its administration, and sometimes this was given them. There was a Brickmakers' Society of Nottingham, not one of whose members could read or write — (we remember the brickmakers of St Alban's in *Bleak House*, and of Hoggle End — 'a lawless, drunken, terribly rough lot of humanity' — in *The Last Chronicle of Barset*) but they hired an outsider to be their secretary. We hear of a barrister, who was also a liberal candidate, taking an interest in a newly formed union of London busmen, and accepting its presidency. Even the railwaymen had first formed a lasting union only with the help of a large shareholder, Michael Bass, M.P. The editor of a local paper in Warwickshire became treasurer of a union of farm labourers. The workers in the jute mills of Dundee were organized to resist a wage-reduction in 1885 by the Unitarian minister of the town. Most of them were women, and where unions of women were formed it commonly happened that the lead was given from outside: Lady Dilke, for instance, when she was wife of the Rector of Lincoln College in Oxford, in 1881 'went around to the women working at the clothing factories and in other trades, and obtained their promises, and she afterwards prepared rules for their organization'.[1]

But such instances had not amounted to much. Whatever the

---

[1] Memoir by Sir C. Dilke prefixed to *The Book of the Spiritual Life*, by Lady Dilke (1905).

JOHN BURNS

BEN TILLETT

latent demand for a lead may have been, there was little supply. On the contrary, the established unionists mostly wanted to keep others out, not rope them in, and especially others whom they looked down on, as they did on labourers and women. They were strongly conscious of a class difference setting them apart, were themselves 'society men' in more than one sense. They did not want labourers or women to form separate unions, because these would stiffen the competition for shares in the employer's total wages bill. They did not want to open their own unions to them because, if they themselves were craftsmen, their most cherished tactic was to restrict entry to the trade, and whether they were craftsmen or operatives they found the essential bond of unity in their occupation, and felt that those in other jobs did not belong.

So it came about that until the 1880's British trade unionism had the characteristics and reputation of the stronghold of a privileged minority. The operatives' unions, particularly the miners' and the textile workers', were too broadly based to deserve that reputation, but it clung to unionism as a whole, and much contemporary discussion of unionism is intelligible only as an appraisal of exclusive and sectional advantage. In 1862 Samuel Smiles[1] wrote of 'trades unions': 'They, in fact, constitute an exclusive body, whose principal object is to keep as many as possible out of their particular trades, and especially to shut out the poor and unskilled from participating in their peculiar advantages.' When John Stuart Mill in 1869 came round to the possibility of unions raising wages, he added,[2] 'it still requires to be asked, whether Unionists are justified in seeking a rise of wages for themselves, which will in all probability produce a fall of wages, or loss of employment, to other labourers, their fellow-countrymen. Still more is this question raised by those restrictive rules, forbidding the employment of non-unionists, limiting the number of apprentices, etc., which many Unions maintain. . . . All such limitation inflicts distinct evil upon those whom it excludes — upon that great mass of labouring population which is outside the Unions; an evil not trifling, for if the system were rigorously enforced it would prevent unskilled

[1] In his *Workmen's Earnings, Strikes and Savings* (reprinted from the *Quarterly Review*), p. 147.
[2] *Fortnightly Review*, June 1869, p. 695.

labourers or their children from ever rising to the condition of skilled.' Similarly Sidney Webb, in 1888:[1] 'Certainly, the workers in some trades have managed to improve their economic position by strict Trade Unions. We are never allowed to forget the splendid incomes earned by these aristocrats of labour, a mere tenth of the whole labour class. But those who merely counsel the rest to go and do likewise forget that the only permanently effective Trade Union victories are won by limitation of the numbers in the particular trade, and the excluded candidates necessarily go to depress the condition of the outsiders.'

But the very year in which Sidney Webb spoke brought an upsurge of unionism that was to extend its bounds in fact and principle. The match girls, the gasworkers and the dockers revealed an unsuspected capacity for action among the unskilled. It was not for nothing that there had now been two decades of general elementary education: not many workers under thirty in 1889 would have been without schooling. This was something new. That women should strike on their own was almost unprecedented. That dockers should have the self-control and steadiness of purpose to hold out for over four weeks had been thought impossible: yet there they were now, disciplined, orderly, resolute. What is more, though their chief leadership came from outside, they found in Ben Tillett a man from their own ranks who could run a union. Others of the unskilled threw up such leaders too — notably Will Thorne and J. R. Clynes. At the same time a missionary spirit animated some established trade unionists who saw unionism as a branch of a labour movement with an aggressive socialist policy. Two engineers, John Burns and Tom Mann, members of the Social Democratic Federation, went down and led the dockers. Branches of unions drew together town by town to form new trades councils with a largely political purpose. That purpose was served, in the new as in the old councils, by holding recruiting meetings, and subsidising and administering new branches.

There were in fact three fields for recruitment. One was that of unskilled generalized labour everywhere, unattached by experience to any one industry. Close to the labourers in part,

[1] In a lecture reprinted as Fabian Tract no. 15, *English Progress towards Social Democracy*.

but on other boundaries adjoining the skilled men, were a hundred patches left here and there in industry between the existing holdings of craftsmen and operatives. Here worked the less skilled operatives, the men on the new machines or rougher jobs, the knobsticks, who none the less had useful experience, and attachment to the trade, and did not call themselves labourers. It must often have been only because they were scattered that many of them had not become organized already. There were even some pockets of really skilled men among them, like the maintenance workers in the Welsh tinplate trade, dyers and woolcombers in the West Riding, and some colliery enginemen. The third field contained certain industries in which few workers of any kind, except some craftsmen engaged on maintenance, were unionized already. This differed from the second field only in that those who were recruited now would not find themselves alongside the fences of already established unionists, but all grades in the industry could potentially join the same union. Transport in various branches, and municipal employment, were the major instances.

One thing was decided by the structure of existing unionism: most of these recruits would have to go into new unions. The established unions saw no point in taking them in. 'The awkward new grades', Hobsbawm has put it,[1] 'could be sent to form unions of their own, which would not complicate or weaken the craftsman's bargains: as the Engineers sent the electricians, the hand-bootmakers the machine bootmakers to form theirs; as the compositors favoured the formation of a separate "printers' labourers' society", and the iron-moulders made no attempt to organize the machine-moulders'. The delegate conference of the Engineers, it is true, did decide in principle to admit semi-skilled machinists, but the branches were generally reluctant to take them in. It was chiefly for them that Tom Mann in 1898 founded the Workers' Union. Despite the new spirit, moreover, old attitudes persisted. When later the national board of employers and unionists in the building industry agreed to admit the labourers to the local conciliation boards, it attached conditions that were like the safeguards of ascendancy in a multi-racial society: any local agreement admitting the labourers

---

[1] E. J. Hobsbawm, 'General Labour Unions in Britain, 1889–1914', *Economic History Review* (2), 1, 2 and 3, 1948–9.

must state explicitly that their admission was of grace and not of right; they should sit only when matters affecting their own interests were under discussion; no man of theirs should sit on any board to hear cases coming up from a town in which their unions had not yet been recognized.

So most of the newcomers to unionism were enrolled, not by existing unions or unions that would consolidate them with other workmen in the same industry, but by general unions which linked them across industrial boundaries with other outsiders like themselves. Farm workers and labourers in steel mills became Dockers. The Gasworkers amended their rules to be able to recruit in a host of industries — brewing and brickmaking, sugar, jute and india rubber, paper and cotton, tailoring and gravedigging. They became general unions.

This is a third main type, that was added now to the unions of craftsmen and operatives. Its novel feature was that it halted at no occupational or industrial boundary. Where there was more than one such union in the field, there had to be some market-sharing if there was not to be conflict, and some demarcation was observed locally; but otherwise there was no limit of region, occupation, or industry. Denied strength through exclusion, the general union sought it through comprehensiveness. The skilled man not only benefited by the scarcity of his skill, but in a strike he had its protection against substitution by blacklegs. The unskilled man's place could be taken by any hungry fellow from anywhere. It often was: as late as 1912, within a month of a stoppage beginning in the London docks the number of blacklegs was put at thirteen thousand. The dockers' victory in 1889 had been won on the rising phase of the trade cycle: it would have been impossible, a contemporary observer noted,[1] in a year of bad trade 'when an unlimited supply of unemployed were being poured out of every depressed industry in London into the sink of dock labour'. The only safeguard was to get all sorts of unskilled men everywhere into one union. As a mere matter of administration, moreover, the scattered groups that entered the general unions needed to unite if they were to pay for a union at all. This was the more so because their dues were low. It was their declared policy at first not to give friendly benefits, for the need to safeguard the reserves for

[1] H. Llewellyn Smith and V. Nash, *The Story of the Dockers' Strike* (1889), p. 43.

these had immobilized some of the older unions: the new ones would have a fund for one thing only, strike pay. But that was a rationalization: the active reason for a small subscription was that most of their members could not afford more. They had one other distinctive feature — they were socialist. The older unions had a tradition that you should keep party politics out of labour questions: these new ones were organized by socialists, and socialism was their aim. The Gasworkers had a declaration of the Marxist faith, drawn up by Marx's son-in-law Aveling; there was never any question of the new unions supporting any candidates but independent labour men. This was a natural consequence of their lack of an entrenched position in industry: instead, they sought a statutory minimum wage, and compulsory arbitration. It was also a consequence of their not being able to pay enough to provide social insurance for themselves, as the craftsmen did: they had to win the welfare state instead. But it also came about because they were not organized at all until men with the socialist faith arose to give a lead, and these men saw unionism as part of a general labour movement and class struggle.

Beside the general union, these years saw the rise of another inclusive type, or striving towards a type, the industrial union. It is the definition of the industrial union in its pure form that its boundaries are those only of an industry: it does not recruit its members from more than one industry, but within that one it takes in every employee, or at least every wage-earner, without distinction of occupation. The second part of that the general unions were willing to and sometimes nearly did provide, in those parts of their field where there was little unionism till they began to recruit — in the gas-works, for example, in municipal employment, and in some branches of transport. But in one such branch, the railways, there was an existing union which, being already confined to the boundaries of one industry, now took on the second characteristic of an industrial union by offering membership to every wage-earner within them: in 1896–7 the 'all grades' campaign of the Railway Servants doubled its membership for a while.

The new unionism had come in with a bang. Within three months of their formation the Gasworkers had demanded from the London companies an eight-hour instead of a twelve-hour day: they got it without a strike, and with an actual increase in weekly pay. Then came the dockers' triumph. The public believed what the new unions proclaimed, that they were essentially militant. But within a year or two this had changed. The triumphs were won on the rising movement of the trade cycle, and the falling followed. Membership dropped away, especially that of the general labourers. The general unions kept going as congeries of occupational groups which filled gaps in the previous structure of unionism, enjoyed some autonomy, and behaved each in its own industry or region as the other unions had long been behaving there. They might or might not obtain recognition from the employers for wage negotiation, and they might live in mutual tolerance or jealousy with their neighbours in the older unions, industry by industry: but their aims and methods were now the traditional ones. The Tyneside Labour Union, recognized by the shipbuilding employers, boasted of its avoidance of strikes. Outside transport the new unions were soon mainly concerned with keeping what toe-hold they had gained. They were not fire-eaters. Soon, like other unions, they began to give friendly benefits, beginning with funeral benefit.

But the movement called the New Unionism was wider than this, and its currents ran through the old unions as well as the new. It brought into industrial relations class consciousness and a faith in socialism. A growing number of wage-earners had it against the boss now not just that he did not pay them more but that he was a boss at all. They believed in the possibility of a different order in which they would no longer work for another man's profit. They looked for a revolutionary change in their status as well as a greater share of the good things other people had so much more of. The old unionists too had new demands now: a minimum based on human needs instead of a wage that fell with the market; the eight-hour day; the right to a voice in workshop management. They were more prompt to back their demands by the strike. We have seen the impact on the boards of conciliation. When the leaders counselled moderation and patience, the rank and file might come out without waiting longer. Duly negotiated agreements they might repudiate as not good enough to take lying down. They would enforce restrictive practices more rigorously.

Employers felt themselves confronted with a spirit very different from what they were used to. The old unions had often been at some pains to be respectable, to show that they accepted the social order, and only aspired to a recognized place in it. In part this was mere protective coloration, and an avoidance of conflict on other points in order to be strong on issues of employment; but it also expressed the spontaneous feelings of men who inherited the traditions of master craftsmen in an older society, and had a status in their own. Many unions had rules not only against seditious talk but against boasting that membership made a man independent of his employer. There were rules, too, to prevent hasty striking. One of the few labourers' unions of long standing, the Glasgow Society of Harbour Labourers formed in 1853, had a rule that 'no strike shall be organized unless decided by a three-fourths majority of the whole of the members of the society, and that only after the matter in dispute had lain for one clear week before the Honourable the Lord Provost of Glasgow, the Provost of Govan, and the Provost of Partick, as a board of conciliation to act between the parties'. The rules of the Scots Railway Servants said that the executive committee must seek to settle disputes by arbitration, and only if the company refused this might they consider the expediency of a withdrawal of labour. Trade unionists who went into politics were mostly Gladstonian, but there were Tories among the rank and file, especially in the cotton unions, which eschewed the party of John Bright and were traditionally true blue. To many of the younger men all this seemed wrong. They did not want merely to speak on terms of mutual respect with their employer, they wanted to take him on and whittle his prerogatives down until they could get rid of him and his profits altogether. They did not want arbitration, least of all by one of their class enemies, they wanted to grow strong and hit hard. They were not prepared to enter into amicable conversations with their exploiters. The existing parties were as bad as one another, run by those whose common interest was to maintain the existing order in which they could live by the sweat of other men's brows: the younger men wanted a party of their own, dedicated to the building of a new order.

The significance of 1889 to contemporaries was not so much that a new type of union arose, as that existing industrial relations began to drive before a gale of novel aspirations and resentments.

8

It was by strikes that the New Unionism had been brought to the notice of the public and had, indeed, discovered itself. What was new was that labourers, even women, could hold out and win. But in other respects the strikes of 1888–90 conformed with a familiar pattern of numerous short stoppages in the rising phase of the trade cycle, and a few stoppages, some of them long, in the falling phase. The last trough had come in 1886, and by the latter part of 1889 there was full employment. That was a phase at which strikes were to be expected, as wage-earners felt some pinch of rising prices at the same time as their employer's business was increasingly profitable, shortages of labour here and there were already causing some bidding up of wages, and there was little fear of not getting one's job back if one struck. By the same token, most employers agreed to some rise without a stoppage, and strikes occurred only when the union reckoned it should get a bigger rise than the employers would go to, or the general raising of wages impinged on a trade which had not itself felt the rise in demand. Nor when they did occur were they likely to last long: they were only giving the system a tap here and there where some friction was holding up the general movement. When depression followed, that movement ran the other way, but now there was much more than some incidental friction to resist the transmission to the price of labour of the change in effective demand. Wage-earners had a natural reluctance to accept a cut in their rate. Some reduction of what their wage would buy they might accept through prices rising while the wage remained unchanged; but a cut in that wage itself, even though prices in the shops had fallen by more meanwhile, was a conspicuous reverse. If the wage really were to follow the market, moreover, it might have to fall a long way, especially in the industries that felt the cyclical movement most: in 1891–2 the miners of South Wales accepted a reduction of $42\frac{1}{2}$ per cent 'off the standard', those of Scotland 50 per cent. At such times the men might dig in and refuse to budge, saying that the first charge on industry should be a living wage for its workers. The employers might accept that, when, as often in building, they

named their price according to their costs, and were not exposed
to the competition of others whose costs had been brought down,
though even there they would feel they must cut their costs if
they were to get work at all. But it was different where, as with
coal, the product had to be sold for what it would fetch in a
market that other districts, and perhaps other countries, were
selling in too. Then a moral claim clashed with a relentless
impersonal pressure. A long, dour struggle might result. The
men usually got the worst of it.

The industries to which the trade cycle brought the greatest
ups and downs were naturally liable to disputes, but there were
other differences between industries. A big stoppage could not
take place except where trade unionism was strong: large
numbers of men could not hold out without it. It might become
strong only as the result of a strike — it was only after the
London dockers had struck in 1889 that most of them joined a
hitherto puny union; the South Wales Miners' Federation arose
out of a stoppage in 1898. Without the strike pay, the leadership
and the discipline that unionism could provide there might be
waves of strikes at times, and here and there a local struggle
might be desperately protracted, but stoppages would not be
big in both dimensions — many men out for a long time. So it
came about that down to 1906 there had been no big stoppage
in farming, or on the railways, or in wool, clothing, food and
drink, shopkeeping, government service, or indeed any white
collar work. Only six industries had had big stoppages: cotton,
coal, boot and shoe, engineering and shipbuilding, the docks,
and building, though because negotiation in building remained
very localised strikes there were typically many and small. But
there was no simple contrast between strongly and weakly
organized sectors. The absence of strong unions was due to
different causes in different places, and the absence of big
stoppages did not necessarily mark harmony or contentment.
There were two industries, moreover, where there had for long
been no big stoppage although unions were strong — printing,
and iron and steel. In printing, strong craft unions enjoyed a
sheltered market. The iron and steel industry, on the contrary,
was exposed to all the winds that blow, but it paid high and
rising wages, more than any other industry it offered the unskilled recruit prospects of advancement to really high earnings,

N

stoppages were disastrously costly because furnaces cracked when they cooled, wages in any case were a small part of the whole cost of production.

Besides differences between industries there were probably differences between regions. The regional differences that appear on the face of a table of man-days lost in disputes do little more than reflect the underlying differences in industrial composition — if mining has a higher rate of loss than other industries, any region with a high proportion of miners will tend to look a stormy one. One way round this is to find what proportion of all the strikers in each year in a given industry were in a certain region, and compare it with the proportion of the whole man-power of the industry which lay in that region; a similar calculation can be made for all industries together. Knowles[1] has made such estimates for a number of British industries and regions in the years 1911–45, and they show marked differences between the propensity to strike of workers in one and the same industry according as they are in different regions. Often the propensity comes out highest where the industry is strongly concentrated — in textiles, Lancashire and Cheshire; in engineering and ship-building (where most of the stoppages were in shipbuilding), Northern Ireland; in mining, South Wales. Similarly for the combined measure: the three regions with the highest propensities, taking all the relevant industries together, are South Wales, the West Riding, Lancashire and Cheshire, but these are regions which also have a concentration of industries with high propensities. Very likely this marks a genuine effect of rever-beration. It is understandable that a fitter in Manchester should be more prone to strike than one in a West Country market town: he is likely to be working in a bigger firm, in any case he has more of his own kind around him to echo and amplify his feelings, his ties with them are stronger and with the rest of the community weaker. Two American scholars,[2] seeking the reason why certain industries have a high propensity to strike in many different countries, have found it here. 'Here is a case,' they say, 'where the totality of common grievances, after they have been verbally shared, may be greater than the sum of the individual

[1] K. G. J. C. Knowles, *Strikes — a study in industrial conflict* (1952).
[2] Clark Kerr and Abraham Siegel, 'The interindustry propensity to strike — an international comparison', Ch. 14 of *Industrial Conflict*, ed. A. Kornhauser, R. Dubin and A. M. Ross (1954).

parts. . . . The members of these groups not only have the same grievances, but they have them at the same time, at the same place, and against the same people. In the more peaceful industries their inevitable grievances are dispersed. . . . The 'mass grievance', not the individual grievance, is the 'source of the greater social difficulty.' Thus the regional concentration of industry may have made for strife through the factor of reverberation.

Very likely there were other sources of regional differences. They may have lain in social structure and custom, in housing, and particularly in the stability and the wholeness of the community — whether men felt they were there by birthright, or had come in as immigrants from a different world, or were children of immigrants. One thinks of the medley of speech and customs in the South Wales valleys, and the Irish and the Highlanders in Glasgow: it was there men believed that 'the workers have no country'. There seems also to have been a difference in the accidents of history. If we believe that the type of leader is determined solely by the type of industrial environment, how can we explain the contrast between South Wales and the North East Coast, whose industrial composition was so similar but whose leaders were so different? It did happen — we may suppose it was determined, but we only know it happened — that on the North East Coast men arose on both sides to counsel mutual respect, and reason in negotiation: Sir David Dale, Sir Benjamin Browne, Sir Andrew Noble; John Kane, Thomas Burt, Robert Knight. One man's initiative would be reciprocated by someone on the other side; no economic storm came to break up the arrangement they made between them; a tradition was established, and drew strength from its own success. Human relations build up like that, but in either direction. Started in the wrong direction, not by malevolence necessarily but perhaps by some twist of circumstance, they can generate ever new conflicts out of the bitter memories of past ones. Each friendly act is suspect as a trap, each unfriendly one is vital to self-defence; and all because that is how it was yesterday.

So far we have been concerned with the big stoppages that made up most of the total of man-days lost. But they were relatively few. The great majority of stoppages were quite small, because they were local — the operatives of one firm out here, two score carpenters in a town there. They were not necessarily brief: the men might have their strike pay long continued by a union whose members elsewhere remained at work, a particular employer might stand obstinately on a point of pride or principle. Nor were they always ended by the men returning to work. It was not unknown for a particular employer to be ruined, or to retire, and his business to be given up altogether; or all his men who came out might get jobs elsewhere — that happened in building when it was busy. On the other hand, he might replace strikers with other men, or give up some part of his business, and in either case refuse to take the strikers back.

It was possible to collect particulars of the issues on which stoppages began. These were not necessarily the same as the causes. In one sense, the ultimate cause of a dispute might be in a general and unformulated discontent, arising from many circumstances of the working life. In another, the causes might be defined as the matters on which agreement had to be reached if work was to be carried on again: but these did not necessarily appear in whatever claim or incident touched a stoppage off, and sometimes no one on either side was clear what they were, and the first service of a conciliator was to disentangle them. But taking the list of issues as they were reported, we find that the staple union issues of wages and conditions of work, especially hours, make up the majority: beside them was a growing class of issues concerning union security — the victimization of a member, or the men's refusal to work with non-unionists; and then came disputes between one union and another about which had the exclusive right to a certain job. These demarcation disputes occurred notably between the craft unions in building, and even more in shipbuilding, where the occupational grouping natural for the building of a wooden sailing ship adapted itself uneasily to the continual changes that brought in and developed the steel steamship.

Though union organization was a necessary condition of big stoppages, they seldom began at union headquarters. It was thinkable that the leader of a union should start a strike for reasons of long-run strategy or power politics, when the men left to themselves would not have moved; but that did not often happen, if only because a leader needed to be extraordinarily trusted for the men to follow him in cold blood into all the hardships of a strike. Usually headquarters did not move until the men were rearing to go, and had in fact in one place or another already come out. The employers who had had to deal with strong unions and who gave evidence before the Royal Commission on Labour in 1891–4 were agreed that the leaders generally exercised a restraining influence. Sometimes they would order their members back, and even expel them, under the rules of the union, if they refused. In a doubtful case headquarters might let a local strike go on without making it official, that is to say, without giving the men strike pay from union funds: their own local committee had then to do what it could to raise funds, particularly through the trades council which brought together representatives of the different unions in a town, and which found one of its main functions here. But if the local action had been taken in defence of the union rate or some cherished working practice, headquarters might endorse it and give strike pay; and if the issue affected the membership in a wider region, would take it up with the employers, and perhaps bring more members out.

Even when he got strike pay, the member needed great self-control and courage to see a long stoppage through, if only because that pay was so much less than his wage — ten shillings a week would be a typical figure, when the craftsman was earning thirty to forty. He might have savings to draw on; after that there was the pawnshop; but sooner or later he would be getting hungry, and, what is worse, seeing his wife and children get hungry too. In practice she could get relief, but under penalty of appearing as a pauper before the relieving officer, with the threat of the workhouse in the background. He, being engaged in a trade dispute, could not, though in fact some Boards had given outrelief to strikers illegally, or under cover of the clause that allowed their officers to give food in cases of 'sudden or urgent necessity'. Continuing and increasing misery might break down the men's resistance, but there were also times when the very pain brought an access of determination. A shipbuilder of the North-East Coast entered into his men's minds when he wrote[1] — as a shipbuilder he takes a demarcation

[1] Colloquy written in 1894, at pp. 326–7 of *Memoirs of John Wigham Richardson* (privately printed, 1911).

dispute as typical — 'Imagine what your feeling would be, if you believed (as if it were the Gospel) that you had a prescriptive right to certain work, of which you were being unjustly deprived, and if you knew that your wife was selling or pawning your furniture, that all your savings were spent and debts being incurred which you could never hope to pay; if you were kept in enforced idleness and bound to report yourself in person every forenoon at the union offices, if your children complained that they had not enough to eat, if awful visions of the workhouse were looming up, and your wife was perhaps being *helped* by kind ladies (curse their condescension!) and that all the while the masters, so far as you could judge, in no way changed their way of life; imagine all this, and you will be able to believe the story that a workman once died of joy when a strike ended. Unless you first realize that the men during a strike grow to look upon themselves as martyrs, and to feel a martyr's exultation, you will never be able to understand how strikes last as long as they do, long after the struggle is evidently hopeless.'

Despite all the loss and suffering that stoppages inflicted on those in and near them, they amounted to very little in the national aggregate. In a bad year they were equivalent to the loss of as much as three days' work on the average for each wage-earner in the country; over the fifteen years that ended with 1907 the corresponding average was about half a day. This way of reckoning, though artificial, gives a sense of proportion, and helps to explain why the public had not been more concerned to prevent or forbid stoppages.

But by 1900 there was no doubt that they were becoming more menacing. The country felt itself confronted with something quite new in 1893, when all the coal pits of Yorkshire, Lancashire, and the Midlands were stopped together. The winter drew on; factories would soon have to stop for lack of coal, townsfolk have nothing to cook and heat by. Gladstone in his last days as prime minister was moved by the threat of suffering to invite the parties to meet his foreign secretary, Rosebery, as conciliator. They did, and he got a settlement. That was a landmark: the first time an industrial dispute had brought the government in. It did so partly because the men had shown such a remarkable power to hold out, from August on into November. Earlier that year fifty thousand cotton spinners had given the country an example of that power too, when they held out for twenty weeks. But they had been left to reach their own agreement at the last, in a memorable all-night sitting. What made Gladstone against all his instincts intervene was that this dispute had halted a large part of a basic industry — that is, one that could not stop without much else stopping too. The miners, like the cotton spinners, had only been standing out against a wage cut that the employers had called for; but in the combination of the large scale of union action with the indispensability of the product lay a potential threat that was not unnoticed on either side.

One dimension of that large scale of action was the area that a union not only held in its own control but would in practice stop as a whole. Hitherto, most disputes had stopped only one district at a time, and unions had been in two minds about extending them. On the one hand there was an advantage of holding a common line throughout, and preventing one district being undercut by another. On the other was the difficulty, so long as district agreements were the order of the day, that members whose own agreement was working tolerably at the time would be loath to plunge themselves into all the hardships of a dispute only for the sake of their brethren at a distance. There was also the very practical consideration, that if a strike were confined to one district the strike pay could be found by the members elsewhere still at work, but if most of them were out it would exhaust their funds quickly. The expansion of unions therefore had not of itself brought a widening of the area of disputes. But several factors did bring about that widening now. A greater militancy made members more willing to come out themselves for the sake of an issue raised elsewhere. The case for doing that was specially strong when the issue was one not of money but of principle: but it was such issues that the rank and file were now raising increasingly — the demand for recognition; refusal to work with non-unionists; the maintenance of working practices; the minimum wage based on human needs. But a dispute about the money wage likewise enforced the need to hold a common line when it was a dispute about a cut: in prosperous times one district might get a rise without being undersold by others that lagged behind, but it was otherwise when demand had fallen below capacity — the men saw then that if they gave way in one district they would have to all along the line. The widening of the area of bargaining must have been powerfully promoted by 'the Great Depression', the trend of falling prices that became apparent when the boom after the Franco-Prussian war broke, and for twenty years, despite two intervals of cyclical revival, continued to press down on the selling prices of the manufacturer, and through them on the wages he paid. The tactics of advance may be to break through where one can, and exploit in depth; but in defence one is flank-conscious. We may conjecture how the tactics of the unions would have developed if their expansion and invigoration had come at a time when wage rises had long been the order of the day. The actual setting was the reverse of that. The seen need was for defence. The method was to widen the area of negotiation. If the years from 1860 to 1890 were the heyday of the district board, the thirty that followed were to see the transition to industry-wide bargaining.

The unions took the initiative in that transition, but the employers toiled after them here as they had done before in the districts. The landmark was another great struggle of the nineties, the engineers' long-drawn dispute through the winter of 1897–8, felt at the time to be 'the greatest struggle between Labour and Capital that this country has ever seen'.[1] One of its significant features was the creation of an industry-wide employers' organization. In June 1896 a Federation brought together some local associations of employers on the north-east coast, in Barrow and Belfast and on the Clyde. When the London unionists claimed the eight-hour day, a London association was formed in May 1897, and at once joined the Federation. A strike began in London; the Federation replied by a partial lock-out; the unions withdrew all their members. Up and down the country, engineering employers drew together to resist the militancy of 'the biggest union in the world', the Amalgamated Engineers: there were 180 firms in the Federation when the struggle began, 702 when it ended seven months later. The settlement left wages to be negotiated district by district, but it laid down various principles to regulate the relations of managers and workmen, and a procedure for discussion of

[1] *Engineering*, 15 Oct. 1897. Quoted here from R. O. Clarke, 'The Dispute in the British Engineering Industry 1897–8: an Evaluation', *Economica*, May 1957.

grievances, that applied throughout the seven hundred federated firms, and came near being an industry-wide agreement.

As such it was the first in engineering, or indeed in any great industry. But if cotton spinning was a separate industry, it had made its own industry-wide agreement in 1893; and a celebrated agreement reached in the boot and shoe industry in 1895 covered the major part though by no means all of it. It is noteworthy that all three of these agreements were reached after an exhausting struggle and resulted in many years of substantial peace. Once they had come together, districts and sections did not break away. No major issue was re-opened in engineering until 1914. There was no general stoppage in cotton spinning for fifteen years. The boot and shoe trade became a showpiece of industrial relations. The transition to industry-wide bargaining seemed a movement towards orderliness and peace.

9

One reason why the dockers had impressed the public so much in 1889 was that they were orderly. Men looked back to the riots in Lancashire in 1878, when an employer's house was set on fire, as the last leap of flames that had burnt themselves out long ago. But soon it seemed that they were taking hold and breaking out again. There was a tension that contemporaries noticed as something new up and down the industrial midlands in the coal stoppage of 1893: endemic rioting and violence, police charging with drawn cutlasses, the military sent for. At Featherstone in Yorkshire a small detachment of soldiers came under a hail of brick-bats as they advanced with fixed bayonets to clear a burning colliery yard: they fired, and killed two miners. That shook a country which had thought such things done with.

There were several reasons why more violent conflicts should break out. One lay in the very extension of the area of disputes, for when so many members of a union were out at the same time their strike pay quickly exhausted its funds, or had to be very small, and hungry men grew desperate. Another lay in the increased participation of the unskilled. More than other kinds of labour, they were drawn into conflict with blacklegs. The craftsmen were saved from that because usually no one else had the skill needed to do their jobs. The miners were protected by a rule in the Mines Act of 1887, forbidding the employment of any man alone at the face until he had had two years underground under supervision. But the unskilled men had only the picket line to rely on. If they were ever to win a strike, they had to meet the imported blackleg and — dissuade him. When their union had only a partial hold, they had to try to stop other men from going on working. There was another factor: in the big towns they would always be intermingled with 'the mob', the destructive and predatory men and women of the slums, who when the crowds were out in a strike would seize their chance to smash, loot and burn. When any big stoppage of the unskilled began now, extra police were sent in, and the military. G. R. Askwith[1] has left a picture of Belfast in a transport dispute in 1907: 'guards at the railway stations, double sentries with loaded rifles at alternate lamp posts of the Royal Avenue, a very few lorries, with constabulary sitting on the bales and soldiers on either side, proceeding to guarded, congested but lifeless docks, and ten thousand soldiers in and about the city. There had been fights in the streets, charges of cavalry, the Riot Act read, shooting to disperse wrecking mobs, a few men and women killed and scores wounded, and the whole business of the city at a standstill.'

But the main source of more violent conflict was that the extension of unionism from 1889 brought it up against employers who did not merely resist it on certain issues but resented its very existence. They resented someone calling himself a union official 'trying to interfere between them and their own men'. They resented the boycott, in which a union in dispute with some other business tried to get their own men to refuse to handle its supplies or products — but this was an expedient to which the union of the unskilled was often driven. They resented likewise another of its expedients — the sympathetic strike, in which men engaged in a dispute and fearful that they could not stand by themselves involved others who had no quarrel with their own employers. In two great industries, shipping and the railways, most of the employers were radically opposed to the unionization of their men. While in some British industries employers worked with the unions in a settled and mainly friendly association that by the end of the nineteenth century ran back beyond living memory, in others they were arrayed

[1] Lord (G. R.) Askwith, *Industrial Problems and Disputes* (1920), p. 113.

THE SPIRIT OF UNREST.

Police Constable. "WHO HAVE I GOT HERE? WHY, A BOTTLE-THROWING HOOLIGAN."
Mr. Punch. "MARCH HIM OFF; THAT'S THE WORST ENEMY OF LABOUR. YOU'VE
DONE YOUR DUTY, AS YOU ALWAYS DO."

(23 August 1911)   Reproduced by permission of 'Punch'

against unionism as a recent invader they were determined to hurl back from its beachheads.

A union refused recognition could do nothing if it could not call a strike. If men who joined it were dismissed and blacklisted it would never grow unless it could enforce their reinstatement. When men, members or not, left their work because of some dispute of the usual kind about wages or the like, the union would come in to take the lead and gain recruits. The employers' riposte was to import blacklegs. By 1900 it was increasingly rare for employers who were in settled relations with unions to try to replace strikers; but those who wanted to break the unions used blacklegs freely.

Several agencies stood ready to supply them. In Lancashire there was a 'free labour' man who had given his life to strike-breaking, he said, because his father had been killed by strikers in Pittsburgh. Bristol had its own brigade, under the command of one Gammy Hunter, established in quarters that were kept provisioned against a siege. A former member of the Amalgamated Engineers ran an Association of Non-Unionists, formed in 1903: he registered men who were ready to go in as blacklegs, and he also helped non-union men to find jobs, presumably with firms that wanted to weaken the hold of the unions in their shops. There was also a Provincial Free Labour Association in Glasgow. But this was a breakaway from the best known agency, the National Free Labour Association. This had begun in 1893. By 1902, at any rate, it was under the wing of a body called the Employers' Parliamentary Council, which brought together a few of the employers who were most actively opposed to recent manifestations of unionism. The Association itself made a show of being a movement of men opposed to the tyranny of the unions, and held an annual congress, but the delegates were hired at five shillings a day, and both the annual report laid before them and the resolutions they adopted unanimously were provided by the Employers' Council. At the close they sat down to a dinner paid for by Sir George Livesey, Chairman of the South Metropolitan Gas Company. The Association was further supported by small subscriptions from some of the railway companies. It was administered by William Collison, a rolling stone, who, after parting company with a union of London busmen he had helped to form, found a position and income for himself in strike-breaking. With his head office in London and five offices in the provinces, he claimed to maintain a register of non-union labour of many trades, and be able to despatch at short notice whatever kind of labour an employer might need to keep his works going, together with a strong-arm squad to deal with pickets. He may sometimes have been able to pick up skilled men who were unemployed and desperately needed a job, but the sort of thing he was good for as a rule is probably better described by the general manager of a railway company, who told two French inquirers[1] 'Two years ago he supplied me in twenty-four hours with the number of men I needed in consequence of a strike among my men. The men in the station at N. had stopped work in sympathy with the gasworkers and labourers in the town. Services were maintained without a break, and that had an excellent moral effect. But the men Collison supplied were mere labourers, and the worst band of ruffians and scoundrels you can imagine. I was delighted to be rid of them'. It was the men whom Collison sent down to the Taff Vale Railway Company whose reception touched off the most famous case in the history of trade union law. It commonly happened, when the strike breakers went down, that they camped inside the factory, or station, or tramway depot, under police protection, and sometimes behind barbed wire.

The Employers' Parliamentary Council had another subsidiary, the Labour Protection Association, which had been set up during the engineering dispute in 1897. Its secretary, who was also secretary of the parent body, told the Royal Commission on Trade Disputes that it was particularly concerned with picketing, and circulated a pamphlet against it which he thought had stiffened the attitude of the bench. Also 'we have a large force of police at our disposal, which we can use at a few hours' notice to send anywhere for the purpose of putting down' interference with free labour.

It was the picketing by the Sailors' and Firemen's Union, founded in 1887 and very active under Havelock Wilson in 1889 and 1890, that made some of the shipowners set up the Shipping Federation then. Its object was to stop the union forcing every officer and man to join, and to ensure that those who did not

[1] P. Mantoux and M. Alfassa, *La Crise du Trade-Unionisme* (Paris, 1903), p. 213, and pp. 321–2.

could sign on as crew without molestation. It was prepared to
treat with the Boilermakers, but not with Wilson, and it made
no secret of its intention to break any strike of his members. One
of its devices was the Federation ticket. Its members would not
engage a man who did not have one. Any seaman could take
one out, and he was not asked if he was a union member, but
he had to undertake to work peaceably with the rest of the crew
whether union men or not. The other main device of the
Federation was the depot ship, in which blacklegs could be
brought to the scene of a strike to make up crews out of reach of
the pickets on shore. With this it won some notable victories.
When his branch in Glasgow collapsed in 1889 Havelock Wilson
came down and in daily speeches outside the Federation Office
pleaded with the men to hand in their tickets: the men responded, and vessels could not get a full Federation crew. Then the
district committee of the Federation brought the *Duke of York* to
the Tail of the Bank as a depot ship and supplied her with
relays of Federation men from other ports, and vessels leaving
Glasgow crewed up as they went out. The strike collapsed.

Among all British employers, the directors of the railway
companies had long stood out by their opposition to unionism
on principle. They found its very existence incompatible with
the discipline that was essential to the safe and punctual operation of their services. 'You might as well have a trade union or
an amalgamated society in the army . . . as have it on railways',
the Chairman of the London and North Western told a Select
Committee on the hours of work of railway servants, in the
nineties. The companies had had no difficulty in recruiting,
especially from farm labourers and ex-soldiers, an ample supply
of men who found their service attractive, and gave them loyalty
and obedience in return for security of employment, relatively
high wages, and good prospects of promotion. But footplatemen
had never been so tractable, and as time went on the relative
attractions of the industry became smaller for railwaymen of all
kinds, and the burden of a seventy-two hour week more invidious. Still the men were scattered along the line, and even
where a number were grouped about one station they were
divided among many grades and duties; so they were slow to
combine. When they first did form unions, in the 1860's, the
management dismissed men right and left for joining. But what

proved to be an enduring unionism took hold when the Railway Servants were founded in 1872, and the footplatemen's union began as a breakaway from them in 1879. The companies would have nothing to do with either: as time went on they became increasingly willing to receive deputations of their own men, but with no outsiders present, that is, no union officers, and letters from union headquarters they generally ignored. When the railwaymen took fire from the New Unionism and pressed their claims anew in 1890, they made some local gains, but won no other recognition except victimization, save on the North Eastern, whose representatives did meet a committee of their own men accompanied by three national officers of the unions as 'advisers'. This was an instance of the conciliatory temper of management that characterized the north-east. The directors of its railway continued to differ from the others, whom they shocked in 1897 by not only negotiating with the Secretary of the Railway Servants but offering to submit the case to arbitration. In the meantime unionism gained its first toehold in the other companies. When in November 1896 the Railway Servants put in a claim which was believed to be backed by the threat of a strike at Christmas, officials of the London and North Western asked their men if they would come out, and those whose replies were unsatisfactory were dismissed at once. A general stoppage seemed likely, when the President of the Board of Trade intervened: the company still would not meet the union, but the President met with each side separately, and mediated an agreement which included the reinstatement of the men who had been dismissed. That was a landmark, and a victory for the union, whose membership doubled in twelve months. But it failed to get the Board of Trade to intervene again when it came in the next year with a renewed claim for recognition and the threat of another Christmas strike — the Board said this would show an 'utter disregard of the convenience of the travelling public'.

The unions fell back, and did little more till 1906. One of their difficulties was typical of much elsewhere in British unionism: they were divided by loyalties of grade and occupation, and could not agree on a common policy. The Railway Servants, though nominally open to all, had in practice been concerned only with the higher-paid grades. At the time of the

New Unionism a separate union was formed for the lowest paid,
and this later arrived at a working understanding with the
Railway Servants. But not so the footplatemen; their union had
the loyalties, and sectionalism, of a craft, and its membership
was solid, and grew steadily, while that of the Railway Servants
fluctuated. If only because a good many footplatemen continued
to belong to the Railway Servants, a common policy was
needed, but a loose federation formed to provide this in 1903
broke down two years later. Meanwhile a union of pointsmen
and signalmen went its own way, and in 1897 a separate union
had been set up for the clerical grades.

There were many other British employers at this time who
shared the unwillingness of the shipowners and the railway
directors to recognize unionism, though they did not necessarily
have any animus against it, if only because it had not yet shown
itself formidable. Arthur Chamberlain, Joseph's brother, may
perhaps be taken as their spokesman. He had no use, he told the
two French inquirers in 1902,[1] for the attack *The Times* had just
been making on the unions, if only because they were not so
powerful as all that. 'On this occasion *The Times* only represents
a clan of reactionary and discontented industrialists, who would
often be better occupied in putting their own house in order. . . .
It's not by a pigheaded resistance to the workpeople's claims
that a business man will get on. Often it will pay him to welcome
them,' and he went on to instance the benefits he himself had
obtained by reducing hours from ten a day to eight. But he
thought the workman's gains were due to economic progress,
not to the unions: these may have sometimes made a rise come
sooner or a cut later than it would have otherwise, but there was
not enough in that to outweigh their tyranny over the individual.
Nor would he recognize them himself. 'In the matter of strikes
I'm uncompromising. I shall always do all I can to avoid them:
I'm always ready to listen to claims, and discuss them in good
faith, and make every reasonable concession. I don't mean
discuss them with the unions, for that I've never done. I don't
recognize the unions as intermediaries between me and my workpeople, but my workpeople can send me a delegation of their
own number as often as they like. If we can't reach agreement,

---

[1] P. Mantoux and M. Alfassa, *La Crise du Trade-Unionisme* (Paris, 1903), pp.
275–81.

then it's a hard and fast rule with me never to give way once a strike has started. We give our people eight days in which to come back. If they don't by then, it is understood that they never will, at any time and on any account.'

10

Some of the lessons of history are taught by what did not happen. There were extensive tracts of British employment where by 1906 unionism had taken no broad or lasting hold. That was the case in all sorts of manufacturing outside engineering and textiles. It obtained also in domestic service, and throughout the distributive trades, and in the clerical employments of banking, insurance, and public administration, and in teaching. The farm workers made up one in seven of all wage-earning men, their wages were low, and more than once unions had sprung up among them and pressed for a rise; yet they had all died away. What was there in these employments to distinguish them from others, and explain why those who worked in them went without the unionism that elsewhere had grown up so naturally?

They may have refrained from it because they felt no impulse towards it, or because they did want it but for some reason or another were unable to achieve it.

We can be fairly sure that those of them who in the general estimation were middle class would just not have been drawn towards unionism, would indeed have thought it beneath them. They had a status which many of them had worked hard to achieve and whose outward marks of respectability they maintained by constant care, industry, and self-control. They saw their position as due to their own efforts and qualities, and would scorn to admit that they could not fend for themselves. Their pride in themselves they nourished by contrast, dwelling much on the uncouthness and fecklessness of the working class, keeping themselves apart. One mark of their superiority was a relative income much higher in those days than now: in a mining village the schoolmaster with £200 a year would have about three times as much as the miners, and it was steady too. Salaries, moreover, much more than wages, kept a customary level, and through the last quarter of the nineteenth century it had happened that a progressive fall in the cost of living had greatly

o

increased what a constant salary would buy. For any one recipient, moreover, it could always be better than constant: the middle-class diet contained the vitamin of hope, there were incremental scales, above all there were prospects of promotion. So the method of payment gave both shelter and stimulus to the sense of independence, and self-respect through self-help.

In their long hours the shop assistants had a disability of a kind that trade unions were specially suited to deal with, and there was in fact a beginning of unionism among them, especially in the co-ops, but it had not gone far. In some ways their job had the marks of middle-class employment: it was clean, it meant applying knowledge to a variety of problems, it usually brought personal contact with the employer, and could afford both a sense of satisfaction and an assimilation to professional status through meeting the needs of the customer personally. It also held out the hope of gaining independence by setting up for oneself. Since most shops were small, the ratio of employers to employed was high, and the relatively large number of alternative employers accessible to each assistant will have given him a greater sense of security. None the less he might have seen advantages in bargaining through a union. If he did, he would not have been held back as much as the book-keeper was by reluctance to put on the habit of a lower class, but there were other factors to stop his union growing. The assurance of mutual loyalty on which unionism depends arises most easily among those doing the same job, but shop assistants were divided among a score of jobs: they thought of themselves as grocers, drapers, ironmongers. In industries where the play of supply and demand upon wages was active and changeable, all the wage-earners could find themselves concerned at any one time with a common issue in their wage-bargain; but the shop assistant's wage was not under such pressure from the market, and his bargain over it depended more on factors particular to him and his employer than on those common to all assistants. A union in those days could hardly have given its members something tangible for their money and attracted recruits unless it could strike, but if a man is to take the risk of handing in his own notice he wants above all to be assured that the others are coming out too, and it is hard to be sure of that when men are working in twos and threes here and there. Many assistants were young women, and wherever these have worked they have had little interest in unionism, because they expect to leave employment before long when they get married. Most of these influences on the shop assistant acted also on the domestic servant.

The smallness of the firm will also help to explain why unionism had taken little hold in much of the manufacturing that was carried on in small workshops, even in great centres of industry. One may add that here, as in retailing, the employer had often begun as a wage-earner himself. There was a saying that the promoted workman made a hard master, but it seems unwarranted by the experience of Birmingham and the Black Country: the wage-earner who had set up for himself had to work hard, and expected no less of his men, but he worked alongside them, and was not removed from them by any distance of class; he spoke their language, and understood what it was like to be in their shoes. Some of the non-unionized plants, however, were quite big. Two circumstances seem to account for them. Many of them did not set on their workpeople the stamp of particular occupations such as provide a bond of union with those doing the same sort of work elsewhere, but employed them in a miscellany of tasks which went by the name of a process or department rather than an occupation. And then, even when they did employ men in occupations that were unionized elsewhere, they were often isolated — the one big firm, typically, in a market town. When a large number of men in the same plight are close together, their grievances grow by reverberation, they become more of a world in themselves set apart from other folk, they have a stronger trust in mutual support. But the workers in the one factory of a country town would see most of other people whose working lives and problems were different from one another and from their own.

The farm workers were different, if only because they had their own passionate and pathetic story of unionism. It can be traced back to the eighteenth century. It had its martyrs, legendary now in the history of British unionism: George and James Loveless, Thomas and John Standfield, James Brine, James Hammett, labourers of Tolpuddle in Dorset, who formed a union in 1833, and were charged with administering unlawful oaths. 'My Lord,' George Loveless wrote on the slip of paper he handed to the judge as the defence of them all, 'if we have violated any law, it was not done intentionally; we have injured no man's reputation, character, person or property; we were uniting together to preserve ourselves, our wives and children from utter degradation and starvation.' They were sentenced to seven years' transportation. What so stirred the country was that they had really been condemned for forming a trade union. It was nothing new for farm workers to be transported. In Botany Bay or Van Diemen's Land the men from Tolpuddle would have joined some five hundred others who had been transported for their part in the rising of the labourers three years before, burning ricks and breaking machines in many a southern county.

Twice later, when unionism in the towns was going through one of its periodic phases of enthusiasm and extension, the villages took the flame. In 1872 it burned up in Warwickshire: the labourers began to hold meetings, got Joseph Arch, hedge-cutter and local preacher, to lead them, struck for a rise, and held a demonstration in Leamington with Joseph Chamberlain's henchman on the platform. The movement spread through most of England south of the Trent, and a national union was formed that had seventy thousand members within the year. Wages rose generally by two or three shillings a week — that is, by about fifteen or twenty per cent. But in February 1874 some farmers of Suffolk began a lock-out which in its turn spread widely through the south; by July the union was broken, its funds exhausted, its ranks divided; a remnant struggled on as a benefit society. Fifteen years later the spirit of the New Unionism kindled the farm workers again, most of all in East Anglia, but unions sprang up too in several southern counties. The setting, we can see now, was far more favourable than that of twenty years before, for then the farmer's selling prices were about to turn drastically down, and now they began to rise; yet less was achieved. In 1893 a harvest ruined by drought was followed by a winter of severe frost; the membership dropped away. By the end of the century trade unionism among farm workers had practically ceased to exist.

It would in any case have found it hard to raise wages. The root of the difficulty was the pressure of population, higher in the villages than elsewhere, because here a higher rate of natural increase impinged upon an unexpansive economy. The villagers married early and had big families; fewer of the babies died than in the towns; every year there were more hands seeking work. But farming could not readily take them in: it was improving its methods, but the improvements usually decreased the amount of manpower needed per acre. The young people could edge themselves into work only by accepting a pittance; or else they must emigrate. That was recognized by Joseph Arch's union in the seventies — Arch claimed that in its first nine years it had helped seven hundred thousand bodies to leave the country — 'Away then, farm labourers, to New Zealand, Australia, and America! that is the only chance for you!' a leading article in the union journal cried. But the migration that took most of the villagers was to the growing towns and industrial areas of their own country. It was in the north that industry had been growing most rapidly, and wages in the countryside had long been far higher there than in the southern counties and East Anglia — a pound a week, say, against thirteen or fourteen shillings. In north and south alike the supply of labour for the farms varied inversely with the demand for labour in the towns, and in the annual hirings of the north the rates that the farm worker could get varied accordingly. But in the south, in villages more remote from industry, the competition of urban demand was not strong enough to break through the farmers' understanding that they should not pay more, except in the times of the most rapid rise in labourers' wages in the towns, such as 1871–2 and 1889–90. In such years trade unions could recruit in the villages because they could go in for a rise and get it. In others, only great strength of purpose and administrative resources could have kept unionism alive. Had these been present, the unions might well have obtained a somewhat higher wage in the south; but the farmers could not pass on higher costs in higher prices, and the bigger wage would have been obtained only for a smaller number of jobs.

Nor was there any strong will to succeed, any natural affinity for unionism in the villages. In part this was due to the backwardness of many labourers — 'they were obstinate, suspicious, and stupid,' Joseph Arch wrote, 'because they were so ignorant; their brains were ill-nourished and so they were dull; their uncultivated minds were like dark lanterns with a rushlight inside.'[1] Something was due also to the opposition of the farmers, squires, and parsons: there were as many humane men among them as elsewhere, but the power they had in the village some of them used vindictively, not least the parsons, for it was commonly the chapel folk who gave a lead to the union. But the happier side of the villager's life will also have had its influence. If he earned less than the townsmen, he did not have the chafing that they suffered in their working life. His own work, of its nature, brought him independence: he set about it in his own way, often alone by himself in the field; he was not driven by the foreman nor paced by the machine, but was drawn on by the claim of the job — the needs of the stock, the rhythm of the seasons. He met his employer face to face, and sometimes worked beside him: the farmer might be a hard man, but he was not a remote power, disquieting because impersonal. 'It is not unusual, indeed, for the farmer and his men to disagree,' we are told of the villages of the upper Thames,[2] 'and I have known them even to indulge in a hand-to-hand fight, and go on working as if nothing had happened; but there is never the dreadful hatred and long-pent-up smouldering passion about the farms as there is in the factory sheds.' The villages had a tradition too of a man's rights, and what a good employer should do. Theirs was an explicitly ordered society, too hierarchical for democratic liking, but giving each man due respect in his place, and uniting all in common interests and neighbourly observances. The world of Flora Thompson's *Lark Rise*, of W. H. Hudson's *Shepherd's Life* and Alfred Williams's *A Wiltshire Village*, is one of hardship, stringent poverty, and too often the workhouse at the close, but it is not one of ignominy, nor of dissatisfaction and fretting restlessness. The industrial wage-earner was drawn to unionism not for its use in the wage-bargain only, but less consciously, out of the vitamin-deficiencies of his working life and his conurbation. To the farm worker labour and neighbourhood alike brought, with exiguous incomes, deep-going satisfactions and reassurances.

[1] *Joseph Arch, The Story of his Life told by Himself* (1898), p. 247.
[2] Alfred Williams, *Villages of the White Horse* (1913), pp. 255–6.

CHAPTER IV

THE DEVELOPMENT OF
PUBLIC POLICY

I

In 1906 British industrial relations were already, in one sense, a mature system, the most mature in the world, for they now had more than a century of continuous practical experience behind them. But in another sense they could hardly be called a system at all, for they existed only where trade unions had grown up. As unions became stable and strong the employers learned to work with them, and a body of customary procedure developed. But where they were still weak and struggling, all was strife or uncertainty; and where they did not exist at all, there were no generally accepted means of settling disputes.

This is remarkable. Parliament had worked out detailed codes for the regulation of factories and mines, and had not been deterred from doing so by the convinced opposition of some of the employers. It had repressed truck and other abuses in the payment of wages. It had removed most of the old inequality of master and servant before the law. It had intervened in many ways to protect women and children in their working lives. To meet the special needs of the unions it had given them a novel, even an anomalous legal status. Yet it had not provided any means of imposing a settlement upon disputes between employers and employed. One might think that it would have been moved by a sense of the same need as it had evidently felt elsewhere, to counterbalance the excess of economic power; or by the opportunity to extend the province of law and order, and so spare the community the losses which disputes imposed. But in fact it was not.

This was not for lack of concern, or experiment: in fact, it had been at some pains to provide a kind of arbitration. Even in the days when membership of a trade union was forbidden by the Combination Acts, some Members had felt that they could not deny the workman the protection of a union against an unjust employer without giving him an alternative means of redress. 'The wisdom and humanity of Parliament', a Committee reported to the House in 1806, 'would shrink from sanctioning the Combination Law if it appeared to them, at the time of its enactment, likely to operate only in favour of the strong and against the weak: if it had any apparent tendency to secure impunity to oppressors, and to give undue advantage to the masters who can combine with little danger of detection, and who can carry their projects into execution with little fear of opposition.' The Combination Act of 1800 had in fact embodied a detailed scheme for arbitration, and when in 1824 the Combination Acts were repealed an Arbitration Act was passed to keep this scheme alive. Its main provisions were taken from another Act of 1800, passed at the request of the cotton weavers, to enable them to get awards that should be legally binding on their masters in disputes about the payment due for work that had been given out for them to do in their own homes; and it was so cast as to apply most directly to this sort of dispute about work already commissioned. As the years went by, the putting out system gave place more and more to factory work; and though Lord St Leonards endeavoured to improve and generalize the procedure, his elaborately drafted Act of 1867 was a dead letter from the outset.

But it would have been a short step to extend this kind of provision to deal with another kind of dispute, which is generally thought specially amenable to arbitration, the dispute about the interpretation of an existing collective agreement. Many other countries today, for example, divide industrial disputes, as our own Royal Commission on Labour did in the 1890's, into 'disputes of interest' and 'disputes of rights'. The first arise when a new agreement is to be made, and the basic wage-rates and conditions of work are at issue: the decision here must depend on market forces, and the organized strength of the parties; it cannot be reached by a judicial process. But when the main agreement has been concluded, disputes will in practice arise from time to time about its application to particular circumstances, and these questions of interpretation are more amenable to judicial procedure. Since, moreover, such disputes seldom extend widely, or raise major issues, the parties to them are more likely to be willing to commit themselves in advance to accept the award of arbitration. In the second half of the nineteenth century it had been common for British industrial disputes to be submitted by the agreement of both sides for decision by some eminent public figure; and in the 1860's one of these, the County Court Judge Rupert Kettle, developed a practice in the Black Country of having the agreed wages and conditions of work set out in detail, so that disputes about interpretation and application should as far as possible be obviated, and failing that be capable of judicial decision. The question naturally arose whether, so far as the established and successful practice of voluntary arbitration was concerned with these 'disputes of rights', it could not be made more general and more authoritative. By one of the provisions of Mundella's Act in 1872 Kettle's system was added to the existing procedure, which employers and workpeople could put themselves under if they chose: if they set up a joint board of the kind envisaged by Lord St Leonards' Act, they could now draw up a written statement of the agreed wages and conditions of work, and undertake that any dispute arising in the course of employment under this agreement should be submitted to the board, whose decision would now be legally enforceable by the penalties of the Act of 1824. In 1894 the Royal Commission on Labour, finding that there was an unsatisfied demand for the redress of grievances about the observance of agreements on wages and conditions of work, considered whether boards of this kind should not be established throughout the country, 'with legal powers to hear cases arising out of existing and implied agreements, or depending on the interpretation of trade customs, and to make enforceable decisions;'[1] and it concluded that, though a general scheme would be impracticable, 'it would be possible to give to Town and County Councils a power of taking the initiative in the creation of special tribunals for defined districts or trades.'[2]

This might have promoted an important development. Much arbitration of this sort of dispute was in fact going on in the latter half of the nineteenth century. More recent years have

[1] Royal Commission on Labour, 5th and Final Report, Part I (Cd. 7421 of 1894), para. 292.
[2] Ibid., para. 297.

seen in the United States the wide acceptance and successful
practice of such arbitration, which is now often regarded as
indispensable to avoid local stoppages. Yet in Britain, instead of
growing, it has diminished, and today, though it does exist, it is
not used widely. This is not because the relevant disputes do not
arise: they arise continually; but they are mostly settled by
direct negotiation between the unions and the employers.

Probably this has come about because British industry, unlike
American, has not developed the collective agreement in the
form most propitious to this kind of arbitration — the comprehensive written agreement governing wages and working
conditions in one plant. In British industry written provisions on
such matters commonly exist in some plenty, but they are
seldom codified in one systematic document, they are usually
supplemented by unwritten custom, and they most often apply
to the whole industry, or a district of it, and not to a particular
plant. The effect is to make the task of the arbitrator very hard.
Unlike his American counterpart, he does not have an explicit
code to apply, a code drawn up, moreover, with special reference to the plant in which the case has arisen; nor does he have
only the working practices of one plant — at any rate one plant
at a time — with which to familiarize himself, for his award will
be watched as a precedent of perhaps industry-wide application.
Experience showed that it might be necessary for both parties to
spend much time in instructing him in the technicalities of the
trade, and even then he might give an unworkable award. The
difficulty would be avoided if the arbitration were entrusted to
someone with a long experience in the industry, but how find
one such who would not be suspect of partiality? A joint board
of employers and workmen in the trade would avoid both difficulties, but be cumbrous. Far easier for the representatives of
the two sides, knowing the trade and speaking one another's
language, to seek agreement by direct negotiation.

Nor, where unions were strong enough to do this, did they see
much attraction in a settlement being legally enforceable. That
appealed only to workpeople whose organization was weak, and
when these demanded arbitration, what they were really asking
for was minimum wage regulation.

Thus there were two kinds of dispute — about the payment
due for work already given out, and the interpretation of existing

terms of employment — for which Parliament had provided schemes of arbitration; but no use had been made of them in modern times.

It was the same with the third and most important kind of dispute, that about the wages and conditions of work which should prevail henceforward. Had the will to use them been there, there were provisions in the Act of 1824 that might have been drawn upon to make a wage award binding, given always 'the mutual consent of both Masters and Workmen' to their being adopted; and this possibility was made clear by Mundella's Act of 1872, which enabled the parties to an agreement about wages and conditions of work to obtain the sanctions of the law not only for the terms of that initial agreement but also for any to be prescribed subsequently by an arbitration. The effect was 'that employers and workmen can practically, whenever they think fit, create, or adopt by agreement, a special tribunal, whose decisions will be binding in all trade disputes, and enforceable by the special powers of the Act of George IV', that is, the Act of 1824.[1] But none of them did.

So it came about that when the Royal Commission on Labour sat in 1891–4, it found no use being made of any means Parliament had provided for settling disputes.

2

This Commission made a wide survey of the conditions of work and the state of industrial relations, and when it came to its final report it had to decide what could be done to improve both. It divided into a majority, and a minority made up of the labour men.

They disagreed basically about the importance of improving the conditions of the wage-earner's working life. The majority thought the existing principles of factory legislation might be usefully extended in some respects — the Home Secretary might be empowered to include maximum hours in the regulations he drew up for the dangerous trades, all occupiers of workshops in certain districts or industries might be required to obtain a sanitary certificate for their premises, new ships should provide at least 120 cubic feet of forecastle space for each seaman instead

[1] Sir Frederick Pollock, in Appx. III to 5th Report of the Royal Commission on Labour, Part I (Cd. 7421 of 1894).

of the present 92, and so on. On unemployment, they thought buyers might reduce some present unnecessary seasonal fluctuations of demand if information were collected to show how orders in the aggregate were varying, and 'public authorities might during more prosperous times prepare plans for works that are needed, but are not urgent; and hold them in readiness for times of depression'.[1] But they were not fertile in suggestions, and generally reluctant to endorse any that would have meant more being done by government — they could not recommend a national system of employment exchanges, for instance, but thought the Labour Department should be prepared to give advice to any private association or local authority that might be considering setting up an exchange.

All this seemed to the minority only vague and scanty. Yet here they were standing before the very crux of their problem — the condition of the people: the people, harassed by unemployment, exhausted by long hours, struck down by industrial injuries and diseases, overcrowded, not less than five million of them sunk below Booth's poverty line. Sidney Webb drafted a report for Tom Mann; they got the other labour men to accept it, and it was sprung as a mine under a Commission that had thought itself unanimous. It propounded a thoroughgoing programme of action along three socialist lines, 'the national or municipal administration of such industries as can conveniently be managed socially, the regulation of private enterprise in industries not yet taken over by the community, and the public provision, through the taxation of rent and similarly unearned incomes, of educational and other facilities necessary for the mental and moral development of all classes of the community.'[2] But it had little to say about industrial relations. 'So long as the mass of the working population remain in their present economic condition, we see no prospect of entirely preventing the dislocation and suffering caused by strikes and lock-outs. We believe that so long as industry is carried on, not with a view to public needs, but for the sake of private profit, and so long as the land, the mines, and the instruments of production are in unrestrained individual ownership, it will be impossible to avoid industrial

<hr>

[1] Royal Commission on Labour, 5th and Final Report, Part I (Cd. 7421 of 1894), para. 312.
[2] Royal Commission on Labour, op. cit., p. 129.

disputes. We do not, therefore, think that any machinery for conciliation or arbitration will put an end to strikes and lock-outs.'[1]

Any recommendations, then, for the immediate improvement of industrial relations, would have to come from the majority. Not many suggestions had been made to it, and they were not far-reaching. One was that such trade unions and employers' associations as chose to should be enabled to acquire legal personality, so that the agreements they made would be legally binding. Another was that the strike and lock-out should be outlawed and arbitration be made compulsory; whether this was done or not, it was also proposed that state boards of arbitration should be set up to which parties might resort who could not reach a voluntary agreement. There were also suggestions for a Higher Council of Labour, made up of representatives of the employers, the unions, and the public, to promote mutual understanding and watch over matters of common interest. The majority were clear at least that they did not want to introduce any element of compulsion. They thought, for instance, that there might be some advantage in a move of 'a tentative and permissive character' whereby town and county councils would be empowered to set up industrial courts to hear such cases as the parties might bring before them voluntarily; but they did not want to create any general system of courts, still less give them jurisdiction over unwilling parties. Nor did they want to set up any new bodies that might compete or conflict with those that employers and unions had been working out for themselves.

It was in these voluntary institutions that they felt they had touched bedrock. A succession of witnesses had shown them how, industry by industry, up and down the country, parties to the wage bargain had been working out the methods that suited their own circumstances, and generally finding, if only by trial and error, a way to voluntary agreements honourably observed. The majority thought they should let well alone. Agreement was the essential, and that is a thing you cannot impose. The tasks and methods of industrial relations were repugnant alike to judicial procedure and imposed settlements. No award or decree could hold wages against the pull of market forces. Other subjects of dispute, such as the employment of non-unionists, or

[1] Loc. cit., pp. 144–5.

demarcation, were equally beyond the reach of positive law. And there was the less need to consider regulation when what was unregulated was working on the whole so well. In fact, though no one mind had planned or law ordained them, institutions and procedures had grown up that provided a healthy body politic for industrial relations. In the perspective of the evidence they had heard the majority found no cause for alarm nor need for intervention. Recent events had created an exaggerated impression of the forces making for change and conflict. Less noticed because so successful, voluntary negotiations between employers and unions were continuing to reach peaceful settlements and foster mutual respect. The aim of public policy must be, without interference, to uphold and extend them.

How it should do this was governed by the majority's finding that industrial relations were at their best when the organization on both sides was strong. This was their chief discovery. It has governed our administrative approach to industrial relations ever since.

In setting it out they agreed that the leaders of a strong union might sometimes initiate a strike as an act of policy when there would have been none if the rank and file had been left to themselves; and that when a struggle did come between two strong organizations, it was apt to be long and costly. But such conflicts came seldom, and the alternative in practice was 'continued local bickerings, stoppages of work, and petty conflicts'. Where organization was strong, strikes would at least not flare up out of some misunderstanding or fit of passion, but would be entered upon only after the issue had been thrashed out. The leaders of associations on either side took a broader view than the immediate parties to a dispute. When a union was strong, that inspired a respect in the minds of employers which made them more courteous to the union's spokesman, who responded with goodwill. Industrial relations had never been more harmonious than in some of the joint boards of conciliation or arbitration, but strong organization on both sides was a necessary condition for their working, because only when it was present would their decisions be observed.

It followed that the way forward for public policy was to welcome the continuing extension of organization, and help the parties to work out their own institutions, so far as that could be done by providing information and advice. There was, moreover, one point in particular at which government could give a helping hand: experience had shown the value, at the right moment, of conciliation, and the majority recommended that the Board of Trade should be empowered by law to inquire into disputes, use its good offices to bring the parties together, and, if both parties requested it, appoint an arbitrator. For the rest, the lesson of experience was negative: there was no useful extension of statutory powers over industrial relations. The present state of the law, which provided protection for individuals while otherwise largely withdrawing industrial disputes from the purview of the courts, was satisfactory. Procedures were best devised out of the experience, agreements were best reached and maintained out of the goodwill, of the parties themselves.

When Parliament came to legislate on its report, it agreed. There were in fact only two kinds of statutory provision that were thought worth discussion. One would give a fresh start to the existing but neglected principle that parties who both of them chose to ask for it in advance should be given legal sanction for the observance of an arbitral award. The first draft of the bill that became the Conciliation Act of 1896 contained some elaborate provisions to this end, but they went out in committee: employers' associations and trade unions that were well enough established to be able to agree on arbitration could usually get the award observed without putting their heads in the legal lion's mouth. The other proposal was that Parliament should require every county to set up what was called a Council of Arbitration, though really its main task was to conciliate: four Bills were brought in to this end. There was in fact a widespread creation of district conciliation boards at this time, and for a moment it might have seemed to contemporaries that they were in presence of a major development that would add a new organ to the body politic. It was, moreover, part of a movement of the times: Belgium in 1887, Germany in 1890, France in 1892, New Zealand in 1894, provided by law for the setting up of such boards. In Britain the London Chamber of Commerce led the way with a carefully constituted board — 'twelve members representing capital or employers to be elected by the council of the chamber; twelve members representing labour, to be elected by the employed; to these shall be added representatives from the separate trade conciliation committees as hereinafter referred to', and so on.[1] In many other towns the chamber of commerce set up a board of the same kind, and sometimes the town council took the initiative — Leicester, for instance, had a 'mayor's arbitration board'. In all, some three hundred local boards were set up. But nothing came of them. Nor was the President of the Board of Trade to succeed when in 1899 he proposed a national board to serve as a court of appeal, and hear cases which the local boards failed to settle: the Parliamentary Committee of the Trades Union Congress promised support, but the Employers' Parliamentary Council replied that they could not see their way to it. The trouble was, these boards had no powers: they could offer their good offices, but were not likely to be as successful in conciliation as a single person whom both parties to a dispute might consider and accept. The most it was suggested they might do if their good offices failed was to hold an enquiry, and publish a report on the causes of the dispute and what seemed to them fair terms of settlement — but what trade would want its neighbours poking their noses into its business in this way? The hope had been that disputants unable to agree but loath to fight it out would gladly come to a board for an impartial settlement; but for either side to be the first to suggest doing so was felt to be a sign of weakness; and no one could be compelled to come.

The upshot was the conviction that there was little that government could do, and what there was had been set out by the Royal Commission. The Conciliation Act of 1896 cut out as dead wood the whole of the three existing arbitration Acts,[2] and even dropped the provision which had appeared in its own earlier drafts that the Board of Trade might promote the establishment of local boards of conciliation. Henceforward the only statutory provision for arbitration was to be that the Board of Trade could appoint an arbitrator at the request of both parties: which it could have done anyhow. For the rest, the Board was authorized to inquire into disputes, endeavour to

[1] Reports of the Industrial Commission on Labour Organizations, Vol. XVII, p. 479, n. 1. (United States: 57th Congress, 1st Session, Document No. 186, 1901).
[2] The Act of George IV, 1824; Lord St Leonards' Act, 1867; Mundella's Act, 1872.

bring the parties together, and provide a conciliator if either party asked for one.

So it was decided that British industrial relations were to consist of voluntary negotiations between employers and employed. Government would not regulate them, save in so far as it had already provided a special legal status for the trade union. When conflicts broke out, it would provide no more than its good offices.

Most of the unions were content with this. Some of them, it is true, wanted compulsory arbitration — those who were making little headway with collective bargaining either through their own weakness or the refusal of employers to negotiate. When Ben Tillett was trying to hold the dockers together in a period of reaction after the fervour of 1889, year after year he put to the Trades Union Congress a resolution for it. Richard Bell of the Society of Railway Servants faced companies that would not recognize his union: he brought in a bill to provide that the wages of railwaymen should be fixed by a court of three, and either side could take the other to it. Such unionists were joined by reformers like Sidney and Beatrice Webb, who wanted compulsory arbitration to enforce minimum wages fixed according to a standard of human needs. But the stronger unions agreed with the chairman of the Royal Commission that lock-outs and strikes were 'the assertion of . . . essential liberties on the part of employers and workmen':[1] they were not prepared to give up their right and power to reject terms of employment they did not like. Their leaders would be preoccupied during negotiations with their responsibility for securing their members' observance of whatever agreement they might make, and would intensely dislike the prospect of being committed to accept terms before they knew what they were. So in the Trades Union Congress of 1906 the stronger unions defeated a resolution in favour of compulsory arbitration for the eighth year running.

But still we may wonder that compulsory arbitration did not commend itself to Parliament as a means of keeping the peace. At the end of the most obstinate conflicts work was resumed on some terms: were these necessarily so very different from those that an arbiter would have awarded at the outset, before all

[1] 5th and Final Report of the Royal Commission on Labour (Cd. 7421 of 1894). Observations appended by the Chairman and others, p. 117.

P

this suffering was incurred? In any one instance, either side might feel with reason that arbitration had given it less than it could have got by direct action; but over a run of years would any shortfalls of that kind come near what they themselves would have lost in stoppages? Above all, there was the interest of the public, of all those outside the dispute whose work or housekeeping it dislocated. The preamble to a bill of 1890 ran 'Whereas the present relations between capital and labour are often most seriously disturbed by strikes, which are prejudicial, on the one hand, to the producing power of the country, and, on the other hand, inflict material hardship upon those who live and sustain their families by labour; and as the majority of these trade differences are ultimately settled by arbitration after much injury has been inflicted upon the respective interests involved: be it therefore enacted' — that all these disputes shall be referable to a court of arbitration, 'whose decisions upon the questions of contention shall be considered final and binding upon all persons concerned.'[1] This was in fact the conclusion that public opinion was about to reach elsewhere in the face of some bitter conflicts. In the year when the Royal Commission reported in Britain, New Zealand outlawed strike and lock-out, and set up a court of arbitration to provide a settlement whenever the parties could not reach agreement between themselves. Here for the first time in history was a court, presided over by a judge with the status of a judge of the Supreme Court, set up to extend the rule of law and order over industrial relations. This was widely noticed. New Zealand became celebrated for a time as the land without strikes. Its example was said to underlie the project of a law for compulsory arbitration that the French socialist minister Millerand drew up in 1901. It was followed by Western Australia in 1900 and New South Wales in 1901. In 1904 the new Australian Commonwealth adopted an Act which outlawed strike and lock-out in all disputes extending beyond the limits of any one state, and set up a new Court to give binding awards instead.

If the British Parliament decided in 1896 not to take that road, it was partly because the cost of stoppages had not been great enough to make it grasp the nettle of enforcement. Stoppages so far had almost all been local: a trade union did

[1] Bill 174, ordered to be printed 3 March 1890.

not expect to have all its members out at once, and could hope to keep strike pay up for those that were; the public did not have its whole source of supply cut off. One instance there had been of a stoppage so extensive as to threaten other industries and consumers over a great part of the country with the loss of essential supplies — the lock-out of the Miners' Federation in 1893; but that had been settled by the conciliatory touch of Lord Rosebery. Otherwise stoppages had not threatened much dislocation, nor had they generally been disorderly.

The objection to forbidding them, moreover, rested not on doctrine but on practicability. In New Zealand and Australia the unions had been weak when the new step was taken: in fact, the title of the New Zealand act began 'An Act to encourage the formation of industrial unions'. Where there were many strong unions, experience suggested that no legal sanctions could make their members work for terms they did not accept. Increasingly the decisions of Boards of Conciliation were being repudiated by the men whose own leaders had agreed to them. Men would work only for terms they accepted as being as good as they could hope to get. Sometimes that acceptance would be wrung from them only by exhaustion; but it could never be ordained by Act of Parliament.

By the turn of the century, then, the British people had decided not to prohibit strike and lock-out, or provide any court to which employer and employed must submit their case if they could not reach agreement by themselves. Yet compulsory arbitration is not basically repugnant to British institutions. Twice it was to be accepted in Britain in time of war. If disputes had been more costly in the 1890's, or the international outlook more threatening, or the unions passing through a phase of weakness, Britain might have come to it then. The experience of those countries that have adopted it in time of peace suggests that when it comes, it comes to stay: everyone complains of it and no one will scrap it. The unions may become strong, but still do not see how they can dispense with it; the move from voluntary settlements to compulsory does not seem such a step in the dark as the move back again. It happened that the great debate on industrial relations which ended in the decision not to have compulsory arbitration in Britain was set going by the New Unionism of 1889, and completed by the Act of 1896; had it been conducted in not very different circumstances, or had the issue remained open to a later day, the decision could have been different, and with it all the later course of our industrial relations.

3

The conclusion that employers and trade unions had best be left free to work out their own agreements implied that if they could not reach agreement they should be free to stop work. But just at this time the law moved powerfully against the strike.

This was the work not of Parliament but of the courts. Parliament itself in the 1870's had drawn up a code whose object was to establish the legality of strike and lock-out while protecting those who would not take part. By 1870 the legality had become doubtful, because any strike or lock-out meant restraint of trade, which was unlawful, that is, a kind of action that the courts could not countenance even if it was not criminal: and a combination which had an unlawful purpose, or used unlawful means, was a criminal conspiracy. But two Acts[1] now put trade unions outside this rule. At the same time Parliament tried to provide that the right to combine in order to hold a strike should not impair the equal right to take no part in it. Public opinion had recently been stirred by reports of how blacklegs were harassed and set upon, sometimes even killed. So the second Act named and proscribed a number of ways in which an unpopular workman might be persecuted: not only by violence or intimidation, or injury to his property, but by persistently following him, hiding his tools, watching or besetting his house or workplace, and the like. But picketing was still allowed to this extent, that attending at or near the house or workplace 'in order merely to obtain or communicate information' was not to be deemed watching or besetting.

This last part of the settlement was soon narrowed, for the courts found that persuasion, however peaceful, went beyond it: pickets might say 'There's a strike on here' but not 'Please don't go in'. This mattered greatly to the unions, because pickets were indispensable in those days when there were more non-unionists working in the firms that were struck, and more men in need of

---

[1] The Trade Union Act, 1871, and the Conspiracy and Protection of Property Act, 1875.

jobs who could be brought in to take the strikers' place: the effect was, as one judge said, 'You cannot make a strike effective without doing more than what is lawful.' Though a later decision gave pickets more scope, their position before the law remained at the best uncertain.

But the settlement of the 1870's was to be upset in deeper-going ways than that: within thirty years the courts had made some strikes unlawful, and all perilous. This has been attributed to the judges' view of the public interest being distorted by the predilections of their class. Such bias is liable to afflict all of us, but we do not have to invoke it in order to explain what happened here. The trouble was that strikes often had other objects and effects than the restraint of trade which the laws of the 1870's had in view. Such restraint was typified by the stopping of a factory for so long as those who normally worked in it were unable to agree with the owners on their wages. This was as natural as the withholding of raw materials by suppliers pending agreement on a price. Only the fact of combination brought in some suspicion of coercion, of inequality of power, and then it was enough to ask, what would the inequality be if the workmen were not allowed to combine? But strikes often had more to them than this merely negative holding back by the two parties to a contract until they had settled its terms, and it was on these further issues that the new decisions were made.

One issue was serious because, though avoidable, it arose frequently in practice — striking in breach of contract. Employees who left their work without due notice were of course liable to be sued individually for damages, but the new law related not to them but to anyone who had induced them so to act. In 1853 the courts had held that to induce a breach of contract, unless there were some justification, was a tort. This now became the basis in law of a number of awards of damages against the officers of trade unions, who were shown to have called their members out well knowing that some of them would be leaving their work in breach of contract.

Another issue was serious because it called in question a basic strategem of the unions — bringing pressure to bear on persons who were not parties to the original dispute. A certain butcher employed non-unionists, and refused to dismiss them at the

behest of the union, which thereupon threatened to strike the
business of one of his customers if this customer would not stop
dealing with him. This was a case of what the Americans call
the secondary boycott. It raises different issues before public
opinion and the law. Public opinion thinks it hard that the
customer who had no part in the dispute should be made to
suffer because of it, and sees in this use of the power of the union
something that goes beyond the withdrawal of labour pending
agreement on its wage, and verges on racketeering. The law
asks, what is the predominant purpose, and if it is to protect
certain interests, are these legitimate? When a union says 'Our
members will not work for less than so much an hour', a strike
may result that damages the employer, and very likely other
people too, but inflicting this damage is not the predominant
purpose, which is to maintain or advance the price of the
members' labour, and this is a legitimate interest of theirs. But
if what the union says is 'We will strike your works unless you
do something to hurt this butcher who won't dismiss his non-
union men', the predominant purpose is not so clear: if it is not
just vindictive, then we must find it in the general strategy of
enforcing the closed shop, that is, stopping men who do not join
the union getting jobs, and is the interest of the members in that
a legitimate interest?

What was essentially this problem, though in a different
setting, came before the courts in 1892, when the House of
Lords had to consider the activities of a combination of shipowners which had been using the boycott and black list to drive
out interlopers and keep certain traffic to its own members: the
Lords decided that the predominant purpose was the pursuit of
trading interests and that the maintenance of a monopoly was a
legitimate interest of the members. But nine years later the case
of the union and the butcher's customer came to the Lords, and
then they found that the predominant purpose was vindictive
and that the maintenance of a monopoly — the closed shop —
was not a legitimate interest. To the layman it is hard to see how
the cases can be distinguished. He must think that the difference
between the judgments lay in the views the judges held about
the substantial social and economic merits of the two cases: that
monopolizing and exclusive tendencies, if nowhere to be
encouraged, did not seem clearly harmful to the public interest

as they operated in the shipping cartel, but as they operated in the trade union they did.

None the less, the courts would still have been unable to mulct the members of the union in damages, if it had not been for another development of the common law. If any one employee of the butcher's customer had given him due notice that he would not go on working for him unless he gave up dealing with the butcher, that employee would have done nothing unlawful. But suppose two employees did this in concert? The answer began to be given that they had entered into a civil conspiracy. The law of civil conspiracy had lately been developed in the courts: it made any combination illegal whose object was something other than the advancement of the legitimate interests of its members, or in the opinion of the Court was unjustifiable. Henceforward men like the employees of the butcher's customer who struck or threatened to strike with any object other than holding out for the terms and conditions of their own employment were liable to be mulcted in damages.

There remained the biggest blow of all. So far, the new law had provided grounds for action against particular men — officials calling workmen out in breach of contract, particular workmen deemed to have entered into a civil conspiracy with one another; but now the courts decided that an action for damages could be brought against a trade union itself. Hitherto the union had been regarded as an association without legal personality — it was not an individual, nor a partnership, nor a corporation. However clearly some action would have given an employer grounds to recover damages if it had been taken by, say, a limited liability company, he could not sue if it was taken by a trade union: if he did try to, the union could simply ask to have its name struck out.

But employers who saw a union coming in from outside, and organizing a strike of their 'own men', particularly resented this immunity: here was a body that gratuitously inflicted heavy losses on them, and had great funds out of which to make reparation, but could snap its fingers at them. So the need for changing this part of the law was much discussed in the 1890's; should not unions be given the right to sue and the liability to be sued? The chairman of the Royal Commission on Labour of

1891–4, in a published draft of the observations which he and some other members appended to the report, suggested that unions should be made legally responsible for their actions, including those of their agents. The proposal was omitted from the final draft, but continued to be kept before the public. In 1900, during a strike on the Taff Vale railway, members of the Society of Railway Servants induced some blacklegs sent down from London to break a contract of service they had made before they set out. It happened that the manager of the railway had a passion for litigation. Against legal advice, he sought an injunction against the Society, to stop picketing. The High Court granted it. The Court of Appeal dissolved it, on the ground that the Society had no legal personality. But in July 1901 the House of Lords restored it.

This is the most celebrated judgment in the history of trade union law. The Court of Appeal had argued, on grounds which seem unassailable, that the legislature would not have been at pains as it was in the Act of 1871 to provide for trustees who could sue and be sued in matters respecting the property of a trade union, if all the time it had intended that the union itself should be able to sue and be sued too. But the Lords rested essentially upon general considerations of public policy. 'Has the legislature', asked Lord MacNaughten, 'authorized the creation of numerous bodies of men capable of owning great wealth and of acting by agents with absolutely no responsibility for the wrongs they may do to other persons by the use of that wealth and the employment of those agents? I cannot find anything in the Acts of 1871 and 1876 to warrant or suggest such a notion.' Even those who welcomed the judgment treated it as not declaring the existing law so much as creating a new and better one.

The effect on the unions was overwhelming. Henceforward if any officer or member committed any actionable wrong, the funds of the union might have to pay for it. The right to strike was not formally rescinded, for it was still thinkable that a strike should take place in which there was no breach of contract and no obstructive picketing, and in which the only object was the advancement of the legitimate interests of the strikers themselves. But these conditions could never be counted on: any dispute breaking out locally was liable to involve the union in heavy damages. Some employers seemed intent on driving their advantage home. The Taff Vale Railway, coming back to the charge, recovered £23,000 from the Railway Servants, who also lost £19,000 in costs. A builder refused to induce his foreman to join the House and Ship Painters and Decorators, or dismiss him if he would not; the union withdrew his men, some of them in breach of contract, and threatened another firm with a strike if it gave him a sub-contract: he recovered £322 from the union. Most remarkable, the Glamorgan Coal Co. and other proprietors sued the South Wales Miners' Federation for withdrawing men on stop-days. Those days were a long-standing institution, whereby when the spot price of coal was falling the men took a day off to shorten supplies; and this was thought to be not unwelcome to the masters. But now the House of Lords found that 'to conspire to procure persons to break contracts is manifestly unlawful; that there was no legal justi-fication in the fact that the defendants had no malice against the plaintiffs, and honestly believed that keeping up the prices of coal would benefit employers as well as workmen; and that the defendants were liable in damages'. And so on. The Courts continued to make distinctions, and dismissed some of the actions brought: when a colliery company sought £125,000 damages from the Yorkshire Miners because of a strike, originally unofficial, in two pits, the Court of Appeal and the Lords held that the union was not responsible for the acts of its branches, nor of its officers when *ultra vires*. But the im-pression was strong and the threat real that any strike would result in the union's funds being mulcted, and there were few strikes.

Out of that Yorkshire dispute, moreover, another judgment arose that seemed to show how far the Lords would go to have the law on the unions. A member of the Yorkshire Miners sought an injunction to stop it issuing strike pay in contravention of its own rules. The Act of 1871 had provided that nothing in it should enable any Court to entertain any legal proceedings with the object of directly enforcing any agreement for the application of a union's funds to provide benefits to members; but now the Lords held that issuing the injunction would not be *directly* enforcing any agreement, and granted it.

The working man believed that 'the Lords' were out to break

his union; and made a note of it. The Labour Representation Committee began to win by-elections. By 1906 the number of unions affiliated to it had trebled.

There was a great debate. A number of issues of statute and common law had come up for reconsideration together — the law of picketing, the doctrine of predominant purpose, the doctrine of civil conspiracy, the legal personality of trade unions. But the contrast between the treatment of the shipping cartel and the trade union under the existing law showed that the real issue was one of public policy. Here, in the unions, were combinations formed to protect men who otherwise, it had been generally agreed, would suffer from an inferiority of economic power. It was generally agreed that these unions had done much good. But they could use their power to strike in ways that were hurtful and oppressive to others, and not solely to protect the terms and conditions of their members' employment, but to advance remoter purposes of strategy and power. Where did the public want to draw the line between legitimate pursuit of the members' own interests and oppressive interference with other people's? and could the law be formulated so that any line would in the practice of the courts lie where it was meant to, and stay put? Those were the substantial issues. It was unfortunate that the debate was precipitated by the Taff Vale case, in which the main issue was the legal personality of the trade union, so that the horns of the dilemma seemed to be, shall unions be made liable to be sued for the wrongful acts of their agents, in which case they will in practice hardly be able to strike at all, or shall their immunity be reasserted, in which case powerful and active combinations will be permitted to hurt others with complete impunity? When the question was posed in that way, practical men could only try to find some middle way in some form of limited liability — by providing, for instance, that only the general or fighting funds of the unions and not funds set aside for benefit purposes should be liable to find damages. The problem would have been better posed as the United States has posed it since: can we distinguish between those forms of union activity that are and those that are not in the public interest — between the ordinary strike and the secondary boycott, for instance, or between the union shop and the closed shop?

4

By 1906 there was only one way in which government was exercising any control of wages: a clause in the contracts it gave out required the contractor to pay the workman who did the work the wages generally accepted for competent workmen in the district. Local authorities often placed their own contractors under the same obligation. But save for any work they might choose to do under such clauses, British employers were at perfect liberty to pay any wages for which men, women or children could be found to work. They remained so although for fifteen years now it had been publicly recognized that the payment of exceptionally low wages was part and parcel of the grave evil called sweating.

Public attention began to be specially directed towards sweating in the 1880's, when the general rise in the standard of living of the wage-earners threw into relief the misery of certain groups whose earnings remained appallingly because exceptionally low. These workers were found especially in bootmaking, tailoring, furniture making, and chain and nail making. Many, but by no means all, were working under subcontract. They worked in small workshops or their own homes: victims not of the factory system but of its absence. The sweated trades were distinguished, said the Committee of the House of Lords which examined them in 1889–90, by 'a rate of wages inadequate to the necessities of the workers or disproportionate to the work done; excessive hours of labour; the insanitary state of the houses in which the work is carried on. These evils can hardly be exaggerated. The earnings of the lowest classes of workers are barely sufficient to sustain existence. The hours of labour are such as to make the lives of the workers periods of almost ceaseless toil, hard and often unhealthy. The sanitary conditions under which the work is conducted are not only injurious to the health of the persons employed, but are dangerous to the public. . . . We make the above statements on evidence of the truth of which we are fully satisfied, and we feel bound to express our admiration of the courage with which the sufferers endure their lot, of the absence of any desire to excite pity by exaggeration, and of the almost unbounded charity they display towards each other in endeavouring by gifts of food and other kindnesses to alleviate any distress for the time being greater than their own.'[1]

The cause of this misery emerged fairly clearly from contemporary inquiry: these workers were helpless, either to make use of the labour market and move to better jobs elsewhere, or to stand up for themselves and hold out for a minimum where they were. Without training or resources, incapable of finding or perhaps keeping better paid employment, they were equally incapable of uniting to demand from employer or buyer a price which would yield them a subsistence in such work as they could do. Under the lash of hunger, they could only keep themselves alive from day to day by taking what work was given to them at whatever price the putter-out set on it, or by offering their products to the public at whatever price would enable them to meet the competition of others no less pressed to sell. In technical terms, their work was in inelastic supply to particular employments, and they had no reserve or transfer price. Beatrice Webb, who herself had worked in sweat shops of the East End, showed that it was not the contracting system that was the cause of the sweated workers' misery, nor did the contractor or subcontractor for whom they worked usually wax fat at their expense: those of them who sold direct to the public were no better off, while other types of worker were earning good wages under sub-contract. It was rather that the contracting system was often the only way in which work could be brought to them at all. But it did none the less expose them to a special danger: for the contractor went as low as he reckoned he must to get the contract, and then set their wages accordingly, and they were too exhausted and unlettered to combine in a union which would insist on a minimum rate of wages and so put a floor under all the tenders. 'It is mostly in public contracts that they grind down the worker,' a journeyman tailor of Glasgow told the Lords' Committee.[2]

If those were the causes of the trouble, what was the remedy? Something could be done by changing the law so as to bring the foetid workrooms under more effective sanitary inspection; but the root of the matter was the starvation wage, and remedies for this were harder to find. Everyone agreed that whatever raised

---

[1] Fifth Report from the Select Committee of the House of Lords on the Sweating System (169 of 1890), paras. 175–9.
[2] Fourth Report (331 of 1889), p. 10.

the stamina and resources of the sweated workers themselves
would help to break the vicious circle of poverty breeding
helplessness, and helplessness breeding poverty: but the question
was how to make a start. The House of Lords Committee
thought that co-operative productive societies might help, and
for the rest could only hope for the growth of 'well-considered
combination amongst the workers'.[1] Here again was an inquiry
reaching the conclusion that the best practicable development
of industrial relations lay in the growth of responsible trade
unions.

Yet, at the best, this growth would take much time, especially
as so many of these workers never met one another but worked
each in his own home; and in the meantime the only way in
which wages could be raised was by some imposed regulation.
But from this the best informed and most humane thought of the
time drew back. The presumption of the most authoritative
economic doctrine was strongly against it. John Stuart Mill, for
example, still in 1890 by far the most influential British economist, had devoted two pungent chapters of his *Principles* to popular
remedies for low wages, and demonstrated, as he thought with
complete finality, that one fatal flaw was in them all: so long at
least as the labourers retained their present tendency to pro-
create, whatever raised their income, or offered them a
guarantee of maintenance despite the unemployment which
higher wages would cause, would lift some of the present checks
on procreation, and lead to such an increase in their numbers as
must force down their earnings again to a level at which 'death
or prudence' sufficed to stop further growth. 'No remedies for
low wages have the smallest chance of being efficacious, which
do not operate on and through the minds and habits of the
people.' It is true that Mill himself in his last years had modified
his conclusions, and that since his death in 1873 other economists
had reached a very different view of the labour market. But the
new ideas had not yet percolated far, and in the meantime the
old presumption that interference with the market rate of wages
could only be mischievous was reinforced by the working maxim
that though restrictions on the work of women and children
were permissible, there should be no interference with the terms

---

[1] Fifth Report from the Select Committee of the House of Lords on the Sweating
System (169 of 1890), para. 186.

on which grown men chose to sell their labour, no regulation even of their hours of work.

Beyond these general principles, and giving pause to practical reformers who would not have been deterred by abstract doctrine alone, were all the awkward possibilities which presented themselves as soon as the enforcement of a higher wage was considered as something that might be actually done here and now for a given group of workers. Since the employer or middleman in the sweated trades was generally not making any great profit himself but was pressed down by competition no less than his workers, he could pay higher wages only if he charged more for his product: but then, would the public buy it, or would he not be undercut by the factories, and especially, in a country devoted to free trade, by the foreigner? Even, moreover, if a number of workers kept their employment at the higher wage, there would be some slower or less skilful workers whom it would no longer pay to employ: if a man could get work at 4d. an hour, are you to say he must not work at all because no one should have less than 6d.? There was also the practical problem of delimitation: no practical man supposed there could be a general or national minimum wage, or maximum working day, but short of that, how could you confine regulation to particular groups or trades or places, without driving industry away, just as the silk industry had once been driven out of Spitalfields, and without inviting undercutting from unregulated workers who would now find it worth while to enter the trade? This problem was specially vexatious at a time when differences between the rates of pay for a given kind of work in different places were generally much greater than they are today. In one trade factories paying relatively good wages might be found side by side with sweat shops and homework in which earnings were miserable. The accepted rate for carpenters was 10½d. an hour in London and less than 5d. at Falmouth. How could any uniform rate be made effective? If separate rates were promulgated for different sections of a trade, how could they be arrived at, and if they raised the cost of labour in any section, would they do anything but drive its trade away to another?

These were all serious questions. In the light of experience, we can now make some assessment of their practical consequence, but we cannot look down on those who found them hard to answer in 1890, for they are of the same kind as always perplex us when some change in our economic arrangements is under consideration. We can draw up the list of eventualities to be considered, but we cannot quantify them; we cannot tell in advance which of a number of equally real possibilities will be substantial and which inconsiderable in practice; we can foresee the difficulties of administration, but cannot tell which will be solved as we go along and which be obstinate. In 1890 the general presumption was that the conceivable difficulties of wage regulation would in fact prove insuperable. The House of Lords Committee did not even consider the possibility of attempting it.

There was one way, however, in which it thought something effective might be done, not to enforce a general minimum, but to prevent the wages paid to the weaker workers being depressed below whatever rates prevailed in the greater part of the trade. 'We are glad to find', it said, 'that efforts are being made to put an end to the grave scandal of sweating in the making up of Government contracts for clothing and accoutrements': it was a point to attack, both because some of the worst sweating occurred in contract work, and because public authorities ought to set an example. The Committee endorsed no particular proposal, but exhorted all public authorities to 'take every precaution in their power to ensure fair and reasonable terms to the worker'. 'Practical experience alone', they added, 'can determine how this result may best be effected.'[1] What came of this is of interest, because it provided the only kind of action government took to influence wages.

Two possible forms of such action were being tried out about the time the Committee reported. One was to insert actual wage-rates in the contract, and require the contractor not to go below them. The public authority might fix these rates out of its own knowledge of trade practice, or might ask those who tendered to state the rates they proposed to pay, and select its minima in the light of these statements. The London County Council included in each contract one schedule of wage-rates and overtime rates, believed to cover all the trades required, and another of maximum hours of labour. The second form of

[1] Fifth and Final Report from the Select Committee of the House of Lords on the Sweating System (169 of 1890), para. 203.

stipulation did not prescribe wage-rates or hours, but only required that, for example, 'the wages paid in the execution of this contract shall be those generally accepted as current in each trade for competent workmen in the district where the work is carried out.' This is more comprehensive, and flexible; liable to be indefinite, and consequently hard to enforce; yet also attractive, because simple enough to be generally enjoined and adopted.

It was this form, consequently, that Parliament endorsed, by a resolution agreed to without a division in 1891: 'In the opinion of this House it is the duty of the Government in all Government contracts to make provision against the evils which have recently been disclosed before the House of Lords' Sweating Committee, and to insert such conditions as may prevent the abuse arising from sub-letting, and make every effort to secure the payment of the rate of wages generally accepted as current for a competent workman in his trade.' This became known as the Fair Wages Resolution, though it required wages to be fair only in the sense that they should be not less than those generally prevailing, whether high or low, in the trade, and, in practice, the district. The Resolution was observed not only by Whitehall but by many local governments. The drafting of the necessary clauses, and still more their interpretation and enforcement, gave much difficulty, but the general view was that there was a change for the better: within the considerable ambit of work for central and local government sweating was checked and more work was given to the good employers. If in one way the Resolution did not go very far, moreover, in another it marked the acceptance of a principle, and the invention of a procedure: government could hardly itself fix wages, but where in a given trade and district certain wages were recognized as reputable, it could require that they be paid by all employers.

The recognized terms would often be considered such because they had been worked out by employers' associations and trade unions. Implicit, therefore, in the Fair Wages Resolution was the principle that government might intervene to raise wages, in so far as it required all employers to observe terms which had been agreed between representatives of workmen and employers, and which therefore might be expected to be high enough to provide a living wage, but not so high as to ruin the trade.

Evidently this principle might provide a way of stopping some of the sweating which the Fair Wages clause did not touch.

The same possibility was also implicit in the hope of the House of Lords Committee that trade unions would grow up among the sweated workers: for why should a rise of wages negotiated by a trade union be welcome, when one imposed by government would be dangerous? If the difference were only one of flexibility, and the nice adjustment of rates by those who had a close knowledge of the trade, then witnesses before the Committee had suggested how government could avail itself of these advantages of voluntary bargaining. Lewis Lyons was a tailor's machinist, who had kept his own paper, *The Anti-Sweater*, going for eight numbers: he suggested that 'the rate of wages should be fixed by a Board of Tailors or a Board of Bootmakers to rule that particular trade. In the old City Guilds each company had its board where disputes of trade were settled by them. . . . This Board of that particular trade would know the value of the labour time, the amount of time expended in producing a certain commodity; this board understanding the technicalities of it would know what rate of remuneration should be given for that labour time.' 'Do you mean', he was asked, 'that the masters and men should form a kind of board to decide what the rate of wages should be?' 'That could be done,' he said.[1] William Hoffman, once a foreman in a boot factory, and now a journalist on *The Shoe and Leather Record*, made the suggestion, which he thought would ultimately abolish the whole of the sweating system, 'that there should be a similar arrangement to that which was accepted and entered into at Northampton last year. There employers and workmen, after considerable conflict, have agreed that there shall be a uniform rate of wages, that is, that a certain boot of a certain description is worth so much making, whether it is made for A or for Z. By this means competition cannot be carried on at the point of prices, which is exacted simply from the wages of the men.' Northampton had not only this uniform price list, but a joint board of arbitration. But both had been instituted only after a strike which the union had been able to sustain for over three months.[2]

[1] First Report from the Select Committee of the House of Lords on the Sweating System (361 of 1888), Qs. 1901, 1904, 1905.
[2] First Report from the Select Committee of the House of Lords on the Sweating System (361 of 1888), Qs. 1129, 1135, 1140.

Q

We have seen how this sort of joint board had long existed in Great Britain, and come to be regarded as the best way of fixing wages. When strife broke out in unsettled trades, or when un-organized workers were found to be ill-paid, the natural prescription was to extend the procedure which was working so well already.

As far back as 1848, in the first edition of his *Principles*, John Stuart Mill noted among popular remedies for low wages a plan 'which has found many advocates among the leaders of the operatives, ... that councils should be formed, which in England have been called local boards of trade, in France, 'conseils de prud'hommes' and other names: consisting of delegates from the workpeople and from the employers, who, meeting in fair con-ference, should agree upon a rate of wages, and promulgate it from authority, to be binding generally upon employers and workmen.' But where the workpeople had no effective union, this development was possible only if Parliament took two steps: it must set up the joint board by its own initiative, itself pro-viding the spokesmen whom the workpeople could not find for themselves; and it must compel all employers to pay not less than the board prescribed. But this was intervening in the labour market much farther than any Victorian Parliament would think it prudent to go.

None the less it remained a traditional policy among the unions, and in the 1880's it received a new impetus, when the spotlight was turned on sweating. At this time also it was given a definite form in the mind of the remarkable man by whom it was later to be persistently brought before Parliament.

In 1885, Sir Charles Dilke had been generally regarded as a future Prime Minister. Grandson of a man of letters who had been proprietor of *The Athenaeum* and friend of Keats, Hood and Lamb, son of one of the principal organizers of the Great Exhibition, he had had a brilliant career at Cambridge, and gone round the world, and written a book about his philosophy of empire which had had an immediate success. At the age of twenty-five, in 1868, he headed the poll in the new constituency of Chelsea. He was assiduous in the House, a student with an unusual capacity for work, a Radical with his own convinced line in home policy and a special knowledge of foreign affairs. After the election of 1880 Joseph Chamberlain wrote to offer him 'a thorough offensive and defensive alliance. . . . My own feeling is that if you are stronger than I am in the House, my influence is greater than yours out of it, and therefore that, together, we are much more powerful than separated; and that in a short time, if not now, we may make our own terms'[1] — that is, terms with Gladstone. In fact, in 1882 Gladstone came to the conclusion that it was Dilke who would have to succeed him as Leader of the House, and in order to give him training he brought him into the Cabinet as President of the Local Government Board. 'I never knew a man of his age' — Sir George Trevelyan wrote — 'hardly ever a man of any age — more powerful and admired than was Dilke during his management of the Redistribution Bill in 1885.'[2] In 1886 a week of evidence in a divorce case indicated that he had made a practice of illicit relations. *The Times* recorded his fall, shameful, complete and irretrievable.

But some of his friends stood by him. Joseph Chamberlain supported him with courage and tenderness during the trial, and never broke their friendship off. There was also a widow with whom he had an understanding known as yet only to a few friends — Emilia Francis Strong, whose marriage with Mark Pattison, the Rector of Lincoln College, had suggested to George Eliot the marriage of Dorothea and Casaubon in *Middlemarch*. The news of the charge against Dilke reached her when she was lying sick of typhoid at a hill-station of Madras: she cabled to *The Times* the announcement of their engagement. They were married, with Joseph Chamberlain as best man, before the case came into court, and they remained inseparable until she died in 1904. Through her, Chamberlain persuaded Dilke to come back to politics. In 1892 he was returned for the Forest of Dean, and he sat for it until his death in 1911. From the miners in his new constituency he went on to meet miners in many other fields, and Mabon organized a torchlight procession to welcome him to the Rhondda. He became a spokesman of the unions. 'From 1870 to this date,' Dr Gore, then Bishop of Birmingham, said in 1910,[3] 'one man has stood for all the great causes of industrial progress, whether for the agricultural

---

[1] Gwynn and Tuckwell, *Life of Sir Charles Dilke* (1917), I, 304.
[2] Gwynn and Tuckwell, op. cit., II, 159.
[3] Gwynn and Tuckwell, op. cit., II, 342.

labourers, or in the textile trades, or in the mining industries, or with the shop assistants. That man is Sir Charles Dilke.'

Part of this work was his advocacy of Trade Boards. Several sources had contributed to his conception of them. One was John Stuart Mill — not the Mill of the *Principles*, but Mill in the last four years of his life. In Avignon he had read the young Dilke's book of travel and empire, and wrote to the unknown author, 'it is long since any book connected with practical politics has been published on which I build such high hopes of the future usefulness and distinction of the writer.'[1] When he came back to town he at once got Dilke elected to the Political Economy Club, and the two entered into the relation of master and disciple. We do not know what views Mill was then propounding about wages, but we do know that his mind had moved on from its old anchorage, and Dilke's own incorrect statement[2] that Mill in his *Principles* considered the possible application of Trade Boards to home work, and said that cheapness of goods is not desirable when it is due to low wages, may well indicate the drift of Mill's thought during their discussions between 1869 and 1873.

A second source of Dilke's conception lay in Australia, which he had visited in his world tour. To the Jubilee in 1887 came Alfred Deakin, then leader of the liberals and Chief Secretary of Victoria, later to be prime minister of the Australian Commonwealth, and he discussed with Dilke a proposal for trade boards which was being advanced by the uncrowned king of Victoria, David Syme. Son of a Scots schoolmaster, Syme had trained for the ministry, but he lost his faith, worked on a Glasgow newspaper, then set out to seek his fortune in the goldfields, first of California, then of Australia. He found none, for the rich claim he staked at Mount Egerton was jumped; but eventually he did become rich, as editor and proprietor of a Melbourne newspaper, in which he championed the interests of the urban wage-earner in Australia against the landowners and the importers. He wrote an essay, *Outlines of an Industrial Science* (1876), which sets out to show that wrong conclusions are reached when economic processes are lifted out of their social setting for

---

[1] Gwynn and Tuckwell, op. cit., p. 70.
[2] Report of the Select Committee on Home Work (246 of 1908), Minutes of Evidence, Qs. 3920-2.

separate study, and pleads that government should consciously guide and direct economic affairs, in the interests of justice and development. 'Is it desirable,' he asked, 'from an individual point of view, that a certain act should be performed? Then the individual should perform it. Is it desirable, from a social point of view, that a certain act should be performed? Then the state should perform it.' There are a science and an art, he said, of industry, as of other activities, and 'the art of industry is Industrial Legislation'. More particularly on wages, 'all attempts', he wrote, 'to settle the wages difficulty by Supply and Demand have hitherto ignominiously failed. If capital takes advantage of labour at one time, labour takes advantage of capital at another. . . . In all disputes of this nature the claims of capital and of labour should be taken into consideration and equitably adjusted. . . . The true solution of the wages difficulty is to be found in the Courts of Arbitration, where the principles I contend for are fully acted upon.'

When Deakin got home he drew up a bill for trade boards, which he sent to Dilke, and in 1896 the first boards were set up in Victoria. Two years later 'the subject was supposed to be sufficiently ripe in Britain', Dilke said, and he had a bill for British trade boards drafted on the same lines.

There was yet another source of Dilke's advocacy: his wife. As a girl, she had been a pupil of Ruskin, and her life's work was the study of the history of French art. She was said to be the best dressed woman in England. But she worked assiduously for the protection of women in their working life — especially for those in the dangerous trades, handling white lead and phosphorus, but also for those in every kind of sweated work. It was to her unwearied persistence, no less than that of her husband, that Beatrice Webb attributed the final establishment of the trade board.

So, we may reflect, among the properly intellectual sources of the trade board movement were the minds of Mill, and of Ruskin, and of a Scots theologian in the vortex of a gold rush. As Mill's life went on, he came to believe more and more in the capacity of human society to grow, and of human nature to grow with it, so that he could no longer predict men's reactions to some new measure with confidence, and would allow that the measure might do something to change the men themselves.

Ruskin, though he did not understand the political economy he assailed, was really saying something valid and necessary — that an abstract science cannot of itself prescribe rules of conduct, which must have regard to the whole nature and object of man. It may have been the workings of the quest for gain among men abstracted from the ties of a settled society that convinced Syme of the need to intervene in the market as might be necessary to build a good society. The common element was the thought of intervention as constructive.

The bill which Dilke had drafted was first printed in 1900. It followed the familiar pattern of a Conciliation Board with an independent chairman, but provided that the representatives of employers and employed might be appointed by the Home Secretary, and that when a board fixed the minimum rates they should forthwith be binding on all employers, under penalty of fine, and be enforced by the factory inspectors. No trades were specified, but the Home Secretary was empowered after inquiry to appoint a board for any trade in any district.

The bill was printed again annually, but there was never a second reading debate. At the outset of 1906, there it rested. Perhaps interest had waned since the great inquest into sweating sixteen or more years ago had found no practicable remedies except the Fair Wages Clause. The trade unions meanwhile had become concerned mainly with their own position before the law, and the restoration of the effective right to strike. Nor was Dilke himself a powerful advocate. Even at the height of his influence there had been noted in him a lack of the power to kindle enthusiasm; and now, though he was assiduous and well informed, he must have carried with him also some aura of ineffectiveness, diffused by the knowledge that he was barred from office. His speeches lacked power; in personal relations, though he was not ostracized, he would have met some distance and reserve. Yet still, he may have been the best advocate available. There was probably no member of the House who in his own or his constituents' behalf would have opposed a rise in sweated wages, in itself; but if it was to be brought about by the intervention of Parliament, then it aroused apprehensions in the House, it appeared as the thin end of a wedge, it raised a forbidding issue of principle. A new House, a new campaign against sweating, and a new limitation of the project, had to come before action was taken. In the meantime, save only for the Fair Wages Clause, the fixing of wages remained outside the scope of public policy.

5

Once again it is instructive to reflect on what did not happen. Parliament had done much to give business a framework. It had provided general limited liability, and developed the law of the company, regulating the functions of shareholders and directors. It had intervened within the firm to impose a factory code for safety, health and welfare; it had limited the hours of women and children, and latterly, on the railways, even those of some men; it had regulated the mode of payment of wages; it had developed the law of the contract between employer and employed. But it had not attempted to provide any general form of constitution for the firm. In recent years various countries have at least tried to enact some elements of this sort of constitution. The United States, for example, has provided for the holding of elections among the workpeople of a firm, to decide which union shall have the right to represent them, and has laid the management under a legal obligation to negotiate with the one they choose; it has also promulgated something of a code of behaviour within the firm by proscribing a number of unfair labour practices. Other countries have laid firms under an obligation to provide some form of representation of their employees, or enter into joint consultation with them: Western Germany in 1952 adopted a law with the stimulating title of 'a law for the constitution of the firm'. The British Parliament of the nineteenth century was willing to devise and enact new constitutions for local government: it reconstructed the boroughs, and set up county councils in a clear field. The interests of the householder in his neighbourhood are not greater than those of the workman in his firm. Why did Parliament provide a constitution for the one and not the other?

The question implies that the constitution of the firm would have contained an element of self-government, or at least of employee representation. A legal structure of the firm of course there was: we know that it vested control in the hands of the proprietors of part at least of the capital, and related the workman to them by contract not status. In this it seemed to be following the natural order. Capitalists hired labour, not labourers capital. Could it be otherwise?

From early times the endeavour had been made to have it otherwise. The self-governing co-operative workshops of Robert Owen and of the Christian Socialists were attempts to break away from the authoritarian structure of the firm, from having the wage-earner work under the orders of capitalists and subject to dismissal by them. They tried to give him within the firm the status of a citizen, and to ensure that he hired the capital he needed as he might rent a building, without subordinating himself to the lessor. 'Hitherto,' wrote John Stuart Mill in 1852, 'there has been no alternative for those who lived by their labour, but that of labouring each for himself alone, or for a master. But the civilizing and improving influences of association, and the efficiency and economy of production on a large scale, may be obtained without dividing the producers into two parties with hostile interests and feelings, the many who do the work being mere servants under the command of the one who supplies the funds, and having no interest of their own in the enterprise except to earn their wages with as little labour as possible. . . . There can be little doubt that the *status* of hired labourers will gradually tend to confine itself to the description of workpeople whose low moral qualities render them unfit for anything more independent: and that the relation of masters and workpeople will be gradually superseded by partnership, in one of two forms: temporarily and in some cases, association of the labourers with the capitalist; in other cases and finally in all, association of labourers among themselves.' Mill believed this because of the success of various systems of sub-contracting, profit-sharing, and co-operative workshops, especially in Paris, and he went on to describe them. He included one English experiment which was noteworthy because it used the structure of the joint-stock company to give employees a share not merely in profits but in management. Henry Briggs, Son & Co., a colliery firm in Yorkshire, in 1865 converted their business into a joint stock company, and induced their men to take up shares: there was provision for profit-sharing, of a kind subsequently familiar, but the remarkable thing was that in 1869 the miners who were shareholders were invited to elect one of their number to be a Director. Various experiments of these kinds went on, especially in profit-sharing and co-partnership. Profit-sharing provided commonly that for each unit by which the dividend on the ordinary shares exceeded a fixed percentage, a bonus at a certain rate should be paid on wages: in itself this left the structure of the firm unchanged, and only provided for a kind of group bonus as a supplementary method of wage-payment, and yet it did give the wage-earner a different status within the firm, because it recognized his claim to share in what hitherto had accrued to capital alone. Co-partnership proper was said to exist only when part of the capital of the firm was owned by the workpeople, and in schemes of co-partnership they were usually given some help or stimulus to take shares up.

In 1913 a bill was introduced into the legislature of Massachusetts to oblige all corporations to divide between shareholders and employees all profits in excess of a return of five per cent on the current market value of the capital. Later a bill was to be introduced into the House of Commons that would have made provision for co-partnership a condition for the enjoyment of statutory powers such as limited liability by all new companies in Britain. It was a sufficient reason for no such measures being enacted that most shareholders and directors did not like them at all. None the less we may ask why they had not been more advocated.

The basic reason was that the wage-earners had not shown the capacity to manage, still less to develop, any business but co-operative retailing, and some branches of manufacturing that found their market assured therein. From its effective start at Rochdale in 1844, 'the co-op' had spread widely if unevenly, and grown, until by the end of the century its sales amounted to more than £50 millions a year, at a time when the whole wage bill of the country was getting on for £700 millions. This limited success was still remarkable, and the co-operative societies were pointed out as striking examples, like the trade unions themselves, of the ability of the wage-earners to provide from their own ranks administrative ability and disinterested devotion. But these resources served only to run a kind of business that by its nature called for little innovation, technical knowledge, organizing drive, or risk-taking, so that it could be sufficiently administered by a part-time committee and some whole-time managers retained at modest salaries. Through the 'divi', and the natural loyalties of its members, it had a tied clientele; it dealt mainly in the steady staples of consumption. Nor did it broach the problem of self-government: its workpeople were wage-earners working like other wage-earners for an employer, and were often explicitly denied a member's voice in the management. When the retail co-operatives embarked, through the Wholesale Society, in various branches of production, they appointed managers who had substantially the same authority as other managers to hire and fire and take charge in their workshops. The movement as a whole showed the capacity of wage-earners, in a limited and unadventurous field, to assume the functions of the employer and hire other wage-earners, but was no evidence of capacity to develop other sorts of business, and did nothing to transcend the subordination of wage-earner to employer at the place of work.

Attempts to do more than this there were, but they had not gone far. The long endeavours of middle-class idealists to work out some form of self-government in industry — Vansittart Neale alone had lost £40,000 in the attempt — had issued in a number of small productive societies maintaining self-managing workshops. But these amounted to little more than extended partnerships, in industries where equipment was simple, and some individual workmen retained their independence: there was no instance of any substantial factory being built up and owned by those who worked in it. The Central Co-operative Board, in an address to the workers of the United Kingdom, said 'We call your attention to a means of improving your own position, the greatest and most important means of all, which you appear, strangely, to overlook — self-employment. We want you to make the profits on your own work raise you up generally in proportion to the degree in which you help to produce them, instead of raising up only a few persons. . . . Why do you not set about this great work earnestly?' The answer was twofold. Few men have the temperament and talent to build a business up, and those that do prefer to keep it in their own hands. Self-government was not propitious to vigour and progress in the management of business.

Those must be the reasons too why the trade unions, although they often had a considerable capital to invest, did not do more to by-pass the employers whom many of the members believed to be exploiting them. They had in fact been drawn from time to time into an attempt to set up for themselves. After the Engineers' strike in 1852, Vansittart Neale had bought the Atlas Engineering Works in London, within half a mile of the head office of the Amalgamated Engineers, and production was begun there with a view to the union taking it over; but one member of the council objected so strongly that the project was given up, with the loss of the whole purchase price and debts as well. In the late sixties a building company was formed in London, whose directors were representatives of various building unions, and included Henry Broadhurst the stonemason, later to be secretary of the parliamentary committee of the Trades Union Congress and under-secretary in the Home Department; its shareholders comprised workmen who were as far as possible to be employed by the company; it went bankrupt in three years. In the nine hours' strike of 1871 some Newcastle engineers were helped by a noncomformist minister to set up the Ouseburn Co-operative Engine Works Company. A fully equipped works was bought for £30,000; the men who were to work in it subscribed some shares themselves, and local co-operative societies put up most of the rest of the capital. Orders were attracted at cut prices; there was a strike in one shop; men who criticized the management were discharged; within four years the company went into liquidation. The Northumberland and Durham Miners formed a company in 1873 and bought the Monkwood colliery in Derbyshire: all the capital of £40,000 and more was soon lost. In 1875 the South Yorkshire and North Derbyshire Miners bought the Shirland colliery in Derbyshire for £69,000, finding some £30,000 of capital themselves, and raising the rest on debentures; before the end of the next year the debenture holders took possession, and the Miners lost every penny they had put up. The North Wales quarrymen, locked in a long struggle with Lord Penrhyn around the turn of the century, bought works in other quarries, but failed to make them pay.

One example has been recorded of an employer voluntarily handing over to his workers a part in the control of his business. George Thomson of Huddersfield was a disciple of Ruskin who inherited a worsted manufacture: he gave his workpeople shares, and associated their representatives with him in management. Among those they elected was the secretary of their union. But after Thomson's death the scheme broke down.

These examples are significant. Businesses could be built and run only by efficient managers: enterprise was a factor of production that was indispensable not inimical to labour. It could operate only where, within limits much wider than co-operation allowed, it had executive discretion.

But, it will be said, it was not the man of enterprise but the shareholder who in fact owned the firm, and had the powers of control that went with ownership. That would not hold where men had built up their own businesses, found most of their capital by ploughing profits back, and retained control; but the capital for many businesses never was home-grown in that way, and even where it was, the time would come when more was needed, or the family wished to liquify its assets. Then the scarcity of savings asserted itself: those who had money to lend were able to make their terms, and they would not put it into any risky enterprise unless they kept some control over it. A certain amount of capital could be raised by debentures, which ordinarily gave the holder no vote. But they committed the firm to a fixed charge, in bad years as well as good, and it was more convenient to promise to pay only so much or so little as the realized profit warranted. That could be done only if the lenders had votes in shareholders' meetings. If business did not fluctuate, capital could have been raised contractually, at fixed rates of interest, without conceding powers of control. If those with savings to lend had been willing to hand them over without keeping any control over how they were administered, capital on which fluctuating dividends would have been paid could have been raised on non-voting shares. As things were, it had to be raised in a way that recognized both that yields would fluctuate and that shareholders would want to be satisfied they were not lower than they need be. It was this, and not any provision of the law, that made control attach to ownership. We can imagine a world in which savings were a drug in the market and labour was scarce: then it would be labour that could say, 'If I am to come in to this I shall require a share in the control.' The Victorian world was the reverse of that.

Yet even so we may wonder why labour did not try to make some participation in control a condition of employment. After all, one purpose of the trade union was to enable labour to press certain claims despite its ever-growing numbers, and whenever wages were negotiated the unions might have tried to include in the settlement a provision that would give their members some voice in management. If they did not, it was because the members did not want them to. Many unionists might resent the power of the employer who was seeking his own profit by using them, but when they thought of replacing him, it was by another boss, 'the state', not by themselves. They did not feel they could do it. By the first moves towards it, moreover, they would lose their independence without gaining anything tangible. If profit-sharing was a halfway house, they did not usually want that either. The claim they increasingly put forward was that wages should be based on human needs, independently of the ups and downs of trade: again and again profit-sharing schemes broke down when bonuses paid in the boom vanished in the slump — the Briggs scheme itself, with its miners' Director, had gone in that way. There were many signs that the authority of the employer at the place of work was resented increasingly, but the men wanted to limit it by negotiation, not to assume it themselves. So they did not devise or demand changes in the constitution of the firm.

CHAPTER V

INSTITUTIONS AND PROCEDURES
IN 1906

I

In our account of the development of industrial relations we saw how in three successive periods unions of different types of wage-earner had begun to take hold — first the craft unions, then the operatives', and lastly the general unions. This provides a rough but convenient classification of the trade union world of about 1906.

Most of the craft unions were in four industries — engineering; iron and steel; building; paper and printing — which between them contained three-fifths of all the craftsmen in membership; but there were also many craft unions, albeit small ones, in the woodworking trades. These craft unions amounted to little more than a fifth of all unions in number, yet contained more than a quarter of all members, for at that time they were relatively big. There was, it is true, a rather higher proportion of very small unions among them than elsewhere — such as the Northampton Carpenters and Joiners, with sixteen members, or the Silver Hand Forged Spoon and Fork Makers, with eighteen. But their average size was still substantially greater than that of other types because of the presence among them of a small number of big unions: there were twelve which each had more than ten thousand members, and these between them held nearly three-quarters of all craft unionists. Of the six biggest unions in the country, three were craft unions: the Engineers with more than ninety thousand members; the Carpenters with sixty; and the Boiler-makers with fifty. These are small figures by recent standards, but big by those of the time, when four unions out of five had less than a thousand members apiece.

That the craft unions should have grown so big may be explained by several considerations. The most evident is that having for the most part begun earlier they had had longer in which to grow. But their growth was also favoured by their own nature, by the spontaneous affinity for one another of men trained in the same craft wherever they were. Up to the boundaries of their own craft they could expand without the problems of persuading the diverse to combine, protecting minority interests, and negotiating in different markets. The expansion was also pushed on by the forceful, shrewd and efficient men who came to union office from the craftsmen's ranks. The ablest union leaders in the country in the era of the Webbs' 'New Model' unionism from 1851 onwards were craftsmen, just as the New Model unions themselves were craft unions.

The formation of viable unions of operatives had gone on rapidly from 1850, and half of the unions of this kind existing in 1906 had been founded by the time of the rise of the New Unionism in 1887. But still the other half were the creation only of the last twenty years.

The miners had some big unions, and one of them, the South Wales Miners' Federation, was the biggest single union in the country, and the only one to have passed the hundred thousand mark. But for the most part the operatives' unions remained small, even by the standards of the day. Their skill being less distinctive than the craftsman's they commonly had less sense of trade identity to bring them together across the gulfs between districts and industries. They lacked the resources of money, and often also of personal ability, which the craftsmen could throw into the task of organization. In any case, most of them being younger had had less time in which to grow. So in 1906 they remained sectional, confined often to the workers in one trade and even one district — the Forfar Factory Workers, the Wolverhampton Operative Tin Plate Workers, the Bradford and District Powerloom Overlookers. Even those who by their names claimed a wide scope — some of them destined to grow big later — were still small: the Electrical Trades Union had eleven hundred members, the National Operative Printers' Assistants less than three thousand, the Woodcutting Machinists less than five.

Beside the groups of craftsmen and operatives there was a mixed group of labourers and transport workers. They were much the youngest. The Western Counties Excavators, Quarry-

men and General Labourers went back to 1864, the Manchester
and Lancashire Bricklayers' Labourers to 1869, and there were
others of relatively early origin, but the great majority had
come into being only when a new faith in their ability to fight
their way upwards rose among the unskilled and swept them
into the New Unionism. Yet though they were so young, some
of these unions had already grown to a substantial size: the
Bristol, West of England, and South Wales Operatives had
nearly forty thousand members, the Gas Workers and General
Labourers getting on for thirty. The labourer's very lack of
qualification removed barriers to the extension of his union,
which was 'le club des sans-clubs', and a propensity to ramify
and coalesce was already apparent from which powerful
consequences were to follow.

Beyond these three main groups some sprinklings of unionism
appeared among 'the white-collared' — shop assistants, professional people, civil servants. Much was to come of these
beginnings, but as yet they amounted to little. There were, it is
true, two sizeable unions of shop assistants, one of them solely of
co-operative employees, with nearly thirty thousand members
between them; but even these appeared small in so extensive an
occupation. There were also some unions of musicians and
theatrical employees, assurance agents and clerks. Almost all
these were of recent formation and still small: a National Union
of Clerks had seventy-seven members; even the Railway Clerks
had under five thousand; only in the Post Office were there two
clerks' unions of five thousand or more. There were also some
small unions for supervisory grades or particular duties in the
Post Office: such a title as the Second Class Assistant Inspectors
of Telegraph Messengers (London Postal Service) indicates the
propensity by which the Post Office has been much troubled
ever since, to form separate unions for small subdivisions of the
staff. Perhaps it is the explicitly classified structure of the public
service that makes the servant grade-conscious, and fosters a
minutely sectional unionism.

Trade unionism as a whole had expanded not steadily but in
surges. Until 1870 the membership lay predominantly in the
craft unions, and was very small; just what it was we do not
know, but those unions whose records were tabulated by the
Webbs, and which had between them about a third of all

unionists in 1890, had (so many of them as then existed) less than 150,000 members in 1870, and the Trades Union Congress of 1871 claimed to represent under 300,000 members. Perhaps there were not more than half a million unionists in the country at that time. But in the great boom that followed the Franco-Prussian war a wave rose which may well have doubled the membership within three or four years. That in itself is an indication of how small a part of the field was covered before. In the slump that followed numbers fell off again and fell far, but in 1887 a second wave rose which carried membership to a million and a half by 1892, and after a check in the next depression to near two millions at the turn of the century.

There it remained. That it had not risen further meanwhile marked not the exhaustion of the impulse of the New Unionism but the restraint exerted by the trade depression that followed the Boer War. The membership of trade unions always varied with the trade cycle. When activity was rising employment became more secure, profits increased, employers began to compete for some kinds of labour, the cost of living was likely to go up: wage-earners had an incentive to seek the rises which the movement of the market made it relatively easy for them to obtain, and they had the means to pay their dues. When depression followed there was little prospect of a rise, union or no union; the insecurity of employment made men reluctant to risk a stoppage; dues were harder to find. In such years membership actually fell even when the trend was expansive; the advances were achieved only in the years of high employment.

The trade union world of 1906 was a remarkable mixture of tradition and inexperience. Some unions had a longer continuous history than any others in the world, but more than half had come into existence only during the last twenty years. Most of their members, and many too who had recently joined the old unions, were not the sons of unionist fathers. In shaping constitutions and policies they had the traditions of the older unions to draw on if they chose, but for many of them the old way was not the way forward they were seeking, and they had yet to learn in the school of their own experience. Alongside the old, shrewd unionism of limited aims, here were radical conceptions, rankling grievances, far-reaching expectations.

The two million unionists of 1906 amounted to less than a

R

sixth of all British wage-earners. In one sense this is a small proportion: today the ratio is at least a half. Yet, in another sense, it understates the strength of a unionism which though it lay thin on the ground if spread over the whole land was present in force in some of the most important industries. In fact the comparison with the whole number of wage-earners runs together a small number of basic industries in which unionism was powerful, and a wide range of other employments in which as yet it appeared only sporadically. The union stronghold was made up of five big industrial groups and three smaller ones: mining, iron and steel and engineering, textiles, building, and transport; with printing, clothing and woodworking. These between them held more than five-sixths of all the unionists in the country. Elsewhere there were some trades, in some districts, where unionism was strong, and especially some crafts in which membership was usual, and even compulsory, wherever they occurred. But the sixth of the membership outside the stronghold was scattered among more than half the working population, and left broad expanses almost empty — the remaining factory trades; wholesaling and retailing; and agriculture.

The concentration of membership in certain industries implied a regional concentration in the localities where those industries were chiefly carried on. When the Webbs collected returns of the distribution of trade unionists in 1892, they found nearly half of them in four northern counties — Northumberland, Durham, Lancashire, and Yorkshire. To these we might add Scotland, with more members than Durham, less than Yorkshire. Most of the remaining members were in the manufacturing Midlands, in South Wales, and in London. These districts, moreover, not only held most of the numbers, but were almost the only places in which the proportion of unionists in the population was considerable: outside them, only in Cumberland and Lincoln, Gloucester and Suffolk, did unionists make up more than two per cent of the whole population, or say six per cent of the wage-earners. In the rest of the country they were little seen or heard of, save in a big town here and there.

It would have been taken for granted that the unionists were mostly men. This would not have been so if the same proportion of the women workers as of the men had joined the unions, for then as now the women made up a third of the wage-earners.

But few of them did join, save in the textile trades. There the women members were nearly a half of all unionists. Elsewhere there was only a scattering of them — less than sixteen thousand in all. Women had been admitted to the Trades Union Congress as far back as 1875, but thirty years later there were only two women delegates, and the textile unions which contained most of the women unionists were represented by men alone. There were many reasons for this. Most women wage-earners were in the unskilled jobs, or the small and scattered units of employment like retailing and domestic service, where men also were hard to organise. Four out of five of them would be leaving their jobs to get married before they were thirty, and while they were at work they did not have a man's regard for his job as his mainstay for life, and his consequent inducement to make present sacrifices for future benefits; the more so, because their wages meanwhile were usually only a supplement to the income of their family and not its main source. Those wages were lower relatively to a man's then than they are now — they were commonly 12s. a week, up and down the country, when the unskilled male labourer was getting a pound or a guinea. It was understandable that though women would join a friendly society for its sick benefit, they would seldom keep up union dues.

There was a missionary society, the Women's Trade Union League, whose moving spirits were Lady Dilke and Mary Macarthur. Every year from 1889 to the year of her death in 1904 Lady Dilke visited the Trades Union Congress, trying to stir up interest in recruiting women and break down the prejudices of some of the men against the women being unionized at all — 'Lady Dilke entertained', Beatrice Webb recorded,[1] 'on a large, I might almost say gross, scale — her young women asking every trade union official they came across to champagne lunches and elaborate dinners.' Mary Macarthur was the daughter of a Glasgow draper, who on entering his business became concerned for the shop assistants, and joined their union in 1901; in 1903 she became secretary of the League. Its objects were to spread a knowledge of trade unionism among women, and get unions started which the members would carry on themselves. Mary Macarthur did start not a few; but the difficulty was to find any members with the ability to carry them

[1] Beatrice Webb, *Our Partnership* (1948), p. 48.

on, and they had more chance of survival when they were formed and continued to be run by neighbouring men unionists. Sometimes these organized the women in their own trade, as a defence against the competition of their lower rate of pay — that was how the Society of Women employed in Bookbinding, for instance, and the Union of Women Cigarmakers, were formed and maintained. Sometimes the local Trades Council founded a general union for all working women in the town. But the third, and, it might seem, the obvious way of enrolling the women, was to admit them to the men's own unions. If this had gone on only slowly outside the textile trades it was because the women came up against the same barrier as the semi-skilled and un-skilled men — the craftsmen felt their own advantage lay in keeping them out, not bringing them in. But the new unionism diffused a zeal for unity, and unions were growing now in those trades where the hierarchical division by skill did not obtain. One of the two women delegates to the Trades Union Congress of 1905 was Margaret Bondfield, who came from one of these new and comprehensive unions, the Shop Assistants, Ware-housemen, and Clerks. It was with this sort of union that the future of women's unionism lay.

2

The unions were far from wealthy, even the strongest of them: when we look at their accounts, we wonder how bodies with such small resources could be as effective as they were. The Board of Trade summarized the accounts of the hundred prin-cipal unions of the day, chosen so as to give roughly proportional representation to the unionism of different industries, and containing between them some three-fifths of all unionists. In 1905 these unions possessed less than £5 millions; all the unions in the country probably did not have more than £7 millions; but the friendly societies at that time had £50 millions. The contrast brings home the still restricted hold of unionism on the wage-earners of the country, for it arose from the small numbers of the unionists — only two million of them, against fourteen in the friendly societies — and not from their average holdings being smaller, for with £4 a head they held a little more than the average member of a friendly society. They also held effectively nearly twice as much as their successors were to do in the 1950's:

the £4 would buy about as much as £18 would in 1957, when union funds amounted only to some £9 6s. a head.

But the unions' funds of 1905 were still small in comparison with their own annual outgoings, for they were equivalent as a rule to substantially less than three years' expenditure, and that at a time when the cost of disputes was very low. There had been a steady accumulation in these recent peaceful years, and since the great engineering dispute ended in 1898 a balance of about 4s. a member a year had been put by. But the reserve remained very low: eight weeks' dispute pay for all members at only 10s. a week would generally exhaust it entirely. Some unions, naturally, had more in hand — the Scots Ironmoulders and the Cotton Spinners most of all, with over £11 a head against the £4 average; and the Locomotive men, the Steam Engine Makers, the Shipwrights, and the Engineers, with between £7 and £8. On the other side, necessarily, were unions with much less than the average holding — notably the builders, with no more than half of it, less than eight days' pay for a building craftsman.

These small reserves had not only to take the shock of trade disputes from time to time, but would also be drawn on in many unions to help pay unemployment benefit during recurrent depressions, and in still more to help meet an often mounting total of claims for a range of friendly benefits. The unions made no attempt to cover their actuarial liabilities: most of them were too small for the law of large numbers to apply; they did not join, as conceivably they might have done, to form one common assurance society; and in any case the funds simply were not there. Nor did they usually separate the fund held to meet liabilities for friendly benefit and the fighting fund: save that the miners generally paid a portion of their contributions into Permanent Relief Societies whose finances were separate from those of their unions. It was easy enough to show that by the standard of an industrial assurance company the unions were hopelessly insolvent: yet once established they seldom failed to meet their members' claims, because they had one resource the assurance company quite lacked — when benefits were drawing the funds too low, they could have a whip round. The high level of union income in 1905–6 was attributed in great part to exceptionally heavy levies imposed by the Carpenters and

Joiners on their members still in work, in order to keep up unemployment benefit to the others.

It was members' dues that made up nine-tenths of the unions' income — such was the consequence of the relative smallness of their accumulated funds, of which again two-fifths were kept in too liquid a form to earn much interest. In 1905 the average member was paying about 8½d. a week, or about 6d. in the pound of his wages; but some craft unions collected twice as much and more, and some general labourers' unions less than half — about 3d. a week.

There was a corresponding range in the rates at which benefit was given, and, still more, the extent of benefits provided. But almost all the unions now gave some friendly benefits, at least to those who were willing to pay in something over and above the minimum contribution which qualified for membership and brought dispute pay. The new general unions had made a virtue of necessity at first, and eschewed the friendly benefits for which they had no funds, on the ground that those that did have them were made over-cautious and under-warlike thereby. But the great problem of a union of the unskilled is to hold its members, and one way of tieing them is to get them to subscribe for friendly benefits which they will lose if they leave. If the unions did not get the subscriptions, moreover, the ever busy, ever spreading friendly societies would. So the new unions had generally gone over into schemes of friendly benefit: cautiously at first, and usually beginning, as the friendly societies themselves seem to have done, with the only contingency that is once for all — funeral benefit.

The annual outlay of the unions, on the average of the seven years before 1905, may be expressed roughly as follows, in shillings and pence per member:

	s.	d.
Dispute pay	3	3
Unemployment benefit	6	3
Sick and accident benefit	5	8
Superannuation	3	8
Funeral and other benefits	2	8
Working and miscellaneous expenses	6	4
	27	10

Dispute pay was the one form of assurance which every union provided if it was a trade union at all. The total paid out naturally fluctuated widely — in 1897-8, at the time of the great engineering dispute, the average for all unions had been nearly twice as great as it was in the years that followed. A widespread stoppage would exhaust the funds of almost any union in a few weeks. But widespread stoppages were not expected. Most disputes involved only one district, and many only one firm, at a time, and the majority who stayed at work would pay an extra levy if need be to keep up the benefit of those who were out. It was part of the tactics of the employers in the engineering dispute of 1897-8 to lock union members out in districts not immediately embroiled, so as to prevent their contributing to those that were. But this was exceptional. In calculating what fighting fund they needed, the unions could reckon that most stoppages would be local.

Unemployment benefit was being paid by four out of five of the principal unions. The miners paid little, because they habitually shared shortage of work out among themselves in the form of short time, and they paid benefit only for the minor forms of unemployment which by their nature were concentrated on a few men at a time — stoppages of pits by reason of mechanical breakdowns, accident, or flood. The general labourers, among whom unemployment was endemic, could not afford dues high enough to provide benefit. But most other unions did. The main form had once been travelling benefit: the member out of work and going on the road would get from his branch secretary a card which showed how much he was entitled to draw from each branch he called at — a daily allowance, and the price of a bed; so long as he found no job he had to keep moving, and there was a rule that he must not make a second visit to any branch until so many weeks after his first. Of late it had become more usual just to pay the railway fare to a place where the member had a job or could hope to get one. Understandably, the building trades paid out much in travelling benefit. There were some unions, notably in printing, which paid grants to help unemployed members to emigrate, though sometimes this kind of help was reserved for those who had been victimized or were otherwise in dispute. But the main provision was the 'out of work donation', which a man could draw while he stayed where he was. For a craftsman, it was not usually more than 10s.

a week — a third or a quarter of his wage — and that only for a limited initial period, after which, if he was still out, it diminished progressively. In their power to administer this benefit the unions had a unique asset. It helped them to uphold the union rate against the hungry man's temptation to take work at a secret rebate; and it brought them members, because it was a form of assurance that they alone could provide — only the union branch, with its knowledge of the unemployed man himself and the vacancies in the local market, could tell whether he was 'genuinely seeking work'. Some of the differences in the hold which unionism had gained in different trades can be traced to the different incidence of unemployment: whatever the other pros and cons of unionism in the wage-earners' eyes, it offered help they could get nowhere else to those of them who suffered, or dreaded to suffer, from being out of work.

There was another kind of benefit which in practice was provided by the unions alone, or almost alone — superannuation. Some friendly societies had begun to offer it recently, but it was an awkward sort of liability for a small society to incur — it meant accumulating funds over long years, and the outgoings were of very uncertain extent when they did fall due; while keeping up weekly payments year after year for so remote a return demanded a good deal of self-control from a voluntary contributor. The trade unions, by contrast, need not worry overmuch about funding their liabilities, because they had long since learned to rely on adjusting their dues to cover their outgoings year by year; and they could offer the benefit as part of the return for an inclusive subscription which the member must keep up if he was not to fall out of compliance altogether. There had been an Act in 1894 which provided that if a union paid superannuation at rates not exceeding £30 a year, it might set up a separate provident fund the interest on which would be tax-free, and a number of unions had set such funds up; but the main guarantee of solvency remained the possibility of making the future membership foot whatever might be the future bill. The temptation to attract members by offering generous benefits which would fall due only many years later might conceivably have been great. But in fact it was generally only the craft unions, who did not need to beat the drum for recruits, who had gone in for superannuation, particularly those in metal working, engineering, shipbuilding, printing, and building: save that the miners could subscribe for pensions if they wished through their Permanent Relief Societies. The Engineers alone accounted for two-fifths of all current outlay on superannuation among the hundred principal unions. As far back as 1892 they had instituted a quarterly levy of a shilling a member to be paid into a superannuation reserve fund; their scale of benefit now gave 10s. a week at the top to the member of 40 years' standing, 9s. to the 35 years' member, and so on. It was the general experience that the proportion of superannuated members was rising.

Sickness and accident benefit usually took the form of a weekly payment, but sometimes lump sums were paid in compensation for disablement. Some unions paid for medical attendance. Since 1895 trade unions had been allowed to join the medical associations in which friendly societies were increasingly combining to get doctors' care and medicine for their members. A number of cotton weavers' unions paid no sick benefit but subscribed to the local hospitals in which their members were treated.

The provision of benefits, especially of deferred benefits like superannuation, gave the union executives a strong hold on their members. A man might, in effect, have his life's savings in the union, but he had no 'policy', no 'accrued rights' which he could take away with him if he and the union parted company. If he fell out of compliance through failing to keep up his subscriptions, there was no accumulated fund he could withdraw. If he broke the rules, or failed to follow the instructions of the executive in a trade dispute, he could be lawfully expelled, without having a legal claim to the return of a penny of what he had been paying in, perhaps for many years. If the union simply withheld what was his due, he was prevented by the Trade Union Act of 1871 from bringing an action to enforce his rights under the union's own regulations, or seek damages for the breach of them.

That less than a quarter of the unions' whole outlay went on administration makes them compare very favourably with the collecting friendly societies, which might spend as much as half their income on it. The difference is even more remarkable because the unions were not friendly societies merely, but required their officers to be mainly occupied with trade questions. They did not pay them enough, or have enough of them:

in this sense their outlay on administration was too low, and could the members have been persuaded to double that part of their dues, only about a third on the average of recent years, which went on trade purposes, they should have had good value for their money. But in another sense the low outlay marked a great achievement of honest and painstaking administration by the unpaid officers of the branches as well as by head office. Much of the hold which the unions had gained on the respect of a substantial part of the community was due to the ability which their members had shown in running their own affairs responsibly and efficiently.

A critic of union finances at the outset of 1906 could well have pointed out how slender they were in relation to the potential claims on them — how superannuation was imposing a mounting charge on the craft unions, how reserves bore so low a ratio to turnover, and an extensive dispute would bring a crisis in the finances of almost any union. Certainly there was little scope for manoeuvre here. Yet within it the unions had devised and were now administering daily a comprehensive system of social assurance. The welfare state, as that was to be constructed between 1906 and 1950, did but extend to the whole community the practices and provisions which the unions of 1906 had already tested and developed.

3

The government of these unions showed a great variety.

The simplest form any union could take was the local club: a fraternity of workers met sociably after working hours, commonly at a pub, for conviviality, the discussion of trade affairs, and the administration of a common fund. Their rules provided for the order of drinking not less than of business, and they often elected their chairman evening by evening, from among so many as turned up; but for their work as a friendly society they also needed a treasurer — often the landlord of the pub — and some written scales of contribution and benefit. It was reckoned that there were still as many as 750 single-celled organisms among the British trade unions of Edwardian times.

But many unions that began in this way had naturally reached out to neighbouring clubs and linked up with them. It was common, though not so much so in Britain as in France and

Germany, for the young craftsman to have his Wanderjahre; also men who lost their jobs went off on the tramp in search of work elsewhere; and both sorts of traveller would get into touch with the club of their craft as soon as they reached a new town, and so the clubs were drawn together. When the clubs of a whole region, moreover, were in the throes of conflict, they often appointed delegates to meet together in an informal steering committee at least for the duration of hostilities. It was natural to go on to more durable association, and federation.

While local societies were linking up in this way, other unions were founded — the Society of Railway Servants was a notable example — which gave themselves a wide scope from the first, forming new branches of the one parent union as new members enrolled. When the new unionism came it was even more comprehensive. The majority of British unionists in 1906 belonged to unions which, whether the branches had once set up the centre or the centre had founded the branches, now united under a central administration branches spread over a great part of the country.

Growth to such size and structure encountered the difficulties which scale always raises in government: especially how to combine the executive discretion of full-time administrators with the democratic control of policy by the members generally; and how to balance the centralization of bargaining with a due regard for the particular interests of various regions and sections of membership. In days when most strikes were still local, centralization had this immediate and powerful advantage, that it brought the whole resources of the union to the support of whatever part was in conflict at any one time, and vastly increased the ability of the workmen of any one employer to stand up to him by withdrawing their labour. But this meant that each branch could not be left to engage in what battles it thought fit, and run through other people's money; only approved causes could draw strike pay from the central funds; the question then was, who was to approve? It also meant a head office, and a full-time secretary, who was bound to have the opportunity to exert much influence on the affairs of the union generally; and he might be joined by other salaried administrators, and what the Webbs called 'the informal cabinet of permanent officials' would take shape.

How could this continuous, well-informed, and concentrated power be kept responsive to the wishes of a scattered, partially informed, and only occasionally vocal rank and file? Sometimes the question hardly arose, because most of the members were content to let a strong secretary have his own way, and he was adroit enough not to stir up too much opposition. There were not a few unions of that kind, willing to follow a leader who knew his own mind, in effect run by him. But more often the membership displayed a vigorous repugnance to bureaucracy, and was determined to retain in the big unions as much as possible of the primitive democracy of the small. One way in which that showed itself was an insistence on decisions being remitted from the centre to the vote of branch meetings, and on each branch being entitled to have any proposal it might make distributed and discussed in the same way: the sheer bulk of business to which this gave rise was sufficient in time to render it impracticable, quite apart from the improbability of its yielding consistent policy. Another way was to decide as many issues as possible in advance, and limit executive discretion by comprehensive instructions: much effort was put into elaborating and revising union rules. The obvious course, it might seem, was to make the executive officers responsible to an elected council or assembly, but the difficulty there was the cost of gathering the lay representatives together, and their own inability to leave their jobs for the days of the meeting; the cotton spinners had a rare advantage in the delegates' all being able to get into Manchester for a Saturday afternoon conference. One expedient was to put headquarters under the control of a committee elected by such branches only as were within travelling distance: as late as 1892 the committee of the Engineers had been elected by the London branches alone, and a similar method was still being followed by the Carpenters and Joiners.

But as the incomes of the wage-earner and his union rose, and men could get time off to go to conference, it became possible to bring together periodically an assembly of representatives from all branches or districts. An alternative or supplementary procedure, adopted by the Engineers when they revised their constitution in 1892, was for the members to elect directly a full-time executive council. In one way or another the devices by which representative democracy had combined executive discretion with popular control now became feasible within the union, and the Webbs celebrated their fullest development by the Association of Operative Cotton Spinners — 'a fully-equipped democratic state of the modern type. It has an elected parliament, exercising supreme and uncontrolled power. It has a cabinet appointed by and responsible only to that parliament. And its chief executive officer, appointed once for all on grounds of efficiency, enjoys the civil-service permanence of tenure.'[1]

But this still did not meet all the needs of the rank and file. In those matters which concerned the whole membership it worked well enough: in the policy of the union towards working practices, for example, or methods of wage payment, or the lines of demarcation with other unions, it enabled the members to have policy debated, and executive performance checked. When one of these general issues came up in the daily work of any one member, moreover, he could look to the union for support in any stand he had to take for union principles. But there was much besides this which mattered to him in his working life, and yet in which he was apt to feel that the union did not give him the help and understanding he had the right to expect. The work he was doing might fail to satisfy him, in ways of which he himself had no understanding, but which left him fretful and restless. His peace of mind depended much on his personal relations, on the consideration or hamhandedness with which the foreman treated him, on whether he was working in a friendly and stable group or was isolated or uprooted. Employed often by a concern whose control was remote from him and unknown, yet was liable to reach out and upset his working life, he felt anxious, and had the insecure man's eye for an injustice, was quick to sense a threat. Most men like their work, and like being able to go about it in their accustomed way, but changes in methods and machines were constantly dispensing with old skills, and disordering status. From time to time such anxieties, grievances, and vague resentments seemed to cumulate and reinforce one another; the men in some district would be seething with discontent; and yet the cause was not apparent, no issue had arisen of the kind with which union headquarters was used to deal. So when strife followed, it broke out suddenly; men suffering from a real but undefined sense of grievance

[1] S. and B. Webb, *Industrial Democracy* (1920 edn.), p. 40.

formulated some unreasonable complaint; a trivial incident precipitated an unofficial strike. The men felt they had to take action into their own hands, because the union was no help to them. The officials at headquarters and the national executive were taken by surprise, and found fault with the men for breaking the agreement made in their name. The public blamed the leaders for being out of touch with the rank and file.

These leaders, it is true, could reply then as now, that the government of their union was fully democratic, and if any member had any complaint to state or proposal to make, he could at any time bring it forward at a meeting of his branch, to be transmitted for the immediate attention of headquarters. This was unanswerable, yet really irrelevant, because so often the member could not formulate what was at stake, and the things that were irritating him were not of the kind that union policy and procedure could deal with. The Webbs were, in a way, clearly aware of this. When a workman is selected by his comrades to serve as a representative, they said, 'before he can place himself on a level with the trained official whom he has to control he must devote his whole time and thought to his new duties, and must therefore give up his old trade. This unfortunately tends to alter his manner of life, his habit of mind, and usually also his intellectual atmosphere to such an extent that he gradually loses that vivid appreciation of the feelings of the man at the bench or the forge, which it is his function to express. There is a certain cruel irony in the problem which accounts, we think, for some of the unconscious exasperation of the wage-earners all over the world against representative institutions.'[1] Typically, they called this 'a constitutional difficulty', and found the solution in giving the union a parliament or supreme assembly, in which alongside the salaried officials there should sit many lay members who continued to work at their trade. But the analogy with political government is defective. Debating is not of much use to the member who needs to convey what he finds it hard to express. The parliament of a trade union could discuss general policy, but the sources of discontent included much that touched only particular men in particular places, and could be understood only by those who were with them there.

It might be thought that the member would find the help he

[1] S. and B. Webb *Industrial Democracy* (1920 edn.), p. 56.

needed in his branch. Certainly he could look to it when his
trouble raised a clear issue of union principle: the branch could
take that up, confident of the backing of head office if need be.
But his trouble might not be of that sharpcut kind, and might
be hard for him to explain to anyone who was not working there
with him. The remedy then might seem to be the shop steward,
but that would be to read back the strength and status which
unions generally won later into a period when only some of the
craftsmen were as yet able to use their unionism openly to stand
up to the boss in his own shop. In most trades the time of the
shop steward had not yet come. True, it was usual for the
members of a union in any one shop to appoint one of their
number as collector, or walking delegate, or card-steward, whose
duty was to see that newcomers had a union card or took one
out, but he did not often act as spokesman to management, nor
would his union executive usually have wanted him to put his
oar in.

A third possibility was that the member should make his
complaint to a district officer of his union, who could take action
without fear of victimization, but at the same time was close
enough to him in his daily work to understand the issue. The
trouble was that such officers were few and far between. Only a
big union could afford them at all, and even then it might have
to sack them when its funds ran low at a time of bad trade. The
Boilermakers had appointed whole-time salaried district officers
in the 1860's, but in the slump of 1879 they had had to dismiss
two of them: at the turn of the century, now a wealthy union by
the standards of the day, they had seven district delegates who
between them covered all the United Kingdom. Few unions
were as well off even as that. If a district officer were paid only
as much as a craftsman there could have been one for every
thousand members if they had contributed an extra halfpenny a
week each, but that they were loath to do: they ran their headquarters on a shoestring, and had little to spare for the districts.

What the member saw of the officials he had, moreover, did
not always encourage him to ask for more. The Webbs quoted
from the pen of one who himself had left the bench to become an
official a clear account of how this came about.[1] 'As Branch
Secretary,' he wrote, 'working at his trade, our friend, though

[1] S. and B. Webb, *History of Trade Unionism* (1920 edn.), p. 469.

superior in energy and ability to the rank and file of his members, remained in close touch with their feelings and desires. His promotion to a salaried office brings him wider knowledge and larger ideas. To the ordinary Trade Unionist the claim of the workman is that of Justice. He believes, almost as a matter of principle, that in any dispute the capitalist is in the wrong and the workman in the right. But when, as a District Delegate, it becomes his business to be perpetually investigating the exact circumstances of the men's quarrels, negotiating with employers, and arranging compromises, he begins more and more to recognize that there is something to be urged on the other side. There is also an unconscious bias at work. Whilst the points at issue no longer affect his own earnings or conditions of employment, any disputes between his members and their employers increase his work and add to his worry. The former vivid sense of the privations and subjection of the artisan's life gradually fades from his mind; and he begins more and more to regard all complaints as perverse and unreasonable. With this intellectual change may come a more invidious transformation. Nowadays the salaried officer of a great Union is courted and flattered by the middle class. He is asked to dine with them, and will admire their well-appointed houses, their fine carpets, the ease and luxury of their lives. Possibly, too, his wife begins to be dissatisfied. . . .' And so on; besides which was the very real danger, in those days, of his taking to drink. 'No greater misfortune can befall an energetic and public-spirited Trade Unionist, who on occasions takes a glass too much,' the Webbs wrote in 1894,[1] 'than to become the salaried officer of his Union. . . . Such a man, elected General Secretary or District Delegate, is doomed, almost inevitably, to become an habitual drunkard.' These quotations state the drawbacks at their strongest; but the best of local officials was remote from his members simply because his district was so big. The workman remained conscious of irritations, grievances, injustices in his working life that his union did not seem able to help him with. A problem of communication remained unsolved.

It was one of the problems which arose as unions grew. The other problem which also arose out of growth was how to bring different groups together in one union without too much over-riding of their particular interests.

[1] S. and B. Webb, *History of Trade Unionism* (1920 edn.), p. 467.

So far as these groups differed only because they were in different parts of the country, they proved able to work together well enough through the ordinary procedure of representative government. In early days, before general assemblies could be brought together, the locating of headquarters aroused the jealousy and suspicion that are usual when the capital of a federation falls to be sited, and it was sometimes provided that the branches should take it in turns to be the seat of government, a device which the Journeymen Coopers continued to use even in the twentieth century. But as it became possible to bring delegates in from all parts of the country it was generally found that the members in different regions did not feel particular interests beyond what could be expressed and balanced through the regional system of representation. By the same token, a growing union was generally able to absorb existing local societies of its own kind without their members feeling that some peculiar interest of theirs would be lost in the mass. Even here, however, a difference of local working practices might keep societies apart, as it kept the miners of Durham and North-umberland out of the Miners' Federation; and where differences were not regional merely, but occupational, they offered a powerful and often insurmountable resistance to unification. The parliaments of the cotton spinners and the miners, which the Webbs regarded as exemplary, united in their democracy workers within whose ranks there were few occupational differ-ences: but where were the women from the cardrooms of the spinning mills? and the enginemen in the mines? The sense of trade identity that gave unionism so much of its strength blocked its expansion.

In the discussion of the relations between the unions to which we now proceed we shall see that such way out as was found lay through retaining the mainly occupational boundaries of the separate unions, but linking them in federations.

4

The unions quarrelled with one another frequently, and sometimes viciously.

Naturally they competed with one another for members, and that not among the unorganized alone. Though it was a grave offence under the unwritten law to entice a member of another union away, it was not always clear who was fair game and who not, for unions shot up and died off quickly, men flocked into them during booms and fell away in slumps, and a man who changed his place of work might in any case have to change from one local union to another. Two unions, moreover, might both set out to organize the whole of one trade, or mark out domains for themselves which overlapped, and then one would filch members from the other with a clear conscience, as rightfully its own. 'As for one union poaching from another,' Mr Shinwell has said,[1] 'well, I have about fifty-one years' experience of trade unionism in one form or another and I never at any time found that unions failed to "poach" if they could get away with it. It is a common practice.'

But the great rows arose over things more vital than recruiting — the right to a job, and the union rate. Men who saw members of another union doing work which they regarded as inherently and exclusively their own were confronted with a loss of possible employment, and that perhaps at a time when some of their own number were out of work, and on the funds of their society; and if also the price at which the work was now being done was lower than their own, they were confronted with a threat to their union rate. These demarcation disputes arose not only because the unions claimed overlapping jurisdictions over existing jobs, but also because in the course of technical change these jobs were being altered so as to make changes in their allocation arguable, and quite new jobs arose to open new fields for disputation. That is why they were especially rife in shipbuilding, which from the wooden sailing ship to the steel steamship had undergone in a short span of years a thoroughgoing technical revolution without a corresponding regrouping of the unions. Again, whenever the customary lines of demarcation in two places differed, one union in each of them could seek to extend its own domain by claiming that local practice should be brought into line with old-established rules elsewhere. 'There may even', said the Webbs, 'be an unprovoked and naked aggression, by a strongly organized class of workmen, upon the jobs hitherto undertaken by a humbler section.'[2]

A third source of conflict lay in the jealousy between not

---

[1] House of Commons, Official Report, 542, 13, 23 June 1955, 1561.
[2] S. and B. Webb, *Industrial Democracy* (1920 edn.), p. 508.

different trades merely but different grades. The skilled man did not always welcome the unionization of the labourer, particularly when this gave a spirit of independence to those who worked under him. Confronted with unionism as a threat to his own authority, he could get up on his hind legs like any employer. In the 1880's, the Boilermakers' Secretary related,[1] the platers' helpers in the Sunderland shipyards had become 'so intolerant . . . that instead of the Platers having control of the helpers, or even their own work, the labourers had become complete masters of the situation. They would work when they liked, do just as they liked, hurry a plate away improperly finished, and if a Plater ventured to protest they would boycott him by a refusal to work, ultimately driving him from the locality'. The Platers and Ironshipwrights imported blacklegs and broke the helpers' union.

For demarcation disputes to arise, two conditions were necessary: there must be unions with control of entry to their own trade, and there must be jobs which the men of more than one trade could do. Printing satisfied the first condition, but not usually the second. The whole field of semi-skilled and unskilled labour in manufacturing and transport satisfied the second condition, but not the first. Building, engineering, and shipbuilding remained as the industries in which demarcation disputes were rife, because men of different craft unions were working elbow to elbow there on work of which some part — a part which grew as new methods and materials came in — was within the capacity of more than one craft. Only about a quarter of all union membership lay in this field. But within it conflict was endemic, and bitter, and it caused appalling waste and suffering. It happened commonly that when one union was in dispute with the employer, another union which claimed the job would put its own men in as blacklegs; one of the standing orders of the Trades Union Congress empowered its Parliamentary Committee to hear complaints that this had been done, and suspend, though only for two years, any union found guilty of it. When a dispute could not be settled by argument, one or the other union would down tools, regardless of all the others who got stopped too. In the shipyards of the Tyne, during three

---

[1] D. C. Cummings, *History of the United Society of Boilermakers and Iron and Steel Ship Builders* (1905), p. 111.

years of the early 1890's, there had been thirty-five weeks in which one or other of the chief shipbuilding crafts had been out, and with them many others who had no part nor lot in the dispute, yet who with their wives and children had to suffer deprivation. The main issues over which these battles had raged were, whether the boundary between engineers' and plumbers' work on pipes should be at a diameter of $2\frac{1}{2}$ or 3 inches, and whether joiners should have the sole right to put in wood $1\frac{1}{2}$ inches thick and less.

The obvious remedy for disputes of this kind seemed to be arbitration, which in fact was much used. Sometimes a unionist whose own society was not liable to conflict with the disputants was asked to give a ruling, as Thomas Burt, the leader of the Northumberland miners, was in the Tyne shipyards. Sometimes a judicious outsider was called in: a former judge of the high court of Calcutta, for twenty-two years Reader in Indian law at Oxford, was invoked to divide the work on the Niclausse boiler between the Engineers and the Boilermakers. But an arbiter who was sufficiently detached from the dispute to be above suspicion of partiality might find the technicalities of the trade beyond him. His award, however equitable, might provide an awkward working arrangement. Above all, if any award were rejected, there was no means of enforcing it: despite Thomas Burt's great prestige on the Tyne, when he gave his award the joiners rejected it, and went on strike for fourteen weeks; and it was they who had proposed that he be asked to serve. This was the dilemma of arbitration, in this as in other issues about work and wages: if the parties could be relied on to accept the award, they were usually close enough together to start with to be able to work out their own agreement; if they could not, then there was no way of compelling men to go on working day after day on terms they felt to be unjust.

Evidently a workable settlement was most likely to be reached by the parties' threshing it out themselves, and unions which were thrown much into conflict with one another sometimes had an understood procedure for negotiation, and set up a standing joint committee or the like to which they could resort as soon as each new dispute arose. But experience also showed that these negotiations could be helped by the presence of other unionists from their industry, who could not only fulfil something of the functions of conciliators, and enable the parties to test their claims against the common sense of the industry, but would also make them feel the common interest of their fellow workmen in their reaching a settlement. It had long been customary to bring these disputes before the Trades Council: but the gathering here of all and sundry, and the lack of any suitable procedure, made the occasion one for declamation rather than negotiation; indignant charges provoked angry countercharges; and any attempt by the Council to provide a settlement was likely to result in the secession of one of the unions, or even the break-up of the Council. The Trades Union Congress could deal only with charges of outright blacklegging by one union against another, and even so could not enforce its awards: when three arbitrators appointed under the standing orders of Congress in 1898 found the charge proved that the Engineers had allowed some of their members to blackleg against the Co-operative Smiths of Gateshead, the Engineers simply withdrew from Congress, and they stayed out for seven years. In 1907 the orders were to be amended to cover all charges of prejudicial conduct, but the new jurisdiction proved so embarrassing and ineffective that after only one year Congress went back to the old. The influence of neighbour unions was more likely to be exerted effectively when there was no general meeting, but only so many unions as were concerned in the industry were represented, and the spokesmen were union officers used to dealing with each other in matters of common concern. The settlement of demarcation disputes became in fact one of the main functions and achievements of the industrial federations of trade unions, which had now been growing up for some twenty years.

It was especially the New Unionism, with its enthusiasm for the common cause, that fostered these alliances: more than a hundred of them had been formed in 1890–6. Some, like the miners' that led the way in 1889, brought together unions of much the same occupations in different districts; the majority embraced unions of different occupations in the same industry. Foremost among these were the engineers and shipbuilders, the printing and kindred trades, and the London building trades. Many of the new formations died away, but nearly a hundred were known to exist in 1906.

The typical federation was a working understanding rather than a federal state in the political sense. For one thing, some of its constituent unions belonged to it in respect of only part of their membership, and might belong to other federations in respect of other parts. Its main purpose was to draw up and follow a common policy in collective bargaining, but it did not provide a unified direction: we should think not so much of an army headquarters deploying the corps under its command as of the starter trying to get a number of nervous horses and artful jockeys into line at the gate. The right method of voting in such a federation was carefully considered by the Webbs: should there be a card vote with each union casting as many votes as it had affiliated members, or should each union, big or small, count as one, or should there be some gearing in between? But the question had little practical consequence, precisely because each union retained its identity and its right to secede, and no method of voting could establish a supra-national authority within the federation, nor enforce any decision that some members would clear out rather than comply with. But the existence of a federation did mark the voluntary acceptance by the member unions of an obligation to stick together as far as possible, and particularly to adjust their mutual disputes by agreement within it.

5

Though the unions were jealous of their autonomy, a common threat would draw them together for defence, and from early times the various branches in one town would form a 'strike committee', or 'united trades protection association' to support some of their number in a local struggle with the employers or the law, or to uphold trade union interests before Parliament. These alliances often persisted after their immediate occasion had passed, and by the 1860's it had become usual for any large town to have its trades council. The scope for this sort of council was wide: one would have said it had a great future. It would have a part to play in every local dispute, advising branches that were in doubt what line to take, sending delegates to remonstrate with employers whose own workpeople dared not speak up, raising funds to support strikers, stopping blacklegs coming in or boycotting them when they did, organizing demonstrations, and mediating settlements. It could provide a friendly court in which differences between unions could be argued and adjusted. It was the natural agency for the missionary work of the move-ment, drumming for recruits at large, and founding branches in the trades not yet organized by its own members. It could pro-vide spokesmen for the organized labour of the town, to join the employers or the town council in setting up a local board of conciliation, or organizing relief works for the unemployed, or pressing on the government some measure favourable to local industry. It could put forward labour candidates in the elections for school boards and town councils, and indeed — there was no reason why not — for Parliament itself: a ha'penny a week from the unionists of any town with a member of its own would enable them to support their man at Westminster if they could get him in; the workmen of Battersea maintained John Burns, those of Poplar Will Crooks.

The trades council did in fact have a vitality commensurate with this so long as purely local unions were still important, or branches of a wider union kept a local initiative. In Aberdeen, for instance, in the 1880's and 1890's, the 'affiliated societies sent their leading members as delegates'[1] to the trades council, for it was in practice, and not only in principle, the centre of informa-tion, mutual aid, and common action for all the unionists of the city. Delegates sought advice from it when a claim was pending, and support when a dispute broke out. It had its recognized place in the community, its representatives were invited to civic ceremonies; it organized exhibitions of the industrial arts and made a profit out of them. It reached out into the countryside, helped the farm servants form a union, and engaged a profes-sional searcher of records for the defence of crofters against enclosing lairds. As fervour rose in the 1880's it was active in forming new branches and nursing them; it set up a standing committee 'for the purpose of arranging the better organization of the working classes in the city and district', which drew up a list of the workers without a union; making a start with the seamen it got Havelock Wilson up to address a meeting. In the depression of the mid-nineties it collected relief for the un-employed.

Besides its local role the trade council seemed to have a

[1] K. D. Buckley, *Trade Unionism in Aberdeen 1878 to 1900* (1955), p. 27.

function in public affairs. It was parliamentary business that had led the Manchester and Salford Trades Council in 1868 to convene what proved to be the first of the annual Trades Union Congresses — 'a Congress', as they called it then, 'of the representatives of Trade Councils, Federations of Trades and Trade Societies in general.' It was to the trades councils that they looked first, then to federations of unions, and only lastly to the unions themselves. To this day the title of the T.U.C.— the congress not of trade unions but of trades unions — marks this origin.

Yet in fact the trades councils did not gain influence as time went on, but lost it. The energies and expectations of the local unionists ceased to converge upon them, and radiated outwards instead to their own various headquarters. The basic cause of this was the sense of trade identity of the man in the union ranks, uniting him with men who followed the same trade elsewhere and everywhere, but marking him off from men in other trades even when they were his nearest neighbours. In Britain this separation of the sympathies was able, early on, to express itself in a type of nationwide occupational union: on a small island which already by 1850 had been equipped with extraordinarily good communications by rail, post, and telegraph, the local groupings of each trade could easily reach out to one another, and coalesce in unions which usually covered wide regions, and not seldom the whole country. It followed that when the men of one trade and town were in dispute, the help they could get from the executive of their own union was much greater than any donations their neighbours of other trades might make when the hat was passed round. Nor was this a matter of sympathies alone: it rested also on the contrast of organization — men were willing to make sacrifices to support the cause of others only where they had some voice in the decision to engage in the dispute, and they had that through the control which the executive of their own union kept over its branches, but the local trades council had never gained any such control over its affiliates. The vital lines of communication for each local trade ran to its own district delegates and national headquarters, and the contacts it had with other trades locally were of minor importance for good or ill, might indeed be significant to it chiefly as involving it in demarcation disputes, in which it looked to its own headquarters for support. An able and ambitious young unionist would see his career running from local to national office in his own union, and not through the trades council.

When the major interest of trade protection flowed away from the local council to the national union, the matters of common interest the council was left to deal with were too small to draw in the local leaders, or offset the divergences of trade interest and political outlook between their members: in particular, the councils were often split by feuds over demarcation.

The account of the life of a trade unionist which the Webbs took from the pen of a craftsman, describes how as a young branch officer of his own union he attends his first monthly meeting of the local Trades Council,[1] 'in the large and gaudily decorated assembly room, over the bar of one of the principal public houses of the town. A low platform is erected at one end, with chairs and a small table for the Chairman and Secretary. Below the platform is placed a long table at which are seated the reporters of the local newspapers, and the rest of the room is filled with chairs and improvised benches for the delegates. Here he meets the thirty or sixty delegates of the other Unions. He notices with regret that the salaried officials of the Societies which have their headquarters in the town, and the District Delegates of the great national Unions who are located in the neighbourhood . . . are conspicuous by their absence.' The business begins, there is much of it, and indictments of oppression get a cheer, but as the practical point is reached, again and again the Council does nothing because it is too divided within itself. One union is engaged in a dispute: 'the whole Council has applauded the strike, but when it comes to the question of a levy, the representatives of such old-established Unions as the Compositors, Engineers, Masons, and Bricklayers get up and explain that the Rules of their Societies do not allow them to pledge themselves.' When the delegates of one union accuse another's member of having blacklegged them when they were in dispute, the angry wrangle has to be shelved by reference to a committee which may never meet. 'The Socialist Secretary of a Labour Union submits a resolution calling on the Town Council to open municipal workshops for the unemployed — a project

[1] S. and B. Webb, *History of Trade Unionism* (1920 edn.), pp. 453-7.

which is ridiculed by the Conservative compositor (who is acting also as one of the reporters).' Only where a delegation reports on its representations to an alderman on behalf of the Fair Wages Clause does the new member feel himself in contact with effective action. 'Before the year is up he has realized that, except on such simple issues as the Fair Wages Clause, and the payment of Trade Union wages by the local authorities, the crowded meeting of tired workmen, unused to official business, with knowledge and interest strictly limited to a single industry, is useless as a Court of Appeal, and ineffective even as a joint committee of local trades. At the best the Council becomes the instrument, or, so to speak, the sounding-board, of the experienced members, who are in touch with the Trade Union Parliamentary leaders, and who (at a pay of only a few shillings a quarter) conduct all the correspondence and undertake all the business which the Trade Unions of the town have really in common.'

Though this link by correspondence with the leaders of Congress remained, the trades councils did not keep their seats in Congress itself: in 1892 it decided they should send delegates henceforward only for those unionists who were not already represented through their own societies; in 1895 it excluded them altogether. These changes were in one sense only the by-product of the struggle in which the big unions gained control of Congress, and the unionists proper threw out the politicians like Keir Hardie and Tom Mann. But they would not have come about if the trades councils had had more life in them. This they do seem to have had in Scotland: when the exclusion of 1895 was announced, Aberdeen convened a congress of the Scots trades councils to make protest, and Falkirk followed with another which proceeded to set up its own Scottish Trades Union Congress.

6

As the influence of the trades councils declined, the Trades Union Congress which they had founded changed its function and procedures radically.

It had begun as a demonstration, a rally of well-wishers, and a debating society: it 'will assume', said the initial invitation, 'the character of the Annual Meetings of the Social Science Association,' and among the subjects of papers to be read were such broad themes as 'Trade Unions and Political Economy', and 'The effect of Trade Unions on foreign competition'. At first some of these papers were read by outsiders. But when Frederic Harrison after reading a paper to the Congress of 1883 proposed to take part in one of the debates, he was not allowed to do so; and the address which Lord Rosebery gave to the Congress of 1884 was the last ever to be given by an outsider. In 1895 the rule was adopted that no one might attend Congress who was not working at his trade, or a permanent salaried officer of his union. At the same time Congress went over from its original and primitive method of voting by show of the hands of so many delegates as turned up, to the card vote in which each union was given a number of votes proportional to its affiliated membership, and cast them as a whole. The proposal to do this had originally been made by the Miners' Federation; it was carried with the support of the cotton spinners and weavers, and it gave the miners and the cotton unions between them a third of the votes in Congress.

The only nucleus of organization to remain between the annual conferences had long been a committee of ten, called the Parliamentary Committee, with a secretary, but the secretary's duties did not take up his full time — as late as 1906 the holder of the appointment was at the same time a Member of Parliament and secretary of his own small union — and the only source of funds lay in such donations as the unions chose to make, in response to the appeal which the Parliamentary Committee made to them annually. A regular income was provided for the first time in 1892, when it was agreed that unions should pay affiliation fees in proportion to their memberships. In 1902 the staff still consisted only of one secretary with an office off the Strand and a salary of £300 a year, out of which he paid for any clerical help; but in that year he began to get £250 a year tax free, and have his clerk provided separately; and a raising of the affiliation fee also enabled him to move into larger rooms in Victoria Street, get a new typewriter, and have a telephone put in. In 1904 he ceased to be subject to annual re-election. The office of president was also developed: as a gesture of thanks for hospitality the annual Congress used always to choose as its president a delegate from the town in which it met, but after an especially boring address from one such it provided in 1900 that henceforward its president should always be the outgoing chairman of the Parliamentary Committee. At the same time this Committee itself was given wide powers of exclusion and re-arrangement, in drawing up the programme for Congress out of the resolutions sent in by member unions. The membership of the Committee had never changed much, and since the card vote was adopted it had been dominated by the big unions, but in 1906 a chance was given to the smaller ones when the unions belonging to Congress were divided into twelve trade groups, and one seat on the Committee was reserved for a member of each of the first eleven groups, with five seats for the twelfth group, that of the miscellaneous trades. Thus the big unions could not pack the Committee with their own members; but since the whole of Congress voted for each seat they could still do much to ensure that the kind of man they approved of got in.

In these ways Congress adopted something of the familiar form of a deliberative assembly with its executive and its administrative service. But that service was remarkably small. It is true that the age was one when administration had hardly been discovered as a distinct field of productive activity, with its own science, requirements and potentialities; managers who were masters of their machinery paid little attention to their offices, prime ministers conducted correspondence in their own hands, in all walks of life much was done with a few pens, drawers, bits of string, and cardboard boxes, which has come to claim much more equipment since. Yet even so, the parsimony of the unions is remarkable. At a time when the annual income of the members of the unions in Congress must have been around £100 millions, they were willing to contribute less than £2,000 a year to it. The secretary's £250, about two and a half times the annual income of a craftsman then, caused some outcry in Congress. Well might the Webbs remark upon the crippling disabilities that the reluctance to spend money imposed on the unions. It was because of this, they wrote in 1897,[1] that the Parliamentary Committee had quite failed to assume and discharge the functions of a national executive for the trade union movement. It 'has had practically no means of fulfilling these functions. The central executive of the unions, from whom alone any responsible statement of the trade grievances and proposals

[1] S. and B. Webb, *Industrial Democracy*, Pt. II, Ch. IV (1920 edn.), pp. 226–8.

can be obtained, seldom dream of communicating their desires
to the Parliamentary Committee. This has naturally followed
from the fact that there is no central staff able to cope with such
proposals as have from time to time come in. . . . Nor does it ever
occur to the Parliamentary Committee to attempt to make up
for this deficiency by seeking expert or professional advice for
which Congress has never been asked to provide funds. We
despair of making any middle-class student realize the strength
and persistency of this disinclination of Trade Unionists to call
in outside counsel.' After these words were written, the Taff
Vale decision broke upon the unions, and the Parliamentary
Committee engaged a legal adviser — at an annual honorarium
of £50. Men long painfully practised in making do with small
sums recoiled before larger ones; they were not well acquainted
with the world in which much higher rates of pay than their
own passed current; for them to recognize the proficiency that
went with professional incomes was to accept their own inferiority. Those who have a reasonable confidence in themselves can
allow readily enough that other men will know better than they
about this thing or that: for those who are basically insecure and
goaded by a sense of inferiority it is not so easy.

None the less, there was one field within which the Congress
was active and effective — that of Parliamentary business. It
could be so, in fact, because it was dealing here with matters
whose practical upshot the members of the Committee understood well, and in which they could do much simply by their
own personal contacts. In bringing pressure to bear on members
of Parliament or ministers, moreover, to block one bill or promote another, they were asking other people to do things, not
organizing and directing action to be taken by their own
constituents. Above all, they were working here in a field where,
as nowhere else, a common interest of the unions enabled their
leaders to formulate and follow a policy without raising
questions of their own authority or threatening any union's
autonomy. In substance as well as in form the purpose of
Congress was described by its standing orders, which imposed
only two duties on its executive, apart from conducting the
annual congress itself: '(1) to watch all legislative measures
directly affecting the question of labour; (2) to initiate such
legislative action as Congress may direct.' This executive was

properly called the Parliamentary Committee. The matters on which Congress debated and resolved were almost all, in effect, demands for action by Ministers or by Parliament: improvements, for example, in the Government's own record as an employer; amendment of the Factory Acts, the law of workmen's compensation, the Truck Acts; a bill to limit the hours of work of shop assistants; above all, since the Taff Vale decision, a bill to restore the position of trade unions before the law.

Any alert-minded young wage-earner of the time would have noticed the absence from this programme of projects that would carry him forward on either of the two roads which were now being pointed out to him as the ways to a better world for the workers — direct action by the unions to secure better wages and working conditions and a voice for the worker in the counsels of his industry; and the sweeping away of capitalism by a Parliament which would nationalize the means of production, distribution, and exchange, and set up the socialist state. In fact, both these lines of policy had been advocated in Congress in the 1890's, and both had threatened to split it. True to the law of its own being, setting its own survival above the scope of its activity, with an unconscious astuteness Congress had preserved its unity by establishing a separate channel to carry each of these disturbing currents away.

The issue of direct action was brought to a head by the great struggle on which the Engineers entered in 1897. Congress that autumn instructed the Parliamentary Committee to collect and distribute the aid which other unions might be willing to give. This modest step was, the Committee said, 'a new departure from the ordinary work of Congress, there being no precedent during the past thirty years.' Surely this was surprising: surely Congress might have been expected to organize support for its members in dispute? That expectation overlooks a basic difficulty: no one union will hold its own hard-won funds at the disposal of another unless it can control that other's policy. A voluntary contribution in response to an appeal is one thing, an obligation to contribute quite another. If a hothead knows that any dispute in which he may involve his union will be supported by the funds of others, what is there to restrain him? Why should unions which have taxed their members lightly be able to draw on the resources of those who have made sacrifices to accumulate substantial funds? However just the cause of one union, what benefit will the members of another derive from supporting it? But unions could support one another if they entered into a federation through which they worked out a common policy for disputes. The idea that Congress should itself become a federation of this kind had come up from time to time; the New Unionism naturally seized on it, and in obedience to an instruction by Congress in 1890 the Parliamentary Committee drafted the constitution for it; a fresh scheme was narrowly rejected by the Congress of 1895. When the Engineers' dispute galvanized the attention of unionists again and showed a new power of the employers to organize and fight, Congress in 1897 passed a resolution calling on the unions to form a federation 'to render mutual assistance in disputes, strikes and lock-outs affecting any trade unions affiliated to the federation'. A special committee was elected to devise a plan, and this was put to a special congress to which all unions in the T.U.C. were invited to send delegates. Here, at Manchester, in January 1899, the General Federation of Trade Unions was founded. The Parliamentary Committee acted as the provisional executive only until July, when it handed the reins over to the forty-four unions which had joined the Federation, and which were to make their own arrangements for the governance of what was now an entirely independent body.

Congress was thus rid of the disruptive call for unity in the industrial struggle; and the General Federation carried away with it the frustrating conditions on which alone so much unity as it achieved could be maintained. To induce unions to join it allowed them to retain their independence in the conduct of disputes, and did not ask them to bring their own funds into hotchpotch: so its resources were limited to what could be accumulated from the dues paid to it by its member unions after they joined. They were to be able to draw on their funds at so much a week for each member involved in a stoppage approved by the management committee: a strike by a big union would have broken the bank, and the big unions did not come in. For small unions the Federation did offer a scheme of mutual insurance against being involved in a dispute too protracted for their own funds, but it could survive only if it could ensure that such disputes were rare. In fact, it did survive: it accumulated funds, it paid out benefits; the idea behind it counted for something, and it ranked higher in the estimation of contemporaries than one would think now, looking back; but as a practical force in industrial relations it was negligible. In Congress, however, when the cry was raised for unity on the battlefield, the Parliamentary Committee could say, 'Well, you have the General Federation. . . .' It was a standing demonstration of the impracticability of a high command for the unions.

The other drive which threatened the unity of Congress was that for Socialism. It did so not only because socialism was itself an emotive issue, passionately believed in by some unionists, looked on with as much horror as free love by others; but also because it threatened the established way of getting trade unionists into the House of Commons. This was, to be adopted, or at least supported, by the Liberal party. In the general election of 1892 there were twenty of these Lib-Lab candidates, and ten of them got in; the Social Democratic Federation put up sixteen of its own, and only three got in. In 1895, nine Lib-Labs succeeded, when all twenty-eight candidates put forward by the Independent Labour Party were defeated. Thus the claim that the unions should support labour's own independent candidates offered nothing to those whose object was to get trade unionists into the House to promote trade union interests there: nay worse, it threatened to upset the existing representation by splitting the vote. On the other hand, the claim was insistent, and there could be no doubt in the 1890's that independent labour candidates pledged to socialism were getting more popular support. In 1898 the German socialists polled three million votes and won fifty seats in the Reichstag. From time to time the claim had been made that Congress should put forward and maintain its own candidates, but it had not been willing to find the money. A proposal of this kind came up again in 1899, but now those who were most anxious to increase labour representation would have none of it, for the funds would be controlled by the Lib-Lab Parliamentary Committee. Instead, Congress considered a motion instructing the Committee to convene a conference of 'all Co-operative, Socialistic Trade Unions, and other working-class organizations', 'to devise ways and means for securing the return of an increased number of labour members to the next Parliament'. The miners and the

The Parliamentary Committee of the Trades Union Congress, 1900.

At back (left to right): W. C. STEADMAN (Barge Builders; Sec. of Parly. C'ee. 1905–10); R. BELL (Railway Servants); W. THORNE (Gasworkers and General Labourers); W. B. HORNIDGE (Boot and Shoe Operatives); D. HOLMES (Amalgamated Weavers); W. MULLIN (Card and Blowing Room Operatives).

In front (left to right): A. WILKIE (Shipwrights); E. COWEY (Miners' Federation); C. W. BOWERMAN (London Society of Compositors; Sec. of Parly. C'ee. 1911–23); S. WOODS (Miners' Federation; Sec. of Parly. C'ee. 1894–1904); F. CHANDLER (Carpenters and Joiners); W. J. DAVIS (Brassworkers); with fraternal delegates from the American Federation of Labor—J. M. HUNTER (Illinois Miners); S. J. KENT (Brotherhood of Carpenters and Joiners).

cotton spinners thought that nothing could come of it, and the motion was adopted only by a majority of about five to four; but it can hardly have been unwelcome to the Parliamentary Committee, if only as the convenient disposal of an inconvenient demand.

The conference was held — the occasion is historic and well known — in the Memorial Hall, Farringdon Street, in the City of London, on two days of February, 1900. Little more than half a million unionists, out of nearly two million in the country then, were represented; the Miners' Federation with its reliance on Lib-Lab representation stayed away. The political associations represented were the Social Democratic Federation, the Independent Labour Party, and the Fabian Society. The conference reached agreement because it made no attempt to define doctrine: a sufficient definition of the object was to set up 'a distinct Labour Group in Parliament, who shall have their own Whips and agree upon their policy, which must embrace a readiness to co-operate with any party which for the time being may be engaged in promoting legislation in the direct interest of Labour, and be equally ready to associate themselves with any party in opposing measures having an opposite tendency'. This made sense to the unions, and the socialists did not press for more. In return, the unions agreed to pay a levy of ten shillings a year for each thousand members. To administer this income, a Labour Representation Committee was set up, and the unions now recognized the hold of the doctrines they had not wanted to write large, by giving the socialist associations a majority of seats on the committee, with an I.L.P. delegate, J. Ramsay MacDonald, as secretary.

It was at the next Congress, to which this was reported, that the news came of Mr Justice Farwell's judgment in the Taff Vale case: than which, in the sequel, nothing could have done more to convince trade unionists of every sort that they needed more representation in the House. But the question of what form that representation should take had now been provided for separately from the traditional agenda of Congress, and the Parliamentary Committee as such took no responsibility for it. At the Congress of 1904 a number of resolutions on the Labour Representation Committee were ruled out of order because they purported 'to endorse or amend the constitution of an independent and out-

T

side body'. The President of Congress that year, Richard Bell of the Railway Servants, had his own reason to be glad that a debate was precluded, for he himself would have come under fire in it, as one who had recently supported the Liberal candidate in a by-election. The circumstance shows how Congress in its own proper work was helped by having hived off the disputatious business of politics.

That work of Congress, though so circumscribed, had always been substantial, and had recently gained much in extent and importance.

Traditionally, the Parliamentary Committee regarded itself as having been briefed by each Congress, on returning from which it set about its year's work of bringing the resolutions of Congress to the notice of ministers and Parliament. That was a considerable task in itself. Deputations must be arranged: the Committee reported to the Congress of 1905 how it had waited upon four Ministers and represented the views of Congress to them on many matters, ranging from the law of workmen's compensation to the injustice of charging 2s. 7d. for the death certificate of a member of a trade union, when if he had been the member of a friendly society the charge would have been only 1s. On matters of legislation there was legal advice to be taken from the standing counsel, Edmund Browne, or one of the lawyers in politics, like H. H. Asquith, who were willing to advise the Committee without fee. At the beginning of each Parliamentary term Sir Charles Dilke would arrange a meeting at the House between spokesmen of the Committee and Members who were trade unionists themselves or close sympathizers. Having drafted a bill, the Committee would try to find a private member to introduce it. When a government measure was going through, it would ensure that the views of Congress found expression on the floor of the House and in the amendments considered upstairs. When a matter of special interest to trade unionists was going to be raised, it would send its own whip out to every Member. It printed copies of the division lists, to enable trade unionists everywhere to reward their friends and punish their enemies.

Though this lobbying was so active, it had not until recently gone beyond the instructions given to the Committee by Congress. In 1905, however, the chairman of the Committee reported to Congress that 'for the past two or three years, an entirely new, and, I trust, a welcome departure has been made. For instead of being content with simply registering and carrying out the decisions of Congress, they have taken the initiative on several matters of importance affecting the Labour movement'. He would have been thinking there especially of unemployment: the Committee had not merely acted on a resolution of the last Congress but had joined with the General Federation of Trade Unions and the Labour members of Parliament in drawing up a report on the causes and remedies. It was natural that the Committee should gain in initiative as the range of Parliamentary action in social questions extended. In the 1890's the widest-reaching measure with which the Committee had been concerned was probably the law of employers' liability; but now, with the Taff Vale decision, the whole law of trade unionism had been cast into the melting-pot, and a new Trade Disputes Bill was before the House. By an Act of 1905 a Conservative government had admitted that the relief of unemployment was not a matter only for the Poor Law, and had itself accepted some implicit responsibility for maintaining employment. At every turn a more sensitive social conscience and a greater awareness of the suffering caused by social ills went with a growing belief that these ills were remediable, and that the remedies must be applied by government. Measures which only ten years ago would have been dismissed as impracticable were now debated seriously: the enforcement of minimum wages for sweated workers, for instance, or the eight hours' day for the miners.

Here was a growing scope for the trade unions in politics. The Parliamentary Committee proved equal to the need. It had proposals to make, and a right to be heard. When the Prime Minister made no more than formal acknowledgment of its proposals for the relief of unemployment, its secretary could remind him 'that the members of the Trades Union Congress and the General Federation of Trade Unions, numbering two million of the organized workers of the country, are pressing for a reply'. Congress had bounded its activities to the things in which those workers could speak with one voice. It happened that these things were now of ever growing public scope and consequence. The trade unions were on their way to becoming an estate of the realm. By its assiduity and growing initiative, the Parliamentary Committee had made good its claim to speak for it in the affairs of government.

Yet there was no corresponding development in the internal structure of Congress. Through the twelve months between its annual assemblies, its internal communications depended formally only on the printed reports, the circulars, and the inquiries, which the Parliamentary Committee sent out to member unions; though in practice these would have been supplemented by personal contacts between the ten Committee members and other union officers. The annual Congress itself, though becoming a little more businesslike, remained confused in conception and overcrowded with business. Moving on from its original purpose of a rally, it might have begun to fulfil other functions — the debating of general principles, or the study of questions prepared and documented by a staff, or the review and direction of the actions of an executive; but it was not consciously directed towards any of them. What it did simply depended on what resolutions the member unions sent in. Monday went on ceremonies and formalities. On Tuesday morning the President gave his address, and the rest of the session was devoted to discussing the report of the Parliamentary Committee, which until recently had been rehearsed by the secretary, but now was taken as read. There remained eight sessions, morning and afternoon, which were given up — so much of them as was left after hearing six or seven fraternal addresses — to the discussion *seriatim* of such resolutions as the member unions had sent in. Something was being done now to condense and combine them, but the Congress of 1905 still had fifty resolutions to get through: small wonder that by Friday morning the movers' speeches had to be limited to five minutes and the rest to three. The order in which subjects were taken was decided by lot. A serious debate was still possible on an issue of principle like compulsory arbitration, but it had to take its turn with the London Cabmen's annual protest against the privilege system at railway stations, and a wrangle about where Congress should meet next year. In effect, the agenda consisted of a questionnaire made up of entries sent in by this union and that, and the delegations put Yes or No against each question with their card vote.

For the Webbs the remedy was clear: working as always with a political analogy, they urged the unions to regard themselves as members of a federation, whose government would initiate policy and order the business of the representative assembly to which it was responsible. To turn Congress 'into a useful piece of democratic machinery', they said, 'the first requisite is a strong "Front Bench" of reponsible leaders, who have themselves arrived at a definite and consistent policy. . . . The great officials of the leading trades must realize that it is their duty, not merely to stir up their own branches to feeble and fitful agitation for the particular legal reforms that they desire themselves, but to get constructed the federal organization which alone can secure their accomplishment.'[1]

But a federal government is possible only when the member states have relinquished to it certain powers, however limited, over their own citizens, and the unions joining Congress never did and never could do that. The disabilities of Congress persisted not through ineptitude but because they were inherent in its members' conception of it. In their eyes it never was and never should be a federation, but only an alliance for certain common purposes of bodies which retained their autonomy, and would react fiercely to any threat of encroachment upon it. One might have thought that they could at least have empowered Congress to give binding awards in settlement of their disputes with one another, and in fact there was a rule of Congress which said, guardedly enough, that 'any society engaged in a dispute and considering themselves aggrieved by reason of the members of another society assisting to defeat those on strike, may report the circumstances to the Parliamentary Committee, who may then take such steps as the circumstances may warrant'. The use of 'who' instead of 'which' for the Committee is significant: there were particular men on it who might use their good offices, but it was not a constituted authority. We have already noted how in 1898 the arbitrators it had appointed recommended that the Engineers withdraw their members from jobs properly belonging to the Co-operative Smiths of Gateshead: the Engineers — then the biggest union in the country — simply left Congress, and they did not come

---

[1] S. and B. Webb, *Industrial Democracy* (1920 edn.), pp. 268, 275; also their *History of Trade Unionism* (1920 edn.), pp. 561–72.

back till 1905. The incident reveals the conditions on which alone the Parliamentary Committee could conduct the affairs of Congress. It could exhort member unions, but not give them instructions: it could speak for Congress, but not negotiate for it, because it could not commit members over whom it had no control. There was no element of sovereignty, however small, which they had relinquished.

The causes of this went deeper than the jealousy of each union executive for its independence, and the sense of trade identity that marked off one group from another. These resistances were real, but if they had stood alone they might well have gone down before the strategic advantage of a unified government. The basic obstacle was that the union executives could not delegate powers they did not possess themselves. The political analogy, of state government and federal government, is fundamentally misleading. If the power to coerce is an essential attribute of government then the unions did not have governments at all. True, a member who failed to comply with union policy could be expelled, but when any number of members was at variance with headquarters or with the rest of the membership expulsion was a sanction more dangerous to the union than the member: secession was often easy, breakaway unions could be formed, rival unions were eager to take members over. A common interest had brought men together, they had appointed an executive to pursue the common purpose; they would sacrifice much of their own advantage or opinion for the sake of unity, and might stand by a leader even when they did not like what he had done; but in the last resort they were bound by no lien to this voluntary association, which was their creature not their ruler. It is this protean quality of a trade union that accounts for the difficulty of fitting it into any system of law: at once an organized, unitary body of great power, and a congeries drawn together like a football crowd, streaming off again in all directions. The vote of the majority of union executives could not give Congress power to give orders to them all, because they themselves had no such power over their own members.

It is well for democracy that this is so. If the trade unions had governments endowed with sovereignty and able to enforce discipline, they would be as hard to reconcile with Parliament as the army was in Cromwell's day.

7

We have seen how the Trades Union Congress set up the General Federation as a way of meeting the demand for closer unity without itself bearing the strains that the attempt to unify would bring in practice. It is arguable that the offspring, the scapegoat one might almost say, could have become more powerful than Congress itself. What actually happened to it deserves some further notice.

It had been set up with singularly little discussion. Congress in 1898 was to have given a day to debating its constitution, but the hall it was meeting in was burnt down in the small hours of that morning, and a special Congress was summoned instead for the next January. At the outset this gathering refused to consider the various plans for federation that had been put up — 'the official scheme, Mr Dipper's scheme, Mr Eyre's scheme, the Woolwich scheme, the *Clarion* scheme, Mr Harrock's scheme, the London Trades Council scheme' — and settled down for three days to consider the official scheme alone, rule by rule: an issue of principle could be raised only by moving an amendment to a rule, and there seem to have been only two debates of any general interest — one on the contention that federation should begin with kindred trades and the national body be only a federation of federations; the other on a direction proposed by Mawdsley of the Cotton Spinners, that the committee of the proposed federation 'must not in any shape or form interfere with any Society forming part of the Federation, either in the initiation or management of disputes'; both proposals were defeated. Mawdsley's had at least gone to the heart of the matter: but how could the Federation control its dispute benefit if it could have no voice in the disputes?

Whether advertently or not, the Congress answered this question by giving the Federation no power whatever to restrict its members' actions, but discretion to withhold benefit from them. The crucial rule ran: 'Societies shall be entitled to the undermentioned benefits, providing always that the societies receive the approval of the General Council or Management Committee to any dispute before being entered on.' To this the Congress added an amendment moved by James Sexton of the Liverpool dockers, tacking on the words 'or is afterward approved by these bodies' at the end of the rule: the join was awkward, but the intention to keep a free hand for the members was clear. But what would happen if they became much involved in strife? How could the federation refuse them benefit if their cause was good? How could it pay them benefit if their fight was long? In practice, its Management Committee followed one overriding principle — benefits must not exceed income — and to keep them down it used any pretext it could find. On the very first claim to reach it, it remarked that 'the action of this society in striking without first obtaining the approval of the Management Committee, there being ample time to obtain such approval, would in ordinary circumstances have warranted the Committee in withholding the benefit'. This was not only unsupported by the rules, but actually precluded by Sexton's amendment. Yet the Committee went on to promulgate it as a principle, under the plea that they were giving effect to another rule which said that one object of the Federation was to promote industrial peace and assist in the settlement of disputes — 'I am instructed', the secretary wrote to members at the end of the first year's working, 'to inform you of the following decisions: 1st. That Societies initiating any movement for an alteration in their working conditions, MUST notify the Management Committee, simultaneously with sending first notice of desired alteration to employers. . . . Similarly on receipt of any notice from employers likely to lead to disputes.' '2nd. At the same time, the Committee stressed the need to seek peace by all means, recommending that on any difference arising between Societies affiliated and their employers, every possible method of settling such difference by peaceful methods should be tried; as a means to which the Executive Committees of collateral Societies, who have members working in the shops likely to be affected, should be communicated with, with a view to securing their support and (if desired) assistance in negotiating with the employers.' This was used to withhold benefit from any stoppage that the union could conceivably have avoided. A few days after this letter went out the Committee had before it a claim from the Ironfounders for benefit for twenty-eight of their members who had stopped work in a Huddersfield firm because it had taken on a non-union man. 'Out of a total of 1,542 foundries in the country 587 employed none but members of the Ironfounders' Society, and they naturally desired to retain the shops they had. Under their rules the members could cease work without sanction from the Executive Committee if any privileges they enjoyed were attacked. A long discussion ensued, during which it was ascertained that the man objected to was too old to join the society, but that the district by-rules stated that in such cases one shilling a week should be paid to the society as an acknowledgment. This, it was stated, the man had objected to pay, asserting that sixpence was sufficient. After a somewhat heated discussion, it was moved by Messrs Arrandale and Davis that benefit be granted, Messrs Crinion and Barnes submitting a direct negative. The mover argued that unless benefit was granted it would be a direct encouragement to employers to employ non-unionists; those against granting benefit pointed out the danger there was of the Federation funds not being able to meet claims of this description, and intimated that such disputes should be borne by the societies themselves.' On a division the noes had it, but the ayes being incensed a sub-committee was appointed to investigate the case on the spot. When this reported, it brought out 'the unnecessary haste there had been in resorting to a stoppage of work, without first exhausting the means whereby a peaceful settlement might have been arrived at; the unsatisfactory condition of the town as a whole from a Trade Union point of view in this trade and the extreme difficulty of enforcing the Ironfounders' Huddersfield by-laws in the face of such circumstances; on the other hand it was pointed out that the shops held exclusively by the Ironfounders and the position they had gained should be maintained at all hazards, the opinion held, however, by the majority was that this (under the circumstances) could only be done by diplomacy and tact.' There voted, for granting relief, 3; against, 9. In fact, the clearer the principle, the greater the embarrassment: the Committee could not write a blank cheque by accepting any category of dispute as always and everywhere entitled to support.

The word must soon have got round that there was nothing to be got out of the Federation except chickenfeed. It only supported one struggle of any size — that of the Bethesda quarrymen against Lord Penrhyn — and that it had to let go. For the rest, a list of claims for benefit granted would run like this:

    2 members of the Boot and Shoe Operatives, seeking uniform
        rates in London.

  28 ....ditto, resisting innovation at Chesterfield.

    1 member of the Amalgamated Brassworkers, resisting reduc-
        tion at Huddersfield.

    8 members of the Cotton Spinners' Society, enforcing district
        conditions at Mossley.

  30 ....Amalgamated Society of Engineers, seeking
        advance on the Clyde. . .

and so on. They were all local issues. General wage negotiations,
and disputes bringing a whole union into action, simply do not
appear. There was nothing in the rules to exclude them; but
everyone knew that the Federation could not afford them.

Yet though the disputes with which the Federation allowed
itself to be concerned were mostly small ones, they were disputes,
and by the law of its own being it was concerned with them. In
this it differed basically from the Trades Union Congress, and
came nearer the Continental federations: the essential point was
that it did take part in negotiations with employers. 'During the
last year,' the Chairman told the annual council meeting in
1905, 'they had been called upon on various occasions by affiliated societies to negotiate with employers where the societies
had practically failed to come to an amicable agreement, and
he was glad to say that through the agency of the Federation
they had been able, first of all, to stave off industrial warfare,
and, in the second place, to support, financially and morally,
societies which have been forced to take up industrial battle.'
No doubt the delegation that the Federation sent down was
usually more concerned to get a settlement than a victory, but it
did appear, it did negotiate; and in 1905–6 the Federation took
an active part in a big issue — the claim for weekly instead of
fortnightly pays by the shipbuilders on the Clyde, which at one
time threatened to stop all the yards there. In 1908 the Vice-
President of the Federation, Alderman Gee, himself the Textile
Workers' secretary, appeared with Sexton of the Dockers to
negotiate an agreement for the waterside workers of Dublin. Our
knowledge of what has happened since then in Scandinavia
shows what scope for development there was in this — scope for
the working out of a common wage policy among the unions,
and the participation of officers of the trade union federation in

the negotiations industry by industry, restraining here and reinforcing there. The field was one, moreover, which the Trades Union Congress left entirely clear.

There was another field of great possibilities which Congress was leaving clear — that of union regrouping and recruitment. The Federation was beginning to pay attention to it. In 1906 the Management Committee was suggesting to members that 'the days of individual societies holding organizing meetings are fast approaching a close, and that from the economical, as well as the general result point of view, the united attack upon non-union centres is the up-to-date method. Much good has already been done in this connection, and we have held several extremely successful meetings'. It was also out to foster amalgamation. 'We want', it said, 'more Trade Unionists and fewer Trade Unions. Steps are at present being taken in this direction with respect to at least one branch of labour.' These were modest moves, but moves in a direction where there was much to do. It was not inconceivable even in the entrenched unionism of Britain that a federation should gain gradually in power and authority as it made its way along it.

There was yet another field of activity for a trade union centre, which the Trades Union Congress had relinquished — that of association with the centres in other countries. Congress had burnt its fingers when it arranged an international labour conference in London in 1896: the bedlam, the tribal warfare, the flowing locks and yet more flowing oratory, were intensely annoying, even humiliating to its leaders, and henceforward they had no truck with foreigners — their annual exchange of fraternal delegates with the American Federation of Labour not falling under that condemnation. The newly formed General Federation was able to claim some consequence by moving into the gap, and holding itself forth as the evident counterpart to the federations of unions in other countries. Its Chairman did that as early as its second annual meeting, which was addressed moreover by the Chairman of the Danish federation of unions. The next year, 1902, it sent representatives to Stuttgart for an international conference of national federations, and its own next annual meeting was held jointly with a conference attended by delegates from the unions of seven European countries. The Federation's own reports now began to contain long accounts of the labour movements in other countries, and pictures of their leaders. Here was an opportunity. If the trade unions of the industrialized countries of Europe could arrive at a simple understanding to take action jointly on some essentials of policy, they would not only gain strength in their own countries but become a force in international relations. No one could say yet that this would be beyond them as their own organization matured. If it came about, it would be the General Federation that would take part in it for Britain.

Perhaps that alone happens which alone could have happened, and we can point out the factors which may have condemned the Federation to insignificance from its inception. Its own funds were small compared with its members'. By the end of 1905 they amounted to £125,000: about as much as a single big union would have — the Northumberland Miners, or the Shipwrights, or the Locomotive Engineers — and only the fortieth part of what the hundred principal unions held between them. Some of the strongest unions would not go near it. Its ninety members included the Engineers and the Cotton Spinners, but only seven others of any consequence, and they contained only a fifth of all trade unionists. The boilermakers, the bricklayers, the carpenters, the railway servants, and above all the miners remained outside it. These things seem a sufficient explanation of its ineffectiveness.

Yet there is a danger of reading ends into beginnings, and supposing that the potentialities of the Federation were never greater than its achievement. In fact, in 1900 its potentialities were great. Congress had surrendered to it three fields in which it was free to operate, if a federation could operate at all, and they were fields whose importance was actually increasing and might have been made to increase still more — 'federated' wage negotiation, union recruiting and regrouping, and the international linking of unions. If only it had been more fortunate, in two ways — if more of the bigger unions had given it a trial as the Engineers and the Cotton Spinners did, and if it had found a leader with the generalship of a Bevin: then what might it not have become? Suppose that its leader had manoeuvred early on, in some substantial dispute involving a member union, to get the negotiations into the hands of the Federation itself, whose resources he concentrated upon it at the same time, not

in shillings for a few men here and there but in a mass sufficient
to decide the outcome. Suppose he had devised a method much
as the iron and steel trades found later, for gradually fusing the
unions in an industry without any frontal attack on their
present independence; and so had begun an orderly regrouping
of the Federation's membership industry by industry. Might we
not then be pointing out now how Congress had chosen to
relinquish the leadership of labour, handing over political
representation to one body, and wage negotiation, union organization, and international association, to another; and how it
had reaped the consequences, in the limitation of its own
functions to lobbying, while the Federation grew steadily in
activity and authority? But it was not so. Too many strong
unions had refused to come in at the start, and none had been
persuaded to join since. The officers of the Federation, the
Chairman, Pete Curran of the Gasworkers, and the secretary,
Isaac Mitchell of the Engineers, seem to have been from the
second eleven, finding offices here to which in their own unions
their way was blocked by abler men — Will Thorne and J. R.
Clynes in the Gasworkers, G. N. Barnes in the Engineers. Their
care and caution sufficed to keep the Federation together and
build up its funds, but only at the cost of proclaiming its useless-
ness. An enterprise which could grow only by calculated auda-
city was stunted by prudence and parsimony.

8

Over against the trade unions stood a certain number of
employers' associations. The building industry was in a class by
itself, having as many associations as all the other industries put
together: in 1902 it was known to have 24 federations of
employers and 377 local associations. That left some 26
federations, and 390 local associations, spread over nine other
industries.

We know much less about these employers' associations than
about the unions: they shunned publicity; though instances of
them went back to the early days of the industrial revolution
they had no continuous history; they were not a cause, a movement, and they had no doctrine, no literature.

There were, it is true, some associations of old standing,
formed to lobby at Westminster, or limit competition between

their members, which took on the function of presenting a common front to the unions. As far back as 1803 a general meeting of the Master Papermakers at the George and Vulture Tavern, Cornhill, London, resolved that it was 'highly expedient the whole of the Trade should be formed into one general Society, under the Denomination of, The United Society of Master Papermakers of Great Britain, associated solely for the purpose of resisting the illegal Combinations existing amongst their journeymen'; and the 'solely' was there only to keep them on the right side of the law which then forbade combinations of masters to fix wages no less than those of the men, for in fact they already had a Committee, widely supported by the papermakers of the south, which had been active in lobbying against the excise duty on paper and trying to regulate the price of rags. But associations of that kind had become rare among British firms. The coming of free trade removed what was their chief object in many other countries — lobbying for the tariff. A trade particularly subject to control might have its protective association, like the London Master Bakers', which required that when a loaf was bought from any member for the purpose of analysis he should at once inform the Committee, and make available to it a sample of the flour; and which also worked for the repeal of vexatious statutes and the enforcement of the Adulteration of Food Acts. But the general unwillingness of Parliament to intervene in industry made such cases exceptional.

One not uncommon object of employers' associations today is the provision of information, and the carrying on of research so far as that is beyond the capacity of single firms. But research was not in the air then as it is now. Though a number of the employers' associations reviewed by the Royal Commission on Labour included the provision of information among their general objects, not one seems to have included research: the nearest any came to it was the promotion of technical education.

Thus the impact of the unions did not fall upon many existing employers' associations that could now add collective bargaining to their other functions; often, we are told, there was no association among the employers at all until the unions forced one on them. There was said to have been no organization whatever among employers of dock and wharf labour in London until 1890, the year after the great dock strike, when association was provoked by the Dock Labourers' Union forbidding their members to deliver goods to non-unionist carmen. The formation of the Shipping Federation in 1890 was ascribed to the need to resist interference with the shipowners' business by the unreasonable demands and coercive tactics of the Sailors' and Firemen's Union. The master tailors complained to the Royal Commission on Labour that the men refused to recognize their association, though for their part they did recognize the men's union: they thought the men regarded their association as 'an upstart affair', because it had only been in existence for two and a half years, whereas the Society of Tailors had been going for twenty-six years or more. The National Association of Master Builders had been set up in 1878 as the result of the strike which the Manchester carpenters led in 1877 and which lasted throughout the year.

The main reason for the reluctance of employers to combine except under pressure was that they were competitors who sat down together uneasily for any purpose. 'Employers frequently seem to combine rather unwillingly,' the Royal Commission on Labour reported,[1] 'and the trade competition between them often makes it difficult for them to hold together.' 'You cannot get Batley and Dewsbury men to combine for anything,' a witness before an enquiry into industrial agreements said in 1912.[2] Even when an association was kept up there were usually a good many employers who would not come in, or came in and went out as they chose. The secretary of the Patternmakers wrote of the engineering employers in Lancashire, as late as 1906, 'The chief feature of our negotiations with (them) was their lack of co-ordination and consistency. Their local associations coalesced and separated exactly as it suited them. They granted common terms only when and where we could supply the necessary pressure.'[3] Generally it was found that associations formed only under the pressure of some attack by the unions were apt to fall into abeyance, or die away altogether, when the unions were quiet again.

[1] Royal Commission on Labour, Fifth and Final Report, Pt. 1 (C. 7421 of 1894), para. 81.
[2] Industrial Council, Enquiry into Industrial Agreements. Minutes of Evidence (Cd. 6953 of 1913), Qs. 5522–6.
[3] W. Mosses, *The History of the United Pattern Makers' Association, 1872–1922* (1922), p. 133.

The associations formed in this setting, as they presented themselves to the Royal Commission on Labour in the 1890's, naturally showed much diversity. Some were informal, others highly organized. An understanding that there should be consultation with a view to common action when the need arose could exist without any association being constituted; there were bodies like the Fife Coalowners which had no constitution, and normally left each member to deal with his own men, but got into touch with the miners' secretary when any general advance or reduction of wages was at issue; or the coalowners in the county associations for Derby, Nottingham, and Leicester, which existed, it was said, for discussion of prices and wages, but did not require their members to adhere to a common policy, and had no funds with which to support a member under attack. On the other hand were bodies with elaborate constitutions and procedures. The Master Tailors, for instance, who had branches through all Great Britain except London, required each branch to appoint an arbitration committee to which any dispute arising between a member and his workpeople must be reported at once, and failing a settlement by this committee the dispute was to come before a general meeting of the branch, from which if still unsettled it went up to the Central Board; each branch adopted a statement of maximum prices payable to workpeople, and a member found guilty of transgressing this or any other rule was subject to fine, while the Board could make it a condition of any settlement with the unions that they should withdraw their members from his employ. This association, it was said, aimed at applying throughout the country a common wage scale and system of grading. Most associations will have fallen between these extremes, having a written constitution of a simple kind, but relying on custom and unwritten understandings for much of their procedure. Very likely one or more of the associations had by 1906 an office of its own, and a full-time officer, but we do not hear of it, the administration being almost always carried on by the officers at their own works, in what time they could spare from their own business. The associations which lacked development on paper were not necessarily less durable or effective than the others; but the employers' increasing participation in joint councils with the unions was a force making for codification of their own constitutions.

The great majority of the associations were local still, limited to a town, a county, or an industrial region at most, as their names suggest — the Cleveland Ironmasters, the Glasgow Master Plasterers, the Huddersfield Woollen Manufacturers and Spinners. But where the industry extended beyond such bounds of locality the local associations tended to join in federations or become branches of a single wider association. The larger body might itself deal with the unions, or confine itself to providing some services to members who continued to negotiate locally, but even here it would naturally try to co-ordinate policy on issues of principle, if not of shillings and pence. By 1906 a number of bodies had arisen each containing the greater part of all the employers in the industry throughout the country: this was so notably in shipping, engineering, the main sections of the textile industry, and building. But most of these wide federations themselves played no part as yet in industrial disputes, beyond organizing what help they could at the time for their members involved in one in any particular district.

The characteristic origin of the employers' associations in the need to combine for defence set its mark on their procedure. 'Have any of these federations rules as to what is to take place in the case of a strike against any one of the members of the Federation?' — the question, put by a member of the Royal Commission on Trade Disputes[1], envisages the main contingency which the associations were formed to meet. It was answered by Sir Benjamin Browne, the Chairman of the Tyne shipbuilders Hawthorn, Leslie and Co., and a member of four employers' associations, the engineers', the shipbuilders', and the coal trades of Durham and Northumberland. 'When you say rules', he answered, 'we generally go by our own discretion. I would rather say we have customs and we deal with each case on its own merits. . . . Supposing there is a strike in one works, we first of all consider whether the employer is right or wrong, and if he is wrong we tell him he must give way, but if we think he is right we try to meet the workmen and to get the thing settled by peaceable means. In the very large majority of cases that is done satisfactorily. . . . If there comes a stoppage of work at last, we

[1] Royal Commission on Trade Disputes and Trade Combinations, Minutes of Evidence (Cd. 2826 of 1906), Q. 2771–2.

u

sometimes help the employer by pecuniary help, but in some cases, as a last resort, we lock out all the men belonging to that Union. That was done in 1897 with the engineers.' The South Yorkshire Coalowners paid out over £120,000 in the way of such 'pecuniary help' in the ten years down to 1904. Firms might also take on work on behalf of another that was struck; and there was an understanding that they should not take on any of that firm's workpeople while they were out. These practices all applied to a dispute occurring in only one firm, or one or two firms, at a time: if all members were involved in a dispute together, each bore his own costs. Unlike the trade unions, the employers' associations do not seem to have built up funds in time of peace on which to draw in a dispute — the sufficient reason would be that they did not need to do so, as they would hardly be beaten in a struggle simply through lack of cash with which to maintain the essential services of their plants; such a fund would have served only as a dividend equalization account. One purpose of the support given to any one firm under attack was to prevent the unions forcing through a rise in wages by negotiating it with one or two selected firms first, and then demanding that the others follow suit or go one better — the tactics of pattern bargaining and whipsawing, as they are known in America to-day. Incomplete and unstable though the development of employers' associations was by 1906, it had been sufficient already to take a decisive effect on the pattern of British wage negotiation: it was clear now that the unit of bargaining was to be not the single plant or single firm, as it remains so often in America to this day, but at least a whole district of one industry, and sometimes a wider area still.

Though many of the employers' associations provided little more than a mutual insurance against their members' being attacked one at a time, there were ways in which some of them went further. The Shipping Federation was regarded as particularly active against the unions. Its members would employ only seamen who held the 'Federation Ticket', which pledged its holder to sail in any vessel for which he had signed articles even though other members of the crew might prove to be non-unionists, and it had established the use of this ticket against the desperate resistance of the Seamen's Union. It also undertook to supply labour to any of its members whose own men were out — unless, it was said, the dispute was about wages; the implication being that this importation of blacklegs was used only in defence against 'unwarranted interference' with the business of the employer. In other employers' associations, again, it was the practice to circulate black-lists of 'trouble makers'; sometimes there was a rule that no employer should take on a man who had been employed by another member without first applying to that member for information, and one of the objects of the unions in the Federation of Engineering and Shipbuilding Trades was to abolish this 'character note system'. Once entered upon a struggle with a union which they had found specially irksome, the employers might hold out for the unconditional surrender which would in fact mean the break-up of the union. In the industries subject to fluctuations of demand, they might move for a reduction of wages when trade was slack, and apply a general lock-out to enforce it.

Yet after these things have been taken into account, it remains noteworthy that, on the evidence of the unions themselves before two Royal Commissions, the British employers had organized so few attacks upon them. Unlike some American employers, they had not set out in recent years to get rid of unions in their trade altogether. Unlike the Swedish employers, they did not react to the growing strength of the unions by developing an aggressive strategy of their own designed to concentrate their forces upon one union at a time, or to force various unions into a single mould of negotiation — it might have been well for British unionism in the long run if they had.

This comparative tolerance or inactivity does not imply that the employers were more pacific or magnanimous by nature than the workmen: since they were the ones who started in possession of the revenue, and especially of the authority, in which the workman was trying to get a greater share, they had the defensive role inherently. But what does need explanation is why they did not react more sharply when they were attacked. One reason for this was that reluctance to combine with competitors which we have already noticed. For the most part employers' associations were too localized, and their members' loyalty to them too uncertain, for them to be able to take the initiative: when the engineering employers, faced by what they felt to be a basic challenge to their authority in their own shops, improvised a national organization in 1897 to support the London employers by a widespread lock-out, their effort was felt to be remarkable. Typically, moreover, the employer was not interested in industrial relations as he was in production, but regarded them rather as a source from which trouble arose from time to time, to stop him getting on with his proper job; he dealt with it when he had to, and hoped for as much respite as possible before it recurred. Meanwhile he preferred to work at problems that were more intriguing and more under his own control.

There was also a more constructive force. Many employers did now believe that the unions had a necessary function to perform, in fairness to the wage-earner; and others who them-selves would sooner have unorganized workmen to deal with still agreed that if there had to be unions at all, then in practice industrial relations were most orderly when the unions were solidly organized and met a no less solid organization of employers in regular and reasonable discussion. This precept of experience gave to the employers' associations their one con-structive principle, and the main function of many of them was to supply the employers' side of such joint councils. But it was understood that the negotiations should be confined to wages and conditions of work common to all the firms in the associa-tion, and any claim by the unions to have a voice in the way work was done within the shops of any one of them was likely to provoke a sharp reaction.

These considerations go far to explain why the employers set up no counterpart to the Trades Union Congress. When a parti-cular change in the law was being debated an association might be formed to put the employers' case at Westminster. A General Chamber of the Manufacturers of Great Britain had successfully opposed Pitt's proposals for free trade with Ireland in 1785. In the 1870's a National Federation of Associated Employers of Labour was formed to resist the unions' campaign for a legal code: 'in wealth, influence, and representative character,' said George Howell,[1] 'no such formidable organization of capital had ever before been pitted against labour,' but the decisive vote in the House went against it in 1875, it did little thereafter,

[1] G. Howell, *Labour Legislation, Labour Movements, and Labour Leaders* (2nd edn., 1905), pp. 308–18, 379.

and died away. After the great dispute of 1897–8 some of the engineering employers thought of extending their new national federation to include representatives of 'all cognate trades having pressing and immediate grievances with tyrannical Trade Unions'.[1] In the event a separate meeting was called, in November 1898, on the initiative of Sir Benjamin Browne, and an Employers' Parliamentary Committee was set up 'for the purpose of considering and taking action with respect to any Bills, introduced into either House of Parliament, affecting the interests of trade, of free contract and free labour', or with respect to any similar action of central or local government. The intention was to give the Trades Union Congress its counterweight. 'Those who profess through labour organization to speak collectively in the name of labour', Lord Wemyss said at the time,[2] 'are listened to, while employers, as a body hitherto having no corporate organization, are consequently not listened to. It is believed that the formation of an Employers' Parliamentary Committee . . . will make members of Parliament — even Governments — and the Board of Trade see that in Labour and trade questions there are possibly two sides.' But through Lord Wemyss this purpose became associated with others. Born in 1818, he had been a Member of Parliament in the days of Chartism. He had carried through the bill which as the Master and Servant Act of 1867 relieved the wage-earner of much of the oppression of the old law, and he was a signatory of the report of the Royal Commission on Trade Unions which in 1869 recommended some easement of their legal position. But he was noted for his cross-bench mind, he was always against picketing, and as time went on he became increasingly opposed to every form of collective action. Not many employers were of a mind to work with him. Those like Sir Benjamin Browne who had just been through a great struggle with certain unions wanted to keep their end up, but not to engage in any campaign against unionism at large. Many would have liked to see the law changed so as to reduce the existing power of the unions to inflict losses on them, but not many cared about it enough to support a lobby. When any issue came up that did rouse them, they had their own access to Members.

[1] From a circular quoted by Richard Bell at p. 32 of his *Trade Unionism* (1907).
[2] Letter to *The Times*, 18 Nov. 1898.

Nothing came of the Committee that was constituted in 1898. Lord Wemyss may have set up some such body before, and an Employers' Parliamentary Council did now go on for some years under his wing. He told some French inquirers in 1902 that it was maintaining the Free Labour Association, and that it had provided the materials for the celebrated series of articles in *The Times* of 1901–2, blaming the unions for 'The Crisis in British Industry'. But as Arthur Chamberlain indicated, the employers who were active in it were few and unrepresentative.

It remains remarkable that there was as yet no such body as the Federation of British Industry, or the British Employers' Confederation. The reason can only be that there was not yet enough common interest or common business. Different industries, and districts within one industry, and firms within one district, wanted to be free to go their own way. Save for tariff reform there were no active issues of national economic policy: money and banking, the foreign exchanges, the location of industry, the volume of investment, the maintenance of employment and the checking of inflation — that government should be continually occupied with such things, and business men concerned to press their views on government, still lay in the future. Most business men felt then that the less they had to do with government and government with them the better.

9

The wage-earners whose rates of pay were governed by collective agreements still amounted to less than a quarter of all wage-earners. Salaried employees were almost all still outside the scope of collective bargaining, but were half as numerous as the wage-earners within it. Of all who worked for an employer, nearly four in every five made their own bargain with him. How was it struck?

Sometimes the man in need of a job was helpless — 'take it or leave it'. Wherever there was at the moment a single applicant in excess of the number of vacancies, competition between the applicants could conceivably reduce the wage to the lowest amount a man could keep going on, 'the fodder basis'. The sweated trades showed something like that happening; so did the class of day labourers, casual labourers, in the villages. The continual growth of population, calling for ten or twelve, even fourteen more jobs to be added to each hundred in the course of every decade, might have been expected to work in the same way elsewhere. But it did not. Real wages generally had been rising: about 1906 the basketful of goods that the average wage would buy was a third bigger than it had been thirty years before. Yet only a fraction of all wages had been adjusted through collective bargaining.

There were several reasons for this, some that explained why wages were not always being forced down by competition for jobs, others to account for the level of real wages being lifted from time to time.

For one thing, though the rise in the number of applicants was very general, it bore hard only at those points where in the employer's eyes one man was as good or bad as another, so that all applicants were competitors with one another. Where employers had regard to the personal qualities of those they engaged, the man who was known locally as a good workman was in a separate and sheltered class, unlikely to be waiting at the gate, more likely to be able to name his own rate.

But even the rest, who could only take or leave what the employer offered, had some defence in his common decency and his regard for the opinion of his neighbours. His judgment of what was a fair wage would be formed by what had customarily been paid and what other reputable employers were paying now. Thereby an element of self-perpetuation and self-justification entered into the wage-structure: each part tended to remain today what it was yesterday, or to keep a constant relation to other parts; one wage was reckoned fair because it bore a customary relation to a second, whose own fairness would have been established by reference to the first. The notion of a proper rate for the job was upheld even by the unorganized wage-earner, who knowing that he had no second line of defence if he once gave up the customary rate would refuse, up to the last extremity, to take a job for less. Action could be concerted tacitly even where there was no explicit combination. Here as elsewhere the trade union only gave an institutional form and strength to tendencies that were active in the nature of the case.

Thus custom and relativity held wage-rates up even when under the immediate play of supply and demand they would have fallen. This explains the elbow-joint or ratchet effect, as it has been called, the comparative rarity of reductions that appears on a historical survey of wage movements: money wages have gone up often enough; once up they do not fall back much. That has not been true of the industries that have felt the sway of the trade cycle and the fluctuations of export markets, where cuts in the slump were so recurrent that even strong unions could not refuse to institutionalize them through the sliding scale. But even here what was taken off in the slump was usually no more than had been put on in the two years immediately before, and on balance there was a cumulative rise. Generally, money wages that were not for the time being held up by market forces were sustained by forces of convention and equity.

These market forces, moreover, took effect from time to time to raise money wages. In the rising phase of the trade cycle the number of vacancies in some occupations or districts rose for a time faster than the number of applicants, and employers competing for labour raised wages. The same sort of tacit understanding might exist among unorganized employers as among unorganized wage-earners, and they would deem it an unneighbourly act to entice labour by going above the prevailing rate: we hear of that being strongly held by farmers; but it does not seem to have had much effect elsewhere when business was profitable and labour scarce. The trade cycle in fact worked so as to give full employment to semi-skilled and skilled workmen on the average of four or five years out of every nine. In these times money wages rose at the points of labour shortage first, and the rise spread to other sectors as labour was attracted away from them or the claims of relativity were asserted. The general rise was commonly helped on by a rise in the cost of living at the time, stirring men up to ask for more and giving them an argument, but the essential condition was the rise in effective demand as a whole.

The trade cycle apart, demand and supply also operated to maintain and sometimes raise wages in particular industries and occupations. The picture we have had in mind, of a given number of vacancies over against a given number of applicants, holds good of any one day, and expresses a grim truth of the labour market as that is seen by men walking the streets in search of a job, but it leaves out of account the processes which adjust the numbers of vacancies and applicants towards one another. If an excess of applicants lowers the wage, employers have an inducement to use more labour relatively to equipment, and the fall in cost may be passed on to consumers and induce them to buy more of the product. These adjustments are not quick nor automatic: employers may be slow to react; they, or their sales outlets, may not pass lower costs on in lower prices; if these are quoted they still will not raise the sales of some commodities appreciably. But though a reduction in the price of any factor of production does not raise the amount used promptly and predictably, it does exert a pervasive and continuous pressure to raise it: over a run of years the actual number of vacancies for a given type of labour must generally be greater than it would have been if, all other things being the same, the cost of that labour had been higher. At the same time the rate of pay reacts on the number of applicants. Let it fall behind what comparable labour is getting elsewhere, and there will be a lowering first of the quality of applicants for current vacancies, then of their number, and soon some of the old hands will be moving to where they can earn more. Conversely, if the pay is raised relatively to rates elsewhere: offering a little more is commonly the first remedy that suggests itself when vacancies go unfilled. The upshot is that persistent though not always predominant forces are at work to keep the pay of each occupation low enough to give an opening to all applicants, and high enough to maintain their quality and quantity.

This interplay of demand and supply had long been taking place in an expanding economy, in which the demand for labour in most occupations had been growing, but at different rates, and relative supplies of labour were changing, in recent years especially as a consequence of wider education. We have come already upon instances of the changes in relative wages that resulted. Output a head rising in iron and steel but falling in coalmining, the earnings of the iron and steel workers rose relatively to those of the miners. Building entering at the turn of the century a phase of depression in its own long cycle, the earnings of builders lagged behind the general movement. A greater expansion of industry in the North than the South of England drew more labour off from the villages and kept farm wages higher there. Women becoming eligible for more occupations became scarcer in domestic service, and from 1890 onwards the pay of servants rose relatively to other women's wages.

The same market forces also brought about changes in the general level of real wages, in the size of the basketful that the money wage would buy. We have seen how this had been increasing. In practice, it increased roughly in proportion to the rise in output per head of the whole occupied population. When productivity rose at home, or the terms of trade enabled us to get more foodstuffs and raw materials in exchange for a consignment of our exports, and the national product rose faster than population, the bigger product proved to be divided in much the same proportions as the smaller had been, and the wage-earner advanced in step with the rest of the community. This advance was mediated by money wages and prices in various ways: sometimes money wages rose more than prices, sometimes they rose little or not at all but prices fell: whichever way it was, the amount of the relative movement was in practice just about enough to change real wages in the same proportion as output a head generally was changing. This continued to be so in the last twenty years before the war when the rise in output a head was checked.

Changes in wages seem to have been much the same whether or not they were made through collective bargaining. The bargaining power of trade unions and employers' associations did not override market forces. Where each man made his own bargain with the employer, market forces moulded its terms. We could draw a contrast between the wage-earner's position under individual and collective bargaining that would make a wide divergence between the course of wages in the two sectors seem the natural outcome. But in fact there was no such divergence. Alfred Marshall noted in 1892 how wages in Scotland, which used to be very low, 'have already risen nearly up to the English level, as a result of the general tendency of local inequalities of wages to diminish, and in spite of the fact that Unions are weaker in Scotland than in England'; and that 'those occupations in which wages have risen most in England happen to be those in which there are no Unions'.[1]

This does not mean that unions and collective bargaining took no effect on wages, but that any such effects were so small

[1] A. Marshall, *Elements of Economics of Industry* (1892), VI, xiii, 18.

compared with those of other forces that they do not stand out on a simple confrontation of the unionized sector with the rest. What they actually were can only be a matter of judgment. Simplifying greatly, we might assume that before wage-earners were organized they were unable to impose or sustain a stoppage: competition for labour might oblige their employer to pay them more to keep them with him, but they could not strike for a rise; the need to keep a good labour force together might prevent the employer from reducing their rate, but they could not resist a reduction by withdrawing their labour. That does less than justice to the power of unorganized labour to make opposition felt, but let us assume it for the sake of argument. Then the main difference made by combination on both sides will be that there is now for the first time the possibility of a stoppage. Previously, it is true, the employer could always have locked his workpeople out if he wanted to, but there was no reason why he should, for they could not withold their labour collectively whatever wage he announced. Now, however, a stoppage can occur. Whether when it comes it is called a lock-out or a strike is immaterial: the essential is that whichever party is seeking a change in the existing terms can stop the works as an inducement to the other to agree. This other will have to set the cost of a stoppage against the cost of accepting the first party's terms: the former is by no means necessarily the greater, but its existence gives an inducement to concede rather more, or come to terms rather earlier. Thus combination seems to make it likely that whichever party is pressing for a change will get a little more, or get something a little sooner, than it would do otherwise, if it is going to get anything at all. But there seems no reason why this measure of advantage should generally accrue more to one party than the other. Employers faced with a demand for a rise in wages had to set off against any persisting costs of conceding it the loss they might suffer immediately through a strike; but wage-earners faced with a demand for a reduction had also to set off against its cost the loss they might suffer through a lock-out. The sanction, moreover, could not be applied without hurting those who applied it, and so was worth while only when used to reinforce a winning cause. The threat of stoppage only served to shake the branch when the fruit was ripe. The upshot seems to have been that collective bargaining made changes in wages sometimes take place rather sooner, and sometimes go rather farther, than they could have done without it. Since in its absence there were stronger resistances to reductions than to rises, it probably took more effect upwards than downwards, and heightened here and there the existing tendency of money wages to rise cumulatively; but the effect does not stand out.

One powerful influence may seem to have been left out of this discussion. When the leading firms in an industry were all committed to the same minimum wage, they were relieved of that fear of being undercut by competitors which would commonly restrain any one of them from paying more on his own: could not the unions virtually cartellize an industry, and get rises in wages that were covered by higher selling prices, even though the employers would not themselves combine to raise prices? The possibility seemed a very real one to contemporaries. Employers who actively endorsed trade unionism pointed out that it put a floor under competition. An employers' association troubled by the competition of non-members would look to the unions to apply sanctions that it lacked itself. We have seen how in the Birmingham alliances the attempt was made to put a whole trade on a 'cost plus' basis, which was to include both a higher wage and a comfortable profit. But the example also showed that there were great difficulties in the way. The Birmingham alliances failed because some employers would never join them, those that did yielded to pressure to cut their prices, customers went over to alternative products. There were other restraints. Wage bargaining was done district by district, and no one district could make any rapid change in its customary relation with the others. Many firms were selling overseas, or met foreign competition in the unprotected home market, or knew that outsiders would enter the trade if they made it too lucrative. Men generally, producers and customers alike, worked with unquestioning notions of a normal or natural price range that had a strength and fixity of which we have little conception who have seen prices generally trebled in less than half a century. Practical men knew instinctively that they would not get away with 'artificial' values, and resisted factitious rises in cost accordingly. Industry-wide bargaining, at a time when it is not the stability so much as the continuous rise of prices that seems normal, has very different potentialities. Before the First World War the collusive potentialities of collective bargaining had little scope.

So it came about that the course of wages within the sector of collective bargaining was not very different from that outside. One simple consideration reinforces this conclusion. If trade unions had brought an unmistakable gain of income exclusively to those who joined them, it is inconceivable, despite all the obstacles to membership, that four out of five employees would have continued to make their own bargains.

10

The arrangements for collective bargaining varied from the regular sessions of formally constituted boards to meetings that were got together somehow when a dispute arose. Experience showed not only that stoppages were fewer when both sides were organized strongly, but that strongly organized sides got on better if they met regularly than if they waited for occasions to arise. When meetings were regular, claims and grievances came up for attention before a head of resentment had time to build up. The habit of transacting non-contentious business inculcated a businesslike approach to the major issues. Men accustomed to meet and work with one another gained mutual understanding and respect.

But regular meetings were the exception. Often no agreement existed on basic rates. In engineering, though some employers' associations in the Midlands did negotiate district rates with the unions, most employers reserved their right to agree a rate individually with each man they took on, according to what he was worth to them and what they could get him for. If he belonged to the union and they offered him less than the union rate, he was free to decline. As a clause drafted by the federated employers in 1897 put it: 'Employers shall be free to employ workmen at rates of wages mutually satisfactory. They do not object to unions or any other body of workmen in their collective capacity arranging among themselves rates of wages at which they will accept work, but while admitting this position, they decline to enforce a rule of any society or an agreement between any society and its members. The unions will not interfere in any way with the wages of workmen outside their own unions.

General alterations in the rates of wages in any district or districts will be negotiated between the local employers' association and the local representatives of the trade unions or other bodies of workmen concerned.'[1] One of these general alterations might provide, for instance, that each skilled man should now get a shilling a week over and above whatever his own rate was at the time: so much could be negotiated collectively without abandoning the principle that each man's rate must be agreed individually. Of the building craftsmen of Aberdeen we are told that 'by the early nineties it had become an established custom' that the standard rate recognized by the union 'should be paid to not less than three-quarters of the men in the firm while the remaining one-quarter might be paid less';[2] among the three-quarters a good many in practice got something over the standard rate.

In those cases where wages and hours were actually negotiated, the agreement usually covered one district of an industry. Sometimes, it is true, particular firms made their own agreements with a union. In one or two instances, at the other extreme, where an industry or process was largely concentrated in one district, agreements were made that covered most of it — cotton spinning, for instance, and (to a less extent) the boot and shoe trade. Though the rates paid to different occupations were closely linked in practice, they were commonly negotiated separately with different unions. Thus the preponderant bargaining unit was delimited both by district and occupation. The Birmingham bricklayers, the Federated District coal hewers, the North-East Coast patternmakers, the Yorkshire dyers and finishers, the Aberdeen compositors — these were typical 'bargaining areas'.

For matters other than wages and hours, however, there were some industry-wide agreements. The great dispute in engineering in 1897–8 had ended in a kind of peace treaty, which attempted to delimit the acceptable activities of the two sides towards one another, and provided a procedure for dealing with grievances arising at the place of work. Under this procedure a dispute arising in a workshop in any part of the country was

---

[1] Proceedings of conference between the Federated Engineering Employers and the Joint Committee of Affiliated Trade Unions, Nov. and Dec. 1897, p. 142.
[2] K. D. Buckley, *Trade Unionism in Aberdeen, 1878–1900* (1955), pp. 59–60.

liable to be brought to national conference at York. Not all
wage-earners in engineering belonged to a union, nor all
employers to an association, but the agreement did in practice
cover most of the industry, and those who made it would have
liked it to cover the whole. Wages and hours, however, continued to be negotiated district by district. The building industry
followed the same plan.

A distinction had thus grown up between constitutional
questions and grievance procedure on the one hand, and wages
and hours on the other; and industry-wide bargaining came
about in the first before the second. The main reason was that
wage-rates differed so widely from one district to another.
There were at one time thirty-three different union rates for
fitters, and when the rate for a standard week was 46s. around
London it was 24s. in Cornwall. The building craftsman who
got 10½d. an hour within twelve miles of Charing Cross got less
than 5d. in Falmouth. Such differences bespoke a great disparity of circumstances, and even if it had been practicable to
deal with the many districts in a single national conference it
would not have been useful. But rules of conduct were general
and could be dealt with nationally. The dispute of 1897–8 in
engineering had really been about the prerogatives of management — for example, was the decision which man should work
on a certain machine one for management alone, or had the
union the right to a say in it? The principles agreed to govern
such questions were industry-wide in their application, because
an employers' federation had sprung up to make the dispute
industry-wide. This was an instance of organization widening
instead of following the *de facto* area of negotiation. The
negotiation of wages had very naturally spread out over all
the factories in a district, and some sort of meeting of employers
had to be got together accordingly. There was no such direct
pressure of competition to bring different firms into line in
their degree of insistence on the prerogatives of management.
But in the attack on those prerogatives engineering firms had
felt a sufficient common interest to join together and get some
rules agreed to govern conduct everywhere. Hence the paradox
that industry-wide negotiation came about first on questions
internal to the workshop. But where the unions had not yet been
able to make their weight felt so much in the workshop, em-

ployers who accepted wages and hours as legitimate 'trade union matters' would be reluctant to admit that anything else might be negotiated.

None the less, the list of subjects covered by this or that agreement is a long one. The basic provisions for the wage-rate were liable to be divided under several heads: time-rates and piece-rates; minimum rates of earning for piece-workers; higher rates for overtime and shift working. Similarly for hours: the matters to be regulated included not the length of the normal week only but the length and position of breaks for meals, the times of starting and stopping, the arrangements for shift-working, the limitation of overtime, and provision for the time taken to reach the place of work on a building site or at a coal face. Then might come various rules of procedure: how grievances arising at the place of work should be adjusted, what obligations the parties undertook towards one another to maintain the present agreement, and what course they must follow if they wanted to change it, and what they must do if they could not reach agreement. Clauses of this kind, though always liable to be re-negotiated, in effect provided a constitution for the negotiating body. A last main category, where it was admitted at all, contained rules for workshop management, or limitations on the discretion of management: the number of men to be employed on certain jobs; how work was to be apportioned in slack times; lines of demarcation between the jobs proper to different crafts; the number of apprentices to be admitted and how they should be occupied; a rule against enticing workmen away from their existing places by offering more than the agreed rate.

One matter of procedure was also one of some substance: the provision made for ending or re-opening an agreement. There seems to be an advantage in having an agreement run for a stated period only, say a year. This agrees with the conception of the wage as a share in the proceeds which all concerned have an interest in raising as far as is practicable. In this sense an annual review of the capacity of firm or industry to pay is a practical kind of profit-sharing, and can express and strengthen a spirit of mutual confidence and responsibility. Some agreements before 1914 were given a fixed term: the tinplate trade of South Wales brought its agreement up for revision annually, and this was said to be part of the secret of a remarkable record of peace. But more often when a term of years was fixed the object was not to arrange for revision but to put it off as long as possible. An agreement would be concluded for an initial span — in shipbuilding it was three years — at the end of which it would run on unless either side gave due notice to change it. In many industries and occupations the rate of pay had in practice changed so little as far back as men remembered, that the practical way of avoiding disputes seemed to be not to make changes smoothly but to avoid change altogether for as long as possible. Men did not know definitely or generally how much real wages had risen in the last half-century, and going on raising them simply did not present itself as an object of policy. The obvious object was stability, and that did seem to be attainable. Cotton spinning was much affected by the fluctuations of export markets, but the Brooklands agreement in 1893 had provided that rates might be changed only by amounts of not more than five per cent at intervals of not less than one year. That held for seventeen years, and then a new agreement was made that was to remain unchanged for five years, and thereafter be changed only at intervals of not less than two.

Though many matters fell to be dealt with in agreements, the provision made for each was commonly slight or vague: at the best some guide was given to understandings that had to be worked out shop by shop. There were in fact not many issues, beyond the minimum rate and the normal week, that presented themselves in the same form and setting in different firms, and common rules covering a whole district could not provide a detailed code to show what was the accepted course to take in the circumstances of each firm. That could be worked out only by those who knew what those circumstances were and what conflicts of interest lay in them: that is, by the management of each firm working out its own detailed code with its own workpeople. But such agreements firm by firm were not made. What had to be drafted to apply widely could give little practical guidance in particular cases. In the whole increasingly disputed question of which decisions management could take on its own and which only after obtaining the assent of the workpeople, engineering was able to offer the disputants little more than a declaration of co-existence. The national agreement, revised in 1907 from that which ended the dispute of 1897–8, opened with

x

the oracular statement, 'The Federated Employers shall not interfere with the proper functions of the Trade Unions, and the Trade Unions shall not interfere with the Employers in the management of their business.' On the closed shop it said that union members should not refuse to work with non-unionists, and employers should not object to employing unionists: this was the expression of a hope, not an agreement worked out to regulate what was actually going on. On the wage bargain it said, 'employers have the right to employ workmen at rates of wages mutually satisfactory to the Employer and the workman, or workmen, concerned. . . . Unions . . . have the right in their collective capacity to arrange the rate of wages at which their Members may accept work.' There were two issues, it is true, on which the agreement did lay down definite rules: 'there shall be no recognized proportion of apprentices to journeymen;' 'employers . . . have full discretion to appoint the men they consider suitable to work all their machine tools, and to determine the conditions under which they shall be worked.' But both rules were negative, and both ignored, as management firm by firm could not, the active interest of the men in what was done.

It was not on the failure to provide a code for the firm that contemporary discussion bore, but on the problems raised by the ragged fringe of collective bargaining, and the refusal of those nominally bound by the agreement to abide by it.

It often happened that a good many firms did not belong to the employers' association: some in practice followed the agreed wage-rate, but others did not and did not mean to. These firms were sometimes left with the dregs of the labour force, who made a tacit bargain to take less in return for being asked for less, and then low wages did not mean low labour costs. But sometimes these firms employed labour that though not unionized was efficient, and then they threatened to undercut the others; at least they set a narrow limit to what these could concede to the unions. The remedy, much canvassed, was to extend voluntary agreements by law, and make them legally binding on the whole of the employment concerned. The associated employers would have been glad enough to see the others brought into line, and would sometimes urge the unions to get to work on them, but they had a rooted distrust of bringing the government in. When the unionists had gained a partial hold but quite failed to extend it, even what they had was threatened because they could make so little use of it, and then they welcomed the prospect of compulsory powers. But where they already controlled the strongholds they could afford to ignore the rest, did not see why non-unionists should have the benefit of the union rate, and shared the employers' dislike of bringing government into their private business.

The repudiation of agreements by the rank and file had attracted increasing attention as the impatient and aggressive spirit of the New Unionism spread. The trade union leaders could not always refer to the branches each new proposal, or amendment of an old one, that came up in the course of negotiation. They had to go by the settled lines of union policy, and their general sense of what members would accept. Sometimes to get the best settlement open to them they had to accept what had never been put to members, and then they could usually rely on their own standing and eloquence to get their signatures honoured afterwards. But inevitably they were exposed to influences, and had to weigh considerations, that did not touch the rank and file, and they might insensibly move away from it, and misjudge its mood. Any district agreement, moreover, might have very different effects in different workshops or mines, and difficulties would arise quite unforeseen by the negotiators. These surprises apart, it is common in all walks of life for men to be genuinely shocked by the practical application of what they have previously agreed to in general terms. There were some issues, especially in the mines, about which men felt so strongly that they were never willing to authorize their leaders to abate one jot or tittle of their claim. An agreement which the men's leaders could have got across if they had had a say in its application might be wrecked by the use management made of it. When some local dispute flared up men would fling out in an unofficial strike despite the undertaking their union had given that there would be no stoppage until a procedure for conciliation had been exhausted. For all these reasons it happened not infrequently that agreements were laboriously negotiated only to be repudiated by some of the men. The employer had no remedy at law, for the agreement was no contract, but simply a memorandum of the arrangements which the signatories believed those they spoke for would accept as a guide in their individual dealings with one another. The position would be different if the employers' association and the union were given legal personality and enabled to sue and be sued: then any irresponsibility of the rank and file might be visited on the union in damages for breach of contract. But that remedy would affect much more than the disease, for it also carried all the consequences of the Taff Vale judgment. A milder alternative practised by the boot and shoe industry was that each side should deposit a stake, from which it would pay a fine if its members broke the agreement; but unions were unlikely to commit themselves to really heavy fines, and members wild with indignation were not likely to be held back by the thought of a moderate levy on funds already sequestered. The general conclusion was that collective agreements were inherently dependent on understanding and goodwill, not sanctions; that they worked best when unconstrained; and that the remarkable thing was still how well they were kept.

II

The immediate relations between employer and employed at the place of work remained remarkably unregulated.

The only provision made for them in collective agreements was by way of grievance procedure, and this was designed to take disputes out of the hands of those between whom they had arisen. It had been developed by the joint boards of conciliation; we have seen how in engineering and building it was extended over a whole industry before ever there were industry-wide negotiations about wages. Its typical provisions were that if a dispute arising at the place of work could not be settled by those concerned even after it had come before the general manager, then it would go to a works conference, in which a representative of the employers' association and a district officer of the trade union would take part; failing settlement there it would go to a district conference between committees of association and union; and failing settlement again, and supposing organization to have been so extended, it would go to a national conference, between spokesmen for headquarters on each side. In the works conference it was the outsiders who took the leading part, and thereafter the parties to the dispute ceased to appear at all: instead, 'the case' was considered. Experience

had shown that this was an effective way of arriving at a settlement after calm consideration. But if it stopped the parties
fighting their quarrel out, it also stopped them working out
their own ultimate agreement. On any issue they had not been
able to settle between themselves at the first trial they received a
ruling from outside.

Nor had the unions generally any organization to represent
them at the place of work. Two exceptions are notable: the
miners' lodge commonly brought together most of the men
working in the local pit or pits, and its officers could speak for
them to the managers; and in the printing crafts by ancient
tradition the men in each shop formed a 'Chapel', and the
Father of the Chapel was its spokesman. The essential here was
that the branch of the union was delimited by place of work.
But this was not the rule: the general plan was to make branches
up of men living in the same neighbourhood although they
might work in different places, and in a sizeable town the members of the same union working in one and the same shop
would belong to different branches. Questions arising at the
place of work, moreover, were often common to men in different
occupations, but instead of their unionism providing them with
a common front it often sharpened their clashes. At the most,
some unions had accepted or provided for the appointment of
shop stewards, but their role was modest: they were to check the
cards of newcomers and urge them to join if they were not
members already; they were to hold checks to see that the
existing members were paying their dues; they had to keep a
watch generally on the observance of union rules and practices
in the shop, and make a periodic report to the district officer and
his committee. What they were not authorized to do was to
negotiate any issue with management themselves on behalf of
their members.

So except in mining and printing the union seldom confronted
management within the place of work.

None the less, the unionists there had their rules, written and
unwritten, and a tacit organization for upholding them. The
craftsmen of the old school had long enjoyed a substantial independence: they had to be left to do their work in their own
way, and sometimes were much like sub-contractors, even
though they happened to do their work in the employer's shop

rather than their own. Other unionists were under more orders, but they too had their practices, and would instinctively draw together to uphold them against management. These practices served one or more of three purposes, which in modern parlance we call union security, job security, and regulation of the effort bargain.

Union security means the maintenance of the union and of the right to belong to it. Some craftsmen kept a closed shop in the full sense, that is, they would not let any man start in the shop unless he was already a member of their union. More often the existing members kept, or tried to keep, a union shop: a non-member might start work, but he would have to join the union within say a month. An increasingly expressed objection to working with non-unionists was resented by managers as an attempt to dictate whom they should employ. But the issue of membership arose not only in engagements but in dismissals. Sacking for being a unionist, or too active a unionist, would be seen by all as a threat to the very existence of the union. But where the union already had some hold, it would happen rather that the unwanted man was laid off when there was genuine redundancy, but not re-engaged when others were; or fault was found with his workmanship; or a breach of discipline such as had been often enough overlooked in other men was visited with dismissal on him. Then his fellows had to make good the charge of victimization amid a conflict of evidence, and if they struck to secure his reinstatement they could be charged with defending misconduct. Two abstract rights were in conflict: that of the wage-earner to belong to a union without prejudice to his employment, and that of the manager to select his labour force and maintain discipline.

The ever-present fear of unemployment prompted a number of practices whose purpose was to make jobs more secure. One evident effect of restrictions on access to particular kinds of work was to make labour within the ring fence scarcer, and raise its price, but another was to make those who had the jobs more sure of keeping them, and this was a principal object alike of the closed shop, the limitation of the number of apprentices, and the staking of an exclusive claim to certain kinds of work. There were also conventions, observed even by unorganized labour, to limit the amount of work that any one man might do in the day,

and so stop him working other men out of a job: a stint of so
many feet of coal to be cut or so many bricks to be laid, or an
accepted level of exertion. This was one of the sources of ca'
canny. Resistance to overtime went with it: some unions tried to
enforce a rule that overtime should not be worked at all, a rule
adopted by the Boilermakers in 1901 forbade their members to
work it so long as ten per cent or more of them were unemployed. Another way, as it seemed, of keeping up the number
of jobs, was to insist that a certain minimum number of men
should be used to carry out a given task or man a given machine.
New machines that gave bigger output per man threatened that
less men would be needed: wage-earners sometimes refused to
work them, at least with any reduction of complement, and
maintained that they ought to be 'labour-aiding not labour-
saving'. All these were restrictive practices, in the sense that they
kept output lower than it need have been, and therefore kept
wage-earners poorer than they need have been; but the benefit
of abandoning them would have percolated only gradually and
generally, the cost would have fallen sharply on particular men
who lost their jobs.

Restrictive practices also served the object of regulating the
effort bargain. The problem springs from the unavoidable
vagueness of the contract of employment: the wage-earner is to
be paid a certain sum in return for so much effort, but how
much? Effort cannot be measured. True, the results of it some
times can be, and it might seem that at least when the wage-
earner was paid by the piece the contract was explicit; but a
piece-rate is judged by the amount it will enable a man to earn,
and that depends on how hard he is to work. So one element in
a contract of employment is always the making of an effort, and
yet the contract cannot specify the amount of it. 'A fair day's
work' is understood; but the wage-earner puts himself under the
direction of the employer, and he feels that the employer always
has an interest in getting more out of him. He is suspicious of
being chased and sweated. He cannot protect himself by appeal-
ing to the terms of his contract. His defence is to hold back, and
see to it that others hold back too. Some differences in the effort
different men habitually put forth will be accepted, but a man
who does much more than the others is suspect of being a chaser,
secretly paid something extra to set a hot pace for the rest.

Management trying to put in better methods comes up against the fear of speeding up. Doing less work than one could if one chose, and stopping other men working as hard as they would like to, seems surly and mean; yet the wage-earner may see himself obliged to do it, to prevent the wage-bargain being twisted from what it meant when it was struck. If he feels it was unfair he has an added motive to restrict his contribution. That was the justification given for ca' canny in the Seamen's circular that first made the term widely known, in 1896. 'Employers of labour declare that labour and skill are "mere marketable commodities", the same as hats, shirts, or beef. . . . Then the possessors of such commodities are justified in selling their labour and skill in like manner as the hatter sells a hat or the butcher sells his beef. They give value for value. Pay a low price and you get an inferior article or a lesser quantity.'

All these practices were a way of regulating, be it only by obstruction, the relations of management and wage-earners at the place of work. Other issues arising there, though nominally within the unfettered discretion of management, also touched the wage-earner's interests too nearly for him not to claim a voice in them: promotion, for example; discipline; and many matters of housekeeping.

In a settled trade, where equipment and processes and the mind of management changed little, use and wont could decide or obviate such issues, and provide the workshop with an unwritten constitution. Cotton was an example. But since 1890 there had been much unsettlement, especially in engineering. The subdivision of tasks; high-speed and automatic machines; the stop-watch, and the extension of payment by results; a newly probing, pressing mood of management: these broke up the custom of the service, and made the wage-earners wonder what would happen next.

Men whose security was threatened drew together for defence. When piece-rates were set as the various jobs came in, and there was no book of rates, each workman had to make his own bargain, but in practice he would not take a doubtful decision until he had consulted some of his mates, and out of such consultations there grew up piece-rate committees. In other places workshop committees arose to give a lead and hold the line on other questions. The movement was general, but unco-ordinated. It arose as the need was felt, and took such forms as the occasion prompted. Existing shop stewards might or might not be active in it.

New tissue was growing to take the strain where the bodies of the unions were weak; and yet they were loath to accept it. It was hard for any one union to provide for workshop committees in its constitution, because these committees generally had to bring together men from different unions. This fact in itself was a ground of distrust: there was a danger of lines of demarcation being blurred. Whatever the committees did, indeed, seemed more likely to embarrass than to help the union. Its main object had become the enforcing of a common minimum throughout a district, and its method was to negotiate that minimum through its district committee and then set its face against any deviation whether through weakness or militancy. The works committee had no part in district negotiations, but it might slide into deviation. No one was authorized to make or even countenance any agreement with management except the district committee itself. It was the task of the district officers of the union to see that the minimum was observed, and they could not have self-constituted groups of members going behind their backs. As long as the Taff Vale judgment held, a union could be involved in heavy damages through the action of a shop steward, if he was a recognized agent of the union, in bringing a group of members out on strike without due notice, and this must have strengthened the presumption against 'unofficial action'. A union organ within the works, moreover, might prove not too militant but too weak: 'works unionism' carried the taint of the *syndicat jaune*, and there were some works where benevolent employers had set up their own forms of worker representation and the unions could not get in. So the union leaders instinctively distrusted the works committees. These for their own part often distrusted the leaders. When there was trouble at the works the leaders followed the established grievance procedure, but this was inherently conservative. The secretary of the employers' association and the district officer of the union agreed in accepting the custom of the district as their common law, and when a case got to works conference that is what it was judged by: that did protect the wage-earner by making the thrusting manager come back and toe the line, but it could not work out new arrangements to fit new situations. If the case was not settled at works conference, moreover, there was delay, and discussion at a distance, and perhaps only 'failure to agree' in the end. The officials going through with this ritual seemed obstructionist to impatient men in the shops, who denounced evasions and betrayals, and enhanced their own reputation for wildness.

These troubles showed how predominantly the unions had taken shape to deal with those matters only that were common to one occupation wherever it was engaged. Within the workplace itself most of them had developed neither an organization of their members nor a relation with management.

Nor had management itself done much to fill the gap. Two instances are at hand of what was possible. In 1868 William Denny III had become a partner in his family's shipbuilding firm in Dumbarton. He was to be a pioneer of many technical developments — the use of mild steel in shipbuilding, cellular bottoms in merchant ships, an experimental tank for the study of propellers: this last was to lead his firm later to build the first helicopter ever airborne. Soon after he became a partner he instituted a suggestions scheme, with an independent chairman of the awards committee. In 1886 he called a conference of the partners, the departmental foremen, and delegates elected by the workpeople, to revise the rules of the yard. He told the final session that he believed it was the first conference of the kind ever held. 'As civilised nations nowadays,' he added, 'were not ruled by laws they had no hand in making, neither should the workmen of a great public work be ruled by laws which they had no voice in preparing and approving.'[1] Since the Second World War the guaranteed annual wage and supplementary unemployment compensation have attracted attention as developments of collective bargaining in the United States; but it was in January 1907, at a time when technical change threatened redundancy among the employees of the Bradford Dyers' Association, that the Association made a written agreement with them, whereby it was given the right to reduce their number by not more than five per cent, and itself undertook to pay every man displaced, for whatever cause, an amount equal to the out of work benefit he would draw from his union, so that

[1] John Burnett & others, *The Claims of Labour* (1886), pp. 82-4.

he would have 16s. a week in all for the first ten weeks, and 10s. for the next ten.

No doubt there were other instances of the same imaginative and constructive kind; but we know they were not numerous enough to form a general practice. When management generally began to be more concerned with the needs of its own work-people, its initiative was directed to welfare rather than to industrial relations within the firm.

CHAPTER VI

STRIFE 1906–14

1

When Labour swept the country in 1945, one of its first steps was to repeal lock, stock and barrel an Act restrictive of the unions which had been adopted after the General Strike. One of the first steps of the majority in the Parliament of 1906 was to sweep away the upshot of the Taff Vale judgment.

The Royal Commission that had been appointed to consider this law reported shortly after the election. Informed opinion had been agreed that though the unions should be given some shelter from the risks to which the Taff Vale judgment had exposed them, they could not possibly be exempted from all liability to be sued: that immunity they might long have enjoyed *de facto*, but once the Lords removed it, it was seen as too anomalous to be restored. This was the view taken by three of the Commission, including Sidney Webb; the other two were even less indulgent to the unions. The majority held that the immunity had never been conferred on principle, and had been only the unintended by-product of the rule adopted by the Courts of Common Law that damages could not be recovered from anyone not named as a defendant in the action — since every member of a union was a part owner of its funds, and must be held to have lost something if damages were paid out of them, the Courts would not levy any damages on them unless every man jack in the union had been named as a defendant, and this was impossible. But some Judges had suggested a new procedure: they pointed out that the representative action, by which damages could be claimed from the fund held in common by numerous persons if only certain representative figures among them had been named as defendants, could be extended to cover the trade union. Further, in the Taff Vale case, the House of Lords had found that a trade union could in any case be sued in its registered name. 'In short,' the majority said, 'it turns out that the notion of a Trade Union having been intended to be specially exempted from actions of tort is a mere misconception resting on no other foundation than long practical immunity, which was simply the result of defects in general legal procedure that have now been remedied on general considerations of equity quite irrespective of Trade Unions and Trade Union law. And the Taff Vale case shows that, even if the rules of general legal procedure were not available in the case of Trade Unions, nevertheless under the Act of 1871 registered Trade Unions would be liable to be sued in tort.'[1]

So there was no question of going back on Taff Vale. But a union commonly had many members in many places, and it was hard that the funds of all should suffer for the unauthorized action of some one of them, so the law should furnish means 'whereby the Central Authorities of a Union may protect themselves against unauthorized and immediately disavowed actions of Branch Agents.'[2] Also many unions combined the functions of a trade protection and bargaining agency with those of a benefit society, and damages awarded in respect of the first should not fall on the funds held for the second: these when segregated should be given immunity.

The bill that Campbell-Bannerman's government brought in followed the majority in the main principle of not removing the liability to be sued, and it gave the unions only the first of the two reliefs that the majority had recommended, providing in effect that an action for damages against a union should not lie unless the act complained of was committed with the authority of the union executive. But it also gave those acting on behalf of the unions some relief from the additions that the courts had made to the list of actionable wrongs. It dealt with civil conspiracy by providing that if two or more persons combined to do some act in contemplation or furtherance of a trade dispute, this act would not be actionable unless it would be so if one person did it alone. Peaceful persuasion was recognized as a legal object of picketing. Some actions taken in a trade dispute — applying a sympathetic strike or secondary boycott to an

---

[1] Royal Commission on Trade Disputes and Trade Combinations (Cd. 2825 of 1906), majority report, para. 32.
[2] Loc. cit., para. 36.

employer, for instance, or securing the dismissal of a non-unionist workman — interfere with a man's business, or his right to dispose of his capital or labour as he wills: the bill said they were not to be actionable on that ground alone. In saying this it did not go beyond what the House of Lords had already laid down in a decision of 1897, but the immunity was now made explicit.

The House accepted these supplementary provisions, and extended the last to cover also inducing the breach of a contract of employment. But on the main issue the majority wanted a cleaner sweep. Taff Vale had not been a dominant issue in the election, but it had been raised everywhere. The Liberals did not depend on Labour votes in the House, but they did in the constituencies, and most of them had given pledges. Campbell-Bannerman himself, it is said, preferred an outright clause. One such was before the House in a labour bill for whose second reading he himself voted. The bill the Government sent up to the Lords provided simply and completely that an action in tort against a trade union, in its own name or by representative action, should not be entertained by any court.

The Lords, preferring to stand on an issue that would not embroil them with the unions, let the bill through.

Something extraordinary had happened. 'That vast and powerful institutions', the majority of the Royal Commission had written, 'should be permanently licensed to apply the funds they possess to do wrong to others, and by that wrong inflict upon others damage perhaps to the amount of many thousand pounds, and yet not be liable to make redress out of those funds would be a state of things opposed to the very idea of law and order and justice.' Precisely that had been done now. Workpeople who have no quarrel with their own employer suddenly walk out, in breach of their own contracts of employment, because their union says they must stop him supplying some other manufacturer with whom it is in dispute; the stoppage is prolonged, and he suffers very heavy losses: he has no remedy against the union. A man who wants to go on working during a strike is knocked down by a picket the union has posted, and is crippled for life: the picket, if identified, may be punished for assault, and may be required to pay to the victim such damages as his own means permit; the funds of the union may be immense: the victim cannot draw a penny from them. Nor is the immunity of the union confined to trade disputes: alone among the press of the country the journals of trade unions can libel a man without his being able to recover damages from the proprietor. The Trade Disputes Act of 1906 declared that the union, like the King, could do no wrong.

The Crown has lost that immunity now, but the union has it still. We may well ask why. Perhaps the ultimate reason cannot be given without exploring the relations between the categories of law and the changing structure of society. But the immediate answer is, this anomaly was the price paid for the right to strike. In practice, if the funds of a union are liable to make good the damage caused by wrongful acts done on its behalf, it will lose heavily from time to time, and can never enter upon a trade dispute, even in ultimate self-defence, without apprehension of losing heavily. The remedy, it may be said, is to make sure that wrongful acts are not done: as the law stood after Taff Vale a union could still conduct a great strike, and so long as no wrongful act was committed the greatest loss suffered by em-ployers or public would not enable anyone to recover a penny from it. But a union with many thousands of members in many places cannot exercise effective control over all the actions they take on its behalf. Especially when so many strikes were partial, or fought by the importation of blacklegs, they were likely to bring some struggle on the picket line. The liability to an action for damages was not inherent in strike and lock-out in principle, but it was in practice. So long as it was there the most conser-vative and orderly unions would hesitate to enter upon any stoppage. But for eighty years now the principle had been accepted that men might combine to withhold their labour in order to maintain or advance its price.

This case for the settlement of 1906 was reinforced by the knowledge that the new statute was not a leap in the dark, but only restored what had been the state of affairs *de facto* if not *de iure* for thirty years before Taff Vale. Under that dispensation industrial relations had improved, and they had improved most where the unions were strong. The lesson was that industrial peace was in practice most likely to be maintained not by the sanctions of law but by the goodwill of free agents.

To this we may add that discussion had failed to devise any

satisfactory halfway house between the liability Taff Vale imposed and complete exemption. The suggested provision, for instance, whereby a union would not be liable for wrongful acts unless they were committed by, or with the authority of, its executive, or without subsequent repudiation by it, would have enabled unions with forethought and ingenuity to cover themselves against most claims: the difference would be only that the position was trickier.

None the less the regime of immunity had brought enough hardship to unoffending men for the Taff Vale judgment to be welcomed by many as the overthrow of an abusive power. Hardship was inflicted especially by the sympathetic strike or secondary boycott against those who were not parties to a dispute, and by the sanctions the unions applied against non-members. The remedy that had been found was to enable the sufferer to sue the union for damage. When that particular remedy was found objectionable, the suffering came to be regarded as irremediable in principle. But this was unnecessary. British law could have done then what American law does today, and safeguarded the right to withhold labour in combination pending agreement on the terms of employment, while forbidding other practices that make oppressive use of union power.

2

It was the railwaymen who had taken the knock of Taff Vale, and been most hampered by it afterwards: a union in settled relations with the employers could do something even if it had to be chary of striking, but a union refused recognition could do nothing at all. Now the railwaymen had a green light again, and at once they moved forward. In 1907 the country faced the imminent prospect of a stoppage of all its railways. That had never happened yet. It threatened a trial of strength approaching civil war. If it came about, men did not see how life could go on.

A sufficient cause of the railwaymen's discontent was that for twenty years they had been falling behind other wage-earners. Down to the 1880's they had been relatively highly paid, as one would expect in an expanding industry; but in the last twenty years industrial wage-rates generally had risen by a quarter, and theirs by hardly five per cent. Their hours, though somewhat reduced, remained exceptionally long: in 1907 the predominant week was of sixty hours, and not a few worked seventy-two, whereas the engineers and the builders had won the fifty-four-hour week in the 1870's. One reason for this relative recession was that the age of expansion of the railways was over: now they were rationalizing, economizing, and using more powerful engines and heavier trains so as to save labour. An expanding industry is likely to build up a labour force with a high proportion of younger men; when expansion stops these become in time a high proportion of older men, competing with one another for promotion and blocking the way of those who joined after them. So it came about that after the 1880's work on the railways lost the prospects of promotion that had once made it attractive.

But the check to the demand for railwaymen would hardly of itself have brought all the worsening of their comparative position that they actually suffered: they laboured also under a disadvantage that might almost be called accidental. At the end of the 1880's Parliament had taken in hand a general regulation of goods rates. The original object had been to hold them down, and the new schedules only prescribed maxima; but most of them when authorized proved to be higher than actual rates hitherto, and when they came into effect in 1893 most companies put their charges up to them. The indignation of traders at this, coming as it did after nearly twenty years of predominantly falling prices, was very great, and the next year Parliament adopted an extraordinary Act, laying it down that if someone should complain to the Railway Commissioners that any rise made since the end of 1892 was unreasonable, the burden of disproving that lay on the company, even though the rate lay below the maximum that Parliament itself had approved. The effect was to clamp most rates down in perpetuity. But precisely at this point the tide of prices turned, and year by year the railways had to pay more for their coal, their steel, their timber. In the 1880's their working expenses had always been less than 55 per cent of their receipts; by 1900 the ratio was up to 62 per cent. Dividends came down. At a time when a rise in the cost of living made it natural for the wages of railwaymen to go up too, the companies were under mounting pressure to keep them down.

Y

This was a principal reason for the obstinate refusal of all the companies except the North Eastern to recognize the unions. Something was due to the tradition of discipline in the service, and something to the railway directors being an unenterprising lot — Charles Masterman, who was to see something of them from the Home Office in 1911, said they struck him 'as distinctly inferior in capacity and energy to most other big business men they had had to deal with'.[1] But they would hardly have become so different in labour policy from most other big employers if they had not been in a cleft stick: they stuck to their traditional policy of not recognizing the unions because otherwise they thought their costs would be raised against rigid revenues. The remedy might have seemed to be to go to Parliament with the unions' support and ask for permission to raise their charges so far as was necessary to cover higher wages — such permission as was in fact to be given in 1913. But the Taff Vale judgment came, and brought them years of peace, and made them think they could go on as they were.

That was all changed by the Trade Disputes Act. Already in 1905 the members of the Railway Servants had been calling on head office to launch a national all-grades movement. Both terms had pointed meanings. Whereas hitherto each company dealt separately with the pay of its own employees, now the union was to seek a single agreement covering all the railways in the country. Whereas hitherto the pay of different grades had been fixed separately, and the men themselves had been grade-conscious, now they were to stand together and demand improvements for each and every grade. In November 1906 a conference drew the programme up. All its claims depended on one of them: 'the time had arrived when the members of the Society insist upon recognition of Mr Bell and the other head officials by the railway companies to negotiate on their behalf.'

Richard Bell himself was a moderate and cautious man: though he had entered Parliament under the auspices of the Labour Representation Committee in 1900, he had incurred the wrath of the left by supporting the Liberal against the Independent Labour candidate in a by-election. He moved cautiously now. When his request for a meeting, simultaneously submitted to all the companies, was rejected by all except the North

---

[1] Lucy Masterman, *C. F. G. Masterman. A Biography* (1939), p. 213.

Eastern, he did but repeat it. It was rejected again, as was the plea for recognition that the Locomotive Engineers had made quite independently. In the summer of 1907 it became apparent that the resentment of union members was mounting fast and high. The companies stressed what a small part the unionists formed of all railwaymen, and their spokesman Lord Claud Hamilton appealed for the support of the public in 'the stand we are making to preserve for ourselves and the staff we employ the right to continue to enjoy the privileges of free citizens, untrammelled by the coercion and tyranny of an outside, irresponsible body'. In July Bell approached the companies for a third time, with no more success. In October his union voted overwhelmingly for a strike.

There was only one way, Lloyd George as President of the Board of Trade advised the Prime Minister, to avoid catastrophe, if the Directors refused conciliation. 'We must, when Parliament meets, at once introduce a measure making arbitration in railway disputes compulsory in all cases where the Board of Trade consider the nature and magnitude of the dispute warrants such a course being adopted. . . . The Conciliation Act itself is a poor thing. It is only the knowledge that there is something behind it that will induce the Directors to pay any attention to it.'[1] Against the advice of his officials Lloyd George intervened, and it was the employers he went for. He would put to them a plan for joint boards of conciliation on the pattern of coal, and iron and steel — 'failing that, the steamroller,' he told his brother. 'The Companies must give way on that point I am definite.' Ten days later he wrote, 'All day with the Directors. In the morning I had to threaten them. Told them that there must not be a strike on any account.'[2] He brought the union leaders to the Board of Trade, but still the employers would not deal with them. The two parties sat in separate rooms, and even when by going to and fro he got their agreement, the employers would not sign a joint statement, but each side gave its adhesion separately.

Nor did the scheme itself require the companies to recognize the unions. It provided only that company by company, and

[1] Quoted from Frank Owen, *Tempestuous Journey: Lloyd George, his Life and Times*, (1954), p. 155.
[2] William George, *My Brother and I* (1958), p. 212.

section by section, boards of conciliation should be set up, in which employees who had been elected by their fellows would meet some of the managers immediately concerned, to discuss wages and hours, so far as these could not be settled in the usual way. If the sectional board could not agree, the issue would go to a central board for each railway, and if this could not agree, it would go to a single arbiter. How he would hear the case was for him to decide: the agreement said nothing; if he chose to hear the men's side from the lips of a union officer, he could.

In fact, it was expected that he would. The companies had saved the form, the union had won something in substance. Its officers could still not deal with management, but in practice they could get management taken to arbitration on any issue of wages and hours, and they were not debarred from themselves appearing before the arbitrator.

The Locomotive Engineers and the General Railway Workers adhered to this agreement the same day. The North Eastern railway was not a party to it, but later set up a scheme of conciliation by direct agreement with the unions, other than the clerks, whose unionization it resented and tried to repress.

Lloyd George's settlement in 1907 was a landmark in more ways than one. Once before, in 1893, the government had been brought in by the shortage of essential supplies consequent upon an industrial dispute, but the stoppage in the coal industry then was by no means complete, and supplies were exhausted only gradually: this time the dislocation was expected to be so swift and overwhelming that the mere threat of it was enough to bring the Government in. And it intervened now not to conciliate but to force a settlement on the employers under threat of special legislation. At a time when most of the institutions of industrial relations were confined to particular districts, it imposed common institutions on virtually a whole industry. Once again an industry-wide agreement on procedure had been reached before there was any industry-wide bargaining.

3

Save for a notable extension of workmen's compensation, the Government had achieved little as yet for 'the condition of England question': in the next four years it laid the whole foundations of the welfare state. Mostly this was the work of 'the terrible twins'. On the reconstruction of the Government in April 1908, Lloyd George became Chancellor of the Exchequer and Winston Churchill President of the Board of Trade. Experimentally minded, combative, kindled with the thought of a new social order, these two picked up the ideas and improvised the agencies of a nation-wide attack on destitution. By impulse Lloyd George was Labour. His account of one conference has been recorded.[1] ' "There", he said, "were the employers on the one hand, plump, full-fed men, well dressed — men who had never known what it was to go short in their lives. On the other side were the men, great gaunt fellows, pale with working underground, their faces all torn (drawing his own nails down his cheeks) with anxiety and hard work." He made a sort of gesture of dismissal. "I know which side I am on when I see that sort of thing," he said.' Churchill's impulsive sympathies were partly Tory, and he was ambivalent towards labour when it was in revolt and his strategic responsibility for maintaining supplies or deploying the forces of law and order aroused the warhorse in him; but with his humane and venturous imagination he entered into the lot of the poor, and when he met the men's leaders he warmed to them with his outgoing friendliness and his liking for a bonny fighter. 'Slightly bent, hesitant of speech, almost an apologetic manner, youth left in mobile features, ready for boyish fun, the cares of office sitting lightly on a good-sized brow, eyes that sparkle with a wistfulness almost sweet' — that was how Ben Tillett saw him in the dock strike of 1911.[2] 'If patience and courtesy, if anxious effort and sincerity count for respect, then Winston Churchill is entitled as a man to gratitude.'

The measures Lloyd George and Churchill took up were mostly to be found in the stock of proposals assembled by the unions. When the unions recovered their effective freedom to strike in 1906, they turned (save the railwaymen) not to industrial action but to Parliament. The report of the Parliamentary Committee to Congress in 1907 said 'One lesson, at any rate, can be enforced from the Parliamentary work of the past eighteen months, and that is the political power that lies in the hands of labour. It is overwhelmingly within the competence of labour to alter the present unequal state of society. . . . We urge

---

[1] Lucy Masterman, *C. F. G. Masterman. A Biography* (1939).
[2] Ben Tillett, *History of the London Transport Workers' Strike, 1911* (1912), p. 35.

our members to take up the following social and industrial reforms:

1. Miners' legal eight-hour day, and a reduction in hours in all trades.
2. Old age pensions.
3. Unemployed.
4. Compulsory State insurance.
5. Land nationalization.
6. Amendment of the Poor Laws.
7. Legal restriction of systematic overtime.
8. Housing of the working classes.'

The Government was now to take action under the first four of those heads, thereby effectively doing something under the sixth as well, and the gesture it made under the fifth involved it in a crisis of the constitution.

One reason for its carrying out the unions' programme was the one they vaunted, their own political power. But there was another. The use of governmental agencies to tackle poverty was a leap in the dark in those days, and there were many wise men who believed it a perilous one. Any government intent on doing something would therefore draw as much as possible from the lessons of other people's experience. This was to be found partly overseas, notably in Germany and Australia and New Zealand, and partly in the practice of our own friendly societies and trade unions. We have seen how the trade unions had already worked out provisions against most of the contingencies that caused destitution: the legislative programme they had in mind was only a generalization, with support from the taxpayer, of the means they had long tried and tested within their own societies of meeting what they knew to be the foremost needs. Any government that sought the same end would have taken much the same road as they even without their prodding it.

But they did prod the Liberal Government continually. Soon after the election one of their delegations had waited on Campbell-Bannerman and Asquith to call for old age pensions, and it was here that the attack on poverty opened when Asquith in his budget of 1908 made financial provision for the Old Age Pensions Bill that Lloyd George brought in. The pensions were to be non-contributory, paid for entirely by the taxpayer. They brought five shillings a week — say a quarter of the labourer's wage — to men and women of seventy who had no more than £21 a year coming in already, smaller sums for those with between £21 and £31, and nothing beyond. If husband and wife were both eligible, they got at most 7s. 6d. between them. By 1913 the annual cost was over £12 millions, nearly half as much as that of the army. Of the many schemes that had long been before the public, most were contributory, and Bismarck's Law of 1889 had shared the cost between workpeople, employers, and taxpayers. But the Danes had had a system of non-contributory pensions since 1891, and a Select Committee under high Tory chairmanship had recommended in 1899 that we adopt something very like it; by now too there was a precedent of ten years' standing in New Zealand. Since, moreover, any self-supporting scheme could pay out next to nothing for twenty years and pensions would have to rest on the public purse meanwhile, the Government took the plunge, and laid them on it in perpetuity.

We are told[1] how the pension transformed the world for the old folk living in daily fear of the workhouse in a hamlet of Oxfordshire. 'At first when they went to the Post Office to draw it, tears of gratitude would run down the cheeks of some, and they would say as they picked up their money, "God bless that Lord George! [for they could not believe one so powerful and munificent could be a plain 'Mr'] and God bless *you*, miss!" and there were flowers from their gardens and apples from their trees for the girl who merely handed them the money.'

Unemployment was next to be dealt with. The last Tory Government had already accepted the principle that the tax-payer's money might be spent on helping the unemployed outside the Poor Law, but the problem was how to help effectively. That was up to John Burns at the Local Government Board, but 'the man with the Red Flag' was a stick-in-the-mud minister, hiding fear of his own incapacity behind his officials' reasons for inaction. So a joint board of unions and Labour members drafted their own bill: it followed a traditional approach in taking the problem to be chiefly one of rehabilitation, and its main proposal was to settle the unemployed in farm colonies. There was an echo in that, going back to Charterville

---

[1] Flora Thompson, *Lark Rise* (1939), p. 100.

and beyond, of a deep longing of the workman whom the growth of population had denied access to the land. But the experiments recently made at Hollesley Bay and Osea Island showed how hard it was to move that way. Meanwhile, however, the boom which had kept jobs plentiful through the first eighteen months of the new government ended abruptly. Some recessions have been gradual, but this one was sharp, and the very rate at which men began to lose their jobs in August 1907 added to the alarm. In 1908 the proportion of wage-earners out of work was bigger than it had been since 1886, the year of Bloody Sunday in Trafalgar Square, and the absolute numbers now were even higher. The resentment was higher still. The Government had to do something.

It would not act, as we should expect a government to do today, to raise the flow of spending on consumption and investment at home: those channels had not been charted yet. But it could do something to help the men who were out of work. Two measures seemed practicable — employment exchanges, and unemployment insurance.

Experiments with 'labour bureaux' went back more than twenty years: in particular, a number of London boroughs had set them up. But they were associated with the relief of distress, so the good workman would not go to them, nor the employer look for him there. Abroad it was very different: Germany was using public labour exchanges extensively, Austria, Belgium, France, Norway and Switzerland had them or were going in for them. The Poor Law Commission set up at the end of 1905 had been instructed to inquire into means outside the Poor Law of meeting distress arising from unemployment, and when its massive majority and minority reports appeared in February 1909 they agreed in recommending a national system of Labour Exchanges. In May Churchill brought a Bill for one before Parliament, it became law in September, and the first exchanges opened the next February. Effective action could be taken swiftly because an exceptional Minister was at the Board of Trade then with two outstanding civil servants, Llewellyn Smith and Beveridge; and also because there was little resistance.

The unions, it is true, had had misgivings. It happened that thereby they first attained the status of an estate of the realm. They had been afraid that the Exchanges would be used to supply blacklegs, or would require men to take jobs below the union rate. Churchill not only worked through these anxieties with the Parliamentary Committee of Congress, but asked it to set up a sub-committee that he could consult continuously on the administration of the Act, and he made the President of Congress a member of the committee of three to which he handed over the filling of all but the highest posts in the system of Exchanges. In fact, many of those appointed were trade union officers — Richard Bell among them, who had led the railway-men through the Taff Vale law suits and the crisis of 1907. The unions must have lost much administrative capacity. But they felt they had a new status: delegations they had sent to Ministers in plenty before, but this was something new.

Once the unions' fears were assuaged, at least no one thought the Exchanges would do much harm, but unemployment insurance was a very different matter. It ran the obvious risks of subsidizing underemployment and pampering the ne'er do well. Even Germany had stopped short of it — there had been no instructive experiment overseas, only a fiasco in one Swiss canton. Though both reports of the Poor Law Commission had looked towards it, the majority thought it needed more consideration, the minority preferred subsidizing the out of work donation of the unions. To set out upon it now was, as Beveridge said later, 'a daring adventure'. But Churchill had daring, and Llewellyn Smith and Beveridge brought unrivalled knowledge to bear, and powerful minds fertile in expedients. They designed a scheme that would confine benefit to men who wanted to be and usually were in work, but were sometimes out of a job by reason of industrial fluctuations. Accordingly it was confined to a limited list of industries where that sort of unemployment was most marked, leaving out the steady trades on the one hand and the casual ones on the other: those it covered contained about one in six of all wage-earners. Since its object, within its practicable enclave, was to help the majority who were not supported by trade union benefit already, it had to be made compulsory and general; but its benefit could be paid through the unions within the industries it covered, and there was provision for a subsidy to unions that relieved unemployment outside them. Unlike old age pensions, unemployment insurance could be made contributory from the first, because there was no actuarial principle in the field to make using one man's current subscription to pay another's current benefit seem improper; so contributory it was made, but the taxpayer added a third to the joint contribution of employer and workman.

It took time to work all this out. It came from Parliament only as Part II of the National Insurance Act of 1911, and the first benefit was not paid until January 1913.

The same Act brought health insurance in. It followed a German model already tried for more than twenty years in practice, and it covered virtually all the wage-earners. In practice it was much more than a scheme of insurance, it was an organization of the medical service with a bigger staff of doctors, and wage-earners now began to get medical care in a regular way unknown to many of them before. It was Lloyd George's adroitness and darting energy that made this rearrangement possible. He would himself have liked a complete national health service: he advanced towards it now up to the limits of the politically practicable. One of the ideas he took up was that it should not by-pass but utilize the existing friendly societies, including those trade unions that gave friendly benefits. The insured were encouraged to join an approved society. That was a powerful argument for the organizer, and one of the reasons why the unions gained nearly a million members in the next two years.

We saw how a higher proportion of children than of grown-ups was in poverty: something was done to help the children now. Already in 1906 an Act had provided for the feeding of hungry children at school. One of 1907 provided for the medical inspection of schoolchildren, after the German pattern. At the same time the first step was taken on a path of utmost social consequence: a higher grant was offered to the secondary schools that would give a quarter of their places without fee to boys and girls from the elementary schools. The education of children from middle-class homes was helped when Lloyd George's budget of 1909 first gave income tax relief for children. By 1914 the number of places in grant-aided secondary schools had been nearly doubled: even at that they provided for less than seven per cent of the children aged fourteen to seventeen in Great Britain. In 1908 came the Children's Act, a charter bringing many provisions together against such evils as baby-farming, maltreatment by drunken parents, children smoking and drinking, vermin on children; it stopped the imprisonment of children under fourteen, and regulated the reformatories to which they might be sent instead.

All these measures tackled the poverty that was brought by life's misfortunes and exigencies, but there was also the poverty simply due to low wages. We have seen how the idea had been worked out of boards to arrive at minimal terms and conditions that should then be made legally binding for particular groups of wage-earners; but also how the campaign for them had failed. Now an Anti-Sweating League revived it, and attention was drawn to the boards in Victoria that had actually been working for ten years without any apparent trouble. An investigator sent out by the Home Secretary reported very cautiously that the experience of Victoria had been 'too brief, too simple, and too exclusively connected with an era of prosperous trade' to be conclusive; the distinguishable effects of the boards on wages were slight; but he was clear that the boards were 'greatly valued and widely believed in' because they gave a sense of security and fairness.[1] He also made the point that they were looked on as a natural extension of the Factory Acts. That was taken up by a Select Committee of the Commons which now investigated the most desperate form of sweating, namely home work, and in recommending a limited and experimental use of boards held that it was as legitimate to enforce a minimum standard of pay by law as one of sanitation or hours of work.

What had once seemed a leap in the dark now appeared only as a short step forward on a familiar path. Churchill took it. Under his Trade Boards Act of 1909 three boards were set up — for Black Country chain making, paper box making, and the making of 'ready made and wholesale bespoke male garments'. There were three independent members in each board, including the chairman, and equal numbers of employers, and persons appointed as spokesmen for the workpeople. When the board, by majority if need be, arrived at a recommendation concerning wages or hours, it went to the President of the Board of Trade; he allowed an interval for objections; he might refer the recommendation back to the board, but could not alter it; in due

[1] *Report on the Wages Boards and Industrial Conciliation and Arbitration Acts of Australia and New Zealand*, by Ernest Aves (Cd. 4167 of 1908).

course he would normally embody it in an order, and then any employer who paid less was liable to prosecution by the Crown and to civil action by the employee for recovery of wages underpaid. The fact that the employee had freely agreed to take less would give the employer no defence.

The experiment was being tried on a narrow front, and even there moved slowly — not till February 1913 was the first order issued. The workpeople it affected were at first almost all women: the trade unions thought little of it accordingly, and made no move to extend it into their own fields of interest — many unionists had as unaffected a dislike as any employer of seeing the Government take a hand in fixing men's wages.

Even if some folk had not been so much too poor, it still seemed to many who stood near the Government that some folk were too rich. An attack on the inequality of wealth by making the wealthy pay higher taxes forms a distinct strand in the Government's policy. It was pushed on by the need to raise more revenue to pay for the attack on poverty, but it was an end in itself. Asquith in 1907 first differentiated between earned and unearned income. True, he did it only by giving a reduction of the standard rate of income tax — from a shilling in the £ to ninepence — to the smaller earned incomes, while withholding it from others. It had indeed long been argued, on the strictest principles of proportionality, that an income which would come to an end with the working energies of the earner, and out of which he had to make provision for old age, should pay less while it lasted than an income from property that ran on in perpetuity. But the implication that the unearned income was somehow less deserved and socially justified leapt to the eye when Lloyd George put his land value duties into his budget, and joined them with a super-tax. The land value duties were far from swingeing — twenty per cent on the 'unearned increment', to be paid when the land was sold, and a halfpenny in the £ on the capital value of undeveloped land; the super-tax was only of sixpence in the £ on incomes over £5,000 — say £15,000 in the money of the later 1950's. But the fury with which these measures were opposed was aroused by the principles they were felt to rest on — that owning was less reputable than earning; that the budget should be used to make incomes more equal.

There was fury again in an outcry against national health insurance two years later. Twice the Albert Hall was packed with women pledging themselves not to stamp their servants' cards. This sort of reaction is not just the normal human resistance to paying more out: its disproportion suggests not so much the reasoned defence of self-interest as the gnawing of an unacknowledged anxiety. In the human heart much is linked with its opposite, and pride in the power of wealth carries with it an uneasy sense of personal dependence. The rich man is like a baby in that the way he lives depends on other people doing most things for him, and when they turn on him he may be as terror-struck by his own helplessness as a baby that feels itself deserted. But for insecurity nature's remedy is aggression.

Some of the well-to-do will also have felt themselves attacked in their self-respect. National insurance implied that they had failed in their accepted duty of looking after their dependents.

4

More time was lost in stoppages in 1908 than for ten years past. But there was nothing out of the way in this: a slump had come, and like other slumps it had prompted demands for wage cuts that were resisted obstinately. In March 1907 Wall Street had fallen, in October there was outright financial panic in America, and Bank Rate in London went to seven per cent for the first time since 1873. British exports had begun to fall, and from August onwards unemployment mounted; by December the 'shipbuilders' order books were emptier than they had been for a decade'.[1] On the North-east coast the shipbuilders gave notice of an immediate wage cut.

The reduction they sought was of five per cent in piece-rates and about the same in the time-rate for the standard week — 1s. 6d. from the skilled man, 1s. or 6d. from lower grades. In negotiations they agreed to postpone 6d. of the 1s. 6d. until March. Most of the many unions agreed to those terms by ballot, but in the nine unions that mostly contained wood-workers the vote was contrary, and their members stopped work, while the others — so many as there were jobs for — went on. So did the members of those unions in other districts, where the employers had not sought a reduction; but after four months of

[1] Sir John Clapham, *An Economic History of Modern Britain*, Vol. III (1951), p. 54.

stoppage the Employers' Federation locked them all out throughout its own area, which included the Humber, East Scotland, the Clyde, Barrow and Birkenhead. Winston Churchill had just become President of the Board of Trade: he brought the parties together and got agreement on an immediate reduction of the full 1s. 6d., but with provision also for the setting up of 'permanent machinery' for future negotiations.

Meanwhile the engineering shops on the North-East Coast had been going through similar troubles. The employers had given notice, actually before the shipbuilders, of the five per cent and 1s. 6d. cuts. But with the patternmakers and the ironfounders they had boards of conciliation, and both boards decided on a cut of only 1s., while one of them also decided that the percentage cut should be only $2\frac{1}{2}$. Most of the twenty-five other unions settled for that. But three of them, the Amalgamated Engineers, the Steam Engine Makers, and the Machine Workers, were parties to the procedure for the avoidance of disputes which had been adopted when the great stoppage ended in 1898. They followed that procedure to its end in national conference, where they agreed to submit the 1s. and $2\frac{1}{2}$ per cent cut to ballot of their members: there was a big majority against acceptance, and they stopped work in February. Lloyd George was then still at the Board of Trade. He got into touch with the officers of the unions and with two leading employers, Sir Benjamin Browne and Sir Andrew Noble, and he got the unions to ballot again, on the proposal that work be resumed forthwith, the existing rates of wages continuing until Easter, when a referee should decide whether there should be a cut or not. Twice the majority rejected that. The stoppage went on until August, when the employers threatened that if the dispute was not settled forthwith they would lock out all members of the three unions in their works throughout the country. The Amalgamated Engineers asked Churchill to arrange a meeting. The officers of the three unions could get no concession, and agreed to recommend their members to take the cut and go back to work, though with the promise of a later conference to set up improved negotiating machinery. They must have known they were beaten, but even now the membership accepted their advice only by 4,609 votes to 3,739. They went back to work on 24 September, seven months after they came out.

The stories of these disputes have been worth telling in some detail because of some common features they reveal. These appear also in a third dispute, in cotton — the employers in an export industry calling for a cut; some of the unionists accepting but one union rejecting it; the employers threatening and this time actually enforcing a lock-out, not of the resistant union alone; a settlement reached by conciliation, this time by the Mayor of Salford, with the full cut of five per cent but this postponed for three months; a later meeting at the Board of Trade agreeing that future negotiations should be held under an independent chairman appointed by the Board.

These features suggest some reflections. That employers should demand wage cuts when sales fell off was common form: its inevitability, at least in the industries that fluctuated most, had long been recognized by the use, explicit or implicit, of the sliding scale in mining and iron and steel. But that the demand should be maintained through stoppages lasting as long as seven months calls for explanation. The employers would not have held out like that if it meant losing much profitable business: the question is why the men held out, for they knew that the industry was depressed, and even had they averted the cut in the end it would have taken them nearly twelve years more to make good the loss of seven months' pay. The probable answer is twofold. For one thing, the younger men especially were increasingly unwilling to agree that pay must fall when profits fell. They held that the payment of a wage determined not by supply and demand but by human needs and common decency should be a first charge on their industry. In the good years that industry made profits enough; let it draw on these to tide it over the bad. If capital claimed the reward of risk-bearing then let it bear the risk, not cast it on to labour. To cut the existing wage was the more indefensible when a rising subjective standard of living made it appear scandalously low already. Beyond that, secondly, there was the aversion of either side to giving way to force even when what was conceded was not unreasonable in itself. The sliding scale had worked in part because it worked impersonally: if it reduced or raised wages it did so by the law of its own being, not at the imperative of either side. But where there was no such agreed criterion of wage changes, the side that gave way today was just giving way, and once prised out of its trenches might be pushed back farther still. What was at stake was not a shilling a week but a principle. Once you begin appeasement, begin paying Danegeld, you have given up your independence, you must expect one demand to follow another.

It was really this that had brought the Labour Department of the Board of Trade to its faith in the efficacy of 'machinery'. The immediate inducement was that generally the machinery did work: industries with formally constituted agencies and procedures for their negotiations generally did reach more peaceable settlements than those which left the course of negotiation to the event. But the underlying reason for this experience seems to have been that an established routine reduced the fear of just giving way. It did not in itself, like the sliding scale, provide an impersonal criterion of the appropriate change in wages, but it was impersonal in its due procedure: both sides in following this were accepting an obligation, not throwing their weight about, nor manoeuvring to get the sun in their opponents' eyes. Here was a ritual. In adjusting conflict the function of a ritual is to enable each side to give way without feeling the other has forced it to. Those who followed this one were still bargaining, but both sides gave their eventual agreement as in duty bound, and not at the point of the pistol. This was made explicit when the machinery included a decision in the last resort by an independent referee or chairman, but even without that it provided an assurance against being rushed and dictated to. We have seen how the benefit the board of conciliation brought in this way was felt most clearly at the outset, and there were often disappointments later. But faith in the boards rode over the setbacks: it had prompted the settlement of the great dispute on the railways in 1907, and apart from the railway boards some sixty-seven other new boards were set up between the welling up of that dispute and the end of 1909. It was in pursuance of accepted doctrine that in each of the three big disputes of 1908 the Board of Trade guided the parties towards 'permanent machinery'.

Another common feature of these stoppages will have been noticed: in each of them some unionists came out while others stayed at work, or wanted to stay, and many who had no part in the dispute lost their jobs because of it. This was the outcome of those who worked side by side, but in different occupations, being organized in different unions. As more of the men became unionists the difficulty increased, but could be met more readily by the unions forming joint committees or confederations through which to bargain in concert. The effect was to widen the area of bargaining.

These disputes also show this area being widened in another way: when some of the members of an employers' federation were in protracted dispute with certain unions, the whole membership would threaten to lock-out all the unionists. The sense of common interest in resisting the unions was strong enough in these instances to make business men whose own firms were going on working while some of their competitors were stopped willing to stop their own firms too. Probably this cohesion of the employers was correlative to the belligerence or apparent unreasonableness of the unions they had to deal with, and it was exceptional, but where it did appear it made for more inclusive and more centralized negotiation.

The slump that had caused the trouble in 1908 had come in from abroad at a time when there was no sign of recession in Britain itself. Though severe it was brief. In 1909 there were no more great struggles over wage cuts. Instead, coal-mining became much disturbed by an Eight Hours Act.

Some of the miners had already achieved an eight-hour day: in Fife and Cumberland the hewers worked only eight hours 'from bank to bank', that is, inclusive of winding time and time of travel underground; in Durham and Northumberland their shift was only seven hours. In Lanarkshire and Yorkshire, Somerset and the Forest of Dean, it was a little more than eight hours, but not much. But elsewhere it was nine hours or more — in North Wales, Staffordshire, and the Midlands; most of all in Lancashire, and in South Wales where on four days a week it was 10½ hours. But these were only the hewers' hours: the lower paid men and lads on haulage and other jobs away from the face worked longer. In Durham and Northumberland, for instance, the coal the hewers cut each day in two shifts of seven hours was hauled and raised by lads working one shift of ten hours. The long hours of darkness into which the lad was plunged made a powerful impression. Robert Smillie, the obdurate leader of the Scots miners, had begun as a hand-pumper when he was sixteen.

z

With another lad he manned the pump continuously in two shifts of twelve hours; at either end of the shift they had half an hour's walk, bent like 'a half-shut claspknife'; they changed shifts at the week-end, and then once a fortnight he was on without relief for twenty-four hours from six on Saturday evening to six on Sunday, alone in the pit except for a man at the pumping station by the shaft. 'There is always a movement of some kind going on in the mine-workings,' he recounted later.[1] 'A fall of stones makes a terrifying noise in the awful hush and grave-like gloom; the constant drip, drip of water, in a shallow, damp mine such as this was, produces an eerie effect.... The rats knew very well that I was alone and became bold and impertinent, approaching me in twos and threes, standing only just out of my reach, a hungry look in their bead-like eyes.'

The cotton men had gained a famous victory against long hours in the Ten Hours Act of 1847. We have seen how Parliament acted in 1893 to reduce the excessive hours of railwaymen. When the Miners' Federation was formed in 1888 the New Unionism was rising, and one of its aims was the statutory eight-hour day. The Federation adopted it, and together with the abolition of the sliding scale made it the spearhead of its forward policy. A bill reached second reading in 1892, and almost annually after that it was brought before the House. Joseph Chamberlain and Lord Randolph Churchill spoke powerfully for it, and three times it passed the second reading, but it was never allowed to go through. The trouble was it was opposed not only by the coalowners, led by D. A. Thomas of South Wales, but by the miners of Durham and Northumberland: for here the lads on haulage could be brought down to an eight-hour shift economically only if they were divided between two shifts a day and the hewers between three, and that, with its night shift and upheaval in the home, the hewers would not have at any price. So Durham and Northumberland stayed outside the Federation, and their spokesman Charles Fenwick, secretary of the Trades Union Congress from 1890 to 1893, opposed the Eight Hours Bill in the House.

It was implicit in the verdict of the electors in January 1906 that the Bill should now go through, and already in May it reached second reading; but the Durham and Northumberland

[1] Robert Smillie, *My Life for Labour* (1924).

men moved an amendment, and the owners could argue with force that to shorten the working day at a time of falling output a man, rising costs, and increasing competition overseas, would cause much trouble. So the Government, though sympathetic, would not move until a departmental committee on the probable economic effects had found that though what on the average would be a reduction of a tenth in the hours a man spent underground would bring output down in the short run, there were various effective ways of restoring it later. The Government now brought in its own bill, and it became law at Christmas 1908, but it did not give eight hours 'bank to bank', only eight hours exclusive of winding times, which on the average added half an hour to the time spent below.

That was a disappointment; and in any case it now became apparent that any general limitation of hours must upset many of the miners. Of the hewers it benefited only some, and even these now missed their traditional freedom to offset lower tonnage rates by cutting more tons. It was the lower paid and younger men who gained most, but they found traditional arrangements upset, particularly their breaks for meals. Everywhere working practices had to be changed and customary time-tables adjusted. The great gap in British industrial relations showed here, the lack of means of communication and negotiation between management and its own workpeople firm by firm: it caused great trouble now, even in an industry where most of those who worked under one management belonged to only one union and the union branch was often coterminous with the pit. What happened was that the owners and the union officers negotiated agreements in advance, district by district, and these were sometimes ratified by a ballot of union members; but they had to run in general terms, much that was important had to be worked out pit by pit, and often the managers simply posted notices stating what the new arrangements would be. When the men had a first taste of them, the next day they would not go down. The Act came into force in most fields on 1 July 1909: on the 2nd, strikes began in Yorkshire and South Wales. In Durham and Northumberland it came into force at the New Year of 1910: on 3 January strikes began there that lasted into April.

In the end, new working practices were threshed out and

adopted. In Warwickshire, for instance, thirteen thousand men had been stopped by a dispute over the length of a mealtime: men and management agreed it should be not less than fifteen minutes nor more than twenty-five, and put their case to Winston Churchill, who awarded twenty. Most of Durham, but only part of Northumberland, came on to the hated three shift system. The troubles were long remembered, by some as an example of the rank and file unionists' indiscipline and disregard of agreements, by others as a display of high-handedness by management. We, looking back, may see them as an instance of the limitations of industry-wide regulations, and the need to provide for communication and negotiation firm by firm.

5

Later in 1910 the miners at the Ely colliery at Tonypandy in the Rhondda refused to accept the rates offered them for opening a new seam, and were locked out. The men at five nearby pits also controlled by the Cambrian Combine struck in sympathy on the 1st November. Most of them stayed out until the latter part of August the next year, when they went back on terms they could have had before they struck. So described, this Cambrian strike seems like many another save only for its unusual length, but in fact it was a prologue to the omen coming on.

For one thing, it showed the increasing economic tension in the coal industry. The root of the trouble was a progressive fall in output a man, apparent since the end of the 1880's, and due mostly to the working out of the best seams and the loss of working time and strength as shafts went deeper and faces lay farther from the shaft. The consequent rise in costs was not offset by a sufficient extension of demand: the price of coal did rise, but not more than wholesale prices generally. Meanwhile a number of measures added to costs — the Coal Mines Act of 1896, workmen's compensation in 1897 and 1906, a coal export tax in 1901, Home Office regulations about timbering and haulage in 1902. Then came the Eight Hours Act. South Wales was one of the coalfields where it cut deep: output a head was said to be down by thirteen per cent in the Cambrian pits at the end of 1909, and as there had been no rise in rates the hewers' earnings would have fallen in the same proportion, while the

day-rate men lost overtime. When negotiations were opened for
a new wage agreement the next spring the South Wales Miners'
Federation tried to make that good, and they asked the Miners'
Federation of Great Britain to back them with the threat of a
national strike, as it had backed the Scots miners against a
threatened cut the year before, but it would not: this time the
issue was a rise, and the local leaders had no stomach for a fight.
They came back to recommend acceptance of the employers'
offer, and on a ballot they got a majority for it: it gave an
immediate rise in rates, such as was in any case due on the
recovery in selling prices, but little else the men cared for.

In particular, it did nothing to meet them on their grievance
of 'the hard place'. The hewer was paid according to the
tonnage of coal he cut, and only the large clean coal at that.
There was a rate for each seam, supposed to be so adjusted to
the relative ease or difficulty of working it that with a given
effort a hewer would earn the same amount in a shift whichever
seam he was in. Adjustments of this kind could work fairly
enough in the men's experience as long as a seam ran true, but
there was trouble when the hewer came on soft coal or a roll or a
fault — then his earnings must fall unless the manager made
them up. In South Wales the practice was for the manager to
allow a 'consideration' of so much a shift, fixed by him after
inspection of the difficulty. His judgment depended also on the
capacity of the pit to pay. Some of the better-paying pits shared
their profits with their men by liberal 'con'; when costs had to
be kept down 'con' was vulnerable. From the turn of the century,
managers were in fact under pressure to keep down costs:
especially so, it was thought, when the ownership passed into
the hands of a combine like the Cambrian. Required to reduce
the cost of dead work, managers bore down on the hard places.
When a miner claimed in the County Court that he was entitled
to the rate of 'con' customary in his pit the judge ruled that
allowances were paid *ex gratia* and could form no part of the
contract of employment. It was the rate for a particular kind of
hard place, a new seam at its opening, that started the Cambrian
dispute.

But the increased stringency of management was only part of
the story: there was also an increased militancy of the men. The
Cambrian dispute revealed a new temper in the younger men, a

blazing anger, a bitter determination to enforce new claims. For their established leadership and its traditional methods the new militants showed a withering contempt. The wage settlement of the previous spring had set up a Conciliation Board with Lord St Aldwyn as independent chairman and William Abraham — Mabon himself — as chairman of the men's side. This board now appointed Mabon and the chairman of the employers' side to act as conciliators, and in October they published agreed terms of settlement giving the men rather more than the employers had offered at first: the men rejected them. A deputation from the Executive of the Federation came down to urge acceptance on the strike committee: it refused. G. R. Askwith of the Board of Trade held meeting after meeting, and tried to build on an assurance by the chairman of the Combine that he had no intention of reducing average wages at the Ely pit, but the strikers would look at nothing but a minimum wage fixed in shillings and pence. The Miners' Federation of Great Britain got the strikers to ballot on the terms reached by Mabon in October: its delegates were hooted in the street, the terms they commended were rejected almost unanimously.

In part the men were uncompromising because they stood for a principle on which compromise was not possible: either there would be a guaranteed minimum for the hewer in a hard place or there would not. But they chose to stand on that because they were in a mood to stand. Their strike committee held their allegiance by its implacable enmity to the employers. The rest of the South Wales coalfield had decided not to come out in their support, but it was in a ferment. In the course of 1911 an unofficial reform committee grew up whose members held a socialism far removed from the jolly fellowship of Robert Blatchford, the hygienic bureaucracy of the Fabians, or the idylls of Keir Hardie: their analysis they drew from Karl Marx, their strategy from Daniel de Leon in America and Tom Mann newly returned from Australia to preach syndicalism. They drafted their programme, *The Miners' Next Step*. It condemned the conciliation board because it made gentlemen and M.P.'s of the men's leaders and set them above the rank and file. It advocated industrial action, to be pursued by unions which united all grades and occupations in each industry under one fighting command to maintain an unremitting offensive against the employers. The immediate objects were to be the minimum wage and the reduction of hours: they were to be fought for with the *grève perlée*, the irritation strike — going slow, working to rule, petty sabotage of all kinds — and pressed home till the whole of the employer's profit had been wrested from him. The ultimate aim was the taking over of all industries by the workmen themselves.

Here were a dogma, a diagnosis, a will to power and a plan to seize it. A revolutionary centre had formed that, if enough men had felt the same elsewhere, could have seized national power.

In the summer of 1911 it looked for a time as if just that would happen. A week before King George's coronation in June the seamen and firemen at Southampton came out. Their national union had its programme but this strike was not ordered from headquarters: it was spontaneous combustion, and the transport workers in many ports were ready to follow — first Goole, then Hull, and Manchester, where eighteen unions made a compact not to go back till each and all were satisfied; ship repairers' labourers in Cardiff, engineering labourers in Manchester; near the end of July the dockers, coal porters and carters of London. What the men wanted was often hard to tell; to the employers it seemed the upheaval was simply revolutionary; but, port by port and trade by trade, settlements were reached by raising wages.

Many disputes continued none the less into the blazing heat of that year's August; and then a new revolt broke out — the railwaymen of Liverpool struck. They gave their reason as discontent with the working of the conciliation scheme of 1907. That roused railwaymen all over the country; they were smouldering with resentment against lagging wages and the denial of recognition to their unions. It was they, too, who once again had been made what seemed to them the first victims of a legal attack on unionism: at the end of 1909 the House of Lords had granted a member of the Railway Servants named Osborne an injunction to stop his union spending its funds on political purposes, and so, it seemed, to stop railwaymen ever pursuing in the House again such a campaign as had relieved them from the Taff Vale judgment. Their executives could not hold them, and gave them their heads by suddenly issuing an ultimatum giving the railway companies twenty-four hours to agree to meet them or suffer a national stoppage. They held off long enough only to meet the Prime Minister himself. He was intensely concerned by the continuing international crisis that had begun when Germany put a warship into Agadir at the end of June. He spoke sternly to the men, offering them a Royal Commission to investigate the working of the conciliation scheme, but warning them of the grave responsibility they would take if at that moment they paralysed the railways. George Askwith, sitting beside him, 'longed to pull his coat tail' as 'he saw the jaws of the Northerners stiffen'.[1] The men retired, came back, and said no. 'Then your blood be on your own head,' said Asquith, and left the room. The executives sent out two thousand telegrams to their branches: 'Your liberty is at stake. All railwaymen must strike at once.'

Never before had all the railways been stopped. Men did not see how the life of the country could go on. Conflict was all around them that summer, and not with Germany only. Forty thousand women had just marched from the Embankment to the Albert Hall to demand the vote. In the struggle over the powers of the Lords, the Opposition had concerted disorder and howled Asquith down in the House. A fortnight later Carson had risen there to prophesy Ulster's appeal to arms against Home Rule. When a dispute broke out around the docks or the mines, rioting, fire and looting began too. When Askwith got down to Hull, he 'heard a town councillor remark that he had been in Paris during the Commune and had never seen anything like this: . . . he had not known there were such people in Hull — women with hair streaming and half nude, reeling through the streets, smashing and destroying'.[2] On 15 August troops fired on rioters in Liverpool and killed two. Within two days, it is said, all the gun makers of St James's and Pall Mall sold out their revolvers. In the small hours of the 18th, the day the general railway strike began, Winston Churchill and Masterman drove round the streets of London, watching the cavalry and infantry marching in through the hot darkness. There was a fight expected in the London docks that day, for the shipowners were going to bring in their *Lady Jocelyn* full of blacklegs to unload a cargo. On the 19th a crowd attacked a

[1] Lord (G. R.) Askwith, *Industrial Problems and Disputes* (1920), p. 164.
[2] Lord (G. R.) Askwith, *Industrial Problems and Disputes* (1920), p. 150.

Tonypandy in the Rhondda, November 1910: Barricaded Shops (Above); Strike Pay Being Given out in a Chapel (Below). The inscription is from II Chron. vii, 12, "I have chosen this place to myself for a house of sacrifice."

train at Llanelly: the Worcesters fired and two men were killed. The crowd returned to the train, took liquor from it, and wrecked the shops of two magistrates; when the goods shed was being looted it caught fire, and a van of gunpowder went up and killed five. The same night, and for five nights afterwards, the crowd in some of the Welsh mining towns went for the Jews, pillaging their shops and houses: on the 22nd it was reported that Jews were fleeing from Tredegar and Ebbw Vale by every train.

It is worth setting these things out to make clear the gnawing unrest men were suffering then, and the conviction borne in on many that catastrophe impended: they felt themselves in a parched forest where the clink of a flint anywhere was enough to start an inferno. The sense of social tension near to breaking point, aroused by the revolt of the young men the year before, continued to haunt responsible minds through the years until the war, and formed part of the setting of their disputes.

Yet it was only part. No other industry came out now. By the end of August the processes of conciliation had achieved a victory and the major disputes were at an end. Churchill had the *Lady Jocelyn* stopped below the port. Lloyd George actually got the railwaymen back to work after only two days. He used the Agadir crisis to make the employers give way, and they deputed two of their number to meet the union leaders — actually to meet them: it was the first time they had ever done it, and this much achievement of recognition was the essential gain on which the men went back to work, pending the report of the Commission. When this appeared in October, its recommendation for the improvement of the boards did not go far enough for the unions, but the companies holding that the unions had promised to accept the report would not meet them to negotiate amendments. Recognition seemed an open issue again. But then the Commons unanimously adopted a resolution that the parties ought to meet. They did, with Askwith in the chair. As part of the settlement they reached it was provided that the secretaries of conciliation boards, who on the men's side might now be trade union officers not being employees of the company, could accompany the men in deputations: by such a face-saving indirection did the companies at last agree to bargain with the unions' spokesmen.

Two Acts of Parliament in 1913 added to the railwaymen's gains. The Railway Traffic Act made good a promise the government had given during the negotiations: it set railway rates free at last from the standstill of 1894 by instructing the Railway Commissioners to allow rises needed to cover costs incurred in improving labour conditions. The Trade Union Act reversed the judgment in Osborne's case and allowed trade unions to spend their money on politics, provided they kept their political fund separate and allowed any member who did not wish to contribute to it to contract out. This Act was of general import, but the railwaymen had a special interest in it. Not only was it they against whom the Taff Vale and Osborne judgments were both given, but so long as their unions were refused recognition by their employers they depended more than most wage-earners on Parliamentary action. A recent instance had concerned the clerks. The North Eastern, which had long been alone in recognizing the unions of the operating grades, took strong exception to its clerks joining unions too, and warned them that if they did those expecting promotion would not get it, and those who had it already would be taken down. The Railway Clerks got the Labour members to block a private bill promoted by the North Eastern; at the end of five weeks it gave way, recognized the union and withdrew its ban.

6

The national strike on the railways had not long been settled when plans were made for a national strike in the mines. The increasing pressures from both above and below which had made the 'con' a burning issue in the Rhondda had raised the claim for a minimum wage in other fields too. In October 1911 the Miners' Federation declared for a district minimum or a national strike. In some districts the owners accepted the principle, Warwickshire adopted seven shillings a shift forthwith; but in other districts the owners rejected the claim out of hand. On 20 December the Federation decided on a ballot, by 18 January 1912 this had given a majority of four to one for a strike. On 2 February the claim was formulated, on the 7th a meeting with the owners reached deadlock, on the 26th the whole Federation struck.

In this rapid assumption of the industry-wide offensive some have seen the influence of South Wales and the doctrine newly preached there, but a sufficient explanation lies in the force of example. In the other great industry that was in a cleft economic stick, the railways, by threat of strike the men had made the Government impose a whole system of joint boards on the owners in 1907, and with only two or three days of national strike they had just made the Government oblige the owners to admit trade union officers to negotiations. The miners themselves had recently won from Parliament the limitation of hours they could not wrest from the owners. It was natural to infer both that it was easier to get industry-wide regulation from the Government than improvements district by district from the employers, and that the way to get it was by the industry-wide strike.

This inference was strengthened by the first reactions now. There was a widespread feeling that the strike would be a disaster that must be averted at all costs. A hundred and seventy mayors met at twenty-four hours' notice in the Mansion House and declared their profound anxiety. The Prime Minister and three other members of the Cabinet held hearings of the two sides, though the miners did not come until after the strike had begun. As with the railways, the Government was feeling for proposals which without seeming unreasonable to the House would go far enough to be acceptable to the men, and which it would then impose on the employers. But it could not find them. It accepted the principle of the minimum — Asquith even had to deny that in his address to the miners he had said that there should be a minimum in every industry — but it thought that what the minimum meant in shillings and pence could only be worked out district by district, and it did see the force of the owners' objection that if hewers were secure of a wage independent of their effort their output in the aggregate would certainly fall, so it said there must be safeguards against abuse. This did not suit the miners at all. They had drawn up a schedule of district minima in money, and coupled with it a national minimum of 'five and two' — not less than five shillings a shift for every man underground and two shillings for every boy. It was that or nothing for them. Among their spokesmen was George Barker, one of the new militants from South Wales. At the conference that drew the claim up he had declared, 'I have very little faith in a Government which is supported by 632 capitalists and landowners. We are going to bring out the resources of the labour movement to try and wring from the oppressor a fair and equitable wage for the toilers of the country.' Asquith asked him now in his imperturbable way 'You are out for the money, Mr Barker?' Barker said he was not going back without it. But the Government's ultimate weapon was legislation, and it could not conceivably try to fix wages in shillings and pence by Act of Parliament.

So the strike went on, and had to until the miners would accept a settlement without their schedule and their 'five and two'. Taking strikers together with those who were laid off for lack of fuel, soon there were reckoned to be near two million out of work. When the strike had lasted a fortnight the Government brought the two sides together again: four days of conference ended in failure to agree. Thereupon the Government decided to bring in a bill embodying its proposals, though it had no assurance whatever that the miners would go back when the bill became law. The stock machinery was to be installed: in each district a joint board was to be set up, with an independent chairman, to fix a minimum from time to time. There was no national minimum.

The bill was brought in on the twenty-third day of the strike, 19 March. Two days later Balfour for the opposition moved its rejection; the motion was defeated. In committee, the Government majority threw out most of the coalowners' amendments, and the Labour amendment to insert the miners' schedule in the bill, but when the amendment to insert the 'five and two' was called, Ramsay MacDonald indicated that if the miners got this they might withdraw their claim to the schedule. Sir Edward Grey seized the chance to get negotiations re-opened. For a moment the two sides even met face to face again. There was no hope of agreement. The miners proclaimed that the bill would not get them back to work unless 'five and two' was in it in black and white. The Government decided to throw out the 'five and two' and go ahead. At the third reading Asquith, who had stood so often impassive while the opposition hurled abuse at him, was so moved that he became hardly audible. ' "I speak under the stress of very strong feeling," he said, with an effort. Hesitating between his words, he asked Parliament to pass the

THE FINAL ARBITER.

The Spectre of Famine. "IF *YOU* CAN'T SETTLE THIS, *I* WILL."

Reproduced by permission of 'Punch' (27 March 1912)

Bill as the only possible solution in a great emergency. "We have exhausted all our powers of persuasion and argument and negotiation," he added swiftly, as though he would deliver the words before agitation checked him. He struggled to control himself. Tears were in his eyes. Then he said, in thick, low, halting tones: "But we claim we have done our best in the public interest — with perfect fairness and impartiality." [1] The opposition voted for the bill. The Lords, following their policy of not throwing out measures to help the trade unions, let the bill through without a discussion. On 27 March it became law.

Then it was up to the miners. Their weakness was their own power of destruction. By now, we must suppose, their leaders who saw how the rest of the community was suffering must have been appalled at the damage the strike was doing. They decided to ballot members, though without giving a lead themselves. In some 450,000 votes there was a majority of about 40,000 for staying out. The leaders argued that a recently adopted rule requiring a two-thirds majority for starting a strike must also apply to keeping a strike on, and declared this one over. By the second week in April the pits were in full work again.

A main lesson was that a big strike is too indiscriminately destructive to be a useful bargaining weapon. But some held that this time it had achieved a great victory: Keir Hardie jumped for joy in the House when the principle of the minimum actually became law. Others, angered by the surrender of the 'five and two', or embittered by what the district committees did and did not do when they got to work, wanted to renew the battle with a stronger nerve. Both saw yet more linking up of unions and enlargement of the strike as the way to yet greater power.

A first step was to join the unions in each industry together. The Eight Hours Act, though it had decided against the Durham and Northumberland men the issue which had long kept them out of the Miners' Federation, had at least decided it, and they had now come in. The Railway Servants were unable to bring the Locomotive Engineers in, but in 1913 they did unite with the signalmen's union and a union of general railway workers to form the National Union of Railwaymen. Tom

---

[1] From a contemporary account by a journalist, quoted and corroborated by Lord (G. R.) Askwith, *Industrial Problems and Disputes* (1920), pp. 216–17.

Mann had been able to practise what he preached when in 1910 he and Ben Tillett brought several unions together in the Transport Workers' Federation.

But in 1912 the transport workers learned the limits of the strike that is not supported from without. In May the lightermen, dockers and carters of the port of London came out, spontaneously, as they had done less than a year before: this time, so far as an issue could be disentangled, it was refusal to work with non-unionists. The chief employer was the Port of London Authority which Lloyd George had created: under the chairmanship of Lord Devonport it was unyielding. The Government held conferences with both sides, and proposed the standard remedy, a joint board of conciliation: for once it was the employers who refused. After six weeks of strike the Commons debated a resolution that the parties should meet, but, in a free vote, the majority for it was only three to two, and the employers simply announced that they adhered to their decision to agree to no conditions before the men went back. The suffering around the docks was now terrible. Blacklegs were being gathered in by the thousand — to this day there are men in Dockland called 'twelvers'. The year before, Ben Tillett had felt that the hub of England's government had shifted to Tower Hill; now he could only have the meeting there repeat after him 'O God, strike Lord Devonport dead'. Early in August the strike ended in complete surrender. What had gone wrong? Why had the walls of Jericho not fallen as they did the year before? It seemed to be because the movement had not spread. That public opinion was less ready to support the unions when they denied non-unionists the right to work was to be expected: the disappointment was that wage-earners elsewhere had not come out in sympathy. Just before the coal strike that February the Transport Workers' executive had recommended their members to give the miners all the help they could. When the miners struck there had been no work for the coal porters in any case: but now when the porters struck the miners did not come out. A more binding obligation seemed needed.

The miners took the initiative towards it at their annual conference in October 1913. They had had before them meanwhile the spectacle of a general lockout of members of the Irish Transport and General Workers' Union by the employers of

Dublin. This union was the creation of James Larkin, a revolutionary preaching class warfare and direct action, passionate in his hatred, unscrupulous as a man fighting for his life is unscrupulous, incapable of negotiation. The more the British trade union leaders were to see of him that winter, the less they liked him. But what impressed them when the Dublin stoppage began was that the employers, under the able leadership of William Murphy the head of the tramways, were united and unyielding in their determination to break his union. Coming after Lord Devonport's stand that seemed a portent. The formation of a British Employers' Defence Union was now announced, with a proposed fighting fund of £50 millions: there was in fact no more to it than there had been to the other employers' councils that had been got together in the nineties, but it fostered the thought that the sympathetic lock-out should be countered by the trade union alliance. Robert Smillie took the point when he addressed the miners' conference: they instructed their executive to approach the executives of other big unions with a view to co-operative action in support of each other's demands.

In 1914 a scheme for a Triple Alliance of miners, railwaymen and transport workers was drawn up, and it was formally adopted the next year. The text revealed the parties' embarrassment, for it laid them under no obligation to strike together, or indeed to do anything save consult one another before proceeding with a major issue: all its other major provisions were designed to limit their obligations and safeguard their autonomy. None the less it was understood to have pledged all to back the cause of each. Nothing could have been less thought out. That it should ever have been adopted can be explained only by the amount of unemployment among railwaymen and other transport workers that the coal strike had caused in 1912, prompting the thought that if all must be in it together in practice they might as well go in with a will; and by the sense of an impending general clash, a civil war between capital and labour, that was strong at that time of so many clashes. J. H. Thomas of the railwaymen asked in the House why, if Ulster could arm with impunity, his union should not spend its half million of funds on arms too. With the Triple Alliance behind it, it now demanded full union recognition, the 48-hour week, and a five-shilling rise

Hulton Picture Library

London Dock Strike, 1912: Meat Vans leave the Connaught Docks for Smithfield under Police Escort, 28 May

for all grades, failing which it gave notice of a general with-drawal of labour on 1 November 1914.

The two years in which these preparations were going on, from the end of the Port of London strike until the outbreak of war, saw no major industrial conflict in Britain. Yet to contemporaries they seemed no less disturbed than the two years before: small numbers continually striking suddenly here there and everywhere showed discontent to be widespread and turbulent. In 1913 came 'the prairie fire in the Midlands'. While other districts and industries had been convulsed the business men of Birmingham and the Black Country had looked on with some surprise and pity, considering that the employers there were getting the industrial relations they deserved: now their own workpeople flung out. Some girls at Dudley began it, like Bryant and May's girls in 1888: they simply declared they could not live any longer on their wages. In works after works the men followed them out, and a demand was formulated, after the event, for a minimum wage of twenty-three shillings a week throughout the region. Some men were out for three months; three contingents marched to London. The employers, unassociated and unprepared, were somehow got together, and reached settlements with the unions trade by trade. They were surprised to find what a hold the unions had won.

The industrial relations of these last years were in fact dominated by a remarkable extension of unionism: in only three years, from 1910 to 1913, membership rose by two-thirds; on the eve of the war two wage-earners were unionists for every one there had been in 1906. The expansion was accompanied by an increased unwillingness to work with non-unionists, which led to many of the local disputes of the time — some days after the assassination at Sarajevo more than ten thousand men left their work at Woolwich Arsenal because a fitter had been required to set up a machine on concrete laid by a non-unionist. A rise in the cost of living was complained of but not measured until in 1913 a report of the Board of Trade put it at nearly fourteen per cent over the preceding seven years: that seemed to warrant a claim for five shillings a week or so all round. When war came many claims beside the railwaymen's were pending. There had been few strikes that summer, but men felt the unrest mounting all about them.

2A

7

To many observers, especially those to whom all conflict was abhorrent, the last four years before the war seemed a time of remorselessly rising tension, of impending doom. Looking back now, we know that the revolution never came, and have good reason to believe it would not have come even if there had been no war. But we can understand why the industrial unrest loomed so large at the time.

For one thing, it was a quarrel that broke out just when other quarrels were flaring up too. Something had come over people: they divided into irreconcilable camps, they declared their unswerving allegiance to antithetical principles, increasingly they preached violence and resorted to it. There was the vindictive controversy about the powers of the Lords; the mounting battle over Home Rule, and the arming of Ulster; the campaign of the militant suffragettes, with each morning's paper recording a new slashing, burning, or forcible feeding; for good measure at the last even a struggle over Welsh Disestablishment. At every turn someone felt himself wronged to the bursting point. A suffragette threw herself to death under the King's horse in the Derby, a religious maniac went under the favourite in the Gold Cup. If one looked abroad, there was endemic international crisis, and a mounting fear of German armaments, with reports of mysterious aircraft over the eastern counties at night. Events which stir the emotions in the same way boost one another's signals when they are in circuit with one another, and their aggregate effect is greater than the sum of the effects they would take separately. This factor of reverberation must account for much of the fear the strikes inspired.

But they were also ominous because they seemed part of a spontaneous international movement of industrial protest and revolt. A wave of strikes in 1903 had led the Dutch Government to bring in bills forbidding strikes altogether in the railways and public utilities, and the unions proclaimed a general strike to stop them passing. About the same time the engineers of Barcelona struck for the nine-hour day and held out for two months; then a general sympathetic strike broke out, the work of the city stopped and the strikers seized its administration; the troops came in and blood was shed. In Italy in 1904 strikes paralysed the industrial towns; in Milan the Chamber of Labour announced that it had seized power and was conducting the administration in the name of the proletariat; for three or four days there was something like a national general strike. Within a few months, when an ironworks in St Petersburg sacked four men for being unionists, one industry after another in the city struck; on the bloody Sunday of 22 January 1905 two processions of petitioners were mown down. More strikes broke out at that wherever there were factories throughout Russia: Trotsky saw it as an elemental storm that 'charges from place to place, stands stock still, goes round in a circle, at one moment deserts a place and at the next returns to it, then tears off again and hurtles on like a whirlwind'.[1] The trade unionists of France had leaders whose glory it was to be men without a god, a master or a country. When they struck it was to do battle, not bargain: not to win better terms from the employers and better laws from the legislature, but to destroy both. The Government answered them in kind, and they held Clemenceau responsible in 1908 for the killing of twenty strikers and the wounding of more than six hundred. In Sweden the national federation of employers reacted to some local strikes in the summer of 1909 by locking out most of three industries. The unions answered with a general strike that kept three-fifths of the industrial workers of the country idle throughout August; and when they knew themselves beaten and called this off, the original struggles with the federated employers went on, industry by industry, till the end of November. In the heart of New England, at Lawrence in Massachusetts, a spontaneous strike of cotton operatives in 1912 was taken over, and won, by the Industrial Workers of the World, the Wobblies, dedicated to the faith that 'the working class and the employing class have nothing in common. . . . Between these two classes a struggle must go on until the workers of the world organize as a class, take possession of the earth and the machinery of production and abolish the wage system'.

It might have seemed as though wherever industrialism took hold it divided society into two warring camps. But the strife of those years in Britain was hardly of that kind at all. To understand it we must take note of its limits.

It was in fact confined largely to two sectors: unskilled and

[1] W. Sombart, *Der Proletarische Sozialismus*, II, (1924), p. 238.

low-paid labour generally; and all grades of wage-earners in two industries, coal-mining and the railways. Of the great trade union stronghold as that had stood in 1906 singularly little was engaged. Engineering and shipbuilding, iron and steel, building, printing, the textiles, boot and shoe: some of these had their minor upsets, but not one of them a big one. District agreements in engineering began now to provide that there should be no change for three, four or five years.

Then what was it that bore on the disturbed sectors? Of the unskilled we may say that the three years beginning with 1911 were the second wave of the surge that had risen first in 1888: the two had an access of hope in common, a sudden but sustained enthusiasm, a newfound manhood, a rapid recruitment into the unions. Underlying both was the extension of education that had been making a new man of the unskilled worker. But it is as hard to tell why the second as why the first wave gathered just when it did; which means also, to account for the unskilled man having lain doggo, indifferent to unionism and unwilling to strike, for the near twenty years between. It is not as though these had been years of progress: at their end wages generally were buying perhaps five per cent more than at the very outset, and actually less than in the later 1890's. Perhaps it was the rise in the cost of living of about ten per cent between 1908 and 1913 that goaded the labourer into action at the end; but when one remembers what he had showed he could do in the days of the docker's tanner, it is hard to account for his having waited for the goad so long.

Coal-mining and the railways had their own special trouble: in both the management was caught between rising costs and insufficiently rising prices. We have seen how the miner's average output had been falling, whereas the value of coal in terms of raw materials and foodstuffs generally had not risen; and how on the railways the actual rates in shillings and pence had been held down by an ill-considered Act, while costs of fuel, steel and timber rose. In both industries management was sensitive to the least threat of any further rise in its costs, and reacted against unions and unionists with a hostility it would not have felt if it had been able to contemplate higher wages without genuine anxiety. Iron and steel could raise wages more than prices because of improvements in equipment that increased tonnage per man: though mines were making a start with mechanization and railways with electrification they had not yet got far. In such a narrow passage, even had the wage-earner no desire to better his lot, a rise of a few points in the cost of living would bring a head-on collision.

That disputes were concentrated in these particular sectors also explains why they were attended with violence, why news of a strike so often meant the immediate despatch of troops. We have seen how strikes of the unskilled were prone to disorder because hooligans took the chance to loot and because blacklegs were brought in. The labourer, the docker, the seaman, were vulnerable to substitution by blacklegs: often it broke their strikes; the employers resorted to it readily, the shipowners systematically. The railway companies too brought blacklegs in as far as they could, so that if enough drivers stayed at work to keep some trains running the stations and goods yards would be manned too. The miner had no fear of substitution underground, and if there was an understanding with the management about the safety men and the ponies then a miners' strike could be quiet when most effective: but that understanding was lacking or broke down when managers and men were at daggers drawn as they had come to be in South Wales, and then the news that executives were lighting the boilers, or the sight of the pithead winding, would start a rush on the power house. Sometimes, too, management tried to bring blacklegs in to shift coal that was already on the bank. Fights broke out on the picket line, when the police had to get a convoy of blacklegs into the plant, or in the streets, when goods that blacklegs had handled were being taken away. The biggest battles were fought when a crowd of strikers attacked the buildings in which blacklegs were believed to be working, and which a hundred or more imported police defended, perhaps with half a company of soldiers in reserve. When once blood had been shed, fighting with the police might break out wherever the strikers gathered in numbers; and strikers once on the warpath might break into the drink shops. But these extensions of disorder were exceptional. Without the blackleg there would have been little fighting. The unionist had not adopted violence as a policy. It was only that for hungry men to see others taking their jobs was more than flesh and blood could bear.

The British strikers therefore did not have much in common with those on the Continent who seized the town hall; nor did their battles necessarily mark any general trend of the times towards the use of force. If the same number of man-days had been lost in other industries there might have been little disorder.

We may still wonder why those other industries were so little disturbed, for few of them were doing well for their workpeople, whose wages on the average would buy no more when war came than they had done twenty years before. This was in marked contrast to the twenty years before that, in which the wage-earner's basketful had been increased by a third: a rate of progress that would soon have transformed his standard of living, but was then cut off. We know that a similar check occurred at about the same time and persisted down to the war in Belgium, Germany, and the United States, but not in Sweden. The causes are not known definitely, and may not be the same in all countries. But some part was played by a swing in the terms of trade between factory and farm: they moved now against the factory, so that the industrial worker got less food and raw material than before in exchange for a consignment of his own products. A more conjectural but possibly important cause was a check to the rate of technical advance: the rate not of invention and pioneering but of the general application of new techniques, an interval between the widespread harvesting of the economies of steam and steel and that yet to come from electricity, the new industrial chemistry, and the internal combustion engine.

Whatever the causes, there is no doubt about the fact: this was a time when in several countries economic forces were checking the rise in real wages. It is remarkable that this was accepted with so little outcry. Perhaps the outcry was coming when war broke out; but we still have to account for its being so long deferred. One reason may be sheer unawareness of the change. By present standards it was an age of statistical darkness: increasing attention was being given to the cost of living, but if the change in the course of real wages was estimated by one or two specialists, that was as far as knowledge of it had gone. The movements from year to year were small in any case, and not always in the same direction: no clear line of trend would run through men's recollections of them. Knowing little definite about past improvements, men did not then look for more improvement as their due in years to come. The expectation of annual betterment has arisen only in quite recent years. It is perhaps because of this that no simple and reliable relation has been found between the trend of real wages and the incidence of disputes. Over a range of countries and periods it is just not the case that men always or even generally lose less time in disputes when their real wages are rising: it would be in keeping if the failure of real wages to rise did not spark any explosion now.

But a fall in real wages is a very different matter, and if it was to be avoided wages had to be raised. We now know that between 1902 and 1909 the cost of living had risen by four or five per cent, between 1909 and 1913 it rose by nearly nine per cent again. In fact, money wages generally did rise too, keeping pace with the cost of living over the first span, lagging behind the sharper movement of the second but catching it up in 1914. But they rose unevenly, especially for the man who needed the rise most, the general worker. For neither of the processes that have raised his wages in recent years was of much consequence then. There was little competition between employers for his labour even when trade was most active, because of the great continuing growth of population. In the ten years after 1901 the numbers working or seeking work in Britain rose, despite much emigration, by one in eight. Changes in the balance of supply and demand in the labour market take their greatest effect on the general workers, from whose ranks vacancies in more specialized occupations are filled, to whom fall back those who lose other jobs. The employer who wanted more of them at this time seldom needed to bid them away from another firm: there was usually a man waiting at the gate. So the wages of the general worker were not raised by employers' competitive bidding. But neither did the employers often raise them by agreement, even when each for his own part might regard a rise as reasonable: there was seldom any employers' association. In the ports in 1911 G. R. Askwith found 'there was no cohesion among employers, and no section of employers who dared to come forward and give a lead.'[1] 'Prices had been rising,' he said again,[2] 'but no sufficient increase of wages, and certainly no

---

[1] Lord (G. R.) Askwith, *Industrial Problems and Disputes* (1920), p. 177.
[2] Ibid., p. 175.

general increase, had followed the rise. It may be said that employers had waited too much on each other.' He was clear that this was the main cause of the unrest among general workers.

8

Though contemporaries felt themselves confronted with a new problem, they worked out no new policy. For the most part, emergencies were met and ended by the tried and tested methods of the Board of Trade. But in three major crises the Government improvised a new way of settlement, pregnant with consequences.

The tried and tested methods were, to use conciliation as the means of enabling the parties to work out their own immediate settlement, and then help them set up or improve 'machinery' for the more regular transaction of such business in future. G. R. Askwith was the consummate conciliator of the day, telegraphed for when all else had failed, bringing the deep relief of settlement to many an anxious city at the eleventh hour. Ben Tillett sketched him in his *annus mirabilis* of 1911 — 'the patient, plodding man, with pigeon holes in his brains; who listened without sign of being bored or absorbed, who concealed his mind like a Chinaman. Emotionless, except that he would peer through his glasses at someone making a statement of moment, never raising his diplomatic voice, or appearing to hurry over anything; guiding without falter or apparent effort the disputants however heated they may be, himself the inscrutable, patient listener. And such patience! It was more than dour in its persistence and calmness; it compelled by its coldness, and saved us from the bickerings on occasions when the wisest become puny and spiteful.'[1] His first task — it was often half the battle — was to get clear what the dispute was about, and assemble the parties concerned. Argument once joined, he had himself no solution to advocate: it was for the parties to work out their own agreement. His job was to keep their discussion as pertinent as might be, subject always to the need for some ventilational therapy; to seize on any suggestion dropped by either side that might build a bridge towards the other; and to be ingenious in devising ways out of an impasse, but put them out only as suggestions the parties might adopt or reject as they

[1] Ben Tillett, *History of the Transport Strike, 1911* (1912), p. 30.

Jan. 5.
1912

Sir George Askwith

thought fit. When agreement was reached, he would draft its terms very fully. Everyone understood what he had agreed to; he had not been rushed into it, and he identified himself with the decision to accept it.

But now came the second part of Askwith's method: not to go until he had seen at least a start made with better 'machinery' for the future. The sealed pattern was of a joint board of conciliation. We have seen the difference this device had commonly made at its first institution in times past: it very often did the same now. But not always. Its special virtue in the years of rising cost of living was that it enabled employers who were prepared to raise wages if their competitors were doing the same to be assured that they were. It had no special virtue when one side was not prepared to deal with particular spokesmen of the other — the scheme Askwith drew up in Dublin was a dead letter from the first — or when issues of principle arose on which compromise was less easy than on those of shillings and pence — the refusal to work with non-unionists, for instance, on which the employers of the port of London meant to beat the unions, and did beat them, in 1912.

None the less the joint board remained the one constructive proposal before the country. It was used also to settle the two great industries that were in trouble at this time. In each it took a special and limited form: the boards set up by the railways in 1907 excluded trade union officers at first and had no independent chairman; those set up in coal-mining in 1912 were charged only with the fixing of a minimum rate to meet the problem of the hard place. The actually indispensable advantage of the board in both cases was that it was a device by which an extension of collective bargaining could be enforced on the employers from without. On the railways, the employers were obliged to meet their workpeople not in occasional deputation only but regularly and collectively. In the mines, the employers were obliged to accept the fixing of one common minimum rate in shillings and pence as part of the agenda of the district bargaining which they had long accepted for making general changes in the various rates traditionally ruling pit by pit and seam by seam. Both obligations could have been imposed by statute in general terms, just as the Wagner Act in America imposed on employers the obligation to enter into bona fide negotiations with trade unions representative of their work-people: but then complaints of non-compliance come into the courts, a procedure must be provided to settle disputes about which union is representative, a whole positive code of conduct in industrial relations must be developed by statute. British opinion has fought shy of that degree of intervention. Simpler to implant institutions than obligations of conduct — set the boards up once and for all, and leave the parties to use them their own way.

This convenience apart, the boards probably suggested them-selves because of the general faith in their curative powers. This faith showed itself in the setting up after the storms of 1911 of a national joint board, the Industrial Council. The strikes in Manchester in July and August prompted a prominent spinner, Sir Charles Macara, to propose a national court made up of leading employers and trade unionists under neutral chairman-ship, that would hear disputes from any and every part of the country and recommend terms on which they might be settled. Looking for some constructive step to take after that threatening summer, Sidney Buxton at the Board of Trade got the agree-ment of government to such a body being set up, and the Industrial Council was constituted, with a panel of thirteen employers and thirteen trade unionists, and Askwith as chair-man. The idea was an old one: we have seen how the impact of the New Unionism had suggested it in the 1890's, and how various districts had set up courts and councils of just this kind. We also saw how next to no disputants would take any notice of them. The experience should have been instructive, but no one seems to have referred to it. It was repeated now. The first case brought before the Council — the refusal of dockers at Newport to accept an arbitral award — it quite failed to settle. The non-unionist issue now arose in the cotton mills: Sir Charles Macara himself was president of the employers who ordered a lockout without coming to the Council. When the port of London dispute in 1912 seemed to turn upon allegations by both sides that the other had broken an agreement, the Council undertook an inquiry into the keeping of agreements, heard witnesses like a Royal Commission, and published its report. No action was taken on this. The Council died for lack of work.

In very patient hands, conciliation proved enough to settle

the disputes which, though some of them were sizeable, did not threaten to stop a basic industry throughout the country. Those that did the government tackled very differently. In the disputes on the railways in 1907 and 1911 and in the mines in 1912 what it in fact did was to coerce the employers by legislation or the threat of it. Ministers did not leave the dispute to the conciliation service, but took it into their own hands. For its menace to the whole life of the country was felt to be intolerable: an industry-wide stoppage of the railways must be averted at all costs; one of the mines, though not so swift to strangle other industry, could not be let go on long. The sole sanction government could apply to get a settlement quickly was legislation, but even this would work only on three conditions: the terms of settlement must be of a kind capable of being embodied in an Act; they must be sufficiently acceptable to the men to keep them in or get them back if out already; and they must be regarded as not unreasonable by a majority in the House. There was no requirement that they be acceptable to the employers. To Lloyd George, the minister most actively concerned in all three settlements, it was natural to take the men's side — they were the people he had grown up among. But Asquith was not like that, and the Liberals generally drew much of their support from employers: the basic reason for their coercing them now was that in the nature of the case employers can be coerced as the men cannot. This for two reasons: the employers are far fewer in number; what is required of them — to keep their plants running — is generally more capable of enforcement than what is required of the men — to go on doing a fair day's work, day in day out. So the remaining common elements in the three settlements were, the designing of certain institutions to be set up in the industry, and the imposition of these upon the employers.

The issues raised were such that the method could work. What would happen if the men would not resume work except on terms that Parliament would not accept, or that would not enable the employers to pay their way, was left unexplored.

Measures improvised in a crisis opened a new chapter in industrial relations. A new kind of strike had led to a new kind of settlement. The inferences offering themselves to trade unionists were far-reaching. It looked as if the broader the front on which a claim was asserted, the more likely it was to succeed. What could not be won through negotiation with the employers could be wrested from government. In particular, the threat of an industry-wide strike in a basic industry had apparently put irresistible pressure on the Government, and enforced the coercion of the employers. Reflection would qualify this appreciation, but even partial successes of a new formation in its first three engagements were bound to commend it powerfully to the strategist of the trade union offensive. They strengthened the tendency to widen the front of negotiation until it covered a whole industry. They suggested that if the unions in certain basic industries stood together they would prove stronger than any government. Beyond the imposition of particular settlements on the employer they pointed to the day when the government would take his functions over altogether by nationalization.

CHAPTER VII

SEQUEL AND SURVEY

I

The last four years before war came had seen the needle flickering up in many a gauge; yet we know now, there was to be no explosion.

One reason was that most wage-earners were to become better off, those who had been poorest above all. It was remarkable that this should have come about, when after the war we no longer had the food and raw materials which used to come in as interest on the overseas investments now sold off, when export markets had been forfeited, and when many more men than before the war stood unemployed and unproductive. But these losses were offset by a great advance of productivity at home and a favourable turn of the terms of trade in world markets. Productivity was raised by the widespread application of two sources of power that had been only in limited or experimental use before the war — the internal combustion engine, and electricity with its fractional horsepower motors. With these went practical advances in metallurgy, welding, industrial chemistry, and in engineering through the ball-bearing and precision control. It has been reckoned that between 1924 and 1937 the output per wage-earner in British manufacturing increased by more than a third. Meanwhile, in our foreign trade the rhythm of the last hundred and thirty years persisted, and now it was the turn of foodstuffs and raw materials to become plentiful and cheap relatively to manufactures: our shipments overseas were no bigger even in 1929 than they had been in 1913, but we bartered them for more imports. The outcome on balance was an annual product for the average occupied person, in work or seeking it, something like five per cent lower than before the war in the middle 1920's, but five per cent higher in the later 1930's.

After all the damage the First World War had done us that

was something to be thankful for, but if the wage-earners had only kept pace with other people they would have gained little and tardily. In fact they went forward much faster: the basketful that the average week's wage would buy was bigger by about a tenth in the middle 1920's than before the war, in the later 1930's it was up by a third. What is more, this was the payment for a working week that had generally been reduced in 1919–20 from five and a half days of ten hours to a total of 44 to 48 hours, by cutting out the spell that used to be worked on an empty stomach before breakfast.

This relative advance of the wage-earners implies a redistribution of the national income. In fact it appears from what estimates may be ventured that the rate of profit on capital engaged in business remained substantially lower from 1924 onwards than it had ruled before the war; and we know with more certainty that the lag of rents behind the general rise in prices and incomes through the war reduced the share of the landlord in the national income. By processes which no one planned or guided something had come about under effectively conservative government which before the war had been dreamt of as an achievement of socialism: income had been transferred to the wage-earners from the recipients of profits and rents.

But it must be said that the rise in real wages we have considered so far was a rise in the average, and different groups fared very differently. In particular, men in three great industries whose export markets had been cut back were faring worse than before the war — the miners, the men in cotton, the skilled men in engineering and shipbuilding. We cannot invoke the rise in real wages to explain why these men were not fired with the old spirit of revolt. In fact, in all three industries they fought — in engineering in 1922, in coal in 1926, in textiles through five stoppages in 1929–32. They fought, and lost. The lesson of the times was that the money wasn't there: it was no use banging your head against a wall. Their quiet afterwards did not mean content.

It was different in many other callings, most of all among the unskilled, whose earnings had been so low and whose resentment had been mounting so hotly before the war. A great change had come about in differentials: women had risen relatively to men, the manual workers relatively to the white-collared, the unskilled and the machinist relatively to the craftsman. The immediate means had been the raising of all wages by equal absolute amounts to meet the rise in the cost of living during the war: five shillings a week meant at first about fifteen per cent for the skilled man but twenty-five for the labourer. The unions gathering in more and more recruits in those years from among the lower paid could hardly have tried to stem the drift of that. The employers, and the public sense of what was fair in wartime, saw that a given total increase of the wage bill would do more to help those who were worst off if it was divided as an equal absolute rather than as an equal proportionate increment. But these forces took lasting effect only because they were working in the same direction as the market forces of supply and demand. We have seen how education had been progressively increasing the supply of people with skills or the capacity to acquire them, and had correspondingly reduced the relative numbers of those who entered the labour market with nothing but their bodily strength to offer. The greater relative earnings of men and women in the lowest paid occupations corresponded to a greater scarcity.

So the biggest rise came where it was most needed. About 1890 Charles Booth had found a third of all families in London living below his poverty line, not having enough coming in to meet their physical needs even when those were reckoned at a stringent minimum; in 1929–30 a new survey found the proportion reduced to between a third and quarter of what it had been. Of the families with children of school age, Charles Booth found 30·7 per cent in poverty, the new survey 9·5 per cent.

The advance had been helped on by changes that supplemented the rise in wages of the unskilled, and brought benefits to wage-earners generally. The reduction in the number of children was spreading down the income scale: the wage-earner now had fewer mouths to feed, and his wife was not dragged down by repeated pregnancies. The social services which had been set up just before the war came into bearing, and were extended: in the once crippling contingencies of the wage-earner's life he was helped out by health insurance, unemployment insurance and old age pensions. More of his children went on to a secondary school. A great extension of housing provided many more wage-earners with modern amenities in kitchen and bathroom, with a piece of garden and a sight of the sky. Entertainment and fresh interests were brought into the home by broadcasting.

With this material advance went a greater social integration. Already at the end of the last century the widening scope of local government opened to the wage-earner a path of public service, on which he could attain to offices of dignity and honour in the community, with little effective hindrance from social prejudice or his own lack of means. When Henry Broadhurst the stonemason was at the Home Office in 1885, he began the practice of appointing wage-earners Justices of the Peace. By 1895 there were said to be six hundred Labour representatives on borough councils alone. In 1898 Labour gained control of West Ham for two years. Wage-earners who could become magistrates and mayors were not likely to feel themselves outcasts.

The process of integration was now carried farther by a reduction of class differences. There was an economic side to this of which we are sure: as the lower incomes were raised the higher were lowered. The war had brought progressive taxation such as was inconceivable before. Death duties breaking up landed estates displayed the decline of ownership where that had been at its most grandly conspicuous. Inequalities of the income left after tax were reduced radically. But with this also went a change in attitude. 'The democracy of the trenches' was no cant phrase. If it was from the well-to-do families that most of the subalterns came, no rank had a casualty rate higher than theirs. They for their part learned to know the working man, and those of them who returned brought back, as their successors did from the Second World War, a tradition of leadership founded on regard and respect for the men in their charge. The industrial difficulties of the following years found many to feel and say, 'We must stand together now as we did in the war.' There was less arrogance and obsequiousness in manners, less difference in the way a man would speak to those in different walks of life, less segregation by dress. Men felt a need for unity based on understanding, and believed it possible. King George V stood for it: as a naval officer with his own seagoing command he had known the lower deck, and from his accession he had set himself to visit mine and factory and yard, and talk with the men and women there.

This outlook found some practical expression at the place of work. Standards of industrial welfare that some employers had pioneered before the war were observed more widely. The growth of industry in the Midlands and South-East brought new factories with more air and light and more amenities. The extension of personnel management expressed and gave practical effect to an increased regard for the personal potentialities and needs of the workman.

Much is imponderable among the causes, but causes there must have been, for there is no doubt of the effect. Antagonism had been mounting in British society before the war; yet when great stresses were imposed on it in the years after the war it bore them without splitting, and when the blow of a second great depression fell on it, it voted for coalition.

2

The General Strike of 1926 might seem an exception to this rule of increasing integration. But it sprang from no revolutionary purpose, and in fact marked the end of a chapter of bargaining strategy, most of which had been written before the war. A train of events then had given the unionists who could withhold vital supplies and services from the community reason to believe that they could coerce the Government at need; the belief got so much hold that the leaders of the unions could hardly refuse to act upon it when the miners called for help against a major wage cut; but it was no longer founded on fact.

We have seen how as far back as 1893 the suffering caused by a long stoppage in the main English coalfields made Gladstone intervene, but all he did was to provide the good offices of a colleague as a conciliator. Shortly afterwards the Scots miners struck, the employers refused to meet them, and they appealed to Gladstone to intervene again. His letter of refusal contrasted the present state of their affairs with that of the English dispute when he intervened there. 'Both parties', he wrote, 'were then before the Government in one and the same attitude, whereas the telegram you have sent me is written on behalf of one side only, and I doubt whether you would wish me to proffer any request to the Scotch coal-masters concerned.'[1] It was different when Lloyd George was at the Board of Trade or the Exchequer. His personality and policy it was that imposed a settlement on the employers to avert the national railway strike threatened in 1907, settled that of 1911 again by bringing the employers to terms, and in 1912 helped secure the ending of the national coal strike by legislation that imposed the district minimum wage on the employers. The inference was plain, and we saw how the Triple Alliance took it. In 1915 the South Wales miners refused terms that their leaders had provisionally accepted. Their delegates resolved 'that we do not accept anything less than our original proposals, and that we stop the collieries on Thursday next until these demands are conceded'. A Royal Proclamation made it an offence under the Munitions of War Act to do this; two hundred thousand miners stopped work; Lloyd George went down to Cardiff by special train, gave the men what they asked for, and promised that the Government would enforce the terms on the owners.

After the Armistice, when society was heaved about by demobilization and disillusionment, boom and slump, when the railways and the mines came under renewed and redoubled economic pressure, and Lloyd George was Prime Minister, what harvest did he reap? The general strike was proposed as a means of obliging his government to nationalize the mines, and call off the Black and Tans in Ireland. The threat of it seemed enough to stop him helping the Poles against the Soviets. When the miners struck for higher pay in October 1920, the mines being then still under government control, the Railwaymen threatened a nationwide strike unless Lloyd George reopened negotiations within two days. He did so; but on the morrow of the threat he had introduced an Emergency Powers Bill, and only five days later it became law: it gave the government wide powers 'to make regulations for securing the essentials of life to the community' when a dispute threatened to deprive it of them. In March of the following year the coal mines reverted to the owners, who had already given notice of wage cuts. The miners would not take them, and the pits stopped. Within a week the Railwaymen and Transport Workers issued orders for a strike,

---

[1] Letter of 9 December 1893, quoted at pp. 300–1 of P. de Rousiers, *La Question Ouvrière en Angleterre* (1895).

later fixed for the evening of Friday 15th April. That day they cancelled the orders, on the ground that the miners' secretary had indicated in a speech the night before the miners' willingness to discuss a compromise.

That 'Black Friday' was the end of the Triple Alliance. What had happened? In part it was that the slump had set in, and the leaders of the two allied unions would have known that their members had little wish to quit their jobs now in another man's cause. In that cause they must have seen more intransigence than judgment. This time, moreover, the Government plainly meant to resist, and was armed with new powers of resistance. To win by threat was one thing, to engage in open warfare quite another.

But the inference that once the government took its stand a general strike could end only in the defeat of the unions or the overthrow of constitutional government was not clearly or widely drawn: the idea persisted that the withholding of vital supplies from the community was the unions' weapon of the last resort, one they were morally entitled to use at least when they were under attack. The occasion came when, as sterling appreciated and the output of European mines increased, the coalowners sought another wage cut. It seemed at first as if the old demonstration in force would still work, for after the railwaymen and transport workers had undertaken to stop all movements of coal and follow with a sympathetic strike, Baldwin's government announced a subsidy to keep the pits working at the existing wage-rates while a Royal Commission examined and prescribed for the industry. But when this Commission advised that some wage-cut was necessary, the miners refused outright. On the last day of April 1926 the pits stopped. On 1 May a conference of union executives decided almost unanimously to call a general strike. It lasted for nine days, and then the General Council of the Trades Union Congress went to Baldwin and called it off immediately and unconditionally.

The sufficient reason was the same as had stood out on Black Friday. The wonder is only that the General Strike was ever attempted.

Its collapse ended a chapter which had opened nineteen years before. When some unions gained the power to stop not a local part merely but the whole national supply of some vital material or service, a stoppage meant much more than the withholding of labour pending agreement on the terms of its employment, and its sanctions bore not so much on the immediate employer as on all the rest of the community, most of whom were wage-earners themselves. The threat of so much trouble helped a government to make up its mind when it was already well disposed towards the union's claim, and thought it was the employers who were being unreasonable. But let the Government think the boot was on the other foot, let it be prepared to resist: then could the unionists say to their fellow countrymen 'We will starve you, we will be the death of some of you, until we get our way'? — for that is what the plan means if it actually has to be carried out. If the weapon has to be not brandished merely but driven home, then it is as destructive, indiscriminate, and revolutionary as bombardment. Only the exceptional circumstances in which it was first deployed can account for the unions having thought it would serve them.

3

The thirty years since the General Strike have shown so much assuagement of the pangs of the thirty years before, that the question arises how far we have now achieved a solution of the basic problems of industrial relations.

The origin of these problems lies in the growth of population. As soon as there are more children growing up than can succeed to some holding of land or hereditary niche in the establishment of the crafts, the overflow become 'hands', and have to look for work. This means that they have to get access to the use of materials, equipment and technical knowledge. Where these assets do not grow too, the growth of population brings under-employment and dire poverty, as in Tudor England and contemporary Asia, or outright famine, as in Ireland. But even where they grow they remain scarce: initiative, drive and the power to organize and direct are rare gifts; saving should be within the reach of more of us but in practice it proves hard. So those who can give employment are fewer than those who have to look for it. That is why capitalists and managers generally hire workers, and not the other way round. If more men had the gifts of enterprise and thrift the arrangement might be different; but as it is, if most of us are to work effectively or at all we have to become employees.

The status is inevitable; but it can still be galling. We have seen the discontents that arise from the conditions of work. The employee has to put himself under another man's orders, or under those of a remote authority he does not know or meet. He has to forgo the spontaneity and variety of the jobs an independent man will choose to do. Efforts that a man would make readily when he was working for himself become oppressive when they have to be made for the profit of another. And though jobs may rankle, being out of one is worse: there is fear of the sack, and the sense that if two men are competing for one job they are at the mercy of the man who has it to give. This anxiety darkens the wage bargain: to the wage-earner it looks as if he is bound to come off worst if he bargains singlehanded. When those who have jobs to offer owe it to their ownership of property, then the subordination of the employee and his felt inequality of bargaining power merge into the exploitation of class by class.

When modern industry took its rise these effects were prominent: an imaginative observer might well believe that as industry extended, so would they, until they obliterated the traditional features of society in one vast cleavage. Analysing the tendencies of industrialism as he saw it in the 1840's, Marx argued in the Communist Manifesto that wherever it took hold it imposed a grouping and confrontation that superseded all others: the history of the next hundred years would unroll from the conflicts not of nations but of capital and labour. He could claim that he was only projecting trends that were already salient. The hold his doctrine has had on men's minds suggests how it is attuned to their experience. Yet his prophecy has been signally falsified by the event. The holocausts have come from the clash of nation and race, not of 'the two sides in industry'. In two vast countries power has been seized by Marxians, but those were peasant economies, little industrialized: where industry has grown most, social strife has become less intense, and the social hierarchy more fluid.

The reasons for this lie in the development partly of the economic and political structure that provides the setting for the relation between employer and employed, and partly of that relation itself.

We can trace the changes in the structure to no one single source, but the permissive condition for them all has been the rise in the material standard of living brought about by the progressive improvement of the methods of production and the capacity of the workers. Despite grievous fluctuations, the labour market has been dominated by the extension of demand, so that ever increasing numbers have found jobs at a real remuneration that has risen not less than the national product per head. This has brought to many not conveniences and comforts merely but a fuller life. Especially has it pushed back to a narrow pale the daily pain that poverty inflicts: a rise in standards of living that affects many ranks of life in much the same proportion none the less promotes equality when it lifts the poorest across the line between wretchedness and sufficiency. As men become less contrasted in substance they find it easier to give up inequalities in the form and spirit of their relations with one another. Political democracy in turn has used the power of government to minister to the needs of the majority, who are also the most needy, and especially to help their children. The walls of segregation into largely hereditary ranks and calling have been sapped by greater opportunity and mobility. The social distance between one man and another has been reduced. There has been less contrariety within society, and more interpenetration. In the event, the industrialized countries that seemed to be heading for class warfare have achieved a greater degree of equality, measurable and imponderable, perhaps than any other societies we know of save the primitive.

The current of these changes has washed away some of the exacerbations of industrial relations, whose own problem stands clearer than before, less inflamed than it used to be by conflicts of class. But not only has the problem been eased of its aggravations, it has also been met by a growth of expedients proper to itself, arising partly by instinctive reaction, partly by reasoned construction and experiment. Workmen have formed unions. Governments have regulated the workshop and the process of bargaining. Employers have accepted an increased responsibility towards their workpeople. Powers have been counterbalanced, usages have grown up, attitudes have been modified, institutions have been constructed. These things now constitute what is called the machinery of industrial relations. It creaks, and sometimes sticks, but for the most part its wheels turn, and the day's work goes on.

When we come to ask how far the improvement of British industrial relations since 1914 can be ascribed to these two kinds of change, the circumambient and the internal, we can have little doubt that it is the circumambient that have taken most effect, if only because these have been great and the others small. How the structure, balance and manners of British society have been transformed since 1914 we have already seen. In the machinery of industrial relations there has been no such change. The policy of the legislature towards industrial relations has not departed from the largely negative lesson of earlier experience. The scope of negotiations has been generally extended to industry-wide bargaining, but this only by the projection of a trend already apparent in 1914. One new development there has been, of what is called Whitleyism, and the setting up of formal arrangements for joint consultation; but this last may be regarded only as an attempt to fill a gap created by industry-wide bargaining. The system of British industrial relations remains today in its essentials as it was before the First World War. The improvement of these relations since then must be ascribed mainly to changes in their social setting.

It happens that the features we have just mentioned as settled are also features that distinguish British industrial relations from those of kindred countries. On both accounts they deserve assessment at the last.

4

The view that industrial relations go on best when they are voluntary, and that the legislature should give voluntary associations freedom of action without trying to regulate and prescribe for their dealings with one another, was not derived from any aversion to regulation in principle. We saw how the Factory Acts built up a code to regulate the conditions of the workplace. Parliament did not think it enough for the employer to warn the workmen 'If you don't want to take the risk you shouldn't take the job', because often enough the workman had no option. It could therefore extend its control naturally to other hardships which he might have to put up with because of his need for the job, and in part it did so, through the Truck Acts, and some limitation of hours, and latterly even the enforcement of some minimum wages. But it made this extension gingerly, confining much of it to women and young people. The further it moved from the physical conditions of the workplace to the dealings between employer and employed the more difficulty it felt. The problem was not one of principle but of practice — of finding any measures that could be enforced, or if they could would not do more harm than good. Experience seemed to show that men got on with one another best when they were left free to reach their own agreements: even though that meant also, free to fight out their own failure to agree. In some industrial affairs what is remarkable about Victorian Parliaments is the extent to which they intervened and regulated; but not so in industrial relations. These remained a stronghold of *laissez faire*. They are so still today. When British industrial relations are compared with those of the other democracies they stand out because they are so little regulated by law.

This is so notably in the policy adopted to avoid and settle disputes. We saw how discussion and experiment led to the conclusion in the 1890's that industrial relations were most peaceful when strong organizations on both sides met under arrangements they themselves had made, to work out agreements whose enforcement depended mainly on loyalty. If government offered discretionary arrangements they would not be used, if it tried to impose settlements they would not fit. The most it could do was to offer its good offices as a conciliator. To this was added, out of the experience of 1906–14 and the judgment of G. R. Askwith, the belief that there was virtue in having the arrangements for negotiation worked out explicitly and in detail, and that government could help by persuading the parties to set up 'appropriate machinery' and then stick to it. Experience also suggested that failure to agree often arose out of uncertainty or dispute about the facts of the case, and that if these could be set out objectively the parties would find it easier to reach a settlement. When the public was informed of the facts, moreover, its opinion of what settlement was reasonable would bear on the disputants, and this was a powerful sanction in the last resort. Committees of investigation could be set up under the Conciliation Act of 1896. An Act of 1919 added provision for the setting up of Courts of Inquiry. These remain the last resort the community has given itself to deal with an obdurate dispute, and it is remarkably effective. But the Court is really no Court, for it gives no award: it is only a fact-finding and argument-weighing board, whose report should help the disputants to find common ground when they try again.

This is familiar to the British, but striking to the foreigner. What he misses is provision to impose a settlement in the last resort, or bring the public interest to bear upon the terms of settlement. In Australia and New Zealand the parties to disputes are not allowed to turn the sanctions of a stoppage on one another, and the prohibition of strike and lock-out and the provision of compulsory arbitration have claimed 'a new province for law and order'; but in Britain those who stop an industry need commit no offence under the law, and can keep it stopped as long as they think they can get better terms by holding out, even if they are withholding supplies and services vital to the community. A system of compulsory arbitration can hardly stop short of administering, as it has done in Australia, a national wages structure. In Holland, Norway and Sweden the changes to be made each year in wages are guided by central discussions to which the unions and the government, and in Holland also the employers, are parties, and national organizations of unions and employers play a part in the subsequent negotiations; in Britain any suggestion of such co-ordination is suspect, and proposals for a national wage policy founder on the determination of the parties to each bargain to maintain their independence. It has been the policy of government to leave them that independence, because it promotes responsibility, and co-operation can only be given willingly.

There would have been more reason to consider different policies if they made more difference in the event. But prohibiting strikes does not in practice prevent them. The administration of wage levels and wage structures by a central agency is feasible in a democratic country only if it does not diverge far from what the parties reckon they would have if they were left to get the best terms they could from each other and the market. Very various methods of changing wages yield very similar results in countries that are under similar economic influences. Then, since control offers no clear gain, best keep the benefits of letting those who have to work together settle together.

But the lack of legal regulation of British industrial relations shows itself in another sector where the balance of benefit is far more doubtful. The sense that men should be left free to arrive at their own agreements about employment with one another has inhibited the building of a code of law for the institutions and procedures through which those agreements are negotiated. There are many points at which such a code seems needed to define rights and repress abuses. Suppose an employer dismisses a good workman solely because that man is a unionist — is he within his rights? Can he rightfully make it a condition of employment that the workman should undertake not to join a union? If a union inflicts losses on an employer with whom it has no quarrel in order to stop him dealing with another firm with which it is in dispute, should he have redress against the union? A member of a union has paid his dues for most of his working life and is entitled thereby to a retirement pension, but he now breaks a union rule against working overtime, and is duly expelled: ought he to lose all his entitlement? It is recognized that if men cannot agree with their employers about the terms on which their labour shall be hired in future, they are entitled to withhold it in concert: but is there a right to strike with the object of making an employer dismiss a man to whom the strikers have taken exception, or of inflicting hardship on the community so as to make it impose some desired settlement on a dispute to which the strikers are not parties themselves?

The issues which these questions raise are such as the law commonly provides for. They concern the definition of rights and the redress of wrongs. The wrongs may be grievous. One would have thought there was room here for a code of positive law, to define the rights of employer and employed in their mutual relations and prevent them from denying those rights to one another; to protect the individual in his relations with his trade union or employers' association; to define and proscribe practices by employers and employed which are contrary to public policy; and to protect the interests of the public during trade disputes.

But for these issues the British statute book makes next to no provision. Parliament has tried to leave combinations for collective bargaining outside the law as it leaves the village cricket club out. It has been concerned to give them freedom of action, and where they have found themselves constrained it has taken its pickaxe and hacked a cavity in the law to give them scope. But it has not developed any positive code to distinguish what is unjust from what is permissible in the actions of the parties to the bargain. Such rules as there are in this field have come mostly by way of judicial decisions making shift to apply the principles of the common law and the current interpretation of the public interest.

The reasons for the failure to construct a code are intelligible. It is a task of great technical difficulty, in an arena of clashing interests. Where principles are agreed it is still hard to formulate rules that can be enforced and will work in practice as they were meant to. The categories of the law are not readily applicable to spontaneous partial groupings in defence of particular common interests. Its sanctions are hard to apply to tens of thousands of men at once, and were they applicable would still create no willingness to work on terms regarded as unfair. But it is on willingness that good industrial relations depend: if employers and employed are decent and reasonable there will be little trouble, and if they are not, Acts of Parliament will not make them so. In the past, moreover, where the law has borne on industrial relations, as often as not it has made difficulties for the unions, who have concluded that the less it has to do with industrial relations the better; and the rest of the community has not disagreed persistently.

Hence the British tradition. Yet where power exists that can and sometimes, even though exceptionally, does hurt the community and gravely injure individuals, there is a domain for the rule of law.

5

The other salient feature of British industrial relations is the predominance of industry-wide bargaining.

By 1914 the widening of the bargaining area was significant but partial. There were some industries like cotton spinning, the boot and shoe trade, and tinplate, that were largely concentrated in one region, and had worked out what

were at once district and nearly industry-wide agreements —
though Norwich and Kendal, for instance, were outside the
great settlement of the boot and shoe industry in 1895. Engineering and building had made industry-wide agreements about
procedure. But wages and hours in each organized industry
were generally negotiated district by district between the local
employers' association and one craft or occupational union at a
time, or with a number of such unions that had agreed to
negotiate jointly.

Several forces none the less had recently been at work to
widen this bargaining unit by bringing more unionists into it, or
more firms, or both. It is true that neither party to a local
stoppage necessarily gained by widening it: employers and
unionists alike might see their advantage rather in letting their
associates in other districts go on working and so be able to
maintain support for them, as the South Wales coalowners
supported the Cambrian Combine in 1910–11, or the carpenters
supported their members in the shipyards of the North-East
Coast in 1908. By the same token, neither side would always and
clearly be gaining the upper hand if it linked up with more
associates before negotiations began so as to be able to threaten
a wider stoppage. But sometimes both employers and unionists
were moved to extend a dispute or enter into associations that
widened the area of negotiation. The engineering employers
did that in the disputes of 1897–8 and of 1908. In each case a
minority of employers were in obstinate dispute with unions
whose members continued to work for the majority, who at
length locked them out. Those other employers would not have
incurred the cost of that unless the unions' claim or conduct had
seemed so dangerous in tendency as to rouse a sense of common
interest in self-preservation. But the unionists had a more
general inducement to widen disputes and link up the disputants. Though the pressure that strikers were exerting on their
own employers might be greater if other districts of the same
industry went on working, it was galling for them to see the
men of their trade there actually getting higher wages because
they themselves were hungry, as the Scots miners did when the
English Federation struck in 1893. Within one district, if one
union or group of unions came out then the members of the
others were likely to be out too before long: they might as well

link up so as to have a voice in the first decision to come out, and a share in any benefits of the settlement. These considerations had long been leading unionists to enter into federations that linked unions of the same occupation in different districts or of different occupations in the same industry. The spirit of the New Unionism helped that on by a faith in unity and mass regardless of the logistics of bargaining.

In cooler calculations, moreover, there was another factor that worked powerfully for the widening of the bargaining unit, at least until it included all the firms that were close competitors with one another in the sale of their products. For the ability of any one employer to concede a rise in wages, or refrain from a cut, depended greatly on what his competitors were doing, and it had long been found that wages were adjusted more peaceably and employers were relieved of the fear of 'unfair competition' when all observed the union rate. That arrangements should be made for them to do this everywhere had lately become a maxim of public policy. Much of the unrest of recent years had been due to the failure of wages to rise when higher prices of imports were raising the cost of living. Wages did not rise, because demand for the home product did not extend enough, over against an ever-rising supply of labour, to make unorganized employers bid against one another for workmen. But suppose the employers became organized? Would they not be a virtuous kind of cartel, all safeguarded against being undersold because all were pledged and obliged to pay good wages? When disputes about wages broke out and employers were unorganized, the task of bringing them together and of setting up 'machinery' had presented itself to G. R. Askwith simply as one of bringing order out of chaos. But it worked in the first place not because it was orderly but because it made granting a rise so much easier for employers.

Organization was also needed because rates of pay which had long gone their own ways unobserved were now being compared: their differences were found anomalous; you could not adjust one without starting an outcry about another. This demand for uniformity and relativity was an outcome simply of the extension of union membership. It could be met only by organizing a collective agreement and making sure it was comprehensive enough.

These forces making for more 'machinery' were so strong, the wonder is they did not take more effect. The failure of the Birmingham alliances revealed some of the deterrents. The employer was competitive by bent, and disliked giving his competitors a lien on his policy even when that would give him a quieter life. The resistance of customers, competition from other regions or industries, and the presence or threat of foreign competition that there were no tariffs to restrain, all inhibited the running of a trade as a combine by way of collective bargaining. It was for pressure on the government, not wage negotiations with employers, that the broad front had shown itself effective.

But when war came the impulses towards combination were strengthened and the restraints removed. A much more rapid rise in the cost of living called for rises in money wages: they were made at first with a piecemeal variability that outraged the wage-earner's sense of equity. The same contagion of disturbance spread out from the centres where employers had bid up the pay of whatever types of labour happened to be scarce. The membership of the unions doubled in five years. Meanwhile competition was submerged by a general excess of monetary demand: higher prices to cover higher wages ceased to be a threat to turnover, were indeed provided for explicitly by the cost-plus contract. So there was no need for employers to resist the arrangements for comprehensive and uniform wage adjustments that the agencies of government developed as the only way of preventing incessant strikes. In February 1917 it was agreed by the great congeries of employers and unions in engineering that henceforward every four months an arbitral body should consider what change in wages was warranted, and its award should be binding on all firms. The body was called the Committee on Production, and its chairman was G. R. Askwith. The first award gave a rise of five shillings a week to all hands, together with a levelling up to a total of seven shillings of the advances variously given since August 1914. It was thus that engineering entered upon its practice of mounting a national adjustment on basic rates which themselves were the various legacy of the past, district by district. Many other industries now put themselves under the same procedure. Industry-wide bargaining came in, albeit with the connotation that its task was not to settle actual wages but to coordinate wage changes.

So far had this gone in three years that when the Whitley Committee considered its 'suggestions for securing a permanent improvement in the relations between employers and workmen', it assumed without discussion that organization for negotiation and consultation would be industry-wide. Where the employers and workpeople were not sufficiently organized to be able to maintain such arrangements, it recommended the setting up of a Trade Board, and an Act of 1918 extended the original provision for these boards so that they could be set up not solely to protect certain delimited groups of sweated workers but wherever the Minister was 'of opinion that no adequate machinery exists for the effective regulation of wages throughout the trade'.

In these ways it came about that the typical British bargaining unit, which in 1914 was still made up of certain occupations in one district of one industry, had become by the end of the war the whole of the wage-earners in the whole of an industry. This rapid extension had been possible because it had been used to arrange uniform and simple advances that left the traditional structure of wage-rates untouched, and were painless to employers.

It had been possible also for a less transient reason: because it suited the structure of British trade unionism. We have seen how 'the sense of trade identity' provided the bond of union of the wage-earners' associations: men linked up with those doing the same job in other places rather than with those doing different jobs in the same place. So it came about that any one employer in engineering might have a score of different unions in his works. This seems a strange bedfellow for industry-wide bargaining, which links men of different occupations together and divides up those of the same. But in fact the division by occupations promoted bargaining by industry. Because the different occupations in any one employ kept a watchful eye on each other's rates, and the employer's ability to pay varied in the same direction for all of them at any one time, they tended to make a common bargain. But this they could hardly do firm by firm, even if the employer had been willing to treat with them, because they had no organizations within the firm that could join in a federation of all the workmen there. Head offices, however, could work with one another, and whole unions could join in federations even if their local membership could not. So one reason for making the bargaining area the district or the whole industry was that bargaining with any one employer was precluded by the occupational division of his workpeople. Admittedly an agreement made for a wide area could not go into detail, but must confine itself to the provisions, mainly for wage-rates and hours of labour, that were simple enough to be of general application: but this again was not uncongenial to the unions, which could negotiate in common only on the highest common factor of their various and often conflicting interests.

So bargaining for which a number of unions must associate was actually promoted by their occupational separation. But we have seen how the process was also fostered by the attitude of the employers. They strongly resented their own workpeople claiming to argue as unionists with them in their own works, but found the convenience of setting a floor under competition by having the union rate maintained in all firms, and could concede rises or refrain from cuts more readily when assured that their competitors would be doing the same. The limited matters, moreover, that alone could be negotiated for the whole district or industry did but change a datum in their reckonings much as a change in the cost of a raw material would, and did not reduce their managerial discretion nor force them to work in double harness with their own men.

In developing bargaining by district and industry the unions and the employers were both taking the path of least resistance. This alone makes one wonder whether it was in the best interests of either. There are reasons to believe it was not.

For one thing, it left a gap in the firm: usually there was no recognized organ or agent of the unionists there to look after them in their daily dealings with management, and provide management with a means of securing the agreement of the men in measures affecting them. We have seen how workshop committees were springing up before the First World War, and the institution of the shop steward was being extended. During the war the development went on fast, but this marked not the success of the new agencies in filling the gap so much as the

2C

mounting discontent the gap gave rise to in the upheavals of war work. The Whitley Committee, appointed to probe the causes of a now menacing unrest, found them in the gap, and proposed to fill it another way: joint councils should be set up for the discussion of the matters that were of vital and common interest to employer and employed but lay outside the scope of collective bargaining. Their purpose was to give 'to labour a definite and enlarged share in the discussion and settlement of industrial matters in which employers and employed are jointly concerned',[1] and thereby achieve a 'constructive co-operation', 'a frank partnership of knowledge, experience, and good will.'[2] So joint consultation was launched — the formal provision for meetings between representatives of management and the employees to discuss, but not negotiate or enter into agreements upon, matters of common concern, particularly those arising in men's daily work, which are not within the purview of employers' associations and trade unions in their collective bargaining. It has led a hard and narrow life, between the prerogatives of management on the one hand and the unions on the other. Both sides have been split-minded towards it : it offers them both the advantage of some closing of the gap, but managers fear that it will advance the bounds of negotiation and agreement over their executive freedom, the unions that it will by-pass them. It is a kind of double harness, but a sloppy one: trying to achieve co-operation without accepting its constraints. The most pertinent comment on it is that in America, where its agenda is covered by contracts negotiated between the management of a firm and the trade union branch representing the firm's employees, it is not found necessary.

There has been a second drawback of the move to industry-wide bargaining: it has concentrated wage negotiation on a point where little can be done to raise real wages. We have seen reason to believe that collective bargaining does not supersede market forces. The prices at which an industry can sell have generally been limited by the competition of other industries at home and abroad, or by the unwillingness of consumers to buy as much as before at a higher price: then, unions or no unions, there is a point beyond which the wage cannot go without reducing the number of jobs the industry provides. When

---

[1] Cd. 9153 of 1918.   [2] Cd. 9002 of 1917–18.

the flow of purchasing power was rising, and unions found it relatively easy to get advances, the wages of unorganized workers of the same kinds were bid up too. So it came to be noticed that there was little evident difference between the movements of unionists' wages and other workers'; and the differences in the absolute levels of their wages might be as much the cause as the effect of differences in unionization. Charles Booth, the Liverpool shipowner who carried out the great survey of London life and labour, remarked on this in 1913. 'Even as regards wages', he wrote,[1] 'the effect genuinely produced by Trade Unions is questionable. They have, it is true, often opportunely pushed forward a rise or have successfully maintained the rate secured; but amongst the economic bases of wages collective bargaining has played but a small part. The wide range existing in rates of remuneration is surely due to other causes, as are also the general cyclic movements up or down; and it would seem that unionism itself, and the kind of remuneration found practicable, depend upon the scale of remuneration rather than the amount of remuneration on unionism. Undoubtedly stronger organization accompanies higher pay, but in each separate sphere of wage earning, from the highest to the lowest scale of remuneration, I can find no permanent and assured advantage for organized over unorganized labour, either in the earnings or in the security and continuity of employment. The unorganized have indeed been helped by the action of the organized, but what is more marked is that the conditions of employment in both have responded to influences common to the whole field of any industry.'

Since Booth wrote we have passed through phases in which the employer's apprehension of the bad effects of higher prices on his sales has been largely removed. At such times wage claims encounter no stubborn resistance, and industry-wide bargaining may expedite the general rise, by concentrating decisions in a relatively small number of mutually sensitive bodies, and providing an assurance that the rise in costs any one firm is asked to accept will in practice be widespread. But this general advance is so easy precisely because the rise in money wages is to be passed on in higher prices. Real wages are not necessarily raised at all.

[1] Charles Booth, *Industrial Unrest and Trade Union Policy* (1913), pp. 5–6.

The major cause of the rise in real wages that has transformed the condition of the wage-earners in western countries over the last hundred years has been the raising of productivity; but industry-wide bargaining shifts the raising of wages away from the points where it can be connected with this, both as effect and cause. When wage rises are negotiated for the whole industry, the changes which raise productivity in any one firm are not necessarily associated with rises in wages there, and the wage-earner is likely to see them only as disrupting established practices and creating redundancy, for the sake of profits in which he himself will have no share. Save in so far as the standard rate prevents less efficient firms from keeping on as they are by paying lower wages, the pressure for higher wages throughout a whole industry tends to raise prices rather than efficiency.

So it appears that in concentrating upon industry-wide wage-bargaining British unions have deployed their main effort in a field where in the nature of things there is not much ground for them to gain. Meanwhile managers and unions alike have done too little to develop organization and policy where they can do much for both, firm by firm, on the job.

The scope for action here is wide. There is all that concerns the status of the workman: his security of tenure, his rights when promotions are to be made or dismissals become necessary; his safeguards in disciplinary procedure; less palpably, but not of less moment to him, the consideration he receives from junior management, the way the foreman speaks to him. But these are only part of the agenda that opens when agreements are no longer confined to the jejune highest common factors of broad bargaining areas, but can enter into the detail of the arrangements of some one plant — such matters as protective clothing, opportunities for further training, compensation for particular hazards or responsibilities, arrangements for shift working: all the particulars that make up the lengthy provisions of an American 'plant contract'. It is an advantage of this kind of agreement that it is properly arbitrable, as the general understandings of existing collective bargaining commonly are not: for it provides a body of rules drawn up to fit the local circumstances in which the disputes arise, and capable therefore of judicial application to the facts of the case. It is an even greater advantage that these agreements give wage-earners a practical interest in advancing productivity. When wages are negotiated at national level it can be observed truly enough that if wage-earners will give up restrictive practices and facilitate the introduction of improvements, the industry's capacity to pay wages will be raised; but that remains pie in the sky. By agreements within the firm, however, the insecurity from which restrictive practices spring can be allayed, particular changes in work-load or working practices can be directly connected with changes in pay, and where managers and wage-earners together can raise the efficiency of the firm what the wage-earners take out of it need not be held back to what the least profitable third of the industry can afford.

We have seen how it came about that these possibilities were not exploited: there are intelligible reasons for it in the course of history; but in another sense it seems an historical accident, not enforced by any inherent repugnance of circumstance. As one lifts one's eyes from past to future, it seems that in Britain the greatest scope for the development of industrial relations is here. These relations matter most to men when they run between those who work together in the same place. It is only through the understandings developed there that 'the two sides' can approach a working partnership.

BIOGRAPHICAL NOTES

WILLIAM ABRAHAM ('MABON'), 1842–1922. Miner. Organized South Wales miners. Miners' chairman of Joint Sliding Scale Association, 1875–1902. M.P., 1885–1920. Signatory of minority report, Royal Commission on Labour, 1891–4. First president of S. Wales Miners' Federation, 1898.

DAME ADELAIDE ANDERSON, 1863–1936. Clerk to Royal Commission on Labour, 1891–4. H.M. Inspector of Factories, 1894, and Principal Lady Inspector, 1897–1921.

JOSEPH ARCH, 1826–1919. Warwickshire farm worker. Organizer of National Agricultural Labourers' Union: secretary, 1872; later, President. M.P., 1892–1902.

G. R. ASKWITH, 1861–1942. (Sir George, 1911; Lord Askwith, 1919.) Barrister. Worked with Sir Henry James (q.v.). Gave evidence for nine days on trade union law to Royal Commission on Trade Disputes, 1903–6. Aug. 1907, brought in by Lloyd George to Railway Dept. of Board of Trade. Jan. 1909, Comptroller-General of Labour Dept. Chief Industrial Commissioner, 1911–19. Chairman of Industrial Council, 1911.

H. H. ASQUITH, 1852–1928. M.P., 1886–1918, 1920–24. Home Secretary 1892–5. Chancellor of the Exchequer, Dec. 1905–Apr. 1908; Prime Minister, 1908–16.

DR E. AVELING, 1851–98. Advanced Socialist lecturer and writer; professor of comparative anatomy at London Hospital; m. daughter of Karl Marx.

ERNEST AVES, 1857–1917. Sociologist and writer. Co-operated with Charles Booth. Commissioner, Home Office, to investigate Australian and New Zealand wages boards, 1907–8. Special enquiries, Board of Trade, 1909–11. Chairman of first Trade Boards.

A. J. BALFOUR, 1848–1930. M.P., 1884–1922. Conservative leader, 1891–1911. Prime Minister, 1902–5.

GEORGE BARKER, 1858–1936. South Wales miner. Served seven years in Army. District Miners' Agent, 1909. Delegate to T.U.C., 1909–17. Executive Council of S. Wales Miners' Federation, 1910. Executive of Miners' Federation of Great Britain, 1911. For eighteen years on S. Wales Conciliation Board. M.P., 1920–9.

GEORGE N. BARNES, 1859–1940. Scots engineer. Executive of

Amalgamated Society of Engineers, 1889. Its general secretary, 1896–1908. Labour Representation Committee, 1900. M.P., 1906–18. Chairman, Parliamentary Labour Party, 1910.

MICHAEL BASS, 1837–1909. Brewer, Burton-on-Trent. M.P., 1865–86, when raised to the Peerage.

LADY (FLORENCE) BELL, c. 1855–1930. Wife of Sir Hugh Bell, iron-master. Stepmother of Gertrude Bell, Arabian traveller.

RICHARD BELL, 1859–1930. S. Wales railwayman. Organizing Secretary of Amalgamated Society of Railway Servants, 1891; General Secretary 1897–1910. Parliamentary Committee, T.U.C., 1899, 1902–9. M.P., 1900–10. Chairman, T.U.C., 1903. Officer of Employment Exchanges, 1910–24.

WILLIAM BEVERIDGE, b. 1879. Member of central (Unemployed) body, London; and chairman, Employment Exchanges Committee, 1905–8. Board of Trade, 1908. Director of Labour Exchanges and in charge of Employment Department, 1909–16. Published *Unemployment: a Problem of Industry*, 1909. Director of London School of Economics, 1919–37. Report on Social Insurance, 1942.

ERNEST BEVIN, 1881–1951. Born in Somerset. Farmer's boy in Devon. Kitchen boy, van boy, tram conductor, and van driver, in Bristol. Secretary to carmen's branch, Dockers' Union; assistant national organizer, Dockers' Union, 1913. First General Secretary of Transport and General Workers Union, 1922–46. M.P., 1940–51. Minister of Labour and National Service, 1940–5. Foreign Secretary, 1945–51.

ROBERT BLATCHFORD, 1851–1943. Served in Army. Journalist. Became a socialist, 1889. Started *The Clarion*, 1891.

MARGARET BONDFIELD, 1873–1953. Shop assistant. Investigated conditions in London shops, 1896. Assistant Secretary to Shop Assistants' Union, 1898–1908. Chief woman officer to National Union of General and Municipal Workers, 1921–38. M.P., 1923–4, 1926–31. Minister of Labour, 1929–31.

CHARLES BOOTH, 1840–1916. Liverpool shipowner and sociologist. Conducted inquiries published as *Life and Labour of the People of London*, 1891–1903.

ARTHUR BOWLEY, 1869–1957. Statistician. Joined London School of Economics, 1895. First professor of statistics of London University, 1919.

LORD BRASSEY, 1836–1918. Son of Thomas Brassey the railway contractor. M.P., 1868–86. Author of *Work and Wages*, 1872; *Foreign Work and English Wages*, 1879.

HENRY BROADHURST, 1840–1911. Stonemason, and leader of

Operative Stonemason's Society. Secretary of Parliamentary Committee of Trades Union Congress, 1875–Feb. 1886 and Sept. 1886–90. M.P., 1880–92, 1894–1906. Under Secretary in Home Department in Gladstone's administration, 1886.

JOHN BURNS, 1858–1943. London engineer. Joined Amalgamated Society of Engineers, 1879, Social Democratic Federation, 1883. Parliamentary Committee, T.U.C., 1890, 1893–4; its Chairman, 1893. M.P., 1892–1918. President of Local Government Board, 1906–14; of Board of Trade, 1914 until declaration of war.

THOMAS BURT, 1837–1922. Miner. General Secretary of Northumberland Miners' Association, 1865–1913. M.P., 1874–1918. President of T.U. Congress, 1891. Parliamentary Secretary to the Board of Trade, 1892–5.

SIDNEY BUXTON, 1858–1934. M.P. for Poplar, 1886–1914. Helped settle London dock strike, 1889. Postmaster General, 1905–10. President of Board of Trade, 1910–14. Governor General of South Africa, 1914–20.

SIR H. CAMPBELL-BANNERMAN, 1836–1908. M.P., 1868–1908. Chief Secretary for Ireland, 1884. Secretary of State for War, 1886 and 1892–5. Liberal leader, 1899. Prime Minister, Dec. 1905–Apr. 1908.

ANDREW CARNEGIE, 1835–1919. Son of Scots emigrant to U.S.A. By 1881 foremost ironmaster in U.S.A. Benefactor to libraries and education in U.S.A., British Isles and elsewhere.

ARTHUR CHAMBERLAIN, 1842–1913. Brother of Joseph. Chairman of Kynoch's and other companies. For many years chairman of Birmingham Licensing Committee.

JOSEPH CHAMBERLAIN, 1836–1914. Birmingham screw manufacturer. Mayor of Birmingham, 1873–5. M.P., 1876. President of Board of Trade, 1880; of Local Government Board, 1886. Secretary for the Colonies, 1895–1903. Opened protectionist campaign, 1903. Stricken with paralysis, 1906.

LORD RANDOLPH CHURCHILL, 1849–95. Led 'Fourth Party', 1880. Chancellor of the Exchequer, July 1886–Dec. 1886.

WINSTON CHURCHILL, b. 1874. Son of Lord Randolph Churchill. M.P., 1900–22 and since 1924. Dec. 1905, Under-Secretary, Colonial Office. Apr. 1908, President of Board of Trade. Feb. 1910, Home Secretary. Oct. 1911, First Lord of Admiralty, until 1915. Chancellor of the Exchequer, 1924–9. Prime Minister, 1940–5, 1951–5.

GEORGES CLEMENCEAU, 1841–1929. French Radical Deputy, 1876–93. Senator, 1902. Minister of the Interior, 1906, afterwards Prime Minister till 1909, and in 1917–20.

J. R. CLYNES, 1869–1949. Textile worker. Organiser for Gas Workers, 1891. M.P., 1906–31. President of National Union of General and Municipal Workers. Parly. Secretary, Ministry of Food, 1917–18. Food Controller, 1918–19. Chairman, Parly. Labour Party, 1921–2. Lord Privy Seal, 1924. Home Secretary, 1929–31.

WILLIAM COLLISON, b. 1865. Born in east London. Served in army. Formed National Free Labour Association, 1893.

HENRY CROMPTON, 1836–1904. Clerk of Assize, 1858, for 43 years. Positivist. In recognition of services to trade unions, admitted to Amalgamated Society of Carpenters and Joiners. Referee to conciliation board for Nottingham Lace Trade c. 1876.

WILL CROOKS, 1852–1921. Cooper. Chairman of Poplar Board of Guardians, 1897–1906. Mayor of Poplar, 1901. Independent Labour M.P. for Woolwich, 1903; M.P., 1903-10, 1910-21.

D. C. CUMMINGS, 1861–1942. General Secretary of Boilermakers, 1899. T.U.C. Parliamentary Committee, 1902–8; Chairman, 1905–6. Board of Trade Labour Department, 1908. Assistant Industrial Commissioner, 1911.

PETE CURRAN, 1860–1910. b. Glasgow. Worked in engineering shops. Appointed organiser of Gas Workers, 1889. Chairman of General Federation of Trade Unions, 1899–1909. M.P., 1907–10.

DAVID DALE, 1829–1906. Ironmaster, shipbuilder, railway director. President of first arbitration board for iron trade in North of England, 1869. Member of Royal Commissions on Trade Depression 1885–6, Mining Royalties 1889–93, Labour 1891–4.

ARTHUR DEAKIN, c. 1891–1955. Steel worker. Full-time officer of Dock, Wharf, Riverside and General Workers' Union, 1919. National Secretary for general workers in Transport and General Workers' Union, 1932. Assistant General Secretary T.G.W.U. 1935–40; General Secetary, 1945. Chairman of General Council of T.U.C., 1951–2.

DANIEL DE LEON, 1852–1915. Graduated at Leyden. Lecturer at Columbia University, 1872–86. Joined Socialist Labour Party, 1889. Helped to found Industrial Workers of the World, 1905. Split with orthodox trade unionists and founded rival union (1908) in Detroit.

WILLIAM DENNY, 1847–87. Scots shipbuilder. Advocated application of science to industry, suggestion schemes, joint consultation. On Board of Trade Loadline Committee, 1884.

LORD DEVONPORT (HUDSON KEARLEY), 1856–1934. Wholesale grocer. M.P., 1892–1910. Parliamentary Secretary to Board of Trade, 1905–9. Chairman of Port of London Authority, 1909–25.

SIR CHARLES DILKE, 1843–1911. M.P., 1868–86, 1892–1911.

President of Local Government Board, 1882–5. Chairman of Royal Commission on Housing of the Working Class, 1884–5. Resigned from Government, 1885.

LADY DILKE (born Strong), 1840–1904. Wife 1861–84 of Mark Pattison, Rector of Lincoln College, Oxford. Joined Women's Provident and Protection League, afterwards Women's Trades Union League, 1876. m. Charles Dilke, 1885. Represented W.T.U.L. at T.U.C., 1889–94.

J. DOHERTY, b. 1799. Cotton operative. Migrated from Ireland to Manchester, 1816. General Secretary, Federation of Spinners' Societies, 1829; of National Association for Protection of Labour, 1830. Editor of *Voice of the People*, 1831; of *Poor Man's Advocate*, 1832. Became printer and bookseller.

EDWARD VII, 1841–1910. Succeeded Queen Victoria, 1901.

WILLIAM FELKIN, Author of *History of the Machine-Wrought Hosiery and Lace Manufactures*, 1867.

SIR CHARLES FENWICK, 1850–1918. Northumberland miner, 1860–85. M.P., 1885–1918. Secretary, Parliamentary Committee, T.U.C., 1890–3.

H.A.L. FISHER, 1865–1940. Historian. Vice-Chancellor of Sheffield University. Brought in by Lloyd George to be President of Board of Education, 1916–22. M.P., 1916–26. Warden of New College, Oxford, 1926–40.

ELIZABETH GASKELL, 1810–65. Novelist. Wife of Unitarian minister in Manchester. Her sympathy with the textile workers reflected in *Mary Barton*, 1847.

ALDERMAN A. GEE, *c.* 1853–1939. Textile worker of Huddersfield. Built up W. Riding Weavers and Textile Workers, later Textile Workers (Heavy Woollens) General Union; its secretary until 1922. Prominent in formation of General Federation of Trade Unions, 1899; vice-chairman, 1905; chairman, 1910–12. One of the founders of International Textile Workers' Congresses.

GEORGE V, 1865–1936. Succeeded King Edward VIII in 1910; coronation June 1911.

WILLIAM EWART GLADSTONE, 1809–98. Chancellor of the Exchequer 1852–5, 1859–66. Prime Minister, 1868–74, 1880–5 (when also Chancellor), 1886, 1892–3.

CHARLES GORE, 1853–1932. Churchman and writer. Bishop of Worcester, 1902–4; Birmingham, 1905–11; Oxford, 1911–19.

SIR EDWARD GREY, 1862–1933. M.P., 1885–1916. Under-Secretary for Foreign Affairs, 1892–5. Foreign Secretary, 1905–16.

JAMES KEIR HARDIE, 1856–1915. Scots miner. Secretary, Scottish Miners' Federation, 1886. Chairman, Scottish Labour Party,

1888. Independent Labour M.P., 1892–5, 1900–15. Chairman, I.L.P., 1893–1900; 1913. Leader of the Labour Party, 1906–7.

FREDERIC HARRISON, *c.* 1832–1923. Lawyer, writer on philosophy and social questions. Founded Positivist Society, 1870.

GEORGE HOWELL, 1823–1910. Bricklayer till 1864. Chartist, 1847. Leader in struggle for nine-hour day in building trade, 1859. Secretary to: London Trades Council, 1861–2; Reform League, 1864–7; T.U.C. Parliamentary Committee, 1871–5; Plimsoll and Seamen's Fund Committee, 1873. M.P., 1885–95.

SIR HENRY JAMES, (afterwards Lord James of Hereford) 1828–1911. M.P., 1869. Solicitor General, 1873. Attorney General, 1880–5. Raised to peerage, 1895. Chancellor of the Duchy of Lancaster, 1895–1902. Arbitrator in many labour disputes.

JOHN KANE, 1819–76. Ironworker. Became a Chartist. Unsuccessful in efforts to form union, 1842. First general secretary of Amalgamated Ironworkers' Association, 1868–76.

ANNIE KENNEY, 1879–1953. Cotton operative. Militant suffragist. First woman elected to local committee of Card and Blowing Room Operatives, *c.* 1905. Worked with Sylvia Pankhurst in East End, 1913. Imprisoned many times with hunger strike. m. James Taylor.

SIR RUPERT KETTLE, 1817–94. County Court Judge; outstanding arbitrator. Settled seventeen-week builders' strike at Wolverhampton, 1864. Formed a number of boards of arbitration; first president, Midland Iron Trade Wages Board.

ROBERT KNIGHT, 1833–1911. Boilermaker. Secretary of Boilermakers and Ironshipbuilders, 1871–99. T.U.C. Parliamentary Committee, 1875. Established Federation of Engineering and Shipbuilding Trades, 1890.

JAMES LARKIN, 1876–1947. Liverpool Irish. Docker. Strike leader, 1905. Tried to unify Belfast dock workers, and led strikes, 1907. Led Dublin carters' strike and was suspended by Liverpool Executive, 1908. With James Connolly, formed Irish Transport and General Workers, and became General Secretary, 1909. Led Dublin strikes, 1913. President, Dublin T.U.C., 1914. Went to U.S.A., late 1914, where associated with I.W.W., and was imprisoned 1919–23, when he returned to Ireland.

WILLIAM LEVER, 1851–1925. Soap manufacturer. Founded Port Sunlight, 1888.

SIR GEORGE LIVESEY, 1834–1908. As chairman of S. Metropolitan Gas Company, introduced profit-sharing, 1889; co-partnership, 1894. Member of Royal Commission on Labour, 1891–4.

DAVID LLOYD GEORGE, 1863–1945. Solicitor, 1884. M.P., 1890–

1945. President of Board of Trade, Dec. 1905–Apr. 1908. Chancellor of the Exchequer, 1908–16. Prime Minister, 1916–22.

WALTER LONG, 1854–1924. M.P., 1880–1921. Parliamentary Secretary to Local Government Board, responsible for Poor Law work, 1886–92. President of Board of Agriculture, 1895–1900; of Local Government Board, 1900–5.

WILLIAM LOVETT, 1800–77. Cornishman. Rope-maker, cabinet-maker. Secretary of Chartist Convention, 1839. Imprisoned for seditious libel, 1839–40. Tried to unite working-class and middle-class reformers, 1842, 1848. Later chiefly concerned with education.

MARY MACARTHUR, 1880–1921. Secretary of Women's Trade Union League, 1903, and of National Federation of Women Workers. Hon. sec. of Central Committee on Women's Employment. Member of National Insurance Advisory Committee. m. W. C. Anderson, M.P., 1911.

JAMES RAMSAY MACDONALD, 1866–1937. Warehouse clerk, then journalist. Joined I.L.P., 1894. Secretary, Labour Representation Committee, 1900–12. M.P., 1906–18, 1922–35, 1936–7. Leader of Labour Party, 1911–Aug. 1914, 1922–31. Prime Minister, 1924, 1929–31, 1931–5.

MRS J. RAMSAY MACDONALD, (born Gladstone), 1870–1911. Began social work, 1892. Joined Women's Industrial Council, 1894, then National Union of Women Workers. m. Ramsay MacDonald, 1896. Concerned with work for unemployed women, 1905–6.

TOM MANN, 1856–1941. Engineering apprentice c. 1871; joined union c. 1878. Lectured for Social Democratic Federation. Helped to organize gas workers and dockers, 1889. President of Dockers till 1892. Signatory of Minority Report, Royal Commission on Labour of 1891–4. Secretary of I.L.P. c. 1893–5. 1901, went to Australia and New Zealand. Returned as a syndicalist, 1910. Led Liverpool dock strike, 1911. Later, a communist.

ALFRED MARSHALL, 1842–1924. Economist. Professor at Cambridge, 1885–1908. *Principles of Economics*, 1890. Member of Royal Commission on Labour, 1891; on Aged Poor, 1893.

KARL MARX, 1818–83. b. at Trier. Journalist and revolutionary organizer in W. Europe, 1843–9. From 1849 lived in London. Drew up constitution of first International, 1864. Published vol. I of *Capital*, 1867.

C. F. G. MASTERMAN, 1874–1927. M.P., 1906–14. Under-Secretary, Local Government Board, 1908. Under-Secretary, Home Office, 1909. First Chairman, National Insurance Commission, 1911. Financial Secretary to Treasury, 1912. Feb. 1914, Chancellor of

Duchy of Lancaster with seat in Cabinet, but failed to secure re-election to Commons on appointment.

JAMES MAWDSLEY, 1848–1902. Cotton operative. Secretary of Amalgamated Association of Cotton Spinners, 1878. T.U.C., Parliamentary Committee, 1882–97; chairman, 1886. Signatory of minority report, Royal Commission on Labour, 1891–4. Led twenty-week strike in Lancashire, 1892–3. Unsuccessful conservative candidate for Parliament, 1900.

JOHN STUART MILL, 1806–73. Philosopher and political economist. Entered service of East India Company in India House, 1823. M.P., 1865–8.

ALEXANDRE MILLERAND, 1859–1943. French Deputy, 1885–1920. Socialist till 1904, thereafter Independent. Minister of Commerce, 1899–1902. Minister of Works, 1909–10. War Minister, 1912–13, 1914–15. Prime Minister, 1920. President of the Republic, 1920–4.

ISAAC MITCHELL, 1867–1952. Joined Amalgamated Society of Engineers, 1887. T.U.C. Parliamentary Committee, 1897. General Secretary of General Federation of Trade Unions, 1899–1907. Joined Labour Dept. of Board of Trade, 1907. Assistant Industrial Commissioner, 1916. Principal Conciliation Officer, Ministry of Labour, 1927–32.

LEO CHIOZZA MONEY, 1870–1944. Journalist; statistician. Managing Director of *Commercial Intelligence*, 1898–1903. Published *Riches and Poverty*, 1905. M.P., 1906–18. Witness before Select Committee on Income Tax, 1906; on Home Work, 1907–8.

A. J. MUNDELLA, 1825–97. Apprenticed hosier, 1836. Manufacturer, 1848. Formed permanent conciliation board, Nottingham glove and hosiery trade, 1866. M.P., 1868–97. President of Board of Trade, 1886 and 1892–4, and set up its Labour Department, 1886.

E. VANSITTART NEALE, 1810–92. Trained as barrister, and inherited estates. Founded first London Co-operative Store, 1850; Central Co-operative Agency (wholesale), 1851; co-operative iron works, 1852; Cobden Mills, and Agricultural and Horticultural Association, 1866–7. Promoted annual co-operative congress, from 1869; general secretary of its central board, 1875–91.

SIR ANDREW NOBLE, 1831–1915. Physicist, artillerist. Royal Artillery, 1849, for eleven years. Joined Elswick Ordnance Co., 1860, a subsequent component of Armstrong Whitworth, of which vice-chairman, 1882, chairman, 1900.

ROBERT OWEN, 1771–1858. Draper's assistant, later cotton spinner, in Manchester, and at New Lanark Mill (*c.* 1800), where he established improved schools. Founded New Harmony communist colony in U.S.A., 1825–6; Grand National Consolidated Trade Union in England, 1834.

THOMAS PAINE, 1737–1809. Farmer's son. Went to America, 1774; journalist; government emissary to France, 1781. Visited England, 1787; published *Rights of Man*, evading arrest by escape to France. Member of French National Assembly, 1793. *Age of Reason*, 1793. Returned to America, 1802.

E. SYLVIA PANKHURST, b. 1882, younger daughter of Mrs Emmeline Pankhurst. Militant suffragist. Hon. Secretary to Women's Social and Political Union, 1906. Imprisoned many times, with hunger strike. Settled in East End of London, 1913, and developed democratic policy independently of W.S.P.U.

SIR CHARLES PARSONS, 1854–1931. Scientist. Developed the steam turbine. Chairman of several engineering and optical companies. President of Institute of Physics, and of N.E. Coast Institution of Engineers and Shipbuilders.

MARK PATTISON, 1813–84. Scholar. Early supporter of Social Science Association. Rector of Lincoln College, Oxford, 1861. m. Emilia Strong, 1861, afterwards (1885) wife of Sir Charles Dilke.

LORD PENRHYN, 1836–1907. Owner of Welsh slate quarries. M.P., 1866–8 and 1874–80, when succeeded to title. Fought two strikes (1887 and 1900).

WILLIAM PITT, 1759–1806. Chancellor of the Exchequer, 1782–3. Prime Minister and Chancellor, 1783–1801, 1804–6.

FRANCIS PLACE, 1771–1854. London breeches maker. Secretary of his own and other trade clubs, 1793–4. Working behind the scenes and almost unaided (1807–24) secured repeal of anti-combination laws. Prevented their re-enactment, 1825.

W. PEMBER REEVES, 1857–1932. Member of New Zealand Parliament, 1887–96. Minister of Education, Labour and Justice, 1891–6, and enacted a labour code. Agent-General for N.Z. in London, 1896; High Commissioner, 1905. Director, London School of Economics, 1908–19.

MRS PEMBER REEVES (born Robison). Wife of W. Pember Reeves. Author of *Round about a pound a week*.

HANS RENOLD, 1852–1943. Swiss-born, came to England, 1873, and bought small business in Salford, 1879. Invented 'bush roller' chain. Built 'Progress' works, Manchester, 1889; Renold works, begun 1906. Introduced 48-hour week, 1896. Opened personnel department, 1910. Advocated 'scientific management'.

STEPHEN REYNOLDS, 1881–1919. Writer. Worked with Devon fishermen, *c.* 1903. Member of two official committees on fisheries, 1912–13. Resident Inspector of Fisheries, S.W. area, 1914–19.

LORD ROSEBERY, 1847–1929. Under-secretary, Home Office, 1881–3. Lord Privy Seal, 1885. Chief Commissioner for Works, 1885. Foreign Secretary, 1886. Chairman of L.C.C., 1889–90 and 1892. Foreign Secretary, 1892–4. Prime Minister, 1894–5.

B. SEEBOHM ROWNTREE, 1871–1954. Cocoa manufacturer; sociologist. Labour Director of Rowntree & Co., 1897. Published *Poverty: a Study in Town Life*, 1901. Chairman of Rowntree's, 1925–41. Pioneer of 'scientific management' in U.K., and of joint consultation.

JOSEPH ROWNTREE, 1836–1925. Cocoa manufacturer. Introduced social workers into factories and embarked on welfare organization, 1891. Founded New Earswick model village, 1904.

LORD ST ALDWYN (Michael Hicks-Beach), 1837–1916. M.P., 1864–1906. Under-secretary, Home Office; secretary of Poor Law Board, 1868. Chief Secretary for Ireland, 1874–8, 1886–7; for the Colonies, 1878–80. Chancellor of the Exchequer, 1885–6, 1895–1902. President of Board of Trade, 1888–92.

LORD ST LEONARDS (E. B. Sugden), 1781–1875. Barrister. M.P., 1828–32, 1837–52. Solicitor General, 1829–30. Great Seal of Ireland, 1834–5, 1841–6. Lord Chancellor, Mar.–Dec. 1852.

SIR TITUS SALT, 1803–76. Wool Stapler. Founded Saltaire, improved mills and model town for workpeople, 1851. M.P., 1859–61.

JAMES SEXTON, 1856–1938. Liverpool docker. General Secretary of National Union of Dock Labourers, then of National Transport Workers' Federation, 1893–1926. T.U.C. Parliamentary Committee, 1900–23; chairman, 1905. Strike committee, Liverpool docks, 1911. M.P., 1918–31.

DAVID SHACKLETON, 1863–1938. Cotton operative. Secretary of local weavers' associations, 1893–1907. M.P., 1902–10. T.U.C. Parliamentary Committee, 1904–10. Chairman, Labour Party, 1905. President, T.U.C., 1908–9. Senior Labour Adviser, Home Office, 1910–11. National Health Insurance Commission, 1911–1916. Permanent Secretary, Ministry of Labour, 1916. Chief Labour Adviser to the Government, 1921–5.

DR ARTHUR SHADWELL, 1854–1936. Physician; author. Special correspondent of *The Times* in Russia and Germany, during cholera epidemic, 1892. Cholera superintendent, Metropolitan Asylums Board, 1893. Investigated social conditions in Europe and N. America. Published *Drink, Temperance and Legislation*, 1902; *Industrial Efficiency*, 1906.

EMANUEL SHINWELL, b. 1884. M.P. since 1922. Minor office in Labour governments, 1924, 1929–31; minister, 1945–51.

SAMUEL SMILES, 1812–1904. Author; social reformer. General practitioner, lecturing on public health, 1832–8, then journalist. Railway management, 1845–66. Published *Self-help*, 1859. President of National Provident Association, 1866–71.

ROBERT SMILLIE, 1857–1940. Scots miner. President, Scottish Miners' Federation, 1894–1918. Foundation member, Scottish I.L.P., 1888; I.L.P. 1893. President, Miners' Federation of G.B., 1912–21.

ADAM SMITH, 1723–90. Political Economist. Professor of logic, then moral philosophy, Glasgow University, 1751–64. Published *Wealth of Nations*, 1776.

HUBERT LLEWELLYN SMITH, 1864–1945. Civil servant. Lecturer in political economy, 1887–8. Commissioner of Labour, Board of Trade, 1893. Royal Commission on Secondary Education, 1894–5. Permanent Secretary, Board of Trade, 1907–19.

W. T. STEAD, 1849–1912. Journalist. Assistant editor, Pall Mall Gazette, 1880; editor, 1883–90. Founded *Review of Reviews*, 1890.

ENID FRANCES STRONG. See Lady Dilke.

DAVID SYME, 1827–1908. Son of Scots schoolmaster. Landed in Australia, 1852. Bought *The Age*, 1856; took personal control of it, 1860, exercising great influence on economic policy. Published *Outline of Industrial Science*, 1877.

F. W. TAYLOR, 1856–1915. American engineer and inventor. Engineering apprentice, 1875–8. Machine-shop labourer, rising to chief engineer, Midvale steel works, Philadelphia. Consulting engineer in management, 1893–8. Bethlehem Steel Co., Philadelphia, 1898–1901. Unpaid consultant, lecturer, etc. on Scientific Management, 1901–15.

D. A. THOMAS (later Lord Rhonnda), 1856–1918. S. Wales colliery owner; financier. M.P., 1888–1910. President of Local Govt. Board, 1916–17. Food Controller, 1917–18.

J. H. THOMAS, 1874–1949. Railwayman. On Executive of Amalgamated Society of Railway Servants, 1903; president, 1904. M.P., 1910–36. Helped to create National Union of Railwaymen, 1913: general-secretary, 1918–31. Secretary of State for Colonies, 1924. Lord Privy Seal and Minister for Employment, 1929–30. Secretary of State for Dominions, 1930–5; for Colonies, 1935–6.

WILL THORNE, 1857–1946. Born in Birmingham, worked as labourer, came to London as stoker in gas works. Helped to found Gas Workers' and General Labourers' Union: general secretary, 1889–1934. T.U.C. Parliamentary Committee, 1894–1934. M.P., 1906–45.

BENJAMIN TILLETT, 1860–1943. Bristol boy. Sailor; tea warehouseman. Formed small union, 1887. Leader, London dock strike,

1889. T.U.C. Parliamentary Committee, 1892–4. A founder of General Federation of Trade Unions, 1899; on management committee. Helped form Transport and General Workers Union: its political secretary, 1922.

GEORGE TOMLINSON, 1890–1952. Cotton weaver. Secretary, Rishton Weavers' Association, 1935. M.P., 1938–52. Minor office, 1941. Minister of Works, then Education, 1945–51.

SIR GEORGE TREVELYAN, 1838–1928. Historian. M.P., 1865–97. Minor office, 1868, 1881. Chief Secretary for Ireland, 1882–4. Chancellor of the Duchy of Lancaster, 1884–5. Secretary for Scotland, 1885–6, 1892–5.

LEON TROTSKY, 1879–1940. In London with Lenin, then in W. Europe, 1902–5. President of first Soviet in St Petersburg, 1905. Exiled to Siberia; escaped; in London, 1907; then in Vienna and Balkans. Rejoined Lenin, 1914. Commissar for Foreign Affairs in Bolshevik government, 1917, then Commissar for war. Expelled, 1927

BEATRICE WEBB (born Potter), 1859–1947. m. Sidney Webb (q.v.), 1892. Joint author of Minority Report of Royal Commission on Poor Law, 1905–9. See her *My Apprenticeship* (1926), *Our Partnership* (1948).

SIDNEY WEBB, 1859–1947. Civil servant, 1878–91. m. Beatrice Potter, 1892. Active in Fabian Society. L.C.C., 1892–1910. M.P., 1922–9. President of Board of Trade, 1922. Secretary of State for Dominions, 1929–30; for Colonies, 1929–31.

LORD WEMYSS, 1818–1914 (was Lord Elcho 1853–83). M.P., 1841–6, 1847–83. Responsible for revision of law of master and servant, 1867. On Royal Commission on Trade Unions, 1867–9. Founder and Chairman of Liberty and Property Defence League.

J. H. WHITLEY, 1866–1935. M.P. for Halifax, 1900–28. Chairman of Ways and Means, and Deputy Speaker of House of Commons, 1911–21. Speaker, 1921–8.

ALFRED WILLIAMS, 1877–1930. Worked in hammer shop of Great Western Railway works at Swindon, 1892–1914. Served with Royal Artillery in India, 1917–19. Author of five volumes of poems, and several books about the people and countryside of the upper Thames valley.

JOSEPH HAVELOCK WILSON, 1858–1929. Sailor. Founded National Amalgamated Sailors' and Firemen's Union, (afterwards National Union of Seamen) 1887. Friend of Samuel Plimsoll, 1891. M.P., 1892–1900, 1906–10. Helped to organize ship and dock-workers in W. European ports.

APPENDIX ON SOURCES

CHAPTER I: THE CONDITION OF THE PEOPLE

1. *The growth of population*

Secular changes in the purchasing power of the wage: E. H. Phelps Brown and S. V. Hopkins, 'Seven Centuries of Building Wages,' *Economica*, Aug. 1955; 'Seven Centuries of the Prices of Consumables, compared with Builders' Wage-Rates,' *Economica*, Nov. 1956; 'Wage-Rates and Prices: Evidence for Population Pressure in the Sixteenth Century,' *Economica*, Nov. 1957. Ireland: *Encyclopaedia Britannica*, 11th edn., 14.

2. *Changes in the size of the family*

Report on the Fertility of Marriage (Cd. 8678 of 1917). *Report of the Royal Commission on Population* (Cmd. 7695 of 1949); *Census of England and Wales, 1911*, Vol. XIII (1923); A. L. Bowley, 'Earners and Dependants in English Towns,' *Economica*, May 1921.

3. *Internal migration*

Census of England and Wales, 1901, and 1911, esp. Vol. IX (Cd. 7017 of 1913); A. K. Cairncross, 'Internal Migration in Victorian England,' *Manchester School*, 17, 1, Jan. 1949.

4. *Variations in the rate of rise of the standard of living*

The terms of trade: E. H. Phelps Brown and S. A. Ozga, 'Economic Growth and the Price Level,' *Economic Journal*, 65, Mar. 1955. The Atlantic community: Brinley Thomas, *Migration and Economic Growth* (1954). The trade cycle: Beveridge, *Full Employment in a Free Society* (1944), Appx. A; W. W. Rostow, *British Economy in the Nineteenth Century* (1948).

5. *Welfare in the home*

The real income of 1906 compared with that of the 1950's: A. L. Bowley, *Wages and Income in the United Kingdom* (1937); London and Cambridge Economic Service; Ministry of Labour Gazette. Size of household: Bowley and Hogg, *Has Poverty Diminished?* (1925); *Census of 1911, Preliminary Report*, (Cd. 5705 of 1911) and Vol. X. Pt. II (Cd. 7019 of 1913). Dietary: Board of Trade, Second Series of Memoranda, Statistical Tables and Charts, I, *Consumption and Cost of Food in Workmen's Families in Urban Districts of the U.K.* (Cd. 2337 of 1904); *Report of an Enquiry by the Board of Trade into Working Class Rents, Housing and Retail Prices* (Cd. 3864 of 1908); B. S. Rowntree, *Poverty, a study of town life* (2nd edn., 1902); *The Food Supply of the U.K.: a report drawn up by a Committee of the Royal Society* (Cd. 8421 of 1917); *Food Consumption Levels in the U.K.* (Cmd. 7203 of 1947). Drink: *Abstract of Labour Statistics to 1913* (Cd. 7733 of 1915); *Statistical Memoranda and Charts relating to Public Health and Social Conditions* (Cd. 4671 of 1909); article on Drunkenness in *Encyclopaedia Britannica*, 11th edn. (1911). Division of earnings between husband and wife: Michael Young, 'Distribution of Income within the Family,' *British Journal of Sociology*, 3, 4, Dec. 1952; J. Rowntree and A. J. Sherwell, *The Temperance Problem and Social Reform* (7th edn., 1900); B. S. Rowntree, *Poverty, a study of town life* (2nd edn., 1902); J. Hajnal and A. M. Henderson, *The Economic Position of the Family*, Papers of the Royal Commission on Population, Vol. 5 (1950); C. Madge, *Wartime Pattern of Saving and Spending*, National Institute of Economic and Social Research (1943). Phases of stringency: *Report of the Chief Registrar of Friendly Societies for 1906*.

6. *The unskilled labourer*

B. S. Rowntree, *Poverty, a study of town life* (2nd edn., 1902); A. L. Bowley and A. R. Burnett-Hurst, *Livelihood and Poverty* (1915); Mrs Pember Reeves, *Round about a pound a week* (1913); M. E. Loane, *The Queen's Poor* (1910).

7. *The farm labourer*

Lord Ernle, *English Farming Past and Present* (3rd edn., 1912), Appx. IX; B. S. Rowntree and M. Kendall, *How the Labourer Lives* (1913); *Report, Vol. I, on the Physical Examination of Men of Military Age by National Service Medical Boards from Nov. 1st 1917 to Oct. 31st 1918* (Cmd. 504 of 1920).

8. *The wage-earner's house.*

A. Shadwell, article on Housing in *Encyclopaedia Britannica*, 11th edn. (1911); F. W. Lawrence, *Local Variations in Wages* (1899); *Census of Scotland, 1911, Report*, Vol. II (Cd. 6896 of 1913); *Census of England and Wales, 1911*, Vol. VIII (Cd. 6910 of 1913); *Report of the Royal Commission on the Housing of the Industrial Population of Scotland* (Cd. 8731 of 1917); *Commission of Inquiry into Industrial Unrest, No. 7 Division* (Cmd. 8668 of 1917); T. R. Marr, *Housing Conditions in Manchester and Salford* (1904).

9. *Health*

J. C. Drummond and A. Wilbraham, *The Englishman's Food* (1939); Supplement to the *65th Annual Report of the Registrar-General, Pt. II* (Cd. 2619 of 1908); E. L. Collis and M. Greenwood, *The Health of the Industrial Worker* (1921); W. J. Martin, *The Physique of Young Adult Males* (Medical Research Council, Memo. No. 20, 1949); M. N. Karn, 'Summary of results of investigations into the height and weight of children of the British working classes during the last hundred years,' *Annals of Eugenics*, VIII, iv, June 1937; *Report of the Royal Commission on Physical Training* (Scotland), (Cd. 1507 of 1903); Dundee Social Union, *Report on Housing and Industrial Conditions* (1905); *Report of Interdepartmental Committee on Medical Inspection and Feeding of Children attending Public Elementary Schools* (Cd. 2784 of 1905); *Annual Reports of the Chief Medical Officer of the Board of Education*, for 1910 (Cd. 5925 of 1911), for 1911 (Cd. 6530 of 1912); *Report of the Chief Medical Officer of the Ministry of Education for 1939–45* (1947); *New Survey of London Life and Labour, Vol. I* (1930); *74th Annual Report of the Registrar General* (Cd. 6578 of 1913). Care of children: *New Survey of London Life and Labour, Vol. I, Ch. VII* (1930); *Interdepartmental Committee on Medical Inspection and Feeding of Children attending Public Elementary Schools* (Cd. 2779 of 1906); *Report on the working of the Education (Provision of Meals) Act, 1906, for the year ending 3rd March 1910* (Cd. 5724 of 1911); G. A. N. Lowndes, *The Silent Social Revolution* (1937).

10. *Education*

New Survey of London Life and Labour, Vol. I, Ch. VIII (1930); *Statistical Memoranda and Charts relating to Public Health and Social Conditions* (Cd. 4671 of 1909); H. C. Barnard, *A Short History of English Education* (1947); G. A. N. Lowndes, *The Silent Social Revolution* (1937); *Commission of Enquiry into Industrial Unrest, 1917, Recommendations* (Cmd. 8668 of 1917).

11. *The inequality of incomes*

L. G. Chiozza Money, *Riches and Poverty* (1905); E. H. Phelps Brown and P. E. Hart, 'The Share of Wages in National Income,' *Economic Journal*, 62, 246, June 1952; A. L. Bowley, *The Division of the Product of Industry* (1919).

CHAPTER II: THE CONDITIONS OF WORK

1. *The transition from school to a job*

Edward Cadbury, *Experiments in Industrial Organization* (1912). M. W. Thomas, *Young People in Industry 1745–1945* (1945). *Report of the*

Consultative Committee on Attendance . . . at continuation schools (Cd. 4757 of 1909). *Report of Interdepartmental Committee on Partial Exemption from School Attendance* (Cd. 4791 of 1909). Dundee Social Union: *Report on Housing and Industrial Conditions*, 1905. *Report of Interdepartmental Committee on the Employment of School Children* (Cd. 849 of 1902). *Report from the Select Committee on Home Work*, H.C. 1907, (290), VI, 55.

2. *The deployment of the working population*

A. L. Bowley: *Wages and Income in the United Kingdom* (1937), Appx. E; and Special Memoranda 17 and 17A of the London and Cambridge Economic Service (May and Dec. 1926). *Census of England and Wales, 1911*, Vol. X, (Cd. 7018 of 1914), Occupations and Industries, Part I, Table 27. Nos. in factories: *16th Abstract of Labour Statistics* (Cd. 7131 of 1914), pp. 308–9.

3. *Women workers*

Numbers and deployment: *Census of England and Wales, 1911*, Vol. X, Pt. I (Cd. 7018 of 1914). Conditions of work: J. Ramsay Macdonald (ed.), *Women in the Printing Trades, a sociological study* (1904); E. Cadbury, M. C. Matheson, and G. Shann: *Women's Work and Wages* (1906); Margaret Bondfield, 'Conditions under which Shop Assistants Work,' *Economic Journal*, June 1899; J. Hallsworth and R. J. Davies, *The Working Life of Shop Assistants* (1910); Dame Adelaide Anderson, *Women in the Factory* (1922); M. M. Niven, 'The Beginnings of the Institute,' *Personnel Management*, 39, 339, Mar. 1957. W. T. Layton, 'Changes in the Wages of Domestic Servants during Fifty Years,' *J.R.S.S.*, 81, 3, Sep. 1908.

4. *The workplace*

Annual Reports of the Chief Inspector of Factories. Accidents: *11th Abstract of Labour Statistics*, 1905–6 (Cd. 3690 of 1907). Attitude of employers: Lord (G.R.) Askwith, *Industrial Problems and Disputes* (1920) pp. 353–4. Industrial betterment: W. Ashworth, 'British Industrial Villages in the 19th Century,' *Economic History Review* (2), 3, 3, 1951; Budgett Meakin, *Model Factories and Villages* (1905); W. L. George, *Labour and Housing at Port Sunlight* (1909); E. Cadbury, *Experiments in Industrial Organization* (1912); B. H. Tripp, *Renold Chains* (1956). Hours of work: J. Rae, *Eight Hours for Work* (1894).

5. *Unemployment*

W. H. Beveridge, *Unemployment: a Problem of Industry* (1909; new edn., 1931). S. and B. Webb, *The Public Organization of the Labour*

Market (Minority Report of the Poor Law Commission, Pt. II), (1909). W. H. Beveridge, *Full Employment in a Free Society* (1944), Appxs. A and B. The building cycle: Brinley Thomas, *Migration and Economic Growth* (1954), Ch. VII, 7, and Ch. XI.

6. *Changes in machinery*

Sir John Clapham, *An Economic History of Modern Britain*, Vol. III (1938), Ch. 3. A. L. Levine, *Industrial Change and its Effects upon Labour, 1900–14* (unpublished London Ph.D. thesis, 1954).

7. *Scientific management*

Trades Union Congress, *Annual Report*, 1910. F. W. Taylor, *Principles and Methods of Scientific Management* (1911). Alfred Williams, *Life in a Railway Factory* (1915). Sidney Webb, *The Works Manager Today* (1917). R. F. Hoxie, *Scientific Management and Labor* (New York, 1915). H. B. Drury, *Scientific Management* (Columbia, 1918). L. Urwick and E. F. L. Brech, *The Making of Scientific Management* (1946).

8. *Effects of the conditions of work on industrial relations*

Accounts of working life: Alfred Williams, *Life in a Railway Factory* (1915); Peter Donnelly, *The Yellow Rock* (1950); Wil Jon Edwards, *From the Valley I Came* (1956); Robert Tressell, *The Ragged Trousered Philanthropists* (new edn., 1955). The condition of wage-earning: A. E. C. Hare, *The First Principles of Industrial Relations* (1958); T. N. Whitehead, *The Industrial Worker* (1938); F. J. Roethlisberger and W. J. Dickson, *Management and the Worker* (Harvard, 1939); M. S. Viteles, *Motivation and Morale in Industry* (1954); W. L. Warner and J. O. Low, *The Social System of the Modern Factory* (Yale, 1947).

CHAPTER III: THE DEVELOPMENT OF INDUSTRIAL RELATIONS

1. *The first growth: craft unions*

G. Unwin: *Industrial Organization in the 16th and 17th Centuries* (1904). S. and B. Webb, *History of Trade Unionism* (1920 edn.). Board of Trade, *Report on Trade Unions in 1905–7* (Cd. 4651 of 1909). J. H. Clapham, *Economic History of Modern Britain*, Vol. I (1926). D. C. Coleman, 'Combinations of Capital and Labour in the English Paper Industry, 1789–1825,' *Economica*, 21, 81, Feb. 1954.

2. *Operatives' unions and district bargaining*

First three references for Sec. 1.

3. The joint board of conciliation and arbitration

H. Crompton: *Industrial Conciliation* (1876). W. H. G. Armytage, *A. J. Mundella* (1951). J. S. Jeans, *Conciliation and Arbitration in Labour Disputes* (1894). D. Knoop, *Industrial Conciliation and Arbitration* (1905). W. J. Ashley, *The Adjustment of Wages* (1903). E. Brunner, 'The Origins of Industrial Peace: the case of the British Boot and Shoe Industry,' *Oxford Economic Papers*, I, 2, June 1949. W. A. Dalley, *The Life Story of W. J. Davis J.P.* (1914). John Hodge, *Workman's Cottage to Windsor Castle* (1931). *Rules of Voluntary Conciliation and Arbitration Boards and Joint Committees* (Cd. 3788 of 1908). *Thomas Burt, pitman and Privy Councillor. An autobiography* (1924), c. xv.

4. The sliding scale

W. J. Ashley, *The Adjustment of Wages* (1903). L. L. Price, *Industrial Peace* (1887), and 'Conciliation in the Cotton Trade', *Economic Journal*, June 1901. A. G. Pool, *Wage Policy in Relation to Industrial Fluctuations* (1938). U.S.A., 57th Congress, 1st Session, Document No. 186: *Reports of the Industrial Commission on Labor Organisations*, Vol. XVII, Ch. IV. R. Page Arnot, *The Miners: a history of the Miners' Federation of Great Britain 1889–1910* (1949).

5. The Birmingham Alliances

E. J. Smith, *The New Trade Combination Movement* (1899). Alan Fox, 'Industrial Relations in 19th Century Birmingham,' *Oxford Economic Papers*, 7, 1, Feb. 1955. David Solomons, 'Uniform Cost Accounting — a Survey, Pt. I,' *Economica*, 17, 67, Aug. 1950. P. Mantoux and M. Alfassa, *La Crise du Trade-Unionisme* (Paris, 1903).

6. Difficulties of the joint boards

Royal Commission on Labour, 1892, *Summary of Evidence* (C. 7421–I of 1894), Gp. C, Pt. I, hosiery, and Pt. II, china and earthenware. Royal Commission on Trade Disputes and Trade Combinations, *Minutes of Evidence* (Cd. 2826 of 1906). See also Sec. 3 and last ref. under Sec. 4.

7. The New Unionism

E. J. Hobsbawm, 'General Labour Unions in Britain, 1889–1914,' *Economic History Review* (2), 1, 2 and 3, 1948–9. H. A. Clegg, *General Union* (1954). H. Llewellyn Smith and V. Nash, *The Story of the Dockers' Strike* (1889). Will Thorne, *My Life's Battles* (1925). Ben Tillett, *A Brief History of the Dockers' Union* (1910); *History of the London Transport Workers' Strike, 1911* (1912); *Memories and Reflections* (1931).

8. *Stoppages*

K. G. J. C. Knowles, *Strikes — a study in industrial conflict* (1952). Sir John Clapham, *Economic History of Modern Britain*, Vol. III (1938). *Annual Reports of Labour Dept. of the Board of Trade on Strikes and Lock-outs.*

9. *Sources and centres of conflict*

G. Howell, *Trade Unionism New and Old* (1891). Lord (G.R.) Askwith, *Industrial Problems and Disputes* (1920). Royal Commission on Trade Disputes and Trade Combinations, *Minutes of Evidence* (Cd. 2826 of 1906). P. Mantoux and M. Alfassa: *La Crise du Trade-Unionisme* (Paris, 1903). W. J. Shaxby, *The Case against Picketing* (1897). L. H. Powell, *The Shipping Federation: a history of the first Sixty Years*, 1890–1950 (1950). G. C. Halverson, *Development of Labour Relations in the British Railways since 1860* (Ph.D. thesis, University of London, 1952).

10. *Sectors with little unionism*

Joseph Arch: the story of his life told by himself (1898). E. Selley, *Village Trade Unions in two Centuries* (1919). Reg Groves, *Sharpen the Sickle!* (1949). Flora Thompson, *Lark Rise* (1939). W. H. Hudson, *A Shepherd's Life* (1910). Alfred Williams, *A Wiltshire Village* (1912). D. Lockwood, *The Blackcoated Worker* (1958).

CHAPTER IV: THE DEVELOPMENT OF PUBLIC POLICY

1. *Public provision for settling disputes*

Councils of Conciliation Act (30 and 31 Vic. C. 105). Arbitration (Masters and Workmen) Act (35 and 36 Vic. C. 46). Royal Commission on Labour, *Fifth and Final Report*, Part I (C. 7421 of 1894), including Appx. III. Conciliation Act (59 and 60 Vic. C. 30). Lord Amulree (W. W. MacKenzie), *Industrial Arbitration in Great Britain* (1929).

2. *Findings of the Royal Commission on Labour, 1891–4*

Report of the Commission, as in Sec. 1.

3. *The Courts and the strike*

Beatrice Webb, 'The Failure of the Labour Commission,' *Nineteenth Century*, July 1894. N. A. Citrine, *Trade Union Law* (1950). O. Kahn-Freund, Ch. II, Legal Framework, in A. Flanders and H. A. Clegg, *The System of Industrial Relations in Great Britain* (1954).

Report of the Royal Commission on Trade Disputes and Trade Combinations (Cd. 2825 of 1906). F. Bealey and H. Pelling, *Labour and Politics 1900–1906* (1958).

4. *The enforcement of minimum wages*

Fifth Report from the Select Committee of the House of Lords on the Sweating System (169 of 1890). Beatrice Webb, *My Apprenticeship* (1926). *Report of the Fair Wages Committee* (Cd. 4422 of 1908). S. L. Gwynn and G. M. Tuckwell, *Life of Sir Charles Dilke* (1917). *Report of the Select Committee on Home Work* (246 of 1908). J. A. la Nauze, *Political Economy in Australia* (1949).

5. *Why had Parliament not provided a constitution for industrial relations within the firm?*

A. Williams, *Co-partnership and Profit-sharing* (1913). Benjamin Jones, *Co-operative Production* (1894).

CHAPTER V: INSTITUTIONS AND PROCEDURES IN 1906

1. *The size of unions and union membership*

Board of Trade, *Report on Trade Unions in 1905–7* (Cd. 4651 of 1909). S. and B. Webb, *History of Trade Unionism* (1920), Appx. V. A. L. Bowley, *Wages and Income in the United Kingdom* (1937), Appx. E. B. V. Humphreys, *Clerical Unions in the Civil Service* (1958).

2. *Union funds and benefits*

Board of Trade, *Report on Trade Unions in 1905–7* (Cd. 4651 of 1909). Geoffrey Drage, *Trade Unions* (1905). Article on Friendly Societies in *Encyclopaedia Britannica*, 11th edn.

3. *The government of the Unions*

S. and B. Webb, *Industrial Democracy* (1920 edn.). Article on Trade Unions in *Encyclopaedia Britannica*, 11th edn.

4. *Conflict between unions; federations*

D. C. Cummings, *History of the United Society of Boilermakers and Iron and Steel Ship Builders* (1905). J. Lynch, *Skilled and Unskilled Labour in the Shipbuilding Trade*, in *Report of Industrial Remuneration Conference* (1885). S. and B. Webb, *Industrial Democracy* (1920 edn.). Board of Trade, *Report on Trade Unions in 1905–7* (Cd. 4651 of 1909), p. xlvii.

5. *Trades Councils*

K. D. Buckley, *Trade Unionism in Aberdeen, 1878–1900* (1955).

6. *The Trades Union Congress*

B. C. Roberts, *The Trades Union Congress 1868–1921* (1958). Annual Reports of the T.U.C.

7. *The General Federation of Trade Unions*

Report of the Proceedings of the Special Trades Federation Congress which was held at St James's Hall, Manchester, January 24th, 25th and 26th, 1899. Annual Reports of G.F.T.U.

8. *Employers' Associations*

Royal Commission on Labour, 1892; *Summaries of Evidence* (C. 7421–I of 1894), Organizations. Royal Commission on Trade Disputes and Trade Combinations, 1903–6. *Minutes of Evidence* (Cd. 2826 of 1906), Appendices. Industrial Council, Enquiry into Industrial Agreements. *Minutes of Evidence* (Cd. 6953 of 1913). D. C. Coleman, 'Combinations of Capital and Labour in the English Paper Industry, 1789–1825,' *Economica*, Feb. 1954. G. Howell, *Labour Legislation, Labour Movements, and Labour Leaders* (2nd edn., 1905). P. Mantoux and M. Alfassa, *La Crise du Trade-Unionisme* (Paris, 1903).

9. *The fixing of wages within and without collective bargaining*

Board of Trade, *Report on Collective Agreements* (Cd. 5366 of 1910). A. Marshall, *Elements of the Economics of Industry* (1892), VI, xiii.

10. *The arrangements of collective bargaining*

Collective Agreements between Employers and Workpeople in the U.K. (Cd. 5366 of 1910). Henry Clay, *The Problem of Industrial Relations* (1929), Ch. I. Industrial Council, *Report on Inquiry into Industrial Agreements* (Cd. 6952 of 1913). W. Mosses, *The History of the United Pattern Makers' Association 1872–1922* (1922).

11. *Relations at the place of work*

Sidney Webb, *The Works Manager Today* (1917). G. D. H. Cole, *Workshop Organization* (1923). A. B. Bruce, *The Life of William Denny* (1888). *Denny, Dumbarton 1844–1932* (1932). *Collective Agreements between Employers and Workpeople in the U.K.* (Cd.5366 of 1910).

CHAPTER VI: STRIFE 1906-14

1. *The Trade Disputes Act, 1906*

Report of the Royal Commission on Trade Disputes and Trade Combinations (Cd. 2825 of 1906). O. Kahn-Freund, chapter on 'The Legal Framework' in A. Flanders and H. A. Clegg, *The System of Industrial Relations in Great Britain* (1954). N. A. Citrine, *Trade Union Law* (1950).

2. *The railwaymen, 1907*

J. W. F. Rowe, *Changes of Wage Rates in certain industries during the last 30-40 years* (London Ph.D. thesis, 1923). M. Alfassa, *La Crise Ouvrière Récente des Chemins de Fer Anglais* (Paris, 1908). Frank Owen, *Tempestuous Journey: Lloyd George, his Life and Times* (1954). Lucy Masterman, *C. F. G. Masterman, a Biography* (1939).

3. *The foundations of the welfare state, 1908-11*

Reports of the Select Committee on the Aged Deserving Poor (H.C. 296 of 1899). Lucy Masterman, *C. F. G. Masterman, a Biography* (1939). Sir John Clapham, *An Economic History of Modern Britain*, Vol. III (1951), Ch. VII. W. H. Beveridge, *Unemployment, a Problem of Industry* (1930 edn.). W. J. Braithwaite, *Lloyd George's Ambulance Wagon* (1957). *Report on the Wages Boards and Industrial Conciliation and Arbitration Acts of Australia and New Zealand*, by Ernest Aves (Cd. 4167 of 1908). *Report of Select Committee on Homework* (House of Commons, 246, 1908). B. C. Roberts, *The Trades Union Congress 1868-1921* (1958).

4. *Wage cuts and the miners' Eight Hours, 1908-9*

Lord (G.R.) Askwith, *Industrial Problems and Disputes* (1920). Board of Trade, *Report on Strikes and Lockouts in 1908* (Cd. 4680 of 1909). *Final Report of Departmental Committee appointed to inquire into the probable economic effect of a limit of eight hours to the working day of coal miners* (Cd. 3505 of 1907). H. Stanley Jevons, *The British Coal Trade* (1915). J. W. F. Rowe, *Wages in the Coal Industry* (1923).

5. *The Cambrian stoppage, 1910-11; the seamen and dockers, the railwaymen, 1911*

David Evans, *Labour Strife in the South Wales Coalfield 1910-11* (1911). Lord (G.R.) Askwith, *Industrial Problems and Disputes* (1920). H. Stanley Jevons, *The British Coal Trade* (1915). Ness Edwards, *The South Wales Miners' Federation* (1938). Ben Tillett, *History of the Transport Strike, 1911* (1912). G. C. Halverson, *Development of Labour Relations in the British Railways since 1860* (London Ph.D. thesis). *Report of Royal Commission on Railway Conciliation and Arbitration Scheme of 1907* (Cd. 5922 of 1911, 6014 of 1912–13). J. H. Thomas, *My Story* (1937).

6. *The coalmines and the Port of London, 1912; the Triple Alliance; the Midlands, 1913; the growth of unionism*

D. H. Robertson, 'A Narrative of the Coal Strike,' *Economic Journal*, Sept. 1912. R. Page Arnot, *The Miners: a history of the Miners' Federation of Great Britain 1889–1910* (1949). Lord (G.R.) Askwith, *Industrial Problems and Disputes* (1920). *Report upon the present disputes affecting transport workers in the Port of London and on the Medway* (Cd. 6229 of 1912). H. Gosling, *Up and Down Stream* (1927). A. Wright, *Disturbed Dublin: the story of the great strike of 1913–14* (1914). *Report of an enquiry by the Board of Trade into working class rents, housing, retail prices and rates of wages in the principal industrial towns of the U.K. in 1912* (Cd. 6955 of 1913).

7. *The causes of the strife, 1910–14*

W. H. Crook, *The General Strike* (1931). S. and B. Webb, *What Syndicalism Means*, published as a supplement to *The Crusade* by the National Committee for the Prevention of Destitution, Aug. 1912. A. L. Bowley, *Wages and Income in the United Kingdom* (1937). E. H. Phelps Brown and S. J. Handfield-Jones, 'The Climacteric of the 1890's,' *Oxford Economic Papers*, 4, 3, Oct. 1952. Commission of Inquiry into Industrial Unrest, *Reports* (Cd. 8662–9 of 1917–18).

8. *Public policy towards disputes*

Lord (G.R.) Askwith, *Industrial Problems and Disputes* (1920).

Chapter VII: Sequel and Survey

1. *Why no revolt followed*

H. Nicholson, *King George V: his life and reign* (1952). Sir John Clapham, *An Economic History of Modern Britain*, Vol. III (1951), Epilogue. R. S. Sayers, 'The Springs of Technical Progress in Britain, 1919–39,' *Economic Journal*, 60, 238, June 1950. L. Rostas, *Comparative Productivity in British and American Industry* (1948). A. L. Bowley and J. C. Stamp, *The National Income 1924* (1927). E. H. Phelps Brown and S. V. Hopkins, 'The Course of Wage-rates in Five Countries,' *Oxford Economic Papers*, NS 2, 2, June 1950. E. H. Phelps Brown and P. E. Hart, 'The Share of Wages in National Income,' *Economic Journal*, 62, 246, June 1952. E. H. Phelps Brown and B. Weber, 'Accumulation, Productivity and Distribution in the British Economy, 1870–1938,' *Economic Journal*, 63, 250, June 1953. H. A. Clegg and Rex Adams, *The Employers' Challenge* (1957). *New Survey of London Life and Labour*, Vol. VI (1934).

2. *The weapon of the stoppage of essential industries*

H. A. Clegg, *Some Consequences of the General Strike*, Manchester Statistical Society, 13 Jan. 1954. R. Page Arnot, *The Miners: years of struggle* (1953). J. H. Thomas, *My Story* (1937).

3. *How far have the basic problems of industrial relations been solved?*

A. E. C. Hare, *The First Principles of Industrial Relations* (1958).

4. *The negativism of British public policy towards industrial relations*

O. Kahn-Freund, chapter on The Legal Framework, in A. Flanders and H. A. Clegg, *The System of Industrial Relations in Great Britain* (1954). C. Grunfeld, *Trade Unions and the Individual* (Fabian Research Series No. 193, 1957).

5. *The predominance of industry-wide bargaining in Britain*

The coming of industry-wide bargaining: Henry Clay, *The Problem of Industrial Relations* (1929); Ministry of Reconstruction, Committee on Relations between Employer and Employed (Whitley Committee), *First Report* (Cd. 8606 of 1917–18), *Second Report* (Cd. 9002 of 1917–18). Comparative features of British trade unionism: W. Galenson, *Contemporary Labor Movements* (New York, 1952); A. Sturmthal (ed.), *Contemporary Collective Bargaining in Seven Countries* (Ithaca, N.Y. 1957); R. A. Lester, 'Reflections on Collective Bargaining in Britain and Sweden,' *Industrial and Labor Relations Review*, 10, 3, Apr. 1957; M. Derber, *Labor-Management Relations at the Plant Level under Industry-wide Bargaining* (Univ. of Illinois, 1955). The effects of trade unions on wages: A. Marshall, *Elements of the Economics of Industry* (1892), VI, xiii; Charles Booth, *Industrial Unrest and Trade Union Policy* (1913); R. A. Lester and A. M. Ross, 'The influence of unionism upon earnings,' *Quarterly Journal of Economics*, Nov. 1948; H. M. Levinson, *Unionism, Wage Trends, and Income Distribution 1914–47* (Michigan Business Studies, 1951); Clark Kerr, 'Trade unionism and distributive shares,' M. Bronfenbrenner, 'The incidence of collective bargaining,' H. M. Levinson, 'Collective bargaining and income distribution,' all in *American Economic Review*, 44, 2, May 1954; Lloyd Reynolds and Cynthia Taft, *The Evolution of Wage Structure* (1956); J. T. Dunlop (ed.), *The Theory of Wage Determination* (1957); Clark Kerr, *Productivity and Labor Relations* (Univ. of California, Institute of Industrial Relations, 1957); M. Bronfenbrenner, 'The Incidence of Collective Bargaining once more,' *Southern Economic Journal*, 24, 4, Apr. 1958.

INDEX

PRINTED IN GREAT BRITAIN BY ROBERT MACLEHOSE AND CO. LTD
THE UNIVERSITY PRESS, GLASGOW